THOU SHALT FORGET

Indigenous Sovereignty, Resistance and the Production of Cultural Oblivion in Canada

Pierrot Ross-Tremblay

Published by the University of London Press

Human Rights Consortium, Institute of Commonwealth Studies,
School of Advanced Study, University of London, 2019
https://hrc.sas.ac.uk

ISBNs
978-1-912250-09-7 (paperback)
978-1-912250-28-8 (.mobi)
978-1-912250-29-5 (.epub)
978-1-912250-42-4 (.pdf)

University of London Press
School of Advanced Study
University of London
Senate House
Malet Street
London WC1E 7HU

Cover image: Paul Ross Sr in front of his house in Essipit, with family members (his daughter-in-law, Angèle Vallée, on his right, and his son, Joseph Ross, on the back cover of the book) and visitors who are seated (Musée du Bas-Saint-Laurent, Rivière-du-Loup Fonds J-Adélard Boucher, NAC jab0486f mbsl.qc.ca).

HUMAN RIGHTS CONSORTIUM | SCHOOL OF ADVANCED STUDY UNIVERSITY OF LONDON

Contents

List of figures

Acknowledgements

This book is the result of several years' work that began with my first doctoral reflections in 2005–6 at the Institute for Development Studies in Geneva, continued during my PhD studies at the University of Essex (2007–12) and rounded off at Laurentian University in Sudbury (2014–19). This book could not have come to fruition without the love of my family who supported, encouraged, trusted and defended me, from beginning to end – especially my life partner, comrade and colleague, Nawel Hamidi – a person with a heart of gold who has always encouraged me to stand up, hold my head high and tell it as it is, especially in the face of injustice and the worst outrages. This book is yours also.

To my boys Pishimnapeo (Shams), Maikan (Ushen) and Lounès, this book asked a lot of you in absence and silence, too much perhaps. But your dad wrote it with the conviction that it would nourish the little Essipiunnuat that you are and will become. Your Innu heritage is a treasure, never doubt it. To my exceptional parents, Réal and Claude-Andrée, you have been consistently generous, protective and good counsel from the beginning, providing unwavering support. Be assured of my complete gratitude. Thank you to my brother Dario who has always been there to support and accompany me on our ancestral territories to refresh and keep the vision clear, on the calm seas and during storms. The camaraderie and humour of my cousins and hunting partners, Pascal, Anton, Fred, Martin, Yannick and Christian, helped me greatly in my daily life in Essipit, thank you. Thanks to my aunts, uncles and extended family, including my brothers-in-law and comrades Riad and Fares. We are a wonderful family. Many sacrifices on the part of our relatives were necessary before it was possible for me to give birth to this book, in what proved to be a somewhat difficult labour. I am indebted and deeply grateful to you. This work is also yours.

I would like to express my deepest gratitude and love to the Essipiunnuat, from all generations, and especially to those who lived through the Salmon War and agreed to share their stories and thoughts. You have taught me and transformed me by your affection, your stories and your wisdom. In all humility, I have done everything in my power to be faithful to your spirit and your words. Thank you to the Elders who guided me, informed me, and helped me avoid the pitfalls and dangers of researching my own community, especially when the subject was the traumatic conflict and issues of memory and forgetfulness touching the very heart of internal colonialism. Your sound advice, always consistent with the expression of truth for the purposes of healing and justice, has made all the difference in this book. Investigating our own cruelties is sometimes difficult or even dangerous but you have given me the conviction that to be honest and to say things as they are has a higher value than the benefits of remaining silent on what must be voiced. I have learned that by following your advice, we arrive at the end of the road with some scratches, but lighter of heart. Thank you for the courage of your words and for your patience with a young researcher who sometimes lacked experience. This book is above all a tribute to the Essipiunnuat warriors, especially those who have since left us for the great land and whose portraits in this book are testimony to the legacy of our ancestors – this book is dedicated to you. I am thinking of warriors such as my nimushum Paul Ross Jr (Ti-Paul), Jean-Noël Ross, my uncle Marcel Ross, our cousin Serge Moreau, Uncle André Ross (Pet), André (Ti-Nours) Ross, Uncle Romeo and Uncle Arthur. Tshinashkumitnau.

Thank you to everyone for your stories. Whether you work for the band council or criticise it, support or oppose modern treaties, thank you for your courage speaking out. I have learned as much from those who encouraged me to pursue the search for truth as from those who have done everything in their power (some Essipiunnuat and some not) to prevent this book from seeing the light of day. By their love, the first gave me the resolve, the inspiration and the conviction to pursue publication. Thanks to them, future generations will know how far their ancestors were prepared to go in order to defend their heritage and ancestral sovereignty. By their relentless efforts, the second group offered me invaluable insight into the production of forgetfulness and ignorance, how the deep forces of psychological colonialism impact upon our relationship with the past (truth) and the Earth (life). It is where the opposing current is strongest that the salmon finds a way to bounce back and return a little closer to where it was born. Every obstacle, every dam erected on the way, became a source of crucial information to the last. The second group also taught me how to guide future researchers in looking at their own communities, and how to put the love of truth, honesty and bravery above the short-term interests of pleasing the authorities.

Over the years I have received many teachings from my Innu brothers and sisters from Natuashish, Sheshashit, Pakuashipit, Unamen Shipu, Natashkuan, Ekuanitshit, Ushat Mak Mani Utenam, Pessamit and Mashteuiatsh, and from other First Peoples, including our brothers and sisters Wendat and Atikamekw Nehirowisiw. I would like to heartily thank Elder and Professor Malcolm Saulis for his teachings on our medicines, our ceremonies and the moral and spiritual qualities required to be a good person and a circle keeper. These profound teachings have nourished and guided me. I am indebted to all the writers and thinkers of the First Peoples, such as the late An Antane Kapesh and William Commanda, Charles Coocoo, Leroy Little Bear, Georges Sioui, Shanipiap Sioui-Mackenzie, Joséphine Bacon, Évelyne St-Onge, Élie Mestokosho and great allies and transmitters of knowledge who were generous with me, such as

Rémi Savard, José Mailhot, Sylvie Vincent and Paul Charest, and not to forget the great researcher and mentor Sylvie Poirier. I am especially grateful to my Innu brothers and sisters from Matimekush-Lac John who welcomed me in the years 2004–6 and supported me in my healing and cultural empowerment process. Thank you to Elder Utshemau Thaddé André, to the thinker and big brother Essemeu Mackenzie and his family and to my friend Donnat Jean-Pierre, for hospitality and kindness. Thanks also to Elder Alexandre Mackenzie, who advised me to pay more attention to the history of my own community as early as 2004 and to the late François Penashue Aster, whose stories I had the privilege of hearing.

I would like to thank my Anishnabeg brothers and sisters who welcomed us with kindness, hospitality and humanity to their fabulous and fertile ancestral territories during our stay in Sagamok (Sudbury). Thank you to my friends and colleagues, researcher and educator Darrel Manitowabi, leader Sheila Cote-Meek, the great linguist and thinker Mary Ann Corbiere and the historian and educator Dominic Beaudry. Thank you to the Linklater-Wong brothers, Josh and Ryan, for their deep friendship and to my spiritual brother Ian Desjardins and his family for medicine and ceremonies. Thank you as well to my colleagues in the department of sociology (Simon, Rachid, Parveen, Lynne, Anas, Marianne) of Laurentian for their patience with a director who was far too busy. Nawel, the children and I are also very grateful to you, the Neegan family of Constance Lake FN, for sharing with us generously your beautiful ancestral territories over the past five years so that we could spend time out in the forest and feel at home despite our epistemic exile.

Thank you from the bottom of my heart to my mentor and friend Colin Samson who has been a supporter from the very beginning, first of all during my doctorate at the University of Essex, and then in the process of writing the book. As soon as I heard him at the United Nations in 2005 denouncing the extinction policies and the ongoing genocide, I knew that this man was a great ally of our people. He is faithful to his convictions and to his relationships with us. He and Nicola welcomed me as a family member every time I went to England. Tshinashkumitin also to the Innu diplomat and lawyer Armand McKenzie for introducing me to Colin and advising me to pursue a doctorate with him, as well as to Utshemau and Elder Ovide Mercredi for encouraging me in 2004 to go to the UK to understand the root causes of colonialism in Canada. Thank you to Jeremy Krikler, whose contribution to my thesis committee was beneficial and decisive; he taught me to recognise my own limitations and to overcome them. His keen intelligence, his very rich South African experience and his benevolence have helped me tremendously. Thank you to the great scholar Paul Thompson, whose work, affection and mentorship inspired me enormously. Thank you to my great friend Karen Worcman for all that her work and achievements have contributed both to my research, and to the First Peoples, from the Amazonia to the shore of the Esh Shipu River. Thank you also to Isabelle Schulte-Tenkhoff for her generous advice in Geneva at the beginning of my doctorate. Thanks also to Elder Jacques Kurtness whose experience as an Indigenous university professor in the academic world helped and guided me, and thanks to my friends Gaetane Gascon, Bonnie Campbell and Herman Dworschak for their continuing support. Thanks to my friend and mentor Val Napoleon of the University of Victoria for her presence and constant encouragement. Thank you to my friend Hadley Friedland, who does so much for the First Peoples, for our conversations and encouragement, and to my friends Marie-Ève Sylvestre, Darryl Leroux, Julie Burelle, Mike Paul and Christian Tremblay for their unwavering camaraderie and constant intellectual reinforcement. Thank you to my great mentor Timothy Stanley for his kindness and wise counsel.

Thank you to Damien Short at the Institute of Commonwealth Studies, who believed in the book project from the start and secured its publication. Thank you (and my apologies) to my excellent and patient publishers Emily Morrell and Kerry Whitston at the University of London Press and to Sophie Gillespie and Valerie Hall for their amazing editing. My thanks to those who read earlier drafts of the book, including the fabulous editor and artist Nicola Gray, my Anishnabe sister Deanna Theriault and my friend Howard Waserman, who had to deal with my English at the beginning, poor them. Thanks to all of you for your patience, your constant kindness and your hard work in helping to polish my writing without ever changing its meaning.

Pierrot Ross Tremblay
Ottawa, 4 October 2019

Introduction

Locating the Essipiunnuat

Or in Québec, the Essipit First Nation has developed its tourism and commercial fishery industries, thereby creating local jobs and partnerships with both the private sector and neighboring municipalities.

Statement by Prime Minister Stephen Harper, Crown-First Nations Gathering, 24 January 2012

The white man's law kills the Indian.

William-Mathieu Mark

The group name for the 'Essipiunnuat' is composed of the Innu-aimun[1] idioms *esh* (shell), *shipu* (river) and *innuat* (humans), signifying 'Humans of the Shell River'. These terms are most likely as old as the occupation of the land by the Innu-aimun speakers. The Essipiunnuat named the Esh Shipu river 'Essesipi' or 'Essechipitch'. Notes written by missionaries in the mid 17th century report that local people used the term 'Esseigiou' or 'Esseignou' to define the same river as the one identified by explorers in the early 17th century (Champlain, 1615; Bélanger, 1946, p. 8; Frenette, 1996, p. 11). The Essipiunnuat are also known as *Unipek Innuat*, which means 'Humans of the Sea', for their historical and extensive seal- and whale-hunting activities, and because some of them stayed at a winter gathering place on the coast (Pipunapi, or 'Winter camp').

The Esh Shipu River (now called the Escoumins River) is located in the western part of Nitassinan, the Innu homeland, or area of eastern Québec, just to the east of the confluence of the Saguenay River and the St Laurence. It is situated near the Bay of Les Escoumins, 40 kilometres north east of Tadoussac and 420 kilometres north east of Montreal. The term 'Essipiunnuat', or 'Essipit',[2] refers today to 794 'Indians',[3] locally called 'members', who compose the Essipit Innu First Nation.

1 Innu-aimun is a language belonging to the wider Algonquian linguistic family. There are approximately 11,000 Innu-aimun speakers.

2 Before 1867, the Essipiunnuat were commonly called 'savages', and later 'Indians'. Anthropologists of the 20th century, such as Frank G. Speck, also identified Essipiunnuat as descendants of the former Tadoussac-Escoumains Band. From the creation of the reserve (1892) until the 1950s, the group was called 'Indians of Les Escoumins'. The name then became 'Montagnais of Les Escoumins' until, more recently, it was changed to what is considered to be the 'traditional name' of the people in this region: 'Essipiunnuat', this being the name used by Innu-aimun speakers.

3 Until 2014, the number of band members was 429. The recent McIvor decision of the Canadian Supreme Court boosted the demography of the group to 211 living on-reserve and 583 living off-reserve). See Indigenous and Northern Affairs Canada, https://www.aadnc-

Figure 1. Present-day Innu locations, taken from Rémi Savard, La forêt vive: récits fondateurs du peuple innu, *Boréal, Montréal, figure 1, p. 20.*

On-reserve Essipiunnuat live in a reserved area of 213.7 acres that was created in 1892 as per the provisions of Canada's federal Indian Act.[4] The 'reserve' is now generally referred to as Essipit.[5] The Essipit reserve covers an

aandc.gc.ca/Mobile/Nations/profile_essipit-eng.html, consulted Dec. 2018. More than 70% of the population live outside of the reserve. External Essipiunnuat so far have no right to run for leadership positions, no possibility of voting in elections, and cannot attend general assemblies.

4 A 2017 decision by the Specific Claims Tribunal (*Essipit Innu First Nation v. Her Majesty the Queen in Right of Canada*) ruled in favour of the Essipiunnuat regarding the insufficiency of the lands allocated to them upon the creation of the reserve. As per the decision, Honorable Johanne Mainville stated that: 'the Claimant should be compensated by the Respondent for the different between the 230 acres that were originally planned and the 97 acres that were granted, that is, for the portion situated in Block A and Lot 11 of Range A, and for the loss of use of this difference, with interest.'

5 Today, Essipit Band Council positions the group's ancestral domain between La Malbaie River and Porneuf River, on the St Laurence River's northern shore. Their occupation is concentrated *grosso modo* in the hydrographical basin of the Esh Shipu, in a region between the St Marguerite River and the Porneuf River, including the Lake Emmuraillé run-off, Lake à la Croix and Lake des Coeurs. Due to a way of life formerly determined by seasonal migration, occupation of the 'Innu homeland' was much different from what it is now. That said, some band members do not accept these contemporary borders and continue to assert that their ancestral domain extends, in accordance with ancient alliance and relations, to the territories formerly occupied for thousands of years by peoples of the wider Algonquian family and the Innu in particular. Whether or not the band council, instead of the traditional guardians (called *kupaniesh* in Essipit), has authority over ancestral lands and family territories is a major issue in Essipit, as it is for most of the First Peoples in Canada. The band council being a colonial device, it is argued by a large proportion of people who have maintained strong ties with Innu ancestral domain that the band administration only has authority within the reserve and that ancestral lands beyond these borders should be taken care of by traditional family guardians.

area of 1.10 square kilometres, with a population density of 272.4 per square kilometre (Statistics Canada, 2017). As a consequence of colonisation, more or less all Essipiunnuat speak French as their first language, the remaining tiny minority of Innu-aimun speakers (who also speak French as their second language) being composed of migrants from other communities such as Pessamit (Pessamiunnuat) or Mashteuiastsh (Pekuakamiulnuatsh).

On paper, Essipiunnuat governance is based on its general assembly of members, usually held four times a year. In accordance with custom (within the parameters of the Indian Act), the assembly names a chief[6] and three councillors in order to form the band council.[7] However, if it is judged that the band council does not comply with the requirement of the Indian Act, the minister can still legally discharge it. The issue of Innu self-governance, together with the topics of *Innu tipenitamun* (ancestral sovereignty as *responsibility)*[8]and *uetshit takuaimatishun* (self-determination, literally 'propelling and directing our own canoe')[9] remain unresolved and have long been complex issues between First Peoples and the Canadian Crown, as well as within the community itself.

6 Known Essipiunnuat chiefs are Léon Dominique (before 1834); Joseph Moreau (1834); Paul Ross (1904); Jos-Pierre Moreau (1926–46); Joseph Ross (1950–57); Laurent Ross (1957–79); Denis Ross (1979–2012); and Martin Dufour (2012–). For further reflections on Innu modes of governance and traditional decision-making, see Leacock (1997).

7 The band council has no roots in Indigenous philosophy, traditional modes of governance or decision-making. It is a colonial structure that was imposed on the First Nations in Canada, as defined by the Indian Act, in replacement of traditional forms of governance. It was designed to support assimilation and facilitate the cession of land and extinguishing of ancestral sovereignty. A major criticism of the band council system is that, even if the chief and councillors are elected by the members, the council is only accountable to the minister of indigenous and northern affairs. For further reflections on the band council system, listen to Radio-Canada (2019), 'La légitimité des conseils de bande remise en question', Emission Médium Large (in French), https://ici-radio-canada.ca/premiere/emissions/medium-large/segments/entrevue/101853/conseil-bande-autochtone-premieres-nations-pipeline-gazoduc (accessed on 19 Jan. 2019) and see Imai (2007).

8 See Gendreau (2016), pp. 34–5.

9 *Uetshit takuaimatishun* is interpreted here as collective self-regulation and effective self-determination. It literally signifies 'propelling and directing our own canoe', stated here as self-governance. As an informant from Pessamit mentioned, several interpretations might be made in the Innu language. 'My own translation is that the expression means our own autonomy over ourselves. I prefer this interpretation since it includes self-control, self-knowledge, within the limits we must give ourselves, the feelings we may have towards others … to summarise, I believe it is about what we want for ourselves … It might appear a very poetic definition yet this is the very beauty of the Innu language that we can transform it in accordance with what we want to express. It offers the opportunity to incorporate in one expression a quantity of meanings equivalent to what other languages would require a whole sentence to express'. Dana, Pessamit, 2008. As another informant reports, 'It can be understood as what we want for ourselves, and do for it, collectively'. Kevin, Matimekush, 2005.

Erasure, colonial fictions and the 'good Indians'

Contemporary Essipit has been depicted in the media and existing literature by business journalists, government officials, bureaucrats, external researchers, national and international reporters, and marketing strategists as a 'success story', and as a model for other First Peoples in Canada. Essipit's tourism and commercial fishery industries were even praised in a 2012 speech by former conservative prime minister Stephen Harper.[10] Essipit is generally associated with and known for the form of collective organisation it has developed over the last 40 years. As reported by Charest, the former leaders (1979–2016) call it the 'communitarian system', or the 'Essipiunnuat philosophy of community development', which is geared towards 'job creation and self-reliance'. Yet, in spite of the strengths of the local regime and the achievements of the council in the last four decades, these images tend to be one-dimensional and not include long-standing internal criticisms.

External representations of the group are overwhelmingly based on conversations with male 'managers' and 'leaders', people in positions of authority, and people who can exert political and economic control over any members of the group who might express dissenting views. For instance, Charest's assertion that this 'communitarian system' is 'widely chosen and approved, independent of the constraints imposed by the two levels of government' (2009, p. 16) minimises the internal democratic deficit within the community (the systematic exclusion of dissidents and off-reserve members as well as the marginalisation of Elders). It also fails to acknowledge the advanced assimilation of the community into the dominant bureaucratic rational and neoliberal culture as well as the band administration's absorption of the state's definition and colonial grammar. Like other external researchers, Charest, in spite of his experience and reputation for thoroughness and integrity, had hardly any access to alternative views on Essipiunnuat development, or could not report it, particularly the aspects relating to democratic and participative governance or criticism of the regime from an Innu point of view, and epistemology.

Another example of an external representation of Essipit comes from a French journalist, Évelyne Simonnet, who wrote in the early 1980s that Essipit 'triumphed over their third world condition and sense of shame' and metamorphosed into an exemplary 'financially successful, self-reliant, fully employed' collectivity (Simmonet, 1982). Essipit's greatest achievement, according to Simonnet (1982), was said to be the adaptation of 'indigenous values' to 'modernity'.

10 See Harper (2012).

This fictionalisation of the Essipiunnuat condition as having overcome colonialism and 'progressed', and the over-valorisation of its leadership, appear ubiquitous in the literature. Even if they are plainly often commissioned, and are promotional or friendly, these texts and the images of the community they portray are characterised by a tendency to overrate the power of economic development, paid jobs, material wealth and bureaucracy to free a society from profoundly complex traumas, various forms of unaddressed intra-family injuries and a sense of indignity. If there is evidence demonstrating the correlation between the Essipit autonomist movement, leadership, the communitarian system, and a significant decline in the historical marginalisation that has plagued the group, no facts or data show the impact of such actions on the group's psychological condition and its relation to the past and Innu cultural identity. Authors unanimously assume, almost as a mathematical formula, that poverty brings shame and that to accumulate material goods is a valuable source of pride.

They also imply, more questionably, that Essipiunnuat values and their 'similarity' to those of modern Euroquébécois, 'without feather or tent', to use Bernier's (2003) title, might be the most important explanation for their accomplishments, followed by their 'exceptional' leaders. With descriptions such as 'intelligent', 'visionary', 'idealist', 'free from social conformism' and 'capability' in terms of controlling their group, authors have nothing but praise for Essipit leaders' qualities as the cornerstone of the group's 'mastery of its own success'. One American author compares their deeds to the achievements of Gandhi or Rosa Parks in contributing to social change, which is no small comparison.[11]

The growing cult of personality of leaders and their centrality in the local public discourse, and of the former general manager in particular, is best illustrated by a 2016 edition of the band council journal, in which the 'remarkable achievements' of the retiring leader are abundantly praised. The edition includes comments from the well-known Euroquébécois anthropologist Serge Bouchard, and the Québec Liberal Party minister of Aboriginal affairs, Geoffrey Kelly, as well as former consultants hired by Georges. The legacy of the general manager was finely crafted, including a speech of praise for his deeds given by Kelly at the Québec national legislative assembly.[12] It appears to be the culmination of a preoccupation with the myth-making process at the core of the increasingly anti-democratic regime that had developed over three decades. This claimed that the group's present success could be traced back to one root cause only, the 'greatness' of the general manager.

11 See Luc (2009).

12 See *Tipatshimun*, fall 2016 edition.

In the last decade, forestry engineers, who were partly sponsored by the band administration, conducted research on the Essipiunnuat 'preoccupations, values and aspirations', which also leans towards a depiction of Essipit as a model.[13] Another book, by Girard and Brisson (2014), with a preface by the Essipit former chief negotiator, is openly in favour of the current project of a modern treaty being promoted by the administration. Funded in part by the Essipit band council,[14] the book presents a simplified interpretation of the relations between the French and British colonial authorities and the Innu. The preface is characterised by a discourse on the benefits brought by colonisers, absolving them from their deeds of dispossession and their violations of *Innu tipenitamun*. It tends to justify the fiction of a 'shared' sovereignty dating back to Samuel de Champlain, albeit to the advantage of the European conception of the state as contained in the contemporary project of a modern treaty widely criticised for extinguishing indigenous ancestral sovereignty.

> These principles are very similar to those which existed at the time of contact with the French in 1603 and those which the British had preserved in the Royal Proclamation of 1763. The French and British Crowns then wished to start a partnership with the natives of New France and Canada, in order to allow the establishment of a viable colony and the development of a distinct economy, all in a perspective of respect, sharing and peaceful and harmonious cohabitation. For these principles to be exercised safely, they had confirmed them through a nation-to-nation alliance with the First Nations. Hence the term 'Allies' (Ross, 2014).

Such a discourse of absolution, reproducing central themes of the colonial imaginary, serves to feed the Euroquébécois mythology that they would bear less responsibility for colonialism than the English and the Canadians, one long promoted by nationalists, particularly within the context of 'Québécois de souche's national project'. This therefore continues to keep invisible 'what national discourses consistently aim to erase' (Burelle, 2019, p. 172). The Essipit representative is reconducting here a one-dimensional and Euroquébécois

13 The band council supported some research, conducted by forestry engineers, on Essipiunnuat values and the concept of 'indigenous forestry'. The community is presented as a model throughout the study. See St-Georges (2009) and Beaudoin et al. (2012).

14 As for other publications funded and supported by the band council, Girard and Brisson's book reinforces the Petapen grouping's promotion of a modern treaty and its legitimation in the eyes of other Innu communities. As the anthropologist Émile Duchesne observes in his review, 'the authors' conclusion as well as the overall development of the book are placed in support – conscious or not – of the Petapan group's strategy. The heart of the facts brought into the book and the general observation refer more to the communities represented by this grouping. It would have been better to limit the content of the book to these communities or to broaden the scope to include more the strategies and political demands of other Innu communities' (2016).

interpretation at the expense of Innu oral and legal traditions.[15] This type of narrative has been supported by a variety of communication strategies and publications to legitimise the signing of extinguishment clauses included in agreements resulting from the comprehensive land claims process.[16] It aims at fabricating an Innu consent to the surrender and abandonment of *Innu tipenitamun* as a foundation interlaced with the Earth, and as rooted and conceived in their oral tradition. All publications relating to Essipit, in particular those emanating from the band administration's communication branch, are aligned with the official discourse of the band council, promoting the signature of an agreement with the state. Complete control over the group's external image, including through social media, is maintained by just a handful of the band administrators.[17]

In 2016, Serge Bouchard, an omnipresent public figure in Québec, was hired by the band council to write a history of the Innu, with a particular focus on Essipit.[18] This resulted in a very popular yet problematic book called *The Laughing People: A Tribute to my Innu friends* (2017).[19] The manuscript, funded by the Essipit band council and commissioned by its former general manager, was widely promoted by the Essipit communication branch responsible for treaty negotiations. It was strategically presented to the Innu people as a 'gift' from both Bouchard and Essipit.[20] Are Bouchard and his book part of a communication strategy to protect the band council and its former Director General from criticism, as well as to legitimise Essipit's signing of a modern treaty? What is clear is that it effectively serves to reinforce Essipit's image as Innu, in particular through associating it with the Ekuanitshinnuat, as well

15 The mythology of good relations and lasting alliances between the French and the Innu, as well as the fiction of a shared sovereignty, are often used by Québec nationalists to erase their own posture as settlers. Also, there is evidence in Innu oral tradition that the alliance mentioned in Sylvain Ross's preface to Girard and Brisson's book was purely strategic and violated shortly after being made. For more balanced interpretations see Chrétien et al. (2009). For a critical perspective on Québec's representations of the past and First Peoples' sovereignty, see Burelle (2019). On Québec's commemoration of Champlain as a nation-building practice, see Leroux (2010).

16 For critical perspective on the land claim negotiation process in Canada as a continuation of colonialism, see Samson (2014; 2016); Samson and Cassell (2012); Diabo (2012); Pasternak (2016; 2017); Schulte-Tenckhoff (2000).

17 In 2016, the communication division of the band requested that its members communicate with the council before adding any information pertaining to Essipit on Wikipedia, for example.

18 See Bouchard (2016) and Conseil des Innus Essipit, *Rapport annuel* (2016). For a critique of Bouchard's discourse on Québec history and relations to First Peoples, see Burelle (2019) pp. 57, 70–1, 74, 79–82.

19 Bouchard and Lévesque (2017).

20 It is publicly known that Serge Bouchard is a long-time friend of Georges, whom he praised in a local newspaper in 2016 as a 'great man' to whom he has 'never been able to say no', see http://innu-essipit.com/fichiers/3457/Montage%20final.pdf (accessed 10 Jan. 2019).

Figure 2. 2016–17 marketing campaign, taken from https://www.grenier.qc.ca/nouvelles/7949/ vacances-essipit-devoile-as-nouvelle-identite-visuelle (accessed 20 May 2015).

as proposing the community as a 'model' to be followed by others. The book, although well-written and entertaining, remains stale because it is clearly a tool to manipulate the Innu, who are asked to swallow a political strategy rooted in the anecdotes of the famous anthropologist and his flattery of local leaders. It draws a romantic veil which helps, consciously or not, to control local interpretations, and to silence and erase further internal critical voices, diverting attention from the harsh truths of the leaders' relationship with their own past. Both this and the Girard and Brisson book are examples of 'mercenary work' which give overwhelming power to authority in the production of group stories, and a unified interpretation. These projects are also led by Euroquébécois, who, in spite of their openness and good relations with local managers, tend to frame Innu history through the lens of Québec national history and trauma, a perspective that is also favoured by both Innu and Euroquébécois Essipit band administrators. In Julie Burelle's view, 'settler-colonial societies have long depended on a rewriting of history to legitimise their existence', which leads to a failure to 'unsettle Québec's settler-colonial past' and contribute to perpetuating 'settler-colonial domination in the present'. According to Burelle, Bouchard's discourse and performances are determined by 'his desire to be made innocent of his settler-colonial complicity' (2019, p. 81). She adds that his 'poetic license with history' would allow him to 'champion Indigenous people and simultaneously use them to affirm whites' innocence' (2019), p. 83.

Essipiunnuat who dared to criticise Euroquébécois hired by the band and imbued with the Québec imaginary and selective memory, and who were at times taking decisions related to Innu culture and symbols, found themselves accused of being discriminatory towards Euroquébécois and even of being 'racists' and not 'liking the whites'. As an example of stratagems employed to maintain control over the Essipit's representations of the past, in 2008 the previous band general manager, Georges, had hired historian Pierre Frenette to write the group's history at the same time as I was carrying out research for my PhD.[21] Meanwhile, Georges warned me that my research 'would upset some people'. The phenomenon of the band administration and their leaders hiring research professionals from various disciplines was described as 'mercenary' (Garneau, quoted in Charest, 2005, pp. 13–14). According to Charest, the transfer of knowledge for remuneration would greatly impact on the production of local knowledge in communities:

> It is regrettable that too often the results of this type of production of knowledge remain more or less secret, thus putting the lamp under the bushel ... Thus, in my opinion, too tight control of research can affect not only the quality of work done, but especially their diversity. Some issues, however, of major importance, such as power relations within Aboriginal groups and communities, may not be acceptable, whereas from a strictly scientific point of view they are essential to analyse in order to understand all the internal dynamics of these groups and their external relations. Enclosed in narrow corridors and subject to prohibitions and even self-censorship, research can certainly not produce comprehensive and well-grounded analyses of the Aboriginal reality. (2005, pp. 13–14)

The administration's depiction of the community is best illustrated by its 2016–17 marketing campaign, conducted on behalf of the corporate branch of the band council. It demonstrates how indigeneity has been commodified and how 'Innu' has been used as a brand.[22] The campaign continues to market Vacances Essipit, a branch of the band Enterprises, as a tourist destination. What may seem innocent enough – even funny and engaging at first – powerfully illustrates the misappropriation of the term 'Innu', as well as a typical pattern of colonial erasure and rewriting.[23]

21 Sadly, Frenette passed away a year into his research.

22 For extensive reflections on the commodification of 'indigeneity', see: Manit (2017), pp. 135–58; Adese (2012).

23 Developed by a well-known Québec marketing firm hired by the band council called Les dompteurs de souris, the campaign makes use of the word 'Innu' to promote Essipit enterprises. In the advertising, the term 'Innu' is linked with 'bliable' to form the neologism 'Innubliable'. In French, 'inoubliable' means 'unforgettable'. One advertisement features a tourist being so aroused by the outstanding beauty of the nature in the area that she is having an orgasm as she pours her coffee. If of relative aesthetic value, this use of the term 'Innu' remains problematic as it concerns the name of a whole people who are absent from the representation. 'Innu', which is a shortened term for 'Innuat' in the Innu-aimun language, means the 'humans'. The term is not only denatured but is reduced to a mere selling strategy, a branding. While promising lasting memories for tourists, the slogan achieves the internal erasure of the term 'Innu', by twisting its meaning in French.

External accounts of the community often portray it as having come into existence only when the former leaders took office 40 years ago. It is as if there is an absence of a group 'self' before that time (Simonnet, 1982; Anderson, 1999; Bernier, 2003; Gaudreau, 2006; White, 2008; Charest, 2008; Luc, 2009; St-Georges, 2009; Beaudoin et al., 2012; Bouchard, 2017). This repetitive discourse, which is reasserted in contemporary imagery, deserved further investigation. It also echoes the colonial fiction of the group's absence of history before the creation of the reserve. But if these proofs do not exist, it is because no researcher has been able to give voice to the Essipiunnuat themselves. None of the previous research has examined the full spectrum of community life. Too often it has neglected a particular age group, aspect of social status, or has lacked the scope to look at the emotional health of the people, their self-perception or relationship with their past.

The overwhelmingly positive external view of the Essipiunnuat as presented in previous research calls for a deeper, internal, independent and critical perspective, based on people's experience, cultural memory[24] and stories. Such an approach would show that financial prosperity does little to erase the memory of misery or trauma; shame and self-hatred can take surprising forms when we attempt to banish them. Such circumstances are likely to generate internal tyranny actualising suffering and subjective amnesia (a desire to forget as well as an inner command to forget), and severe intergenerational consequences. No matter how deep a truth is buried, it will always seep out. The Elders we met repeated over and over again the importance of facing the truth and looking back at the past as a prerequisite for effective decolonisation. Although it might seem desirable to forget and escape the story of 'why', we can seldom achieve this. Forgetting acts like a drug that momentarily comforts but does the user little or no good in the longer term.

Catching oblivion: a genealogy of amnesia

> In order to exist, man must rebel, but rebellion must respect the limits it discovers in itself – a limit where minds meet, and in meeting, begin to exist. Rebellious thought, therefore, cannot dispense with memory: it is a perpetual state of tension. In studying its actions and its results, we shall have to say, each time, whether it remains faithful to its first noble promise, or if, through indolence or folly, it forgets its original purpose and plunges into a mire of tyranny or servitude.
>
> Albert Camus, *The Rebel*

At its outset, this research, which began as a PhD at the University of Geneva, was about documenting Innu historical resistance to colonialism and

24 Cultural memory is defined by Assmann and Holscher as 'all knowledge that directs behaviour and experience in the interactive framework of a society and one that obtains through generations in repeated societal practice and initiation' (1988).

endogenous conceptions of a right to self-determination in the face of internal colonialism in Canada. The project was based on the assumption that the best way to prevent the genocide of vulnerable micro-groups was to empower them to defend themselves and their ancestral domain. As the project developed, it became clearer that I could test this most effectively by studying the experience of my own community (Essipit).

Like many Essipiunnuat of my generation, I had been forced to live most of my life off-reserve but I had maintained my connections there.[25] My mother's community membership was re-established in the 1980s, just like mine, after the Canadian parliament passed Bill C-31, which partly changed the practice of women being excluded based on marital status in accordance with the Indian Act.[26]

On returning to live full time on the reserve in 2006, I observed that my lack of knowledge about the group's past was widely shared by members of my generation, whether or not they had lived off-reserve. It seemed to me that this cultural disconnection was the first problem that needed to be tackled if the Crown were to be prevented from further violating the ancestral normative order. How could people resist the invalidation of their ancestral conception of sovereignty, the limitations to their freedom, and the commodification of their culture if they themselves were ignorant of what needed protecting? What are the links between the cultural genocide experienced by the Essipiunnuat and the idea that our *sui generis* conception of Innu tipenitemun as sovereignty, responsibility and freedom does not exist? Cultural oblivion, brought about in part by genocidal policies internally reproduced, means that groups affected are more likely to relinquish rights and surrender *Assi* and ancestral lands.

In 2007, some of the older Essipiunnuat informed me of an event that occurred in the 1980s – of which I had vague childhood memories – called the Salmon War. My interlocutors, including Elders, considered this event to be the most important in the history of the group and the most significant in their own lives; a pivotal moment that supposedly reinvigorated and empowered them. The leaders, in particular, depicted it as the genesis of all the subsequent developments that had been undertaken by the community. My preliminary investigations into the Salmon War revealed an event which pointed to a wider story of resistance by First Peoples to policies of extinguishment, and an assertion of sovereignty. This led to the decision to re-orient my PhD as

25 For some elements of my autobiographical memoire, see Ross-Tremblay (2015), no. 5, pp. 214–31. I returned to live permanently in the community in 2006 with my wife, children and parents.

26 For more information on the topic, see Canada., Erasmus and Dussault (1996). G., & Dussault, R. (1996). Report of the Royal Commission on Aboriginal Peoples. Ottawa: The Commission; Palmater, P. (2019), 'Canada continues to deny sex equality to First Nation woman and children', Rabble.ca, (consulted January 23, 2019).

a community-based and participative oral history of the Salmon War and to document how my own community dealt with the forces of colonialism in the 1980s. The account of resistance and empowerment would be valuable for other vulnerable groups facing similar situations. My principal contacts at that time were leaders and other individuals in positions of power in the community (at the band council where I worked as a negotiation advisor from 2007 to 2009) who fed my assumption that the Salmon War was mainly an experience of collective self-empowerment.

However, tripartite conversations with Jeremy Krikler and Colin Samson, my PhD supervisors at the University of Essex, led me to the realisation that there were other voices and perceptions of the community, and its systems and past that might be being overlooked. My own need for acceptance following time away from the group had made me vulnerable to indoctrination and inclined to an essentialised and mythologised Essipiunnuat memory that tended to legitimise the current social order. This was to be a cornerstone of the research project: psychological colonialism had made us relatively blind and deaf to the cultural treasure to which we are heirs and I could hardly ignore the state of our inner condition or fail to investigate why it came about.

The focus of my research shifted towards investigating the relationship of the group to its past, the intergenerational implications of this, and the reasons for it, rather than an exploration of the past itself. It switched from being an oral history project/sociology of local development to a mnemohistory focusing on the production of amnesia.[27] This new approach was to require a challenging level of self-reflection, since I was still working at the time as a negotiation advisor for the band council.[28] The discoveries I made and the obstacles I met on the road to truth-telling and rememorisation were to become precious data in the documentation of a multifaceted example of cultural oblivion.[29]

The privation of cultural memory among the youth as a phenomenon was clearly impacting on our cultural identity as Essipiunnuat, but above all it was

27 It was to become my PhD thesis, completed in 2012: 'A Genealogy of Amnesia: Memory and Forgetfulness in Essipiunnuat's Narratives of the Salmon War (1980–1).

28 I stopped working for the negotiation sector of the band council at the end of 2009. At the same time, I volunteered to write a strategic vision for the cultural sector, which was submitted a month later. It was entitled *Pour nos pères et nos enfants: occuper le territoire de la mémoire et du rêve* [For our fathers and children: to occupy the territories of memory and dream]

29 Meanwhile, I undertook a journey of personal healing and cultural empowerment, through nutshimit ('life in the forest'). These long periods of time alone in the bush (generally two weeks) became indispensable in order to investigate in myself the phenomena that I wanted to understand in and with my people. This proximity to the earth, to oneself and elders' teachings was the antidote to being overwhelmed or devoured by the complex social phenomenon I was trying to understand within the reserve. Rooting myself epistemologically more deeply brought an important phase of psychological decolonisation; I was then able to take a more insightful look at the deeper, and often fiercely hidden, causes of our human condition as Essipiunnuat, and better assess our relationship to colonial institutions and culture.

jeopardising the cultural continuity of the group. How can First People resist attempts to extinguish their ancestral sovereignty if younger members have relatively little idea that this legal order even exists? What were the sources of self-ignorance and a far-reaching amnesia about the group past, despite a clear willingness and need to know? Part of the response to this enigmatic rupture of transmission, symbolised by ignorance of the Salmon War, had to be sought partially in the previous generation and their silence. For this earlier generation, especially those who had participated in the Salmon War, the event had been a pivotal point in their lives and the group's memory. Mnemonic practices pertaining to the event would be rich material for shedding light on this intergenerational concern.

Preliminary investigation revealed powerful experiences of cultural revitalisation and the re-emergence of an Innu conceptions among the group at the time of the Salmon War. Yet on closer examination there was an uneasiness about the event, about the past and also about the current condition of the group. A complex code of silence was revealed during the first meetings with those taking part, that from the very beginning revealed evidence of strong systemic and political barriers to remembering, and of forms of in-group control in the present that were casting a shadow over the past. Indeed, there was a tendency among a majority of interlocutors to assume that the community had 'no past' before the Salmon War; stories about the group were more or less entirely articulated in accordance with the chronology set by the current regime, particularly its former general manager. A first look at the stories also echoes some profound and intriguing silences.

The fundamental enigma in *Thou Shalt Forget* concerns the phenomenon of cultural oblivion, its sources, mode of production and effects, as experienced by the Essipiunnuat. It is assumed here that the weighty effects of cultural genocide and its impact of intergenerational trauma, breaks in cultural transmission related to experience of the Residential Schools, the absorption of Québec nationalist mythologies, and the advanced internalisation of the Crown representations of the Indian-as-object (that was to be internally redesigned as 'simulated Indian' or 'simulacrum of indigeneity') are all determining features of the current condition of the group. A trend towards moving away from what is 'Innu' – a propensity to abandon it, to step away or disconnect from it, with collateral effects such as cultural anaemia, was observed among the younger generation. The existence of a discourse on the invalidity of Innu knowledge as a point of reference was noticeable among this group too, as revealed by the interviews and in conversations that occurred mainly between 2007 and 2012 with 15 Essipiunnuat aged between 25 and 38 years old.[30] As will be shown

30 I belong to this generation and I suffer, to varying degrees, from the same psychological and cultural phenomena experienced by other young Essipiunnuat. It is sometimes difficult to see the social phenomena that we are facing ourselves, especially cultural oblivion, because

later, in addition to these conversations with the youngest, which helped to identify the extent of the phenomenon of forgetfulness, were added in a second phase more formal interviews with thirty people from previous generations (of which 20 who agreed to be recorded).

A journey in truth-hunting: intergenerational silence, discontinuity and amnesia

Research on young Essipiunnuat mnemonic practices shows evidence of an advanced form of collective memory loss and enigmatic absence of Essipiunnu memory in self-identity. This is best illustrated by the near-complete ignorance among my generation about the Salmon War, a pivotal episode in the lives of generations of Essipiunnuat (that is, for their parents and grandparents). One young Essipiunnu, for example, who was five when the war started, had never been told anything about it:

> I was five or six years old and my memory is that I am sitting with my mom and … it's not funny, it's serious and there are guns around … I don't know if I've seen my dad leaving the house with guns, I don't know if I've seen people passing by with guns … I don't even remember if I heard gunfire … but I know that there were guns involved. I didn't know what was going on and we didn't know what turn it was going to take. So my memories are summed up like that. It was serious, there was an element of danger … but ... I didn't know why, it's really also about the feelings of my mom … because my mom knew what was going on … but you see, I've never talked about it again with my dad, nor with my mom, or with anyone else … so I don't know the details. (Elisabeth, chapter1, ref. 3)[31]

Right up to the present day however, strong emotions are associated with the war. Most commonly, the youngest interviewees would say that they knew something serious happened, but did not know what. This is unsurprising,

we are overwhelmed daily by the enigma we are trying to solve. That being so, the present research aims to shed light on the inner aspects of psychological colonialism based on the valuable knowledge of those who undergo it. As Elder Albert Marshall puts it, 'When you force people to abandon their ways of knowing, their ways of seeing the world, you destroy their spirit and once that spirit is destroyed, it is very, very difficult to embrace anything – academically' (Albert 2015, p. 17). In order to find balance and overcome the condition of being 'incomplete', as find a way to work 'in a harmonious way', Elder Albert proposes a way called 'Two-Eyes Seeing' or 'Etuaptmumk'. This approach, that I've tried to follow in my research, reinforces the capacity 'to see from one eye with the strengths of Indigenous ways of knowing, and to see from the other eye with the strengths of Western ways of knowing, and to use both of these eyes together' (Bartlett, Marshall, M., & Marshall, A., 2012, p. 335). On one hand I thus cross-reference people's views and support and illuminate their rich stories with as many perspectives as possible, from Indigenous and non-Indigenous thinkers, in a transdisciplinary way.

31 The notation of each interview is taken from the classifications assigned by the NVivo software I employed.

since almost all those who took part in the war come across as confused or uneasy in the interviews, saying that it was the most significant experience of their life but that this was the first time they had talked about it. Thus, there is evidence of a shared silence about the recent past, captivating in its intergenerational scope and effect.

If the impetus to study the phenomenon of cultural oblivion came from these early encounters with young people of my generation, all with family ties of one kind or other, it is through interviews and the close study of the previous generation's stories that it is possible to posit a theory about why collective memory loss happened and what the parameters of it are. Breaks in intergenerational transmission of cultural memory, seemingly reaching their peak with the current generation, appear to be the apex of a wider social and historical process of cultural discontinuity experienced by the group over time, which has accelerated in the last century and recent decades (Speck, 1915; Laforest, 1983; Mailhot, 1996; Frenette, 2010, Garneau 2015).[32]

In this context, the task consists of tracing back the genealogy of this apparent cultural oblivion and its 'lineage' (to use Foucault's expression) in order to determine the factors that have led to the current situation. More specifically, the work: 'seek[s] answers to the questions how and why "we" forget, inquiring into those moments and acts of interruption or disruption that are production of oblivion, as well as those that serve to maintain oblivion, such as silence, omission and repetition' (Plate, 2016).

To that end, I had numerous conversations with Essipiunnuat men and women. Yet the book is principally based on the close examination of autobiographical memories of the Salmon War retained by 20 Essipiunnuat who were aged over 38 at the time of the meetings. This allows for a better understanding of this generation's relationship to its Essipiunnuat past and heritage, through individuals' preferences regarding silence, remembering or transmitting. The close study of this generation's mnemonic practices is crucial to shedding light on the group's current cultural condition. This includes the social and historical determinants, as well as the desire for remembrance or oblivion, of its will to continue or to disappear. We return to this later.

People's stories also help us to better understand how cultural oblivion is generated, what the determining factors are, and the main interests in its production (without turning a blind eye to the crucial issue, for many communities, of the role of internal power and the effects on the entire group of

32 For example, when American anthropologist Frank G. Speck visited Essipiunnuat around 1915 during one of his field investigations, he met with my ancestor, an Essipiunnu by the name of Old Paun Rus, or Old Paul Ross in English (1825–1920). The man was already in his mid 80s at the time of their meeting. He became one of Speck's key informants, and is abundantly quoted in his later publications and notes. Speck's field notes, accessible through the American Philosophical Society in Philadelphia, testify to the intensity of Essipiunnuat cultural life in 1915.

the psychological colonialism experienced by the leaders). The social relevance of cultural oblivion is highlighted in large part by its effects on subsequent generations, who are unable to access a collective inventory of experiences and cultural referents. The younger interviewees, each in their own way, voiced concerns about this and its impact on their lives. Conversations with them over the past decade have revealed an intense need to access norms and Innu stories, laws and ceremonies. The majority wanted to know the truth about the past. But they also told of psychological distress – *identity crises, stress, anxiety, alcoholism, drug addiction, depression, suicidal thoughts, homicidal thoughts and self-loathing.* Along with this went an inability to identify the sources of their negative feelings. *One wonders whether the privation of cultural knowledge and memory could be directly related to the psychological phenomena they describe.*

Traditional Essipiunnu cultural values, such as respect, care for others and self-sufficiency are sometimes depicted in discourses as having been lost. Indigeneity is at times linked with weaker racial genetics, inherent health problems, and psychological deficiencies, inclinations to excess, sexual deviance and substance abuse, not only expressing a distance but also a desire to distance. It is not unusual to hear young people speak of 'Indians' as 'others', essentialising indigeneity, producing negative representations, and even making racist statements against Innu (the phenomenon of internal racism as denounced by certain Elders in my conversations with them). More generally, identification as 'Indian' tends to depend on circumstances; a malaise more often replaces moments of pride in expressing an indigenous self. Feelings of non-authenticity, inconsistency and uneasiness, of having an Indian 'card' to play but nothing else, are common. In 2010, a 23-year-old woman from the community informed a French tourist asking about the history of her people that he should look elsewhere, since there were 'no Indians here any more'.

Young Essipiunnuat are far from being alone in being disconnected from a cultural memory and heritage that ought to be theirs. It is a phenomenon experienced by other groups that have been subject to the Canadian and Québécois colonial projects. It is therefore important, although painful, to turn an honest gaze on what is going on in the reserve, not to engage in blame or a smear campaign, but to unveil deeper and often invisible layers of knowledge and experience.

Concerns about the growing intergenerational gap, and weakening cultural identity and collective continuity, have been growing themes of interest in academia worldwide in recent decades. Collective memory loss and its relation to the past, including the discourse on indigeneity, has also become a source of anxiety for the neighbouring Euroquébécois.[33] Although Quebec society is not the focus of this study, it has had and continues to have an important influence

33 See: Leroux (2019) and Caldwell (2017).

on contemporary Essipiunnuat society and other First Peoples of the Québec-Labrador Peninsula (who have by various stratagems been 'Frenchified'), and is therefore referred to sporadically in the text, as it has the potential to make visible the blind spots of the descendant peoples who have settled, over the last 400 years, on the Innu ancestral territories.

Many thinkers have identified this epidemic of forgetfulness as the chief challenge for the continuity of what once was called the 'New World'. In this sense, the Essipiunnuat's experience of cultural oblivion extends beyond the borders of a 0.8 km^2 reserve and the fewer than 300 people living on it, and has a far wider relevance. Yet, the academic arena appears to be struggling with the issue. In this context, the crucial role of indigenous researchers should remain that of voicing problems as formulated by those experiencing them, without minimising their own experience as a source of knowledge.

The phantasm of forgetting: the story of a colonial illusion

> Man is like a salmon, salmon always goes up the river where he was born, this is the real mystery. Wherever a man goes, he never forgets where he comes from. Whatever mileage travelled, the number of cities crossed, no matter how long it takes to find a destination, he never forgets his origins.
>
> Rita Mestokosho, Eshi Uapataman Nukum

When *ushâshamek* (Atlantic salmon) is about three years old, it leaves the river where it was born for its first long journey of thousands of kilometres. The salmon then returns to its native brook, to the exact location of its birth, and repeats the spawning cycle. The Innu poet Rita Mestokosho says in one of her poems that man is like a salmon, since 'he never forgets where he comes from'.[34] Forgetfulness is thus far from absolute. Individuals and groups remain forever connected to the conditions of their beginnings; their deeds, choices and self-representations can never be detached entirely from their own origin in spite of the dams that might prevent them from accessing these spaces. This is well illustrated by Nietzsche's description of the self-designed superhuman's relation to his past, resentfully unable to silence the voices of his past selves; the reminiscences of past will, choices, contentment, deeds and beliefs remain forever connected to the terms of his own birth. Freed from everything he did not choose, he remains the slave of his memory, tied to everything that has made him what he now is (Nietzsche, 1885).

The relationship that a collectivity entertains with the past, what is retained, valued, celebrated or forgotten, is evocative of a fundamental dimension of

34 Mestokosho, R. (1995), Eshi Uapataman Nukum, *Comment je perçois la vie Grand-mère*, Beijbom books.

its current condition, of its symbolic needs, as well as the self-perception of its social and wider historical circumstances. This genealogy of oblivion traces back the lineage of an individual, generational and/or collective propensity to overshadow figures of its experience. Attempts to forget are highly normative and can consist in critical judgements about the self, with major impacts on one's self-identity. To trace back the genealogy of a memory gap, the social, psychological and historical formations of oblivion about specific events pave the way for the discovery of decisive and influential yet unrecognised subjectivities that have shaped its production, including determining commands to forget and the corollary desire to forget in the realm of power.

Autobiographical memories and their intersections give access to common memories and histories, and to the social purposes on which they ultimately depend (Thompson, 2017).[35] Ways of relating to the past and mnemonic practices are relevant to investigation, and life stories and autobiographical memories are now widely recognised as valued material. People's stories offer self-portraits, collective past selves, cultural postures and communalities. The power of stories and their contents in individual lives are the benchmark of their values and norms. Telling and recounting are to sacralise, normalise and standardise; the process generates identities.

Individual readings of group agency contained in personal accounts can be highly informative of the generational and/or trans-group dimensions of collective subjectivity; such narrations have the power to make visible the cultural memory of the narrator used as a resource for the self. Autobiographical stories of a past event give access to the critical experience knowledge of a similar type that forges the social group. The central role of memory of common experience (of 'inventory of experience') in the epistemological formation of a generational unit is a good example: 'The inventory of experience, which is absorbed … from the environment in early youth, often becomes the historically oldest stratum of consciousness, which tends to stabilize itself as the natural view of the world [for each particular generation]' (Mannheim, 1952, pp. 304, 328).

Scrutinising narrations of sociohistorical situations and events can help to investigate micro-groups' relation to their past and to their present and future. It can report on the formation of past generations, their understanding of themselves, and the genuine conception of their values and prejudices. It offers views on how old emotions of the past are brought forward in the present and make visible the new contexts to which they are applied (Hakemulder, 2000, p. 87). What narrators 'want to transmit' is evocative of current individualities but also of group self-conceptions and the selves one could become, would like to become, or are afraid of becoming; it informs on the cognitive manifestation of

35 See also: Thompson (2017) and the excellent book by Releigh Yow (2005). Clinical sociology has been particularly explicit about the benefits of life-story narrative for sociological investigations. See, e.g., Rebach and Bruhn (2001).

enduring goals, aspirations, motives, fears and threats. Ultimately it illustrates the correlations between current self-conceptions and motivations for the maintenance of its normative basics (Cross and Markus, 1994; Markus and Nurius, 1986, p. 954). Autobiographical memory stories shed light on the current self-schemas of narrators, on their organisation of past experiences, and their recognition and interpretation of their social environment. Self-conceptions revealed in narration remain impregnated with cultural contexts and immediate social circumstances, and any assessment of them can be richly informative of communalities and common cultural and social schemes (Markus et al., 1985; Markus and Kunda, 1986).

Social research, to have value and relevance, must be useful to people themselves and should rely as much as possible on their cosmogony (Smith, 1999). Oral history and its methods, and the value that is placed in people's stories and epistemologies, coupled with a detailed study of mnemonic practices, have long proved their usefulness for reviewing official discourse, interpretations and unified dimensions about the past, its narration and sources. It allows for the reaccessing of cultural identification, the spreading of interpretative nets, and easier investigation of current needs, interests and self-perceptions. It offers a space to reinstate points of reference, counter psychological colonialism and reactivate, from the people's own stories, 'the sources of rules and practices that have enabled a group to reproduce in a hostile environment' (Savard, 2004). At its core, this project is a call for research to transcend academia and engage wider audiences to overcome epistemological ghettos and the replication of imposed categories at the service of internal tyrannies. From the beginning, my work aimed to access and make heard people's voices; to optimally generate a confluence of personal, family and community stories into a wider common script entirely nourished by them.

Throughout the research I wished to present people's perspectives faithfully. I wanted to detail their insights into decoding the shadows of our memories and our blind spots. Their words and intuition are intrinsic to the value of this book.

I have tried my best to bring together Essipiunnuat knowledge and stories, and the tools of social sciences, to conduct research 'in a good way', as Elder Albert Marshall suggested, and I hope that my vision of this book being 'for the benefit of all' but especially those who need it most (quoted in Integrative science, 2017) will be an enduring one.

Readings of the stories

The study of autobiographical memories assumes that storytelling reflects the ways in which people's experiences are articulated and how their understanding of life and the world, and of themselves within it, is constructed. Focusing on an uprising, and how such an experience is described in people's stories, was therefore a prerequisite to learning something about those who took part in the Salmon War and the dams between them, their memories and their children's generation. The study of personal testimonies, brief life stories and conversations in relation to the event allows for an understanding of the way in which the Essipiunnuat experienced their fate, how they have coped with it and what they make of it now. They are presented as they were narrated and organised in accordance with the predominant themes and topics. People's stories went through four main readings.

The first reading consists of identifying what people perceive as the sources of the Salmon War, its main determinants, and all the elements that have contributed to its production. The analysis led towards categorising what those taking part identify as the 'objective condition' or the external causes, and then moves towards the 'subjective condition' and collective agency as a determinant. A second reading is about picking out elements relating to self-representations (self-portraits, depictions of others and representations of the group) in the course of the action. The goal here is to access aspects of the group past-self associated with the event and distil its normative charge. A third reading is conducted through the lens of the changes people associate with their experience of the war. The last reading is about searching in the stories, and mnemonic practices, for content evocative of the present time and current condition of the group, including the production of cultural oblivion.

About this book

The first chapter contains some theoretical reflections on cultural oblivion as well as background information (mostly from documentary sources) about the Essipiunnuat and the Salmon War. Chapter 2 identifies the central elements that have contributed to the occurrence of the Salmon War, according to those taking part. These went beyond their own subjectivity. The chapter covers colonialism, the games of Québec government politics, the mentality of the local Euroquébécois of Les Escoumins township, and the actions of radical anti-Essipiunnuat militants. Group agency was identified as a central determinant of the event. This expression of collective subjectivity is associated with references to a common inventory of past experience, the appearance of a movement of affirmation, and the existence of shared objectives that were operationalised through specific and chosen strategies articulated from a symbolic representation of the salmon.

The next chapter examines elements of the group past-self (or elements of the group's past self-identity) associated with the event that were exhumed from people's autobiographical memories. People's self-portraits are evocative of communalities in characters conforming to an emergent norm of commitment (commanders, warriors and supporters), of social background (dual cultural identification, economic dependencies) as well as shared emotions (the pleasures of uprising, the suffering of the subsequent reaction). Representations of others are dominated by the description of ten specific people (idols) who are represented in heroic postures (perilous circumstances, longing for sacrifice, for the good of all) revealing clear common ethical attributes (iconographies) placed in contrast with images of transgressions (irrationality, hypocrisy, non-commitment). Representations of the group (power of solidarity, indigeneity, dignity) confirm features of a group past-self whose aesthetics display characteristics of strength and rebelliousness.

Chapter 4 presents the transformations people associate with the occurrence of war. These accounts suggest four common perceptions of a remodelling of their relational system (fractionation, associations), important alterations of self-identity (indigenisation, cultural reidentification), collective self-empowerment (self-legitimacy, autodynamisation and increased knowledge) and new forms of governmentality (internal re-ordination, perceptions of authoritarianism). The Salmon War is presented as a pivotal moment, resulting in a collective revival, followed by the formation of a post-war regime (albeit on a small scale) exerting political, economical and psychological control – and the emergence of a unified historical interpretation.

The final chapter demonstrates what is revealed about the current condition of the group from looking at how those who shared their stories relate to their past. Studying the stories identifies various 'dams' that distance people from their memories of the war, such as interference from subsequent events (the 1982 agreements, bill C31, the unemployment fare crisis), and other phenomena that contribute to a logic of forgetting (traumas, protection of relations, interests in denial, bureaucratic will to ignorance, erasure and rewriting). However, it also identifies elements of resistance to the vectors of oblivion (emotional reflux, normative charge, reminiscences). A close examination of people's relationship with their past provides background for their current nostalgia (community gathering, Innu way of life, spirit of resistance), social criticism (relations with states, commodification of ancestral sovereignty, monocracy) as well as their views on the current cultural condition of the group (views of reality, need for standards, models to reproduce and avoid). Lastly, it exposes a shared vision regarding the imperative of intergenerational transmission, including what should be transmitted and the best ways to transmit them in order to secure Essipiunnuat cultural continuity in the face of cultural exhaustion. Reflections on the process of investigating one's own community's relation to the past and some keys for researchers to understanding such experience are also explored.

1. The Essipiunnuat, the Salmon War and cultural oblivion

Obsessive preoccupation with bygone triumphs or tragedies substitutes fables of glory or victimization for the chequered pasts we actually inherit. Yet we remain accountable for the whole of our collective pasts. [...] The psychic cost of repressing traumatic memory can be as crippling for nations as for individuals. History is often hard to digest. But it must be swallowed whole to undeceive the present and inform the future.

David Lowenthal, *New York Review of Books*, 14 January 2016

The Innu has always said that he will never cede his rights on the land, he will never go to the government and say 'I don't need the land'. No, the Innu will never say this. There are kids here, they will need it. And later, they will ask questions to the government about the domain of their ancestors.

Elder François Penashue Aster

Cultural oblivion as a phenomenon is fascinating in its scope, its impacts and its complexity. By its very nature it is awkward to investigate. As for ignorance, it is constantly slipping from our fingers and fleeing yet further; it must be looked at through the shadows, in forgotten traces, through whisperings and silences. The researcher disturbs its producers, their secrets, the deeds and past experiences that they believed had fallen into nothingness. Researching oblivion involves digging up skeletons and trying to learn from them. It is not always convenient. But no matter how deeply the truth has been buried, and what was known and felt, it tends to leak into the present. There are always reasons, generally painful ones, why people hide things and strive to make others forget. Abuse and trauma are important, together with fear, guilt, shame and the variety of interests they entail. The colonial authorities (including the Catholic Church) and powers-that-be are impressively gifted at erasing their deeds and rewriting a self-legitimising story that makes the abused responsible for their condition.

Cultural oblivion, particularly that produced in a colonial context that is characterised by internal erasure and rewriting, deserves closer attention. The reserve, as part and parcel of a genocidal project of elimination, is one of the most efficient laboratories for forgetting. The impacts of 150 years of an over-reaching Canadian command to forget remain underestimated. For that reason, Essipiunnuat's relationship with the past can hardly be investigated without considering some of the broader sociohistorical background. From the killing of Essipiunnuat families[1] in the early 19th century, to our displacement in

1 In his conversation with Frank Speck (1927), p. 397, Paul Ross Sr mentioned the fact that Innu families were allegedly killed when merchants who gave them tea contaminated with smallpox.

order to create the reserve, to the contemporary absorption of a Euroquébécois selective memory by our own leaders, the Essipiunnuat experience of forgetting haunts our minds and needs to be told.

After revealing some assumptions about cultural oblivion and tracing back some key social and historical information about the Essipiunnuat, I will introduce the Salmon War, which will lay the ground for a discussion in the subsequent chapters of the mnemonic practices of the contemporary Essipiunnuat.

The study of cultural oblivion

> The overall result sought by colonial rule was to convince the natives that colonisation would lighten their darkness.
>
> Frantz Fanon, *The Wretched of the Earth*

Cultural memory and oblivion

The term 'mnemohistory' is generally used by researchers who are concerned 'not with the past as such, but only with the-past-as-it-is-remembered' (Assmann, 1997). When presented as 'the ongoing work of reconstructive imagination', history revalorises the role of cultural transmission in the production of collective identities. Reception theory applied to history can, then, lead to an increase in sociological relevance; outlooks on and interpretations of the past can reveal the changing set of norms, values and social contexts from which they flourish (Olick et al., 2011, p. 45).

Collective connections with and representations of the past are motivated primarily by the fear of deviating from a set model and by the desire to repeat elements of the past. Cultural memory is defined as 'all knowledge that directs behaviour and experience in the interactive framework of a society' (Assmann and Hölscher, 1988), and becomes transgenerational through 'repeated societal practices and initiation', making a group visible in the present. Based on the group consciousness of unity and specificity, from which it derives its formative and normative impulses, cultural memory offers a ground for the reproduction of its cultural identity. The past in that cultural heritage, and the values that are narrated in its identificatory appropriation, manifest the constitution and customs of a society (ibid., 1988).

The growing field of the historical sociology of mnemonic practices and, in particular, the evocative power of the ways in which groups represent their past in their current condition, deserves close attention (Olick and Robbins, 1998). The need for identity remains the pivot for collective references to the past and the search for cultural referents; narrating the past produces norms,[2] sanctifies identity and therefore ensures that the group maintains a wholeness and cultural continuity (Mol, 1979). Narrating the past is essentially an act of self-identification. The making of history thus consists of producing identity through relating 'what supposedly occurred in the past and the present state of affairs, building meaningful stories for a defined subject, with its own motivations and social circumstances' (Friedman, 1992, pp. 837, 856). This posture validates the power of subjectivity and the importance of considering carefully the production of myth through stories as they reflect 'an imprinting of the present onto the past' (Olick, 2007). Thomas King would say that, ultimately, we are the stories that we tell ourselves (2015).

Forgetting and power

The role of authorities in determining what must be remembered or forgotten is key. The political value created by established authority figures in exercising domination over the production of representations of the past and over interpretations remains weighty. The influence of those exercising power, their command to forget, is decisive:

> The control of the past depends above all on the training of *memory* ... It is necessary to *remember* that events happened in the desired manner. And if it is necessary to rearrange one's memories or to tamper with written records, then it is necessary to *forget* that one has done so. The trick of doing this can be learned like any other mental technique ... It is called *doublethink*. (Orwell, 1954, p. 31)

Selective memory or selective amnesia remains inherent in imperialism and hegemonic practices.[3] As Garde-Hansen and Worcman remind us in their revolutionary work *Social Memory Technology* (2016), if we do not remain vigilant, the risk is great of being affected by the powerful forces that have an interest in forming group memory: 'Without this control and power over narrating the past, communities can become hijacked or coopted for collective memory projects, in which national identity and homogenising discourses smooth over the complexities of multidirectional stories' (2016, p. 191).

The production of the past, the appropriation of cultural referents and the actualisation of 'past' images are classical modes of legitimation, which all act in

2 Cancían defines 'norms' as 'beliefs about what individuals ought to do that become part of a person's motivation through socialization; people come to act in conformity with the norms of their society precisely because they want to conform. However ...norms are perceptions of what actions will lead others to validate an identity (rather than personal beliefs), so that people are thought to conform to norms in order to demonstrate to themselves and others that they are a particular kind of person' (1975).

3 Among others, see Dessi (2008); Chu et al. (1999); Pennebaker et al. (1997); Baumeister and Hastings (1997); Marques et al. (1997), p. 254.

the interests of those in charge. The same event has different values even within groups, and the malleability of cultural identity is often to the advantage of the dominant group (autocrats in particular), especially under colonial rule. The place of wars as founding events in the design of collective self-stories must be carefully considered:

> What we celebrate under the heading of founding events are essentially violent acts, legitimated after the fact by a state of questionable legitimacy; events legitimized, ultimately, by their very antiquity, their time-worn custom. The same events, therefore, signify glory for some, but humiliation for others; one side rejoicing to the other's execration. This is how real and symbolic wounds are stored in the archive of collective memory. (Ricoeur, 2000)

The promise of amnesiology

Oblivion has not been considered for its true value as a manifestation of agency and as a production. Forgetfulness tends to be overlooked, despite its significance in people's lives and its uses for different social purposes. Forgetfulness is as evocative of the normative foundations of a society as remembering; they are both mnemonic practices (Connerton, 2008).[4] Building on the rich history of research on memory, Plate suggests the term 'amnesiology' for those interested in the study of the production of cultural oblivion and the exploration of 'forgetting and forgetfulness not as a failure of memory but as a made condition, produced and reproduced' (Plate, 2016).[5]

This is the approach that I will take here. Cultural oblivion can be revealed in 'disconnections … failures to transmit what is known and … refusal to mark [elements of the past] as memorable' (Plate, 2016). The study of forgetting is concerned with collective traumatic events and strategies for dealing with memories associated with the dual desire to forget and to make forget; or, the struggle around the articulation of truth. It includes institutional and informal forgetting and repression, transgenerational transmission of information about traumatic events and forms of erasure and rewriting of the past in accordance with a chronology geared around conquerors' actions. The modalities of intergenerational transmissions of cultural memory, and the intricacies of collective memory and cultural transmission remain of great interest to this book.

The matter of memory loss following traumatic events and experiences – such as, for example, sexual abuse or war – has a central place in clinical

4 Connerton (2008) identifies seven types of forgetting, corresponding to multiple agents: repressive erasure, prescriptive forgetting, forgetting as constitutive in the formation of a new identity, structural amnesia, forgetting as annulment, forgetting as planned obsolescence and forgetting as humiliated silence..

5 See also, Herzog (2009).

sociology and social psychology. In particular, selective memory and self-deception appear to be treated most widely in these fields. In the case of mass violence, as Stanley Cohen describes in *States of Denial*, perceptions of the past tend to be distorted to meet the agenda of the present; personal memory is contaminated by the passing of political time, and authorities play a major role in enforcing the sense of temporal continuity needed for public order and social control (2001, p. 240).

For individuals and communities with traumatic memories (whether as perpetrators or bystanders), selective memory is often used to escape the past and to forget the suffering that is so closely related to shame and hatred. Those 'recalling', including researchers, often experience degrees of marginalisation and oppression from local authorities. Searching for truth remains a direct threat to the wilful ignorance that is inherent in bureaucratic rationality. As Mcgoey (2012; 2014) argues, the 'cultivation of strategic unknowns' is a great resource for those in positions of power and for colonial institutions.

In the contemporary context of the reserve, social research produces uncertainty due to the very nature of its inquisitive quest into what was not supposed to exist; this unknown object of knowledge is from time to time perceived as a threat to the certainty desired by those who govern and their followers. This is also relevant regarding corporate interests in resource development and extraction (often related to local leaders), investment that naturally requires certainty when it comes to title to the land. In fact, exposing mass silence and oblivion may result in jeopardising the interests of its most ardent producers. Studies of forgetfulness in the context of advanced psychological colonialism, however, have major implications for the indigenous researcher. These include dealing with mostly well-buried factors, and with the reasons they were concealed in the first place. Such frontal stance against the troubled past of our often wounded communities necessarily implies sporadic, unexpected and surely uncomfortable encounters that will, however, be the raw material for developing a more fundamental critical reflection on the relationship First Peoples have today with the past and the land – truth and life, in other words.

First Peoples, colonialism and cultural oblivion

The long tradition of studies on colonialism and the historical practices of collective domination remain relevant for a deeper understanding of First Peoples' contemporary condition and mnemonic practices. Early studies of the psychological aspects of colonialism shed light on the role of cultural amnesia in colonial attempts, through the falsification of memory, the rewriting of historical texts and the extinguishment of what is remembered, to secure supremacy over colonised entities by transforming people and lands into objects. Such scholarly work along these lines remains more valuable than ever in the contemporary Canadian context, where, in spite of symbolic discourse on reconciliation, a constitutional regime genocidal, deeply racist in spirit and imposed on First Peoples remains untouched.

Memmi (1957) used the term 'cultural amnesia' to highlight the links between the apparatus of colonial domination and the debilitating phenomenon of intergenerational disconnections and the identity anaemia that plagues the same groups on which they are operationalised. Dominated, forced into submission, and deeply humiliated, the colonised tend to conform to and mimic the images the colonial society has of them; but assimilation remains a mirage since mainstream society refuses integration. The colonised are therefore confronted, day after day, with the heartbreaking dilemma of remembering and revolt or forgetting and self-annihilation.

The psychological mechanisms of colonial domination, including, at its heart, the distortion, disfigurement and annihilation of the dominated group's cultural memory, have been superbly theorised by Frantz Fanon.[6] As he proposes, the central scheme of colonisation is not only to hold the population under the control of the dominant group, but, by the perversion of its logic, to turn colonised people against themselves:

> Perhaps we haven't sufficiently demonstrated that colonialism is not satisfied merely with holding a people in its grip and emptying the native's brain of all form and content. By a kind of perverted logic, it turns to the past of the oppressed people, and distorts, disfigures, and destroys it … This work of devaluing pre-colonial history takes on a dialectical significance today. (1963)

The dominant group then ensures its sustained pre-eminence by generating the internalisation of a hierarchy of value between two 'essences' of people. The implacable logic of colonialism, its depersonalisation, its collective amnesia, and its production of racialised memory, generates intense psychic crises in colonised groups, which Fanon explains is escapable through a willingness to restore one's dignity and regain one's identity by all means necessary. Yet, the absorption of an essentialist self-conception generates an intense internal contradiction for the colonised; a war based on a racialised concept of the self that contradicts his or her own quest for humanity.

Colonial rule and its types of subjugation push the colonised into the corner again and again; violent insurrections against the colonisers then become almost inescapable. The revisitation of one's past is the most fundamental step in the process of decolonisation, which comes right before entering into

6 See: *Black Skin, White Mask* (1952) [1967 translation by Charles Lam Markmann]; *A Dying Colonialism* (1959) [1965 translation by Haakon Chevalier]; *The Wretched of the Earth* (1961) [1963 translation by Constance Farrington]; *Toward the African Revolution* (1964) [1969 translation by Haakon Chevalier].

the struggle for liberation. This movement towards remembrance is part of a general revalorisation and actualisation of a person's culture[7] symbolised by its songs, poems and old stories.[8]

As elucidated by Maori scholar Moana Jackson (2004), the deep-seated psychological dimension of colonialism affecting First Peoples must be considered in the light of its material basis and the wider historical project of appropriation and exploitation. Colonisation comes with a myth-making process and the reshaping of memory, through the colonisers' production of 'myths' and their strained absorption by the dominated groups. Colonialism, which aims primarily to ensure the pursuit of material benefit and access to resources, needs to legitimise the seizure and guarantee the maintenance of political and economic power of one group over another. Myths thus serve to mask the reality, to justify the status quo and to conceal the tragic extent of dispossession that has shaped indigenous peoples' present and their past. Jackson suggests myth-making as rewriting ultimately absolves the coloniser and secures the basis for the ongoing denial of the rights and obligations of the colonised and the exploitation of ancestral territories.

Studies of colonialism in Canada, conducted by intellectuals from First Peoples, have an increasingly high profile together with speeches on the subject given in universities and the public space and reported on in the media. A new generation no longer accepts that non-indigenous people define them and speak on their behalf equally as much as in literary, art and cinema circles from which a profusion of indigenous perspectives emerge. My goal here is not to expose these fascinating schools of thought, even though their crucial importance is recognised, but rather to contextualise as far as possible the condition of the Essipiunnuat, within the wider framework of Canadian and Québécois colonialism, including in their legal and academic forms.

Canadian colonialism, and its historical accountability for the current condition of First Peoples, is characterised by the production of a deep crisis of identity, political fatigue, multiple dependencies, social disorganisation and economic slump, as Taiaiake Alfred (2004) eloquently reports. According to Alfred, the current human condition in Canada can better be appreciated in

7 Lotman defined culture as 'the totality of non-hereditary information acquired, preserved and transmitted' (quoted in Cobley and Jansz 1997). This definition is complementary to Jimmie Durham's as 'what we know about ourselves and what we want to become'. Durham, in Lippard (1993).

8 The power of remembrance for dominated micro-groups is also one of Sartre's favourite themes, as in his preface to Fanon's *The Wretched of the Earth*: 'Bringing [old stories] alive and introduc[ing] into them modifications which are increasingly fundamental [contributes] to bring conflicts up to date and to modernise the kinds of struggle which the stories evoke, together with the names of heroes and the types of weapons ... The formula "this all happened long ago" [has to be] substituted by that of "what we are going to speak of happened somewhere else, but it might well have happened here today, and it might happen tomorrow"' (1961).

the light of a disastrous succession of events, including Christianisation, forced sedentarisation, ethnocide, the systematic usurpation of traditional modes of governance, dispossession, displacements, residential schools and the abduction and rape and murder of children, and the subsequent intergenerational ruptures and their tremendous effects to-date. Alfred's project – which may have influenced, perhaps more than any other indigenous intellectual, the new generation – involves unearthing the intellectual basis of the state's control over First Peoples, a domination based on the notion of the monopoly of state power and the negation of ancestral freedom and responsibility to the land. Indigenous evaluations of contemporary colonial institutions necessarily lead to the conclusion that the colonial state cannot legitimately determine their futures. Ancestral epistemologies and dynamics of indigenisation produce 'uncertainty' that threaten the authority, monopoly and sovereignty of the state itself, including therefore forms of colonial counter-will and revived desires to erase and bury indigenous referents. We can better appreciate, in the light of this history of deep and lasting oppression exposed by Alfred, to what extent indigenous research and independent investigations in Canada on the issue at stake become a strategic tool and an advanced form of activism, especially when it opens up secure spaces for truth-telling and Indigenous critical postures.

For the Kanien'kehá:ka scholar Alfred, a deeper understanding of the condition of the indigenous peoples in Canada requires wholly recognising the philosophical gap and existing antinomies between the conceptions of Crown sovereignty, as imposed on indigenous groups, its prevailing capitalist ideology and historical project, and the ancestral values of First Peoples. The nature of Canadian colonialism can thus be comprehended by considering its objectives of deterritorialisation, uprooting and disconnection, in order to ensure total conquest and absolute legitimacy, and prevent endogenous resurgence. Continuous control over First Peoples is mainly done through breaking cultural foundations or roots, so that there is 'no memory to store or intellectual base upon which to build a challenge to the empire'. It resulted in a 'spiritual disconnection', a crisis of identity or the impossibility '[of finding] the spirit of ancestors living inside of you'. Ongoing subjection to exogenous norms and their internalisation generates an epistemological collapse preventing the intergenerational flow of knowledge (Alfred, 1999; 2004; 2005, pp. 57,162). The way is then paved for the effective production of cultural oblivion, on a large-scale, through the establishment of solid and permanent dams between First Peoples and their cultural memory and, to use the salmon metaphor, preventing them from returning to their place of birth to reproduce in a symbolical sense and ensure continuity.

The command to forget everything pertaining to one's ancestral domain, cultural memory and self-identity is the powerful tool by which *sui nullius* and the idea of one's own absence can be generated – the absorption of the myth that you have no history and that you are condemned to play yourself in the theatre of your own absence ('a way of life that does not exist', to use Samson's expression). The late elder Herb Nabigon used the term 'hollow tree' to illustrate the effects of colonialism on First peoples and the fact of feeling emptied of one's own spirit (Nabigon, 2006). This colonial erasure was translated, among other things, into mass starvation, the creation of reservations, the abduction of children through the residential schools, theft and trade of babies, forced evangelisation (and the sexual violence and mistreatment by priests that often went along with that), the removal of indigenous women's status and the long-standing manufacture of consent to treaties of extinction and forced cession of ancestral domains. From old stories (*atanukan*) and oral history (*tipatshimun*) to musicians, writers of novels, poets and screenwriters (of documentaries, in particular), and now a new generation of academics, the Innu have consistently denounced colonialism and the fate reserved for their people and Assi ('the Earth') by states, churches and corporations. An exceptionally long history of Innu resistance therefore dates back to first contacts. This can be better understood in the light of forces that have sought to erase it and extirpate it from the very heart of the Innu over the centuries.

Song has been an important vehicle for Innu language, speech and thought from ancient times to the present. One has only to think of Philippe Mackenzie, whose music has influenced a generation of musicians, including members of the group Kashtin. Because they have experienced, often since childhood, the worst of violence at the hands of colonial institutions, the work of these singers eloquently testifies to the deep marks left by erasure policies but also to the role of art in fostering resistance, resilience and reversibility.

As the Innu singer Florent Vollant states, a command to forget, imposed on children in residential schools, signified that 'we were forced to forget who we were' (quoted in Lévesque, 2015).[9] This is the very spirit of Canadian apartheid erected by John A. Macdonald – an absence of memory following genocide and erasure that is echoed beautifully by the acclaimed Innu poet Joséphine Bacon:

> I made myself look pretty
> So that they would notice
> The marrow of my bones,
> Survivor of a story
> That no one tells (Bacon, 2009)

Then, she asserts, in a prophetic tone, her 'dream of a single story, which could dictate without failing, a whole lifetime lived' (Acquelin and Bacon, 2011).

9 V. Audet (2012); K. Bacon-Hervieux (2017).

It is probably the work of the late Elder An Antane Kapesh (1926–94), an early critic of Canadian and Euroquébécois colonialism, who reveals the extent of oppression and dispossession experienced by the Innu. After writing an autobiographical novel in 1976 called *I am a Damn Savage*, praising Innu culture in contrast with the forces seeking its erasure, she wrote the anti-colonial novel *What have you done to my country?* (1979). In it she exposes, with brio and symbolism, the different stages of the history of Innu dispossession. In particular, she uses the metaphor of the Punchinello to personify the colonisers. With great insight, she warns Innu about the risks involved in simulation and playing the settlers' game too much over time:

> Then the child stopped speaking. He got very upset when he realised the importance of the things he had lost. He had lost his entire territory, all the aspects of his culture and even his language. And he knew then that for the future, and until his death, he would have to continue, whether he liked it or not, to play the fool with the Punchinellos and to play to their polichinelleries [buffoons]. (pp. 80–1)

Various attempts have been made to document Innu cultural memory and historical experience. The late Innu historian and ethnologist Jean-Louis Fontaine made a remarkable contribution to contemporary reflection on Innu spirituality and rituals. In his book, *Beliefs and Rituals Among the Innu*, he succeeded with genius in extirpating treasures of ancient Innu spiritual traditions, from writings (*Relations des Jésuites*) known to have marked the greatest wave of oppression and repression of culture. Among these, it is worth mentioning the critical work of Zacharie Bellefleur, Evelyne St-Onge, Céline Bellefleur and Eddy Malenfant, which remains one of the most important contributions to the documentation, produced by the Innu themselves, of their science, language, oral tradition, cultural practices, ways of life, and historical experiences and interpretations.[10] Through Manitu Productions, they have made more than 40 documentaries for television and educational purposes over the last 30 years.[11] Other significant artists include Innu poet Rita Mestokosho, who has a strong and influential voice overseas, and new figures who take an uncompromising look at the Innu condition such as the excellent novelist Naomi Fontaine, who reports on life in her community (and whose novel *Kuessipan* has just been filmed), and the popular actress, poet and activist Natasha Kanapé-Fontaine. The latter is perhaps the one who best embodies

10 Their work, 'dedicated to the Innu nation in which Elders pass on their skills and knowledge to younger generations' is available on the website, 'Nametau Innu: memory and knowledge of Nitassinan' at http://www.nametauinnu.ca/en/culture/nation/detail/64/72 (consulted 26 Jan. 2017). Its short videos include one on the history of the community featuring interviews with members and the former chief, Denis Ross, and another portraying Levis Ross, a captain who has developed a whale-watching business as part of the tourist industry.

11 For more information, see Les Éditions Manitu: http://www.productionmanitu.com/accueil.html.

these strong voices calling for remembering, as a prerequisite to decolonisation, and emphasising the imperatives of overcoming the intergenerational effects of colonial violence and erasure:

> I go back into these lands
> I go back to these bodies
> That today have been erased from the memory
> Have been erased from the memory
> Of our parents. (2017)

What remains most undocumented in the realm of the social sciences, however, is the internalisation of colonialism, the forms of abuse and the wounds within the community as a result of colonialism, and the inner phenomenon of suffering and transgressions favouring intergenerational ruptures, erasure and oblivion. With the exception of the excellent work of Radio-Canada journalist Anne Panasuk (2018), who exposed the extent of priests' abuse in communities as well as the phenomenon of sexual violence perpetrated within communities today, little research is available that gives voice to the Innu themselves in connection with their realities, and with forms of internal oppression in relation to the past.

It is worth mentioning, however, the excellent novel *Kitchike*, by the Wendat novelist Louis-Karl Picard-Soui, who exposes with intelligence and perspicacity the power relations within the First Peoples communities situated in the south of the province of Québec. His novel exposes with humour but great realism

Figure 3. Innu family on the edge of the St Lawrence River, near a village today called La Malbaie, dated 1863 (Alexander Henderson/Library and Archives Canada / PA-149709).

the forms of internal tyrannies, incarnated by an all-powerful leader with an autocratic style of ruling, including inflicting humiliation.

Some of the research in this area has striven to echo Innu perceptions of their current condition and the phenomenon of cultural oblivion among them. For the sociologist Colin Samson, mnemonic practices among the Innu must be considered in the light of the Canadian state's wider programmed extinguishment of the Innu. The tragic and traumatic consequences of this are best illustrated by the daily lives of the people of the Natuashish and Sheshatshiu communities. The tragedy experienced by the Innu, including intergenerational ruptures in transmission and forms of cultural oblivion, are widely produced by a regime of power that is destined to eliminate the Innu systematically. The clear relations between the historical regime of power destined for the First Peoples and their current condition, as a historical production, are widely kept silent and denied by both the Canadian and Euroquébécois colonial societies (Samson, 2001; 2003; 2006; 2008; 2010).

The anthropologist Rémi Savard has provided valuable insights into Euroquébécois' complexes and their own cultural representations and perceptions of the Innu over time, characterised as they have been by ignorance and a disregard for indigenous culture and worldview for more than four hundred years. Witnessing the government's historical attempts to assimilate, erase and annihilate Innu cultural memory, Savard (2004, p. 112) concludes that for the Innu, the consideration of their history and remembrance of their old stories (*atanukan*) form the backbone of cultural continuity. This reactivates 'the sources of rules and practices which have enabled the group to reproduce in a colonial environment that has long dreamt of seeing it disappear'. Recalling these stories today is an assertion of sovereignty and its actualisation in ancestral terms.

Both Savard and Samson have demonstrated how the current transgressions experienced by the Innu are directly linked to Canada's historical genocidal policies and attempts to extinguish these groups and usurp their ancestral sovereignty, above all in order to secure corporate interests (Savard 1971; 2002; 2004, p. 68). These wide-ranging, direct encounters echo some key Innu perspectives and conceptions about the relationship between their past and current situations.[12]

The Ordeal of Truth

Literature on cultural memory and oblivion is concerned with the role, power and value of heritage and remembrance for groups, and their continuity.

12 Among others, see the linguistic, anthropological, ethnological and oral history of scholars such as Mailhot (1996), Vincent (1994), Bouchard (2004) and Charest (2003). The colossal and respectful work devoted to the Innu word, left by the filmmaker Arthur Lamotte, should also not be forgotten, including important archives containing hundreds of interviews.

Concerns with the past are generally presented as a collective demand for memory, a willingness to access the *truth* about history or a dynamic of cultural assertion. Delving into stories of yesteryear can generate the normative power of past stories and past selves and their potential actualisation, enabling people to create their own culture of relatedness. Gazing into the past allows for differentiation with respect to the present, and for reassessment and reevaluation of the current cultural condition and social order. One way or another, remembrance signifies eruptions of the past and its leaking into the present; a 'terrorism of veracity' well exposed in Nietzsche's work.[13] Yet, a posture of truth in relation to the past remains a prerequisite for transgenerational transmission and increased collective agency.[14] As an Essipiunnu Elder states:

> The most powerful tool today when we speak with the young people is the truth. We have to shake them. They will be shocked at first, they may not like it and may get away from you. But they will eventually come back. Because they will think about it and will know that you're honest with them. This is how we should speak with the younger generation if we want to communicate something to them.[15]

Memory, amnesia and remembrance remain a central theme in art, especially in contemporary cinema. These productions tend to resonate with the quotation from the beginning of Israeli filmmaker Ari Folman's animated *Waltz with Bashir* (2008): 'We may forget the past, but the past won't forget us'. Either as victims or oppressors, coloniser or colonised, protester or statesman, individuals and groups remain connected with the social circumstances that led them to seek oblivion. Directed amnesia, with its preferred medium of silence, and produced oblivion are fragile and not absolute, to the chagrin of all those who struggle to forget and to make others forget.

It is certainly perilous to resort to 'history', 'archaeology' and 'anthropology' in research focusing mainly on mnemohistory, amnesiology and how Essipiunnuat stories report the group's relationship to its own past and present. This is especially true when such an exercise requires that we rely on the same colonial and written sources, while trying to question the validity of erasing Innu epistemology and memory in favour of pleasing Euroquébécois. Likewise, there is a tension when we self-censor to protect settlers' fragility. It seemed useful to refer briefly to existing documents, especially taking into consideration the small number of references to Essipiunnuat that are available. These sources are particularly helpful when it comes to documenting and deconstructing the colonisation processes and its effects, from first contacts until today.

13 The expression is a subtitle in the book *Vie et vérité : textes choisis* (Nietzsche, 2001).

14 See Ramos (2010); Iniguez et al., (1997, pp. 238–9); Dessi (2008); Nietzsche (2001).

15 Personal communication, Innu Elder, Sep. 2009.

The aim of this section is therefore to summarise existing data on Essipiunnuat and their ancestral domain, and to use all the available written material pertaining to Essipiunnuat, irrespective of the discipline, in order to support and complement people's knowledge and stories. While some sources are weaker and more questionable than others, the crossover of disciplines, data and stories certainly helps towards better comprehension of the context and circumstances of the eruption of the Salmon War in the 1980s.

This research was conducted, from beginning to end with, by and for Essipiunnuat themselves and it was engineered with and governed by the explicit goal of 'assisting in cultural maintenance', to produce a more 'inclusive' and therefore more 'complex form of knowledge'. By making Essipiunnuat's stories and knowledge its first source, facilitating the articulation of Essipiunnuat epistemologies emphasising relationality and relational accountability, this research thus tends to subscribe to the indigenous standpoint theory and embraces indigenous research methods (Foley, 2006; Nakata, 2007; Wilson, 2008).

The Essipiunnuat: contexts and circumstances

We were told that before the reserve, we had no history[16]
Elder Elise Ross

But the night of oblivion will not come.
Tahar Djaout

A significant amount of information exists that pertains to human occupation of the area which corresponds to what present-day Essipiunnuat consider to be *Nitassinan* ('our homeland' or Innu ancestral domain in Innu-aimun).[17] Archaeological literature reveals human occupation of the hydrographical basin and banks of the Esh Shipu river, where Essipit is located today, dating back approximately 8,000 years (Plourde, 1993, quoted in Charest, 2009).

There is also evidence that small seasonal groups, who used stone tools, came to the area to benefit from the abundant resources provided by the sea. (Chevrier, 1996, p. 103; Frenette, 1996, p. 9). An analysis of the last two

16 From an interview with the late Elder Elise Ross (Laforest, 1983).

17 During interviews, some older Essipiunnuat contested the way the term 'Nitassinan' is used in the context of modern treaty negotiation by lawyers and band administrators. This approach would not correspond to ancestral Innu vision and would come too close to the Eurocanadian concept of property and frontiers between Innu groups, which includes the possibility of cession and alienation of the land. In their view, the Innu homeland could not be divided and given over exclusively to a few Innu, who would wrongly award themselves the power to alienate the land contradicting First Peoples' collective and shared obligation to 'Assi' (the Earth) and future generations.

thousand years of occupation in the high northern shore region demonstrates the continuous presence of small local groups occupying the interior, as well as the upper areas of different hydrological basins and the coastal littoral, according to seasonal migration (Chevrier, 1996, pp. 107, 114).

A rich Innu oral tradition preceding the period of contact with Europeans in the mid 16th century, but testifying to these encounters, has been transmitted from generation to generation. Consequently, the seasonal migrations of the Innu, which led them to the shores of the Esh Shipu, preceded the imperatives of the fur trade. Summer gatherings were important times for decision-making, diplomacy and trade as well as ceremonies. Until forced sedentarisation, Innu had an ancient way of life based on a cycle of subsistence conditioned by seasonal rhythms. People shared their time from autumn until spring in small familial units in the interior, coming down to the coast along ancient paths in the summer in order to gather together in multi-familial units on the banks of the salmon rivers: 'the smallest and best articulated units … constituted of less than one hundred individuals closely related to each other, and each of these groups would occupy the mouth of a different river, for which they were generally named' (Savard, 2004).

Transgenerational transmission of Innu oral tradition takes three main forms: old stories known as *atanukan* (what must be transmitted), *mishta-aiatshumun* (historical events) and *tipatshimun* (events that have occurred in one's life). Old stories take the form of epic stories that reveal fundamental components of Innu cultural memory, ranging from science (innu-aitun), ontology and cosmogony, to philosophy of law and governance, botany and zoology. This ancient oral tradition – containing insights into first contact with Europeans, about political alliances, conflicts and perceptions of the European endeavours on their lands – is remembered and has been partly written down.[18] The innovative work which has compared, for example, archaeological finds and archives with contemporary Innu oral accounts on the founding of Québec City demonstrates the acuity of Innu ancestral memory, especially when compared with documentation from the early 17th century, which was often falsified and rewritten by the authorities (Chrétien et al., 2009).

In addition to oral history and tradition, contacts between the Essipiunnuat and explorers, merchants, priests, bureaucrats, and more recently researchers, over the last 400 years have left important written and oral evidence behind. For example, early colonisation of the Innu ancestral domain, in particular

18 The immense documentation of the Innu oral tradition carried out by Rémi Savard, José Mailhot and Sylvie Vincent should not be ignored. They and others, who were concerned with not reproducing colonialism in ways of doing research, were important 'transmitters' of Innu cultural memory, at a time of great turmoil and intergenerational ruptures. Having made a significant contribution to the cultural continuity of the Innu, they tend to be highly respected in communities.

the foundation of Québec, is vividly depicted in Innu oral tradition. The perspectives this contains differ, however, from the French interpretation. If for the French, their arrival foresaw the establishment of a New France, it sounded more like a catastrophe for the Innu. It appears that relations between the Innu and the French began in trade and mutual curiosity, but they rapidly transformed into power struggles, war and conflict and a lack of respect for Innu consent, reflecting the French cover-up of their imperial intentions (Chrétien et al., 2009). This original bewilderment is well demonstrated in new analyses of the 'alliance' of 1603 that occurred in Tadoussac (on contemporary Essipiunnuat ancestral domains) – one that was agreed between the French and a wider grouping of people of the Algonquian family, including the Innu. The alliance was allegedly based on trade and defence agreements already negotiated between traders and the Innu (Trigger, 1981).[19] Innu oral tradition recounting what happened next demonstrates the insincerity of the French and the lies they told (Chrétien et al., 2009), and confirms a Jesuit intention which translates as a 'cross ... erected on these lands in order to take possession of it' (Fontaine, 2006). It must also be said that the arrival of French settlers, followed by the English, marked the beginning of human trafficking of which the Innu women were the first victims. In the light of 400 years of history, Champlain's affirmation that 'our boys will marry your daughters, and we will make only one people', used over time to embellish Euroquébécois colonialism, has sinister resonances today.

The first documented contacts with Basque fishermen date from the 16th century (Turgeon, 1986). In his *Des Sauvages*, published in 1615, the explorer Samuel de Champlain is one of the first Europeans to describe the Esh Shipu river and the people he met in the area, including the *utshemau* or great captain, Anadabijou (1993 [1615]). The Jesuits meticulously documented their first contacts with the Innu in *Relations*. These documents offer insights into the Innu way of life, including their spirituality, despite the strong 'cultural filters' and intentions of the priests. More importantly, they reveal that the Europeans were greatly motivated to take over the continent. They also report the Jesuits' eagerness to obtain, at all costs, the conversion of First Peoples, which resulted in repeated attacks on Innu ancient rituals and ceremonies as well as the progressive inculcation of a culture of family violence and the imposition of patriarchy. The Jesuits were teaching the parents to physically punish their children and husbands to beat their wives (Hamidi and Kanapé-Fontaine, 2018, p. 14). In *Relations* the Jesuits described their early efforts at evangelisation between 1632 and 1672. These writings broadly reflect European intentions and cultural representations of the local populations. Contemporary Innu interpretations of their actions sustain that the long-lasting and intense

19 See also Frank Christopher's film *Dead Reckoning: Champlain in America* (2009).

efforts to indoctrinate local groups provoked 'the alteration, even the gradual disappearance of a whole cultural world' (Fontaine, 2006). Slowly but surely, 'the new religion wormed its way up to substitute itself entirely to the old one, inserted to become the only truth' (Fontaine, 2006).

The archives of trading posts are informative about the comings and goings of the Essipiunnuat over a long period, and of the types of businesses and relations they undertook with the traders. Trading posts were established in the region from 1670 onwards (Dufour, 1996, p. 17), and the presence of First Peoples on the Esh Shipu river in the late 17th century is well documented (Nouvel, 1664; Bélanger, 1946). The increased interest of the French in seal and salmon at the beginning of the 18th century also led them to develop further their contact with the *Unipek Innuat*, the 'Humans of the sea', referring to members of these groups who spent winter by the sea in order to hunt seal (Dufour, 1996).

French interest in dealing with the local population resulted in the establishment of a permanent religious mission in 1720, with a chapel at the local group's winter camp, Pipunapi (Bélanger, 1946, p. 14), to be followed five years later by a trading post. This post generated more than six hundred sealskins and more than 90 barrels of oil annually (Parent, 1985, p. 824). The diminution of animals in the region increased Innu interest in seal hunting and their presence at Pipunapi, a site that was abundant with seal (Parent, 1985, pp. 753–4).

Traders' attempts to impose a monopoly on local groups led competing agents to undertake stratagems destined to significantly weaken the local population. For example, a violent incident occurred in 1760–1 when Tomas, the son of Miskout and Gertrude Tchiskoué, was reportedly murdered in the area of the Esh Shipu river by the captain of an English schooner (Bélanger, 1946, p. 15). In the words of the old Innu patriarch, Paul Ross Sr, interviewed by Speck, traders allegedly introduced 'tea and bread into which one had put the small-pox' so that 'the poor Indians all fell down dead in a short time' (Speck, 1927). Indeed, the notorious General Amherst's policies in the 18th century of using bioterrorism against First Peoples and to 'try every other method that can serve to extirpate this execrable race' (Amherst, 1763) remains central to contextualising that historical period for First Peoples.[20] Canada has a long history of mass violence towards First Peoples.

The controversial transfer of the French titles in 'New France' to the British Crown – an infringement of Innu consent – and its effects on *Innu tipenitamun* (Innu ancestral sovereignty), are intrinsic to the question of the legal value of the Great Alliance of 1603 in international law. If *Innu tipenitamun* has been translated as 'sovereignty' within the context of contemporary language,

20 For more information on Amherst's bioterrorism, see also D'Errico (n.d.).

Figure 4. Les Escoumins township c.*1912 (from family archives).*

the referential in which the concept takes root is far from the European conceptualisation of land and power (Savard, 1981; Gendreau and Lefèvre, 2016). In fact, abstract words such as 'property' or the legal concept of 'fee simple', do not exist as such in Innu-aimun (Mailhot and Vincent, 1979). *Tipenitamun* carries the meaning of responsibility, management or control over something, and *kanauentamun* means guardianship over something (Ross-Tremblay, Motard et Vincent, 2015). *Tipenitamun* refers to an intergenerational approach to relating to *Assi*, and must be understood outside a bureaucratic conception of land title (CAM, 1993). Because of the indivisibility between being 'Innu' and 'Assi', identifying with the idea of consenting to the extinguishment of Innu *tipenitamun* would ultimately mean self-annihilation. *Tipenitamun* is used to refer to

> the relation of a Mayor with his city, of a Minister with the domain under his jurisdiction, of Band Chief with the member of the Band, of parents with their children, of God with humans, and, in the context of Innu religion, of Master-spirits with the animal species they control (Mailhot and Vincent, 1980).

Innu tipenitamun thus refers primarily to the old legal order and philosophy of law reflected in the old stories.[21] Therefore, talking of Tshakapesh constitutes, 'a solemn affirmation of sovereignty since it is a reactivation of the very sources

21 On the topic of Indigenous philosophies of law see Savard (2004), Friedland and Napoleon (2016), Borrows (2016; 2019).

of the rules and practices that have allowed the group to reproduce in a colonial context having always dreamt of its disappearance' (Savard, 2004, p. 168).[22]

With the transfer of French possessions to the English Crown in 1763 came an uncertainty about the status of these lands and the dynamics of their appropriation. The description 'Indian territory' even appeared in the royal proclamation, and state appropriation of these same territories thereafter tends to demonstrate that the conquest (as remembered in Euroquébécois historiography) includes French possessions going far beyond the tiny strip of land along the St Laurence River where they applied their law and exercised their sovereignty (Lacasse 1996; Morin, 1997). As subsequent history shows, these were the first steps of a systematic attempt to invalidate *Innu tipenitamun* and to put into operation a transfer of responsibility over the Innu ancestral domain. Yet, Innu legal tradition pertaining to the land has continued to the present day, in spite of state attempts to domesticate indigenous rights (Schulte-Tenckhoff, 1998) and to obtain consent for the relinquishing of ancestral sovereignty.

The northern shore of the St Laurence River, which the French king gave to his 'best' subjects, was transferred to English merchants who took over the trading posts that were rich in fur, wood, seals and salmon, and led to a tremendous impact on *Innu tipenitamun*. From the mid 19th century, the Hudson Bay Company (HBC), operating from the old King's Post at Tadoussac, exercised a monopoly on the activities surrounding indigenous territories (Panasuk and Proulx, 1979, p. 4).

Until 1842, lands beyond Tadoussac were open to trade and the establishment of trading posts, but they were closed to settlers and land speculation and were still exclusively occupied by Essipiunnuat. The collapse of the fur trade and a growing interest in timber in the early 19th century resulted in the fierce appropriation and capitalisation of these lands, with catastrophic effects for the Essipiunnuat. This moment marks the beginning of their marginalisation and the collapse of their economic self-reliance, which would culminate in them being confined to a 0.5 km^2 reservation near the mouth of the Esh Shipu in 1892. The HBC pronouncement that it was the sole tenant of all fur trading posts within the Saguenay-Lac-Saint-Jean and Côte-Nord regions, without considering the Innu ancestral occupation of these lands, or *Innu tipenitamun* and consent, was the company's most gloomy forecast (Mailhot, 1996). From the Act of Union of 1840 onward, there is evidence that the Canadian government engaged in a vast programme of reduction of First Peoples and the extinguishment of their sovereignty in order to establish the supremacy of the

22 Tshakapesh is a hero in Innu oral tradition and in the oral traditions of other members of the Algonquian linguistic family of Turtle Island or North America. See Bellefleur (n.d.). For more information on contemporary conversation around the Innu conception of sovereignty, see Lefevre and Gendreau (2016).

Figure 5. Old Paul Ross Senior (from family archives).

Crown (Savard, 2002, pp. 26, 30). The reserve system, constitutionalised in 1867, was to become a privileged device to monitor the indigenous population and to create, in the words of prime minister John A. Macdonald, a British North America 'purified from Mongrel races'.[23]

In the 1820s, the HBC intensified its commercial salmon fishing activities on the Esh Shipu, which was still a favourite summer gathering place. At that time, many families chose the Esh Shipu as a place to settle each summer because of its rich wildlife and abundant salmon (Mailhot, 1996). The first representative from the HBC, who was to become a settler, was sent in 1825. With the end of the King's Post in 1842, the official colonisation of the Essipiunnuat ancestral domain began, operationalised through coordinated actions by the state, the Church and the traders. The resistance of the Essipiunnuat to colonisation is well documented in successive petitions that were sent to the Crown, in which the tragic consequences of violating Innu consent, *Innu tipenitamun* and the

23 See the report of Royal Commission on Indigenous Peoples (1996) and the report of the Truth and Reconciliation Commission (2016). On John A. Macdonald's supremacist views and the project destined to annihilate First Peoples and their cultures in Canada, see Stanley (2014).

Essipiunnuat way of life, cultural practices and economy are explained. The destruction of ancestral hunting grounds had a particularly negative impact, as it made the Innu way of life impracticable (Laforest, 1983, p. 31).

One hypothesis, based on conversations with community members and previous research, is that the HBC employee and French settler Joseph Moreau sold 'his new property' in the area to which he had been sent – it surrounded the Bay of Les Escoumins which had been the oldest continuous gathering place for Essipiunnuat for thousands of years – to a François Boucher, who was then able to construct a lumber sawmill with the Têtu family (Frenette, 1997). Moreau had married an Innu woman[24] and is likely to have signed the surrender of the land. Even though he was a settler, he became 'chief' of the band in 1834, a practice favourable to land speculators and timber companies, and that was encouraged by the Crown to shape indigenous surrender of their ancestral domain at that time. In the mid 1840s, the Boucher & Têtu Corporation built a dam on the river and a mill factory on its banks and organised the establishment of the town of Les Escoumins. Two years later, the town had 286 inhabitants (ibid.). Despite pressure from local authorities, Essipiunnuat continued to occupy their ancient gathering sites in the bay of the newly established village, until the authorities forcibly displaced them.

Control increased over the Essipiunnuat as the Crown put into operation the Gradual Civilization Act, which aimed explicitly to 'civilise the savages and manage their goods in order for the country to continue its maximum development' (Pennefather, 1856). Meanwhile, lumber activities and land speculation on ancestral hunting grounds severely reduced Innu self-subsistence, with terrible consequences for their self-determination. Pennefather concludes by mooting the possibility that the 'Indian problem' could be solved in less than ten years, in order to avoid further costs for the government over time, and, in parallel, allow optimal exploitation and revenues from First peoples' ancestral domains. His report recommended the repatriation of Indian affairs to the colonial government in order to favour local property developers, to force all Indians to cede their lands to the Crown without their consent, and to promote the eradication of indigenous languages, the abolition of their political institutions and the annihilation of their right to self-determination.

In 1857, through diverse legal procedures, Canada formalised the incapacity of 'Indians' and the abolition of their self-determination (*uetshit takuaimatishun*).[25] State actions also provided the priests with new tools to operationalise their project of completing Christianisation through sedentarisation. Added to the pressure of migration, forestry activities were

24 Marie Vollant (1813–38).

25 *Act to encourage the gradual civilization of Indian tribes in this province, and to amend the laws relating to Indians*, 20 Victoria, c. 26, sanctioned 10 Jun. 1857, quoted in Savard (1992).

significantly reducing the presence of animals, the possibilities for hunting and fishing, and transactions over indigenous ancestral domains were reducing even further access to territory and the capacity for auto-subsistence.

The road was paved for transferring the Essipiunnuat to a reserve – preferably, for the Crown, in the newly created reserve of Pessamit, planned to be the 'Indian capital'. In the early 1860s, the canton of Les Escoumins was officially created (Létourneau, 1985, p. 43), as was the Betsiamites reserve (now called Pessamit). The church authorities were of the opinion that civilisation was harmful for the Indians and that they must be prevented from any contact with 'white' people (Frenette, 1995, p. 26). As 'Indian and lands reserved for the Indians' came under federal jurisdiction in accordance with article 91 (24) of the new constitution, the 'creation of Canada' in 1867 officialised the usurpation of the Innu ancestral domain as conceived by them as an obligation towards *Assi* and future generations (Morin, 1997; Savard, 2002; Ross-Tremblay, 2016). The Indian Act ('An Act respecting Indians') was created with the assumption that 'the Indians' would all soon disappear in accordance with an effective operationalisation of newly created state devices (Savard, 1992). In order to prevent any rebellion resulting from the settlers' invasion of ancestral domains, the federal government put into action stratagems for the replacement of traditional political institutions by structures modelled on colonial local authorities.[26] The government also used treaties elsewhere in the country to concretise the usurpation of Indigenous sovereignties.

A road was opened between Tadoussac and Les Escoumins and speculators became very active in the area. Local officials requested that the Crown buy the lands occupied by the 'savages', who were 'not improving them'. Although little information exists pertaining to the condition of the Essipiunnuat between 1870 and 1890, the negotiations involving speculators, local officials and federal bureaucrats that contributed to the creation of the 'Indian Reserve of Les Escoumins' in 1892 are partially documented. In the summer of 1892, a contract was signed for the purchase of lands to establish the reserve: $162.75 for 97 acres, of which $62.75 went towards interest incurred from 1881 onwards (Frenette, 1995, p. 31).[27]

Official archives are silent about the displacement of the Essipiunnuat from the site of Les Escoumins to the actual reserve. The only evidence found, in a private council file, says that from 1899, the 'Indians of Les Escoumins' were

26 *Act for the gradual enfranchisement of Indians, the better management of Indian affairs, and to extend the provisions of the Act thirty-first Victoria*, chapter 42, 32–3 Victoria., c. 6.

27 The creation of the reserve in 1892 was the object of a particular land claim. For more information, see Innu First Nation of Essipit *v.* Her Majesty the Queen in Right of Canada (2017), consulted on https://decisia.lexum.com/sct/rod/en/item/230117/index.do. Essipit won its claim in 2017 in the court decision Innu First Nation of Essipit *v.* Her Majesty the Queen in Right of Canada, 2017 SCTC 1.

henceforth allowed to receive direct monetary assistance from the Department of Indian Affairs, but that this would be distributed at the hands of Charles E. Bélanger, the main industrialist in the region who had established himself in the Bay of Les Escoumins, and who possessed forestry concessions in the Esh Shipu hydrographical basin as well as the sawmill in the village (Private Council, 1927).

If information about the Essipiunnuat following the establishment of the reserve is limited, accounts by the American anthropologist Frank G. Speck pertaining to Essipiunnuat culture and way of life, gathered during his successive journeys among them in the early 20th century, remain a rich testimony to Essipiunnuat cultural vitality at that period. His accounts of the Essipiunnuat's ancestral domain, their familial hunting grounds and their usurpation, published in *Anthropos* in the 1920s, was used for the contemporary Essipiunnuat land claim.[28]

In 1927, the American review *Anthropos* published the results and analyses of Speck's investigation into the familial territories of various groups, including those of the Essipit region, or people he refers to as the Tadoussac-Escoumains Band. He revealed data gathered in the Essipit area in 1915 on the geographical limits of the group, and ethnographic and topographic information on the region. In his report, he mentions that the band of Tadoussac and Escoumins merged to form one entity, despite the presence of two Innu families in Tadoussac in 1915. The Tadoussac band held the name of *Waca-t'cèkwilnuts* (people of the gulf') and the Saguenay River had the almost identical name of *Wacatscékoci-bu* (river of the gulf) (Speck, 1927, p. 11) According to Speck, this band identified itself at the time as *Ecsi'biuci'bziwilnlits'* or *Ecsi'pi'w-ilnuts* (Human of the Brook Shell River). In his view, the people of what he called the 'Escoumains Band' are the successors of ancient bands that occupied the high northern shore region (from Tadoussac to Québec) but who left in the last three centuries; their 'errant families being traced to … the Escoumains bands', the only operating band of this region. Interestingly, he attributed the absence of a band in Tadoussac to the penetration of settlers into the interior and to the presence of various private hunting and fishing clubs (ibid.).

The names of the families occupying parts of the Innu ancestral domain located by the High and Low Saguenay river are by a large majority associated with the Essipiunnuat; some information concerning the origins of the hunters of the Tadoussac band was added and provides some clues concerning the displacement of the families. In the case, for example, of the St Onge family, Speck maintains that Paul St Onge was the chief of the ancient band of Tadoussac. However, in the mid 19th century, Paul St Onge is established one kilometre east of the Esh Shipu. Census data from Duberger from 1844 identify

28 For a critique of the coloniality of Speck's work, see Leacock (1997).

him as willing to become a farmer, which corresponds to the figure of the 'good Indian' highly valued by the colonial institutions of the time. Duberger believed, according to his report, that 'the other Montagnais will do the same [as St Onge] and follow the example of the numerous English, Irish and Canadian settlers who are to join them'. Contrary to the Bacon and Dominique families, who we know settled on the Pessamit reserve, the St Onge family is not mentioned any further in the subsequent 20th century census data on Essipit and the high northern shore regions. But what about the Anglée, Napentie, Nicolas and Denis families, who were all at a certain period clearly identified as having close links with the Essipiunnuat?[29] According to the anthropologist Jean-Pierre Garneau (2015), migration to Pessamit and other communities, as well as natural mortality, would be the main determinant for the reduction of the community to the two main Ross and Moreau families. Garneau's report for the Land Claims Tribunal in the case involving Essipiunnuat – despite its shortcomings – offers one of the most exhaustive descriptions of Essipiunnuat families history to date.

Speck's recording of Essipiunnuat linguistics, kinship, cosmogony, rituals and beliefs, for example, and of the ethical attributes of the group, provides some rich evidence of Essipiunnuat connection with Innu ancestral culture and referents of the wider Algonquian family (Speck, 1918; 1921; 1927). Speck's archive, available at the American Philosophical Society in Philadelphia, include

29 A list of these families was documented but unpublished in the research conducted by Laforest in 1983. Despite the great value of Mr Garneau's work and his contribution to the documentation of Essipiunnuat family histories, we tend to question his interpretation on two particular points. The first concerns Old Paul Ross's mother, baptised and renamed 'Marie Sauvage' by a priest in Tadoussac. Unfortunately, this interpretation was reproduced in Serge Bouchard's book, which was widely distributed in Québec, entitled 'the laughing people'. Garneau questions Frank G. Speck's assertion, based on his interviews with Old Paul Ross, that Paul's mother was a Cree of Moose Factory in northern Ontario, where his father, Simon Ross, had stayed. It seems that Paul Ross Sr's words are too easily disqualified in favour of the priest's version in Tadoussac who erased, for reasons unknown, the name of Paul's mother. This information is vital to the Ross family's search for their 'missing' grandmother. Paul's mother was renamed 'Marie Sauvage' at her baptism in Tadoussac and no other information about her exists, other than Paul's story about his mother, as reported by Speck. The fact that he and his mother were adopted by the Essipiunnuat in no way justifies mutilating their ties with the Eeyou who are deeply bound in different ways to the Innu. As with Paul, the Ross family's memory gives value to the integrity of their family history and defends their interpretation of it.

The second element in question is how Joseph Moreau, a former HBC employee who settled on the shores of the Esh Shipu river around the 1820s, appears as someone exceptional, a model of a French-Canadian descendant now entirely integrated into the Innu world. This interpretation tends to erase his role as a settler, while making him stand as an example of a 'good marriage' between an Innu woman and French-Canadian man. Nothing proves that his actions were so exceptional, especially since he was allegedly to take advantage of his family ties with the Innu to become 'chief' of the band and then to 'sell' Essipiunnuat's ancestral domain to the lumber companies. It resulted in accelerating colonisation and the village of Les Escoumins being established.

fieldnotes of interviews with Paun Rus Sr (or Paul Ross, quoted earlier), 'another patriarch of the Escoumains band', that contains information on ancestral medicine, botanic knowledge, art and oral tradition. It includes interviews with other Essipiunnuat who reported a unique version of the *atanukan* (the epic story about Tshakapesh) thousands of years old. As mentioned previously, the old man also informed the anthropologist of a possible mass killing of Essipiunnuat in the middle of the century before, allegedly at the hands of traders trying to impose their monopoly. The patriarch locates this occurrence at 'Whitefish Points' (known to the French as Pointe Sauvage) (Speck, 1932). Eleanor Leacock (1997) criticises Speck's research and discourse pertaining to Innu conception of land tenure, and his underestimation of the transformative effects of colonialism. In particular, she mentions that Speck 'did not consider the loss of political independence or the greatly reduced access to lands' in his analysis (p. 153). Indeed, Speck and other anthropologists 'tried to do by fiat what the Jesuits had tried and failed to do in the 17th century: transform the Montagnais from a people who honoured collective rights to lands into individualized property-holding families' (ibid.).

Demographic and industrial statistics reveal the scope of the upheaval experienced by the Essipiunnuat in the 1920s. The region faced a demographic boom, fast-paced industrialisation and a society that was increasingly modelled on capitalism. Changes in the group's way of life were noticeable during the 1920s (Conseil des Montagnais des Escoumins, 1994.) Firstly, migration occurred; in 1924, only 28 people were living on the reserve, a number that was to drop to 21 in 1934 (Boudreault, 1994, p. 29; Charest, 2003, p. 91; Indian Affairs, 1883–1917). Official documents report hostility towards the Essipiunnuat from Les Escoumins township. One letter illustrates, for example, attempts to get rid of the group, and other documents demonstrate Escoumins officials' misappropriation of funds destined for the building of an Innu school, which was a plan they had opposed.[30]

The burden of whiteness, civilisation and progress

The spread of the lumber industry's activities over the Essipiunnuat ancestral lands and hunting territories, and the tremendous impact this had on the group, remains the most significant occurrence of the period examined above. The disastrous impacts of the destruction of the ancestral lands was partly documented in some research commonly known as the *Great Research*, which was commissioned in the late 1970s by the Conseil Attikamekw-Montagnais

30 A letter from citizens of Les Escoumins was sent to the mayor asking for the displacement of 'Indians'. There is also proof of a case being opened which concerned money having been allocated for the construction of a school in the community that was diverted for the benefit of the village; all Essipiunnuat children were then forced to go to the neighbouring Euroquébécois township's school.

Figure 6. Ushashamek or Atlantic salmon moving up the river of their birth to breed.

(CAM), which brought all the Innu and Attikamekw communities together and was responsible for undertaking negotiations with Canada and Québec in respect of the Innu self-determination and ancestral domain.

The report on the Essipiunnuat conducted by Laforest in 1983, and included in the *Great Research*, summed up the existing information on the issue of land occupation, and enriched and gave context to the 30 interviews he conducted with hunters and trappers, giving priority to the older generation. The report provided evidence of the deep ruptures in the natural and cultural balances formerly in place caused by lumber exploitation, the construction of forestry camps, the great influx of workers, the migration of animals further north, as well as racist attacks in the forest:

> The lumber industry increasingly broke the natural equilibrium of ecosystems; they could not trap in certain sectors during the cutting, but also afterwards, so that Essipit ancestral territories were systematically ruined: they were cutting everything, destroying the lakes; there was no longer any food for the animals ... there was nothing left. ... They were also causing a lot of fires with their negligence (Laforest, 1983).

The report shows how the majority of Essipiunnuat who had not worked in the lumber industry during the hunting season before 1920–30 had been systematically forced to do so, subsequently becoming dispossessed, deterritorialised and disconnected from their lands and the remaining precious elements of their ancestral way of life (ibid.). Meanwhile, an intensification of

Figure 7. Sawmill and dam built on the Esh Shipu river (from a postcard, family archives).

Canada's policy of assimilation and extinguishment of indigenous cultures and sovereignties during and after World War Two was also observed. In the same area there was an emergent resistance movement personified by, among others, Jules Sioui (*wendat*) and William Commanda (*anishinaabe*), who organised and mobilised people to counter the ongoing policies of genocide imposed upon First Peoples (Shewell, 1999). Notably, Sioui was in touch with the Essipiunnuat families' headman, who allegedly supported his initiatives.

Archives, local newspapers and the few interviews conducted with Essipiunnuat about the post-World War Two period commonly report, between the 1940s and 1970s, the tragic consequences of more than a century of marginalisation. These are economic uncertainties, high rates of unemployment, almost complete dependency on big corporations and Euroquébécois society to earn a living, the long-term exile of heads of families, with catastrophic consequences on transgenerational transmission, and a harsh life on the reserve. During this period the local language, innu-aimun, was partly erased and hidden from the community and when reportedly there arose in the group feelings of self-hatred and of shame at being Essipiunnuat. As an Elder remembers, 'When we were young [in the 1950s] nobody wanted to be an Indian. Certain people among us were so ashamed that they were willing to ask for emancipation' (Essipit, 2007).[31]

Memories of that time are hazy; in my conversations with some interviewees there are notable mentions of mistreatment, alcoholism and sexual abuse. The latter – also related (but not only) to some Catholic priests living sporadically

31 See also: Conseil Des Montagnais Des Escoumins (1994) and Anderson (1999).

Figure 8. Essipiunnu Marcel Ross raising a net during the Salmon War.

nearby – remains a taboo in the small community. These psychological wounds from childhood experienced by some Essipiunnuat impact upon the group's view of the past. Concerns were raised by one individual I spoke to that research in the community might unearth secrets pertaining to transgressions and abuses, but this person would not tell me about that period.[32] Information on the 1970s suggests a severe collective economic dependence and a widespread psychological phenomenon of surplus-powerlessness.

In the late 1970s, the main lumber company left the village of Les Escoumins and the village experienced a decline in population after many years of growth. Unemployment among the Essipiunnuat reached 30 per cent (20 per cent in the Québec northern shore region), leading to a general collective disempowerment that was directly related to a century-long process of marginalisation (Mailhot, 1996). As for many other First Peoples, the late 1970s and early 1980s appears as a time of revival for the Essipiunnuat, coupled with some contentious politics. It is in this context that an Essipiunnuat radical movement emerged in the early 1980s, led by a cell of newly graduated university students. The process of decentralisation, requested by the CAM and finally accepted by the Crown, gave a boost to the actions of their movement as they were finding new opportunities for creating jobs, were mobilising members and dynamising a process of autonomisation and collective self-empowerment with significant elements of cultural reinvigoration.

32 Personal conversation with Anon., Apr. 2010.

An accurate portrait of their heritage remains to be painted, however. If various studies have at times approached the material aspects of Essipiunnuat colonialism, the absence of documentation on the psychological and cultural dimension of colonialism's impact on the group, its historical consciousness, its self-image and collective identity (conveyed particularly through its oral history and people's stories) is glaring. Despite this silence, existing material includes data pertaining to the context of the group's ideology, the new society it wanted to create and how they enabled it.

The recent retirement from public life of these leaders, and the generational shift it entails, paves the way for more critical research on their governance that is currently absent from the literature. As for representations of the group itself, the depiction of the leaders and of their heritage is unidirectional and without any critical perspective. A special edition of the community journal dedicated entirely to 'the great man' (this is how Georges is described by Serge Bouchard in the community journal) best illustrates this glorification of the 'leader' (Première Nation des Innus Essipit, 2016–17). This new generation of leaders, who have exercised control over the political and economic life of the group for more than three decades, were also affected by the intergenerational traumas inherent in the colonial experience, and their actions need to be contextualised.

At another level, their lives and actions, which have profoundly marked the group condition, were also tinted by their own experience, which, in some cases, revealed a profound ambivalence to Innu cultural heritage. Therefore, it is imperative that the new movement they initiated and the regime that followed must be reflected upon in the light of a number of factors. These include the sociohistorical background of its emergence, the heavy psychological colonial heritage and the cultural disconnection that the group has experienced over a long period. These include profound traumas, marginalisation and disempowerment, as well as forms of surplus-powerlessness not foreign to radical cultural and memorial discontinuities, and the internalisation of colonial referentials impacting directly on collective self-image.

In the light of what is now known, can we stick to the narrative that the community had *no history* before the 1980s, and that in the chronology of action the establishment of a new regime was the foundation of the group's very existence? People's stories are much more subtle and complex than that, and this book aims to contribute to a critical approach able to give voice to multiple social interpretations.

The Salmon War

In the late 1970s and early 1980s, Innu and other Algonquian groups (such as Abenaki, Anishinaabeg, Atikamekw, Eeyou, Malecite and Mi'gmaq) of the

Québec–Labrador peninsula began to meet more frequently and strategise in order to assert self-determination and ancestral sovereignty, for which they received increased international support. The rise of indigenous nationalism during this period resulted in expressions of discontent, intolerance to colonial oppression, and a general radicalisation on the issue of territorial rights and the reappropriation of ancestral lands taken earlier in the century. Development on these lands without their consent was contested and denounced as illegitimate, and there was a reconsideration of their relations with the Canada and Québec states, and with mainstream Québec society as well as intergenerational shifts within communities. Times were volatile, therefore, and with great potential for conflict.

All over Nitassinan (the Québec–Labrador peninsula), indigenous assertiveness destabilised state–indigenous power relations. Innu claims to sovereignty and the recognition of their ancient legal order touched the Euroquébécois ontologically; it was the very legitimacy of their settlement on the continent that was being questioned. In general, the Euroquébécois, and particularly the nationalists, were widely reproving of Canada's colonial policy towards them and had developed, over time, a consciousness of being an oppressed and colonised people. The emergence in the public sphere of an indigenous discourse from groups inside of the province, in which francophone Euroquébécois were now represented as settlers and oppressors, was hard to receive and to bear. Québec nationalism had been on the rise since the late 1960s and was at its height in the early 1980s. The Parti Québécois was in power, and a referendum on Québec independence from Canada was organised on 20 May 1980 but was lost, and as a result many Euroquébécois were disappointed and bitter.

Indeed, Québec was implementing a vast industrial strategy of occupation of its 'national' territory, including mega-dam projects in large northern areas indigenous groups claimed were theirs. Innu claims of sovereignty were generating a shadow of 'uncertainty' over Québec's intentions. The CAM was uncompromising; the Innu would never accept the extinguishment of their rights accepted by the Naskapi, Cree and Inuit groups through the James Bay Agreement. It was sacred and non-negotiable. In Québec, if muzzling the 'Indian' resistance was increasingly a tough option, negotiating Innu sovereignty was an achievement that was far from being 'trendy' in public opinion.

The Salmon War occurred in this complex context. The issue at stake supersedes the mere theme of ancestral salmon fishing and encompasses the very question of the Innu condition and the Essipiunnuat in particular. It involves issues of sovereignty and rebellion against the authorities and the laws perceived as not applicable to Innu people. To generalise, the Salmon War corresponds to a series of violent episodes, centred on the issue of salmon

Figure 9. Québec Police force intervening in Listuguj, June 1981 (Obomsawin, Alanis, Incident at Restigouche, *National Film Board, 1984)*

fisheries, that occurred between indigenous groups and the Québec state, but also involving Euroquébécois villagers. It reached intense peaks during the summer fishing seasons of 1980 and 1981. The feuds left a heavy scar on the small community of Essipit and those involved refer to the episode as the 'most significant moment of their lives'. Perceived as a cathartic time for the group, the conflict is apparently now identified by its members as the main source of the community's subsequent revival and increased self-reliance. As with other Innu communities who live by a salmon river, the war looms large in Essipiunnuat political memory. This current research, however, focuses entirely on the Essipit community.

Ushâshamek (salmon) has an important cultural significance for the Innu, and particularly for the Essipiunnuat (Mailhot, 1996; Chevrier, 1996; Charest, 2012). Salmon has been vital for subsistence from the beginning of human occupation of the hydrographical basins of the Esh Shipu river (Charest, 2012, p. 36). For more than four thousand years, groups that spent most of their time in the interior have frequented the coastal regions. Their subsistence during those stays was predominantly based upon the availability of aquatic animals, seals, birds and fish, with salmon being one of the main food sources (Plourde, 1993; Chevrier, 1996; Richard, 2006). In Innu classification, Atlantic salmon are aquatic animals, *Namesh*, and are answerable to an animal master named *Mishtinâk* (Clément, 1995).

The abundance of salmon in the Esh Shipu has been identified as a major explanation for a significant indigenous summer presence on the shore of the river. Smoked salmon was also used during long journeys within the interior to reduce the need for hunting and fishing (Mailhot, 1996). Salmon fishing is perhaps the most ancient activity practised on the coast (they are harpooned at night by the light of a flame-lit torch; Mailhot, 1996). This practice has been inherited by every generation because a vast amount of data about salmon is held in ancestral knowledge, its external and internal anatomy, its locomotion, environment, seasonal phenomena, and its reproductive activities (Clément, 1995).

Ancestral salmon fishing in the Esh Shipu was drastically impacted by the construction of a permanent dam from 1846. Charest's research shows that the consequent destruction of the river over time increasingly blocked salmon access to it such that the fish had most likely completely disappeared by the 1920s. Charest summarises information produced by archaeologists, explorers, visitors, priests, fisherman and other academics since the period of contact up to now. The processes that led to the disappearance of the salmon are therefore well known, but they also led to the Innu being excluded from practising their most important ancient activity and mode of subsistence.

Charest's research demonstrates the long process of the Innu being dispossessed of their ancestral rivers and the steps that led to communal action being taken to combat this, since all Innu on the coast were facing similar situations. Research by Anne Panasuk and Jean-René Proulx, in particular, contextualises the Salmon War well (1979, pp. 203–17).[33] The taking away of the salmon over centuries, by corporations and authorities, symbolises the wider disregard for indigenous sovereignty in this part of the world, as well as the location of its reassertion. Although Québec had been implementing a policy of suppressing private fishing clubs since 1969, rivers with a salmon population were often excluded. In 1977, outfitters[34] and sports clubs, often owned by rich business people, were still in control of the best rivers, which were often guarded by armed men. Even if some Innu groups had signed agreements with the government in relation to their fishing activities, many conflicts and restrictions remained. The government was trying to evade the wider question of *Innu tipenitamun* over *Nitassinan* (Panasuk and Proulx, 1979).

In 1978, without any known consultation having taken place with the Essipiunnuat, the Québec government created the ZEC *(zone d'exploitation controlée) Nordique des Escoumins.* This new administrative device served to decentralise the management of a large part of the group's ancestral lands into the hands of local Escoumins people, therefore reinforcing the state of Québec's authority. The goal of the ZEC was also to increase public access to Québec's tourist, fishing and hunting activities. This project, in an underhand way, directly increased the presence of sport hunters and fishermen on the land,

33 Panasuk and Proulx (1981) also produced an MA thesis at the University of Montréal about Innu fishing rights on Québec northern shore rivers.

34 In Canada, an outfitter is 'an enterprise that provides recreational services and infrastructure in exchange for remuneration for recreational purposes related to the practice of hunting, fishing or trapping. These companies also often provide a service of accommodation, equipment rental and guide. By extension, the term outfitting is used to designate the land occupied by the establishment' (Gouvernement du Québec, n.d.).

but the new state policy was being put into operation without consulting the indigenous people.

Local Escoumins leaders and some local residents were radically opposed to any Essipiunnuat participation in the initiative. The new indigenist movement perceived the situation to be the conclusion of a long process of having their sovereignty buried. It was also a final chance to reassert their historical rights. Québec's increased structuration of Innu ancestral territories culminated with the announcement that the Esh Shipu and its remaining salmon were to be managed exclusively by the provincial government, and implemented by agents in collaboration with a local committee composed of Escoumins citizens. For the Essipiunnuat, this was the last stage in a long sequence of being pushed back.

In the media reports of the time, the Salmon War was analysed by considering a series of elements: the disappearance of the river's salmon population due to the polluting practices of the Consolidated Bathurst Company; the Essipiunnuat actions pressuring the government to recognise their ancestral rights through the symbolic spreading in 1980 and 1981 of a net east and west of the dock near the Bay of Les Escoumins; the non-recognition of indigenous ancestral rights by local Euroquébécois, on the basis that the group should be 'integrated into the dominant society' and had no rights outside of the reserve borders (Radio-Canada, 1981); and the metamorphosis of their crusade into a movement of Innu and wider indigenous affirmation of *tipenitamun*. The event is predominantly presented as a scientific debate over the management of a river and its salmon population – yet the dispute is also associated with an 'ethnic' fight between 'whites' and 'Indians'. This conflict is presented as having been revived by Innu non-compliance with Québec legislation, and, more significantly, in terms of an emerging indigenous national movement of decolonisation more widely contesting the Québec state.

According to these sources and documents from the time, the Salmon War in Essipit of 1980–1 began with the installation of a community net by the Essipiunnuat on 12 June 1980. It was placed at the mouth of the Esh Shipu river, near the Escoumins dock, provoking anger from those who lived in that village. They began to pressurise the government to prevent the Essipiunnuat from fishing. This jeopardised local authorities' efforts since 1977 to restore the river's salmon population. A group of villagers and their representatives denounced the indigenous activities as illegal and called for the state to get involved in saving the river, and to stifle any indigenous resurgence. The newspapers informed the public about these interactions between the Essipiunnuat, other Innu communities, the state of Québec (as represented by the wildlife agents, bureaucrats and the provincial police) and local Euroquébécois. In conjunction with a background of disputes around authority over the land, this resulted in various government interventions and the erection of blockades, leading to negotiations but also violent clashes between June 1980 and July 1981. This all culminated in direct confrontation between the two groups and a hostile intervention of approximately two hundred local 'white' people.

The community fishing net was first seized by Québec wildlife agents on 14 June 1980. Some Essipiunnuat then decided to erect a barricade in order to pressure the government, an action which resulted in the interruption of the Escoumins–Trois Pistoles ferry (15 June 1980). A police militia arrived at Les Escoumins and the township adopted a resolution to construct a road to contour the barricade, with negotiations beginning between the Essipit band council and Québec government representatives (15 June). Talks led to an oral agreement, although one article remained unresolved[35] (19 June 1980). The Essipiunnuat resumed their fishing activities, reaffirming their ancestral rights on the river and communicating their intention to the media (26 June 1980). Québec[36] seized the net a second time; the device was then recovered by a group of Essipiunnuat who intercepted the wildlife agents on the road. The wildlife agents' director requested help from the provincial police (10 July 1980). The Essipiunnuat again spread their nets and erected another barricade on 12 July. They received support for their actions from the Algonquin (anicinabe) chief Richard Kistabish and his people, who were located further west of Nitassinan (17 July 1980).[37] The wildlife agents and the provincial police thereafter jointly launched an air, land and sea initiative. Violent confrontations with the Essipiunnuat occurred and firearms sounded; the Québec agents pushed back and the community ended its fishing season (19 July 1980).

35 The two sides reached an agreement in principle. Only one element remained in dispute (no. 8) pertaining to surveillance of the nets and verification of catches. The contentious element of the agreement stipulates that the Essipiunnuat government would designate an individual who would be mandated to first inspect communitarian nets spread on the delimited territory and, in a second phase, verify the number of catches and transmit a statement of the daily catch to the departments. The core issue at stake is the fact that the department wanted one of its agents to conduct these tasks, but the Essipiunnuat government didn't want to cede on this element that implied a lack of trust in them.

36 The use of the term 'Québec' here refers to the Québec provincial government and its representatives.

37 On 17 Jul. 1980, the Essipiunnuat received the support of 3,000 Algonquin through the voice of their representative, Chief Richard Kistabish. The chief declared his people entirely in support of the Innu struggles that, in his view, were taking place in the wider context of indigenous peoples' struggles for respect and decolonisation: 'The governments of Québec and Canada will have to agree to consider the whole issue of aboriginal rights in the country ... For 300 years or more, we have allowed white people ('les Blancs') to do as they please. They dispossessed us of our territories and all that was precious to us. Today, there is a turnaround. We want to bequeath to our children something other than poverty, social and racial injustice. We want our people to survive, and this survival must come from respecting indigenous rights in this country' (my translation). Quoted in 'Les Montagnais des Escoumins ont l'appui de 3,000 Algonquins', in *Le Soleil*, 17 Jul. 1980.

The next year the Essipiunnuat affirmed their rights in the media (5 May 1981). Once again, they spread two nets, in the presence of Innu and First Peoples' supporters. The mayor of Les Escoumins publicly denounced the action on 1 June 1981. The Québec police force then intervened in Restigouche[38] to repress Mi'gmaq salmon fishing (11 and 20 June 1981).[39] The CAM again warned the government of further insurrections if indigenous groups were not allowed to fish salmon (22 June 1981). Québec assured the Mi'gmaq that they would not suffer another intervention (25 June 1981). The Québec minister responsible for the issue at stake then publicly denied the Innu's ancestral rights and legitimised police brutality towards First Peoples (3 July 1981). The Essipiunnuat spread their nets again. On 7 July 1981, between two and four hundred Euroquébécois from Les Escoumins township and surrounding villages mobilised to seize the nets, and there were violent confrontations with Essipiunnuat on the Les Escoumins dock.

Surprisingly, there is little contemporary research on the Salmon War and its place in the memory of Innu groups, despite its significance and the impact it had.[40] The Essipiunnuat, for their part, have been the object of some investigations over the last decades, but nothing of note has been done to assess the psychological and social dimension of their condition. As a result, the complex relationship the Essipiunnuat have with the past, their cultural memory and self-representation, as well as their current condition, has never been investigated. Previous research has rarely focused on the issue, or on the problems articulated by the local people. It has tended, instead, to record elements of the group only through the eyes of the leaders, leaving other critical data in the shadows. This unidirectional narrative and its sources, the internal representations of the Essipiunnuat, and the mode of social control, are central to my study. As these experiences and views can be rich, valid and credible, such a one-dimensional presentation of this group, with an evident focus on the economic issues, obscures important details of how other 'non-influential' members live, feel and perceive their Innu heritage and the community and its needs.

Conclusion

Despite the omnipresence of discourses on reconciliation in the public space, it is still 'taboo' to speak of colonialism, genocide and the historical mistreatment of First Peoples in Canada, and in particular in Québec. Canadian and

38 Restigouche or Listuguj refers to one of the two reserves composed of Mi'gmaq people located in the south eastern part of the province of Québec.

39 See Obomsawin (1984).

40 See McKenzie and Vincent (2010), pp. 103–11.

Euroquébécois nationalists often perceive themselves as belonging to a superior civilisation, and the suggestion that an apartheid system is surfacing at the very heart of their constitution sounds odd and disrespectful. In order to keep a positive self-image, maintaining the invisibility of First Peoples remains more comfortable – a sanitary cordon to protect their fragile representation of themselves from radical cultural criticism coming from within. This is particularly true in Québec, where the francophone majority has a deep and complex relationship with First Peoples' heritage, and with the representations of 'Indians' or 'savages' and their historical role that have been around for a long time. Euroquébécois' representations of 'Indians' and their lands and sovereignty remain awkward and, to use Burelle's words (2014), are characterised by a constant 'settler's moves to innocence'. This is 'in order to obscure its own ongoing settler colonial relationship ... to First Nations whose sovereignty predates that of Québec and threatens the coherence of its national narrative'.

To question the relationship between the Québec national self and local First Peoples is destabilising and can often lead to strong resistance, since it questions the very legitimacy of their own state and the ethnocentricity on which it is based, and is a threat to the foundation of Euroquébécois self-conceptions. These unique circumstances of profound cultural hegemony towards the Innu, and the overall denial of such oppression, added to the discomfort of radical Innu criticism, have major consequences for research. Such an environment of overwhelming epistemic violences can paralyse the body, anaesthetise the mind and make every moment weigh on the act of speaking due to imminent punishment being anticipated. More than a threat, the Innu research object-turned-researcher allows the reemergence of an episteme that threatens to 'pulverise' a culture erected against 'savagery' and celebrating with persistence its own 'whiteness'. Such a society is overwhelmed by a cultural scorbus which makes it desire the symbolic vitamins of several-thousand-years-old cultures that, paradoxically, it cannot help but invisibilise. The society imposed on Innu people has not only a strong propensity to forget, but a reprehensible drive to erase what preceded it in order to perceive itself as 'sovereign'. Yet, the small mirror explorers gave in exchange for a territory that cannot be 'owned' would come to haunt their descendants. Simulated blindness and deafness have their limits. Self-ignorance and denial do not, in fact, change the nature of the relationship between the Innu and the settler population of Québec. The location of Québec's nationalists as a colonised people has weak foundations.

Although the focus of this research is not the French descendants, it is necessary to consider their condition because of their long-term interaction with the Essipiunnuat and the cultural hegemony that has led the Innu to absorb their conceptions, representations, myths and fictions. Looking at Essipit from the inside allows an observation of key dimensions of Québec society and its interaction with Innu referents; an archaeology of Essipiunnuat's own internal conflicts are revealing of wider cultural undercurrents and blind spots.

Historically, research involving First Peoples in Canada has overwhelmingly been used for assimilation purposes and increased domination. State control over research pertaining to 'Indians' has been exercised through funding and the determination of research problems. Among Innu, it has often led to a perception of research being commodified and a stratagem guided by existing authorities that is destined to reinforce and legitimise colonial institutions (when not simply serving the pecuniary or intellectual interests of academics). Today, it is easy to talk about indigenous research as having become an economic activity. These views are far from exaggerated, since research is often for purposes other than giving a voice to any major social concerns such as those experienced by First Peoples.

This may explain why the links between colonialism and the current psychological and cultural condition of the Innu are widely absent in research, even if locally demanded and socially needed. The present research is interested in my family and community's (deeply intertwined) relationship with its past, voiced locally as a crucial concern affecting people in their daily lives, especially the younger generation. It is an investigation attempting to foster remembering in order to better comprehend the phenomenon of collective oblivion and its tremendous psychological effects and legal implications for consent – a rare topic in this area of study.

The Salmon War, as the Essipiunnuat remembered it, was not documented and there was a fascinating silence about it on all sides. The memory of those who took part in the event, and the dynamic of its intergenerational transmission, was therefore a good starting point for tackling the collective memory blank, from a mnemohistorical stance, and within the wider context of its social and historical production. This contribution is on a micro-scale, yet has the potential to reveal a underlying dimensions of a continent apparently obsessed with analogous equations such as those the Essipiunnuat are facing, cornered as they are between a growing gap of memory, forgetfulness and a complex relationship with truth, forged and constantly scrambled by obscure and complex external and internal forces. These prevent them from seeing or hearing, while favouring, often despite themselves, erasure and rewriting.

2. The sources of war: colonialism and the emergence of collective agency

When we revolt it's not for a particular culture. We revolt simply because, for many reasons, we can no longer breathe.
Frantz Fanon, *The Wretched of the Earth*

And after a while, better no talk … they were killing them … You heard of how it was functioning, didn't you?
Pishimnapeo

It changes or we die.
Victor, Essipiunnu

Autobiographical memories of the Salmon War (1980–1) provide ample reports concerning the causes of this major event. These stories are marked by a delineation between the objective conditions (or 'external determinants') and the actions of the group itself as determinants. The target here is thus to access initially the common script pertaining to circumstances of the war and then disentangle discernments of agency and capacity to act. It will then be possible to extricate what has been embedded in people's memories as exogenous historical determinants of the Salmon War and highlight the historical consciousness or past role played by people and the group and its modalities.

A crucial component of people's interpretation of sociohistorical circumstances remains their experience previous to the war and their generational unit or shared experiences. We know that age differences, generational consciousness and access to collective memories markedly influence people's view of the world (Mannheim, 1952, pp. 304, 328); they shape their hermeneutics of what caused the event. 'Event' is understood here in the Foucauldian sense of a crystallisation of past occurrences, with a historical singularity acquired through a particular process. The emergence of an event is firmly attached to the valorisation of its content and a virtualisation that prevents it from sinking into oblivion.[1]

The goal here is to collect in stories the multifaceted historical actors that culminated in the Salmon War by reconstituting, beyond the mere facts, the web of discourses, powers, strategies and practices that caused it. It will then be easier to comprehend the role attributed to collective agency in the uprising, as contained in people's memories, and its potential mystification and re-writing over time to serve a diversity of actors and interests.

1 For further information on Foucault's conception of the 'event', see Revel (2009), pp. 49–53.

A hand strangling us: external determinants

Essipiunnuat in their stories discussed a range of origins, causes, circumstances or agents that contributed to the war breaking out. Sources that were considered external, that did not originate from their own group nor were a result of their own actions and yet were determinant in the igniting of the Salmon War, surfaced in the testimonies. This results in four common elements: Canadian colonialism and colonial violence; the politics and postures of Québec state actors; Euroquébécois-Escouminois representation of and hegemony over the Essipiunnuat; and the existence of organised local anti-Innu militancy.

Constitutional colonialism: the Canadian apartheid

Colonialism is fundamentally about domination and the exercise of control of one people over another. Widely associated with the pursuit of material benefit and access to resources, colonialism has nevertheless a deep-seated psychological dimension. Historically, it has involved the dominant group employing a panoply of tactics to legitimise its hegemony and exploitation, to fabricate consent, mask the reality of dispossession and to seek absolution. Colonialism thus entails strategies of assimilation for increased absorption by the colonised of the colonist's imaginary and prevailing culture, including its selective memory and 'essentialist' representations of the subjugated. The quest for legitimating supremacy has previously led to the dominant group making violent attempts to destroy the memories and cultural repositories of the people who are the object of their actions, aiming ultimately, in the logic of absolute control, to annihilate the past in order to transform usurpation into unlimited legitimacy through rewriting.

The colonisation of First Peoples in Canada involved experiences of uprooting, of disconnection, as well as physical and cultural deterritorialisation in order to secure complete conquest and prevent endogenous resurgence. This was mainly achieved through obliterating First Peoples' cultural foundations, memory and epistemology through an overreaching policy of forgetting and of commanding to forget. These sociohistorical circumstances are reflected in views about the core determinant of the Salmon War, including colonialism, dispossession, domination, violence and decline in auto-referentiality.

The link between the war and colonialism is most significant for the older people taking part, yet it is also mentioned by younger contributors. Those aged over 40 at the time they told their story linked the occurrence of the war with the harsh conditions of the 1950s, as well as the tragic social circumstances of the 1920s which their grandparents had told them of. The stories also report on the conditions endured by the Essipiunnuat in the 1970s, together with earlier phenomena experienced collectively, including the group's forced sedentarisation, interpreted as an infringement of their self-determination (*uetshit takuaimatishun*) and ancestral sovereignty (*Innu tipenitamun*).

The group's historical experience of injustice has been compared to that of the 'Acadians', who were first despoiled of the land where they lived, then deported to New England and the 13 colonies by the British. The Essipiunnuat experienced profound injustice and had politics imposed on them, characterised by the conqueror's cruel and arbitrary absolutism, which framed their collective fate and condition of homelessness:

> When I hear of the deportation of the Acadian, it gives me grief. Us, we are here today and we are still 'deported'. When they want a land, they take it! 'Get out Indians!' It's ours … and when you want to return fire … my god … it's sad. 'The Indians are still there and they don't understand anything!' This is deportation … You can't do what you want. That's why, when they say 'we are a people' ... Yes a people … But a tiny one! And when we affirm it, we are beaten up immediately over and over again. Our case is settled without delay. We are under the rule of arithmetic. That's what it means when you're small. 'Deal with that Indians … we pass first and manage the leftovers.' That's how I see politics. It is unjust. This is all about force. (Édouard, chapter 1, ref. 1)

The growing displacement of the group from the 1830s and subjugation to the authority of the Crown from the 1890s, represented locally by government agents, resulted in the Essipiunnuat being disabused of their local autonomy and sovereignty. Being excluded from administrative decisions that concerned their own governance, they had no choice but to use bribery and collaboration as a way of dealing with the state:

> That is what the government did to you: it parked you in a reserve. You didn't have any choice, they settled you there. You better say nothing otherwise … At that time, it was the federal agents who were in control; you had almost nothing to say. If you were walking with the guy, you were all right … you paid him a drink and ... I've seen things that happened with agents, it was really not funny! If you negotiated something with him and 'fatten' him a bit, you had things. But if you were against his ideas … better not. (Mestenapeo, chapter 1, ref. 5)

Mentions of the mounting disempowerment of the group and its suppression come with assertions about the dispossession of the ancestral domain. This amplified usurpation of ancestral hunting territories and gathering sites by corporations, the Catholic Church and local Euroquébécois, causing sweeping marginalisation, is seen as another characteristic of the group experience of colonialism: 'They took everything away from us. When they needed something, they took the Indians and … pushed them back … Then they had no place left; they took the better spots' (Pishimnapeo, chapter 1, ref. 7).

From the mid 20th century, the usurpation of Essipiunnuat territories took the form of an increased denial of inherent indigenous sovereignty. Such refutation ultimately resulted in the group being persecuted when practising their traditional subsistence activities. From the 1940s onwards, the Innu language (*Innu–aimun*) was systematically banned and the state and church considered the Essipiunnuat to be subject to Québec laws and culture. In addition to the large areas that had been given over to lumber companies since the mid 1850s,[2] the remaining ancestral domain was taken over and monopolised by businesses and corporations who transformed it into private fishing and hunting clubs. It then became illegal and 'prohibited' for the Essipiunnuat to access these various spaces. The deterritorialisation of the Innu was then reaching its peak.[3]

Associated with rising state control and deterritorialisation is the increased feeling of being trapped. Testimonies reveal the establishment of a 'colonial terror' that has caused collective neuroses. In effect, a 'fear factor' became deeply ingrained within the Essipiunnuat. The engagement in the Salmon War is seen as the exteriorisation of this internal repression. With augmented coloniality, being 'Indian' became more painful all the time; being identified as seditious became very costly.[4]

The post-sedentarisation generation began to experience a climate in which everything that was 'Indian' had to be hidden and repressed.[5] This climate of fear was particularly present in the forest where people hunted, trapped and fished as their ancestors had done. Even if convinced of their rights as Innu, people who took part in the war mentioned that their fathers were immobilised

2 It is pertinent to mention that the increasing number of marriages involving Euroquébécois women coming to live on the reserve has led to a particular type of racism within families as well as an increased Euroquébécois perspective when educating children. This subject is highly taboo but arose in the stories. Even though this inner racism has varied widely among families, the testimonies still mention specific families where mothers have zealously applied their duty to 'whitewash' their children and to fulfil the mission, encouraged by political and religious authorities, to 'désauvager' (civilise) the reserve.

3 'At the time, they were selling us a licence as a non-Indian (Euroquébécois) but in fact you couldn't fish all the same. It was all private clubs. It was something, you had no rights! You were taking a licence and indeed, you couldn't fish, you had access nowhere. And our ancestral territory was exactly there. We, our fathers, had always hunted there, by the Moreau River and around. We had always been travelling there. And it became a private club; we were suddenly told "No". They build a road and block our access. That's how it happened.' (Édouard, ch. 1, ref. 2)

4 'My father used to say that before, "you never heard of Indians". It was hidden, it was as if they (the past generation) didn't want to have a problem with them [Euroquébécois]; that was the psychology at that time. And after a while, better no talk … they were killing them … You heard of how it was functioning, didn't you?' (Pishimnapeo, ch. 1, ref. 10)

5 'We didn't talk really about it with each other [about the ancestral territories]. We knew that we needed it and that our lands, they weren't ours anymore … That's where we were ... and my dad had a big family and needed to be employed … if he had raised claims, he wouldn't have been allowed to work, he would have been boycotted.' (Pishimnapeo, ch. 1, ref. 4)

by fears that prevented them from practising ancestral livelihood activities, including fishing and hunting.[6]

From sedentarisation on, there was intense pressure on the Essipiunnuat to put aside their indigenous heritage, to not speak their language and to disown their culture and customs. Forced assimilation into the dominant culture was to produce a form of collective paralysis in the face of repression.[7] Discomfort in identifying as 'Innu' was reinforced by constant experiences with segregation. Feelings of being rejected from mainstream Euroquébécois society on a racial basis is at the core of the older people's inventory of experience.

People remember being 'frightened to say we are Indian' from first starting primary school (Riel, chapter 1, ref. 10). In effect, they confess to the experience of a climate of war from the very moment they were crossing the borders of their reserve. Mentions of Essipiunnuat cultural referents in times before the Salmon War are deeply linked in autobiographical stories with negative and often traumatic experiences.[8]

The ruptures in intergenerational transmission, the distancing from ancestral practices and decreased identification with the reference group, among others, are seen as determining the group's condition in the year preceding the war. A cultural collapse can be clearly discerned associated with successive events and collective experiences of colonialism. Interlocutors depict the Essipiunnuat in the late 1970s as being at a point of cultural self-annihilation, completely assimilated into and similar to the local Euroquébécois. A younger individual acknowledges, for example, not identifying as 'montagnais' or 'innu' prior to their experience of the Salmon War.[9]

6 'In my father's times ... they were saying all the time "We have the right", but they didn't know the "law"... No, they were frightened, they were afraid. No, they didn't go. Because once, my father, he was sitting in our house and he said: "A steak, that would be good wouldn't it?" And pointing at the mountain meanwhile, he said, "The steak is on the mountain over there". He was talking of a moose. That's how he was talking, my father.' (Edouard, ch. 1, ref. 4)

7 'And it was ... the effect of the "white society"'. We had been subjugated to them for a long while. That was the federal policy. If you want to be an Indian, you won't work; you won't have access to professions, the right to nothing.' (Sam, ch. 1, ref. 3)

8 'It is because, me, I started to be at war from the moment I began to leave, to leave the reserve. During our youth, we were refused entry to a hotel, we didn't have the right to enter. What do we call that – segregation? That was it. Where they knew us, around here, we were refused, we couldn't go there. Me, it started there, I've always had a "fall back" since then. They were showing us things you know... "We were friends", but we didn't have a right ... That's why ... We were always rejected this way. That is rejection.' (Édouard, ch. 1, ref. 2)

9 'Before the war, I had the impression that the reserve was a quarter of Les Escoumins. There was no difference. Older people were perhaps seeing differences since they had other experiences, but for me ... we were going to school with people from Les Escoumins, doing sports, you know! We did everything with people from Les Escoumins. There was nothing on the reserve. Really nothing.' (Adam, ch. 1, ref. 6)

Older people's testimonies highlight the post-World War Two ruptures in the intergenerational transmission of Innu culture in Essipit, something that is best illustrated by the disappearance of the language in the space of one generation.[10] People put the cultural collapse of the Essipiunnuat within the wider context of the Canadian Crown's projects and efforts to end indigenous cultural continuity. For example, some interviewees narrate evidences of self-identification as 'Innu' and defence of the Innu language as being met with harassment, humiliation and exclusion.[11]

Moreover, disconnection with cultural memory and the weakening of Essipiunnuat's cultural identity is purportedly correlated in stories with an outburst of in-group conflicts and amplified disempowerment: 'terrible squabbles within and between families.' Increased distancing from Innu culture and referents is thus associated with the erosion of the 'intangible *unité de corps*, all the families together as one' that had characterised the group internal social order until the 40s.[12]

In the years preceding the Salmon War, people's accounts highlight intense inter-familial disputes, mainly between the Ross and the Moreau families around issues pertaining mostly to the distribution of hunting grounds that had previously been shared among them. Effectively, the death of the two main family headmen had supposedly propelled a spiral of conflict that was principally about the possibility or not of selling Essipiunnuat ancestral territories and bequeathing them to Euroquébécois sons- and brothers-in-law.[13]

In the end, a growing distance from Innu cultural referents was to affect the way the Essipiunnuat perceived their rights and the sources of those rights. Knowledge of 'Innu ancestral sovereignty' (*Innu tipenitamun)*, had been transmitted orally from generation to generation. This concept of Innu normativity and laws pertaining to the Earth was still predominant among the

10 'And after I have reflected on all that, I'm still asking myself: "Why didn't he talk to us in Indian [Innu aimun language]?" He talked Indian perfectly, my dad … Uncle Joseph Ross, too; they met and talked Indian only, yes!' (Pishimnapeo, ch. 1, ref. 11)

11 'We have even lost our language [in Essipit] It is very sad, but it's because we were forbidden to speak Montagnais [Innu aimun]: "You stay in Les Escoumins; you don't stay in Betsiamites [Pessamit]. If you want to speak, go to Betsiamites!"' (Sam, ch. 1, ref. 3)

12 'I can tell you, it was all the families together as one … They were meeting. There was yelling, but the family spirit was present. And oop! It disappeared suddenly … Just in our family, the argument between Uncle X and Uncle Y … him, it was all about the "token"; anything to make money. And he did not care whether it was on the back of his brother or not.' (Mestenapeo, ch. 1, ref. 7)

13 'Within the reserve, there was a lot of squabbling even at the level of hunting territories … There were brawls. My grandfather Ross passed away, and the Moreau, it went badly for them too. It was not going well and the families became very divided. Some of them had started to sell themselves … Because until then, nobody had to pay the state for using the small hunting grounds we still had. Historically, familial grounds belonged to the whole group, to the reserve; to the Ross and Moreau families who were, in fact, just one family. But the politics took over our ancient ways.' (Mestenapeo, ch. 1, ref. 6)

pre-World War Two generation, who spoke Innu-aimun fluently and were in constant contact with Innu from other bands, although more intensively so with the Pessamiunnuat.[14]

But the decline of Innu culture among the Essipiunnuat was to change their views on the nature and intrinsic value of their rights, its sui generis definition, and also the imperative of defending it. Cultural decline thus came with tensions within and between families, between those ready to defend Innu collective rights and those seeing them only through the prism of their personal and material interests.

The stories thus suggest a direct correlation between Essipiunnuat detachment and ancestral philosophy as contained in the oral tradition and the internal expansion of capitalist ideology, materialism and individualism. This is associated with intra-group conflicts, collective weakening and a decreased capacity for resistance. That said, people identify their experience of colonialism as an inescapable dimension of the group's situation on the eve of the Salmon War – an essential determinant in the production of that event.

Québec's politics of sovereignty

The politics and posturing of the Québec state, led at that time by the nationalist Québécois Party, are also identified as a major factor in the fomenting of the Salmon War. In fact, the Québec government is now widely regarded as the primary actor responsible for provoking the war, and for creating the general situation of unrest that existed at the time.

If the Canadian state (or the 'Crown') is identified as the prime agent of Essipiunnuat colonisation, the Québec government is depicted in stories

14 Pessamit (formerly Betsiamites, or Bersimis, and Papinachois) is an Innu community (or 'First Nation') located along the north shore of the St Lawrence River at the mouth of the Pessamit River, located 107 km east of Essipit and 50 km south west of Baie-Comeau: see http://www.pessamit.ca. In 1860 the canton of Les Escoumins was officially created (Létourneau, 1985, p. 43). The following year the Betsiamites reserve was created, aimed at isolating the Innu from all contact with 'white' people; according to the Church, 'civilization kills the Indians (Frenette, 1995, p. 26). At that time, some 40 Essipiunnuat were still residing in Essipit. In 1862, the Oblates moved their mission to Pessamit and the original government plan to displace all Innu to Pessamit was taking form – half of Essipiunnuat families moved to Pessamit, provoking a demographic collapse of Essipiunnuat (Mailhot and Vincent, 1979). Only 10 families remained in Essipit (Mailhot and Vincent, 1979, p. 36; Laforest, 1983, p. 4; Boudreault, 1994, p. 29; and Charest, 2009, p. 18.), a number reduced to 8 in 1864 and 6 in 1878; they seemingly migrated to Pessamit (Frenette, 1996, p. 33). People's autobiographical stories confirm that their grandparents had extensive relations with Pessamiunnuat, were travelling to Pessamit by canoe up the coast, and that Essipiunnuat and Pessamiunnuat were very close culturally and shared common views on their history and rights as Innu. Oral testimonies also mentioned continued attempts by authorities and priests to displace Innu from Essipit to Pessamit, presented as the 'capital of the Indians'. Some interviewees mention the fact that Essipiunnuat who wanted to speak Innu-aimun faced racism and were told to go to Pessamit if they wanted to be Indian and speak Innu-amun. People also fondly remember the Pessaminnuat being supportive of the Essipiunnuat during the Salmon War.

as colonialist in asserting sovereignty over the Innu and as having triggered the war.[15] From 1975 and therefore Prior to the Salmon War, Innu groups, represented by the Conseil Attikamekw-Montagnais (CAM), had been undertaking negotiations with Québec and Ottawa over the recognition of inherent Innu sovereignty and self-determination, and the modalities of their operation. Meanwhile, the Québec government, led by the Parti Québécois, was itself engaged in seeking national sovereignty for the Euroquébécois people from the Canadian Crown. The Salmon War, therefore, occurred in this context of competing claims to national sovereignty and independence.

For decades, Innu groups had denounced the negation of their ancestral right to fish salmon and the private and exclusive appropriation of the best rivers by corporations and business. In the late 1970s, such incidents were increasing as the Innu were contesting the private ownership of rivers along the coast of the Québec northern shore and mainstream society's increasing denial of the existence of *Innu tipenitamun*. Growing pressure was being exerted on the Québec government by First Peoples in a context where Québec was modifying its policies, abolishing commercial licences and delegating power to regional authorities called *zones d'exploitation contrôlées* (known as ZEC), composed of locals, to manage riverine ecosystems.

When it took power in 1980, the Parti Québécois decided, without consulting indigenous groups and without their consent, to put in place new administrative devices in order to assert authority over the rivers and salmon fishing. Until then, the Essipiunnuat had been spreading their nets in the sea in front of the reserve. Some family headmen had permission to use nets under Québec commercial licences. The salmon that were caught were generally distributed among the families. The ZEC system had been established on the Esh Shipu River in 1979, and a local committee for the management of the Esh Shipu was named *Comité d'aménagement de la rivière à saumon des Escoumins* (CARSE). No Essipiunnu was invited to join the committee.

In the mid 1970s some of the fishermen from Les Escoumins still had commercial licences and were spreading their nets all around the mouth of the river. But in 1980, new government regulations forced people who had fished the river for years to abandon their activities, and many felt resentful. Meanwhile, under Québec licence, Essipiunnuat families were still spreading nets in the sea in front of the reserve. But as the government was abolishing all licences, it was also cancelling their rights to spread their nets. Central to the Salmon War was the experience of Innu fisherman, Ernest, who went to fish in an area at the tip of the Escoumins dock, just outside the borders of the reserve, in a place where Euroquébécois fishermen were no longer fishing. When he was

15 'It is the government first who did all this shit; it is them who triggered the whole thing in fact. ...' (Tshak, ch. 1, ref. 5)

pressured to stop his activities, the band council called a general assembly of the Essipiunnuat and the decision was made to turn the net into a 'community net'. It was at this point that salmon fishing became a symbol of the struggle for Innu sovereignty.

People on CARSE then submitted a complaint to the Québec government, which responded by sending its agents to seize the net. The Essipiunnuat were convinced, however, of the legitimacy of their actions and their right to fish (Riel, chapter 1, ref. 1).[16] By setting nets in spite of Québec's abolition of commercial salmon fishing, Essipit was affirming that its ancestral rights could not be usurped by the Québec state. Québec, on the other hand, took a hard stance and negated Essipiunnuat ancestral rights beyond the borders of the reserve. Ancestral Innu sovereignty was clearly asserted, and Québec sovereignty was challenged. At the same time, the local Euroquébécois of Les Escoumins were seeing the Essipiunnuat engaged in an activity that they themselves were henceforth prohibited from engaging in.[17]

The government succeeded in seizing the Essipiunnuat's net, but was then faced with resistance and an equally hard stance. The state officials decided to negotiate an agreement with Essipit concerning the fishing activities, and in the summer of 1980 a verbal agreement was concluded, with which both parties were initially content. The Innu spread their nets again, but it was not long before one of their watchmen noticed wildlife agents trying to furtively take it away. The agents succeeded in doing so and left. This mobilised the community into action and more than a dozen men went to intercept the agents on the road as they were on their way back to their headquarters in the neighbouring town of Forestville. They stopped the agents' car and a violent altercation occurred, with the protesters bringing the net back to Essipit.

It is at this point that the event entered its contentious phase and 'the smoke started'. The sudden and unexplained abrogation of the agreement with Essipit is seen as the 'igniting powder'.[18] People's memories of the Salmon War

16 'The Salmon War, it started with the story of the communitarian net spread at the dock. The net had been sold to Essipit by Donald Tremblay, a non-indigenous person. Old Édouard Cyril, he was the first to have this net. He sold it to Donald. And we spread a net there. What happened is that some non-indigenous complained to Québec wildlife agents, saying that we were spreading our nets right in the river … and that we were blocking the salmon's migratory course. But it wasn't the case at all. So we were at the dock and the agent came to try to take off our net. It didn't work since people were entirely opposed to their actions. We told them: "We have a right to fish here, it's an ancestral right, we have no problem, and we weren't hurting the river at all."' (Riel, ch. 1, ref. 1)

17 'It was a net spread on the basis that we were claiming rights that had belonged to us before but that had been transformed into a more commercial basis. There was a commercial net and we were surrounded. There were nets all around, there was not just us who were fishing. And then it was abandoned.' (Mestenapeo, ch. 1, ref. 2)

18 'There were discussions with the mayor of Les Escoumins. But before these discussions we had met with the assistant deputy minister and the minister of fisheries who was also in charge

are mainly comprised of the subsequent confrontations with Québec and its agents. That said, however, the change in the position of Québec, after the negotiations with the minister and the mayor of Les Escoumins, does find some explanation in the stories.

It is alleged that Québec played a populist card and was receptive to local discontentment in Les Escoumins, as well as disregarding the Essipiunnuat and their rights. The repression of a small 'Indian' minority was indeed more popular in public opinion in Québec at that time than any defence or recognition of indigenous rights would have been. Québec's analysis of the situation would therefore have led it to a decision to please the Euroquébécois, and appease their anger, instead of recognising any indigenous rights.[19]

In fact, it is likely that the Québec government believed that the Essipiunnuat would not resist and that the question of indigenous rights would be settled forever; it would be an easy victory, 'Indian revolt' would be suppressed and Québec would take over the rivers. The government strategy was therefore to have the local population putting pressure directly on the group, so that the state would not have to intervene:

> Some of them wanted to make their mark … You know, Québec politics at that time was terrible. They just let things go … The small bureaucrats, what can they do? They were snapping behind their backs, 'Go! Go! Do that!' Those at the top, then, they don't give a damn. This whole thing, it has all been about provincial politics, the government who did not want to hear anything, and who didn't want to think about improving … who haven't taken any means for it. They thought we would submit. And they made a mistake." (Raoul, chapter 1, ref. 3–4)

The events in Essipit occurred at a time when the Québec government was concerned generally with the indigenous contestations about salmon fishing and the management of their respective riverine systems across Québec. At the time, the government was trying to develop close ties with

---

of indigenous rights. So it was negotiated [the agreement], and accepted by the government ... but then it fell apart. We were spreading the net at the dock. We had an agreement. The Amerindian police had brought a large 23-foot canoe … And we were guarding the net, since we had an agreement with the government; we had had talks. So I was keeping the net. At one moment I realised that wildlife agents were at the dock to take off our net … I was alone in my boat. I told the agents: "you won't leave with the net". … The agreement was signed. So that is when they came to steal the net. What happened? They were saying the agreement was not finalised, but we had agreed. When you're dealing with ministers, assistant deputy minister, what is the problem? You ask yourself the question. But they hadn't respected their agreement. So it turned into smoke.' (Mestenapeo, ch. 1, ref. 2 and 4)

19 'The political game was tough. Yes, political manoeuvrings played a major role. At that time, it was much politicised. It was all about politics ... The government preferred to have 2,000 people going to vote for them. So they said "Essipit? Go to hell! We will walk with the politics. Might they put more pressure? Look, we will go on the side of the 2,000; they will make pressure ... The 250 who are in Essipit, we will let them go, let them deal with their own troubles."' (Riel, ch. 1, ref. 8)

the local Euroquébécois associations who managed the salmon rivers. This was particularly true in Les Escoumins, where locally born and resident minister of leisure, fishing and hunting for Québec, Lucien Lessard, who was responsible for the rivers and their management, had links with CARSE members. These close links are generally invoked as the main reason behind Québec's change of direction regarding Essipit and important for gaining an understanding of the reason why the Innu salmon fishing issue came so to the fore.[20]

Québec was in a situation where the state could not intervene directly to crush indigenous resistance but was prepared to do so indirectly at a time when resistance was at its peak in all Innu communities in a general movement to reappropriate their riverine systems. Former participants in the war perceive this in the same way: Québec and its police mobilised the local population to attain their objective of crushing the 'Indian revolt'. People share the view that it was as if the government and the police wanted the local population to solve their problems at the local level (Riel, chapter 1, ref. 4).[21] Stories suggest that the strategy adopted by the government here was to mobilise the local population against the 'Indians' so that they could crush Essipit resistance without the official intervention of Québec.[22]

This all resulted, in 1981, in the direct intervention of more than two hundred local villagers who walked on to the reserve and up to the dock in order to stop Essipiunnuat fishing activities. There were violent confrontations, and

20 'It was not to quibble for the fun of quibbling. It has nothing to do with the fact of saying "ten or fifteen salmon a year". Salmon was a pretext, that's for sure. But we need to reflect on the triggering element behind all that. You know, the discussions with CARSE, the discussion with the MLCP [Leisure, Hunting and Fishing Provincial Ministry] at the time,… Lucien Lessard was the minister in charge at that period, a guy from Bergeronnes [a neighbouring town to Les Escoumins]. You know, there was something …' (Adam, ch. 2, ref. 3) 'We were by the dock at that period. People of Les Escoumins were at Pointe-à-la-Croix and were watching with their telescope what was going on. I think it was all put together ... by the minister. ... If it had been controlled at the very least, local people would have never been allowed to come here, they should have been allowed. But the minister must have organised, with some villagers ... He had chosen all the same people who were able to ...' (Tshak, ch. 1, ref. 4)

21 'It felt as if they had said: You can remove them from there by any means; catch them – us we don't want to go.' (Riel, ch. 1, ref. 4)

22 'We must say that there was a lot of Québec governmental manipulation ... There were negotiations with CAM in regards to the Mingan, the Natashquan River, a lot of things all at once pertaining to the salmon river as well as with the Mi'gmaq, in Listuguj. There were lots of eddies. Everything was moving at the same time. We should also say that the deputy minister of leisure at that period was Lucien Lessard; a guy from Grandes-Bergeronnes, so it's very close ... He tried ... Strategically, they tried ... to have the job done by the local population. "Crush these bastards!" And I have lived it on the dock, and everywhere, in the incidents of war, because we were really at war then, locally [with Les Escoumins]. [We had] no protection from Québec police, and everybody went up! And the community met here at the dock ... there were harsh confrontations. It was wanted. It was the MLCP and the whole thing ... and no Québec police. It was wanted, 200 of them came on the dock. The orders were coming from up there, the order ... Commanded ... well, it was something like, "All right, we won't go right now. Settle this!" It was deliberate.' (Sam, ch. 1, ref. 1 and 11).

this episode is remembered as the heart of the Salmon War. The intervention of between 200 and 400 individuals, according to the different testimonies, from Les Escoumins and the surrounding villages, would have been, to a large degree, coordinated from Québec. Thus, there is the perception that the event degenerated into violence and a war as a consequence of the machinations of Lessard, who favoured the direct intervention of the local population to repress Innu resistance. The minister recruited individuals from Les Escoumins who could mobilise and organise a hostile crowd, in order to lead them to the dock. The policies and actions of the Québec government, particularly of the leisure, hunting and fishing ministry, remain therefore, a central determining feature of the Salmon War within the context of Essipiunnuat autobiographical memories.

The local Euroquébécois: nationalism and racism

A third external source of the Salmon War that people identified concerns the local Euroquébécois population of Les Escoumins. The Euroquébécois' conceptualisation of 'Indians', and the attitude and actions they had adopted towards their Essipiunnuat neighbours since their first occupation of the banks of the Esh Shipu in the early 1820s and the creation of the 'lumber town' (wood entrepreneurs, land speculators and priests) are described as reasons for its occurrence. The Euroquébécois social imaginary would have contained negative depictions of 'Indians', as well as assumptions pertaining to First Peoples' ancestral sovereignties that would have an impact on their receptiveness to Essipiunnuat claims and their interpretation of Innu intentions.

Interviewees describe the episodes of 1980–1 as being a continuation of pre-existing tensions whose origins go back to the creation of the settler town. It is alleged, for example, that the town was actually established on an ancient Essipiunnuat gathering site on top of graves. Tensions between the Essipiunnuat and local villages are thus rooted in the colonisation process, and existed and were felt long before the Salmon War.[23] The creation of Les Escoumins had resulted in the Innu being displaced, without their consent, from their ancient sites located around what is today known as the Bay of Les Escoumins, to the current area of the reserve. This has been neither forgotten nor forgiven among

23 As Maxence says, 'I remember. I knew that there was a tension from the beginning. At that time, I wasn't "indigenous", I wasn't an "Indian", and I wasn't recognised as such. So I knew that there were tensions.' (Maxence, ch. 1, ref. 1). These tensions were felt even more intensively by those who had family ties in both Essipit and Les Escoumins. Indeed, in 1985, the Canadian government changed elements of the Indian Act pertaining to 'Indian status'; so some women recovered an 'Indian status' they had lost when they married non-Indians. So at the moment of the war, some people weren't members of the band despite their family ties with the group on their mother's side, as in the case of Maxence. The children of these women were integrated on the 'band list' of Indian status in 1985 and became 'Indian'.

older Essipiunnuat; for them, the creation of the town remains a misfortune and reminder of their displacement and dispossession.[24]

The attitudes of the local Euroquébécois towards the Essipiunnuat, and their general conceptions of 'Indians' and how these representations have developed over time, have had an impact on the course of the events. Stories imply some Euroquébécois posturing that is distinguished by their denial of the Essipiunnuat as an indigenous group and a widespread hostility to the rights claims. The antagonism between the two groups is widely presented as a racial issue, and has been fed by the villagers' racism towards the 'Indians' (Esther, chapter 1, ref. 2).

Thus the spreading of the salmon net by the Essipiunnuat offered an occasion for the local population to express an already existing racial hatred and jealousy of the 'Indians'; the net merely reactivated old hostilities. Essipiunnuat experiences from early childhood confirm the existence of deeply rooted racist attitudes towards them, transmitted from generation to generation, which were reinforced through the practices of the local institutions.[25] Such prejudices would be translated into Essipiunnuat claims not being accepted, widespread insensitivity to First Peoples' sociohistorical circumstances in general, and in particular to their messages and attempts to inform the public about their rights. This resulted ultimately in a sustained ignorance of Essipiunnuat reality, in order to protect their own representation of the 'Indian' entrenched in their cultural and national discourses. A rising Innu discourse portraying Euroquébécois as colonialists collides with Euroquébécois collective self-conceptions that they themselves were victims of history[26] and that they themselves had been 'colonised' under Canadian rules.[27]

24 'If we go further in history, we weren't a reserve … Yes, we had been bought. If you look at the process, we weren't here. We were at Pointe-à-la-Croix, and we were all around. Well, before, we were moving around; going everywhere we wanted to, so … what they told us [the ancestors or 'tshenu'] is that the Indians were there, at Pointe-à-la-Croix, and all over. Just take Charles Bélanger, "the" very old settler Charles Bélanger. There were indigenous people who were living there where the drugstore is currently located; where the house is, you had a shop. And before, there were indigenous people there. Up until then, we were more than 40 families there; we were many Indians!' (Mestenapeo, ch. 1, ref. 1)

25 'The racists will always be the racists ... I can tell you that when they came to the dock, there were really a lot of racists. Intimidation, attempts to inflict pain on us … They have always been that way. We became used to it. You build yourself a kind of shell. So you have your armour, you talk to them, but at the bottom, you know … All the time, all the time, all the time … It is deep within them. They are educated this way at school by their teachers, at home by their parents … At school, we didn't pay for our pencils. You know "You Indians, you don't pay anything". Take the candies and shut up ... you know.' (Raoul, ch. 1, ref. 7–8)

26 Especially since the nationalists had lost a referendum on Québec independence in 1980.

27 If their circumstances as a colonised people created a need to have an 'inferior Indian' who was, in turn, subordinate to them, their position as a colonialist imposed on them the unsustainable need of a 'non-existent' Indian. This approach is predominant in the narrative on the sources of the war. As Justin explains, a characteristic of the Escouminois-Euroquébécois representation

The intransigence of the local Euroquébécois is best explained in terms of their inheritance of an inability to understand due to the culture and colonised/colonialist heritage handed down through the generations, who lived in what was known as New France. As one person mentions, it was while repeatedly trying to explain to them the purpose of the Essipiunnuat rebellion that he realised they had a mental blockage.[28] Others say the locals' attitude hardened from the very moment the salmon net was spread, and a major shift in their treatment of the Essipiunnuat, even among those who had been friends, contributed to the exacerbation of the confrontation.[29] An increase in the intransigence, and the stigmatisation of everything associated with being 'Indian', was witnessed.[30] Indians were declared guilty of a panoply of issues, and some local Euroquébécois leaders publicly condemned them.

This phenomenon of deep-rooted prejudice is not foreign to the construction of a Euroquébécois nationhood founded on an ideology that places the 'Indian' in the sphere of a being to exclude, not only because he is 'primitive' but because he is dangerous and someone to be frightened of. The need for the Euroquébécois to affirm themselves in opposition to others can be traced back to

of the Essipiunnuat is that 'they think that everything is free for us, that we don't pay taxes and anything, all based on prejudice and ignorance of our real condition, especially when we go out from the reserve.' As he states, it is impossible for them to understand Essipiunnuat circumstances because of their representation of the 'Indian' and the place this representation plays in their identity. For them the phenomenon of assertive Essipiunnuat affirmation was confusing. As Justin says, 'That's what people don't understand. And I think they will never understand; the local villagers, I mean. I don't mean that they may not understand one day ... but we are in 2010 and they still don't understand, and they are now the only ones against us ... It is maybe jealousy of what we have but it is maybe more about that they would have preferred us to stay on unemployment insurance benefits, as our condition at a certain time, just being intoxicated all the time! It would have been easier for them thereafter to say that we do nothing and that we are cowards. In my experience, they had a prejudice from the beginning. Indeed, we have started empowering ourselves. In my view, it bothers them a lot. Thirty years ago, there wasn't much on the reserve.' (Justin, ch. 1, ref. 2–6)

28 'They didn't understand. It was as if colonisation was deep in their genes ... You know, the English, they had been good at it, and the French have had their part of it in the story; "evangelisation", it is rooted deep in them, and everything that it entails. And then we [the indigenous] say, "It will stop, it has to stop." That's how it happened. It was hard for them to understand. You know, they were very used to it, from generation to generation ... you don't know who is the master, when you're not at home' (Pishimnapeo, ch. 1, ref. 7)

29 'They have a wall. They don't respect anything. It is racism. It is racism, jealousy, envy. It is all these things that took over. I had a lot of friends at that period. As the war was coming, oop! No more friends. There were no more friends, then I was a "fucking savage" and this and that, and even if I was trying hard to tell them, they couldn't hear.' (Tshak, ch. 1, ref. 6)

30 'It is to their advantage and they criticise anyway; they are never happy. We would have given them the moon, and they still wouldn't have been happy. By any means, an Indian, whatever he does or doesn't do, they demean him the same. They are therefore all the time against him: "They don't pay taxes; they either don't do this or that". It is part of them and it is anchored. It has always been so ... this is why. Whether you do something or not, they bear you a grudge.' (Édouard, ch. 1, ref. 5)

a fear of being perceived as coming from an inferior culture and being incapable of civilisation. Such a posture could be explained by an internalisation of the policies subsequent to the Durham report from 1839, produced by the British Crown following the repression of the Patriot's movement. It recommended compulsory assimilation into the dominant English culture. One hypothesis is that it led to what could be called the 'Durham syndrome'[31] among the Euroquébécois as a result of their internalisation over time of the idea that they are inferior to the English people because they are, it is said, 'mixed' with the Indians and therefore an 'inferior race'.

Analyses of the construction of images and stereotypes of 'Indians' demonstrate how the Euroquébécois are compelled to assert that they are not 'primitive' and that it is the Indians who are. Recent research tends to validate this critical analysis of Euroquébécois representations of the 'Indian' (Burelle, 2019; Cornellier, 2015; Leroux, 2019), and the strong tendency of Euroquébécois discourse to negate and attempt to delegitimise the inherent sovereignty of First Peoples, as it competes with Euroquébécois sovereignty. This radical critique of Euroquébécois culture is important, since Essipiunnuat share to different degrees the perspective of the Euroquébécois. This is due to internalised racism and advanced forms of psychological colonialism. Because of Québec's long-term cultural hegemony, the Essipiunnuat are also affected by the 'Durham Syndrome'. The 'inferior Indian' is still needed as cement for Euroquébécois self-conception, and as a diversionary tactic so that a positive self-image can be maintained in spite of an often unrecognised colonial bias.

The affirmation of a strong, proud, free and non-supine Indian tends to be perceived as an attack on the frail foundations of Euroquébécois self-narrative and legitimacy, while also generating repulsion and envy. According to Redekop, the fact that indigenous assertion of independence and the quest for autonomy create insecurity among the Euroquébécois, and tend to be perceived as a threat, would reveal that Euroquébécois–indigenous relations are characterised by the existence of a hegemonic structure of violence. The phenomenon is best illustrated by the forms of violence inflicted on First Peoples during the infamous Oka Crisis in 1990,[32] and the extent to which the aggression expressed towards 'Indians' is deeply related to Euroquébécois' cultural identity and plays a critical role in their sense of self (Redekop, 2005).

31 See Ross-Tremblay (2016), *La souveraineté comme responsabilité*; Burelle (2019).

32 The event remembered as the Oka Crisis occurred in 1990 when Mohawks resisted land speculators' attempts, supported by local Euroquébécois politicians, to build a golf course over Mohawk ancestral lands, including a cemetery. It led to violent confrontations between Mohawk warriors and the Québec police, as well as the Canadian army, which was finally called in to suppress the resistance. There was a wave of racism against 'Indians' during the episode. A Québec police officer died during the strife. For more information, see Obomsawin (1996).

Essipiunnuat's testimonies also report the phenomenon of the Euroquébécois' intense jealousy towards First Peoples. This is often invoked as the 'real origin' of the Euroquébécois' tough local opposition to Innu rights, an attitude with its own logic which preceded the salmon conflict. Such envy is said to have subordinate, subliminal roots that would always have manifested in correlation with any advantages given to, or expressions of specificity by, the Essipiunnuat as 'indigenous' or 'Indian'. It is as if an 'Indian' should not have any advantages or be 'better' than a Euroquébécois. Such a gain would be felt as an injustice which destabilised their sense of self and made them vulnerable.[33]

This social phenomenon was noticed by the older Essipiunnuat generations. It is explained by the fact that the 'Indian' is not accepted, but perceived as not truly human. As described by one of the interviewees, the best analogy of the way the Innu are represented within the Euroquébécois social imagination is the case of the 'n word' in American supremacist ideology. Whatever the strengths and qualities of character of Essipiunnuat individuals, they are said to vanish when these persons are identified as 'Indians'.[34]

Another attitude observed among the local Euroquébécois corresponds to them taking a kind of sadistic pleasure in hating 'Indians'. If the stories report a generalised ignorance about First People's human condition and a lack of information among the locals, a tendency to be pleased by discourses denigrating the Essipiunnuat was also mentioned.[35] The theme of manipulation is also repeated in some of the descriptions. Interviewees affirm that due to the negative representations of 'Indians', the manipulation of the local Euroquébécois was easier when it came to questions of indigenous sovereignty and rights. Their cultural imaginary, the intrinsic disapprobation of 'Indians', coupled with being insecure in their own self-image, seems to have led them to be not only more receptive to anti-Indian rhetoric, but more easily mobilised by any local driving forces that were anti-Indian.

Anti-Indian militancy: planning repression

The meeting of various 'anti-Indian' social agents in Les Escoumins and neighbouring villages, with support elsewhere in the province, is reported to

33 'Their jealousy, it is about our rights, our privileges; because we were expressing our indigenous identity. It touched their identity. Yes, it has always been the case, as long as I can remember.' (Pierre, ch. 1, ref. 1)

34 'Me, I've always said that it was about jealousy. The older people were saying the same. They don't accept the Indian! What was it for them? A "n.", a little one. Yet, we were all men.' (Pierre, ch. 1, ref. 7)

35 'There are many ... who were manipulated and who just followed others. When it comes to "Indians", the whites, they are easily manipulated by some people ... often; there are many things they ignore ... When we talk of lands, and territories ... One needs to open one's eyes, but it doesn't always work this way. They have a tendency ... as if it was a pleasure for them.' (Karl, ch. 1, ref. 10)

be another external component contributing to the Salmon War. Anti-Indian militancy, by all accounts, helped to convert a generalised dissatisfaction and reactionary mood into fierce repression and anti-Indian action. Such an organised militancy contributed to influencing local public opinion in accordance with the specific intentions of a range of interest groups such as racial supremacists, provincial politicians, local businesses and ecologists. Early negotiations by the Essipiunnuat with CARSE, aiming to effect a kind of reconciliation before the war, gave them a taste of the type of hostility they were to face.[36]

An anti-Indian fishing group, led by CARSE, was formed with the objective of removing the community salmon net spread by the Essipiunnuat. CARSE comprised diverse groups such as ecologists, fishermen and local business owners (Riel, chapter 1, ref. 1). A double dynamic was observable among CARSE members (Justin, chapter 1, ref. 2–6). On one hand, there were those with a genuine concern for the preservation of the salmon population in the river (Maxence, chapter 1, ref. 2).[37] On the other, the conservation interests often veiled entrenched prejudice, attitudes of racism and/or jealousy in relation to Essipiunnuat rights.[38] People report the existence of some familial clans in Les Escoumins, reputed to harbour substantial anti-Innu sentiments, each of them with their own 'loud speakers'. Some individuals from these clans would purportedly compose a cell that was active before and during the war in disseminating anti-Indian rhetoric.[39]

36 As Ivan explains: 'It's a politics event. The government got involved in that and I don't know why. That's the only reason that I see why it happened. The CARSE used this as a means to put pressure on us, since they were saying that we were destroying the river. In my opinion, that is the only reason.' (Ivan, ch. 1, ref. 3) Essipiunnuat attempts to reach an agreement on the management of the Esh Shipu River and to collaborate were rejected and their rights claims met with a shower of insults about their complete illegitimacy (Sam, ch. 1, ref. 1 and 5). As soon as the Essipiunnuat decided to assert their *Innu tipenitamun* through conducting community fishing, the CARSE accused them publicly of destroying the project to revitalise the salmon population of the river, ongoing since 1977; CARSE then sent a request directly to Lessard's office and that of the local deputy (member of the Québec parliament) to intervene and crush Innu activities. There was a clear matrix of relationships between government officials and the CARSE, which was largely composed of personal friends of the minister. Considering Québec's actions in relation to Essipiunnuat fishing in the light of these dealings, the stories present CARSE lobbying in the province and the favourable response and aggressive postures of Minister Lessard as essential evidence which would explain why the situation degenerated.

37 'What the "whites" were reproaching the Indians for was: "Your net, it hurt the salmon migration, because it caught the genitors right before they enter the river." That was the problem, according to the non-Indians.' (Maxence, ch. 1, ref. 2)

38 'Villagers didn't like that we had spread the net there. So it was "The fucking savages! They take everything from us! They steal everything! The land is theirs! The river is theirs!" The war therefore started there.' (Tshak, ch. 1, ref. 1)

39 'It wouldn't have lasted long … but there was a small cell, the small cell that triggered the village … the S., they are very good at that … the R., not all of them … it was a small gang gathering elements of these families, not just one family, but a small group, it has always been

These forces were indeed seeking direct confrontation with the 'Indians', but were acting mainly behind the scenes as motivators or 'boosters' to direct, guide and coordinate the reaction to Essipiunnuat resistance.[40] They were poised to plan direct action against the group in order to seize the net 'when they saw that the wildlife agents were unable to do anything, or did not want to do anything' (Maxence, chapter 1, ref. 5–6).

The role of local business leaders in fomenting anti-Indian militancy is also reported. The Essipiunnuat's efforts to initiate socioeconomic development during the late 1970s had fuelled misunderstandings between the locals and Essipit. There was a cognitive dissonance between representations of the 'Indians' that had been imposed on the Essipiunnuat for decades and their increased self-definition and self-assurance. Jealousy, which had ancient roots, was reinvigorated by the socioeconomic developments, which provoked an angry reaction from the Escouminois.[41]

Since the mid 1970s, the Essipiunnuat had been proposing initiatives with the intention of accelerating economic development on the reserve. As documented previously, they were also pursuing increased autonomy. This provoked opposition in Les Escoumins, particularly among some of the businesses that were losing out to the communitarian enterprises that had been established on the reserve.[42] Essipit was seeking to revive and diversify its economy and was attempting to develop other projects and initiatives, such as a community centre for young people. As a result, there was growing competition between the local merchants and Essipit's communitarian socioeconomic developments (some small cottages

the same. It's the old ones, they are the worst.' (Karl, ch. 1, ref. 11). 'They were addressing the masses, but above all they were "crowd boosters" that I've named earlier, the shriller, yellers, who were saying things, all kind of things: … "This bunch of fuckers … you will see, it's the end of them, they won't command, they won't rule with their tiny gang, they won't resist the village; and their net … it has nothing to do there"' (Maxence, ch. 1, ref. 5 and 6)

40 As Raoul explained: 'so it's at that moment that the people of Les Escoumins, manipulated by a cell of individuals that we call "boosters", people who were not on the spot and were saying "go ahead, go head, I'll buy you drinks if you go". And the worst talkers were not on the spot.' (Raoul, ch. 1, ref. 6)

41 'They hated us, they hated us; through jealousy but not only through jealousy. It was on everything, I believe. And they observed that on the reserve, things were going up. The bowling alley that we had just built and all that, oh boy! And young people of the village, the whites, were all coming on to the reserve. So they said: "How come that we have businesses, and they don't come in our shops?"; "Indian thieves!"' (Pierre, ch. 1, ref. 5)

42 'Communitarian development had already begun [at the moment of the war]. The community centre was running ... It wasn't embryonic, it was up and running, and the community centre was going, with the pool tables ... We just had two competitors and they had already closed down ... They had been full of drug dealers, and everything. They had a lot of customers, and they all came to us. It was nicer and more secure for young people. Parents knew that at the CCM [Innu community centre], there was discipline, it was more regulated and we would organise a dance party on Friday, and minibuses ... and there was no alcohol and drugs.' (Sam, ch. 1, ref. 4)

for holiday rentals, for example, and a bar). So, if for Essipit salmon fishing was a highly symbolic and fundamental issue pertaining to principles and rights, in Les Escoumins it was, above all, a question of potential income for local entrepreneurs.[43] By various means, Essipit was slowly increasing its economic development, but on a communitarian basis. The local business community therefore, indeed saw the 'Indians' as potential competitors who would exert a negative impact on their profits.

On the ground, Essipiunnuat affirmation through fishing rights was intruding upon the local Euroquébécois sense of self, but it was also raising questions about the restoration of the river that was predominantly being driven by economic interests. The village had experienced significant economic difficulties since the closure of the local mill, and local Euroquébécois entrepreneurs, very active in CARSE, had developed a business model through which the revitalisation of the salmon population in the river (seeded with salmon smolt in order to increase spawning runs) would attract sport fishermen and generally improve the local economy, moving it way from subsistence and primary industry towards a more tourism-based economy. Some had even built small lodges in order to exploit this anticipated tourist traffic. These people were therefore active members of the CARSE, in the expectation of gaining from the revival of the river.[44]

A nucleus of individuals was openly seeking a war with the 'Indians' (Pierre, chapter 1, ref. 6)[45] and were ready to reward those who would engage against them.[46] Such anti-Indian militancy, together with Canadian colonialism,

43 'At that time, CARSE was requesting that we stopped fishing so that they could do economic development.' (Adam, ch. 1, ref. 2)

44 'Non-Indians thought they would become rich with that. Some had already built lodges by the river, some cottages by the river. They were planned … They were protecting their goods; well, not so much their goods as their interests. There were many reasons there.' (Sam, ch. 1, ref. 13)

45 Pierre states that 'the whites wanted the war so that we come to play their game; what "they" wanted. For us, it was just to have the privilege recognised to spread a communitarian net.' (Pierre, ch. 1, ref. 6). Essipiunnuat attempts to be co-manager of the river were refused. So, there was no possible agreement between CARSE and Essipit since the non-participation of 'Indians' was a matter of principle for the former. According to interviewees, and as discussed earlier, Québec's and CARSE's call for the repression of 'Indian' activities is seen as a key element in the unfolding of the war. The Essipiunnuat saw the setting of the nets as the start of the war, since it provoked an anti-Essipiunnuat movement. If this movement became widespread in the village, it received additional impetus from a group of local people, allied with a group of inveterate racists and others who considered Essipit economic development to be a threat to their financial interests or to be unwelcome competition for any present or future business affairs. These individuals, allied with the Québec state, considered it in their interest to mobilise the local population against Essipit. By disrupting the native fishery, they could 'head off' any impending 'Indian' insurgency.

46 According to Tshak, some business owners were involved in mobilising villagers against the Essipiunnuat. The distribution of alcohol was one way of getting local villagers involved in direct action against the Innu (Tshak, ch. 1, ref. 3).

the actions of the Québec government and the local Euroquébécois idea of 'Indians', is regarded as a crucial element in the making of the Salmon War.

Hope in our hands: faces of group agency

Participants[47] correlate their own subjectivity with the occurrence of the Salmon War. Manifestations of agency are reported in the stories and interpreted as having nourished the outbreak of the war. Those interviewed undoubtedly grant a central role to their own individual actions in the war, and the confluence of them with shared views and actions. Four leading components emerge from the stories as having made up its underlying factors: acts of reference to a common past, and collective experiences and memories; the surfacing of and belonging to an internal movement; the existence of common objectives; and the participative development of strategies.

A growing consciousness

Stories pertaining to the genesis of the Salmon War are impregnated with references to the group's past and its historical circumstances. They also reveal a role played by images of the group and their influence on people's motivations, choices and assessments of their condition just before the war. Collective memories remain powerful resources for collective action; they offer points of reference (Blühdorn, 2006) that contribute to 'reactivat[ing] the sources of rules and practices' (Savard, 2004, p. 112). They are thus central to the establishment of cultural identity and its defence:

> Memory of the past plays a crucial role in the transmission of cultural identity. In every society and every country, the collective memory transmitted to the young by the elder generation, through a variety of channels, influences their perception of their cultural identity and values, and their willingness to invest in them – with major economic as well as political and social consequences. (Dessi, 2008, p. 2)

People speak openly for example, about their concerns on the eve of war that they might be repeating the mistakes of the past, and on the other hand of the importance of ensuring the continuity of cultural norms. Their stories expose common themes in this auto-referentialisation: attitudes that hint at a historical consciousness shared by those taking part, and at images of the group and its situation in the frame of historical time. In the early 1980s, these mnemonic practices, concerned ways of relating to the group imaginary that undeniably fuelled motivation and inspired commitment and a sense of

47 The term 'participant' is used in the book to mean those who took part in the Salmon War and not those who participated in the research.

shared purpose. Connections to a commonly remembered past influenced Essipiunnuat's perceptions and actions, and they deserve closer attention.

In the context of the Salmon War, the past is often used as a point of reference concerning the nature of collective indigenous rights. Awareness and defence of these rights are presented as inseparable from the oral tradition and cultural memory that carries them from generation to generation. People articulate their views about Innu sovereignty based on the teachings they received from their parents, grandparents and ancestors. Access to this knowledge, widely based on collective remembrance and intergenerational transmission, is conditional on an accurate conceptualisation of *Innu tipenitamun*. Indeed, the acquisition of such data, and the historical consciousness it carries, is a prerequisite for resistance and non-consent to its extinguishment.[48]

For the older people particularly, but not only for them, any representations of Innu laws and normativity pertaining to ancestral territories clearly arise from a unique cultural frame of reference widely shared by First Peoples, especially those of the larger Algonquian family. They defend a vision of indigenous ancestral sovereignty articulated around respect for Assi ('the Earth'). This is generally represented in stories as an obligation to protect the earth for present and future generations, and as the source of an indigenous way of life based on responsibility, freedom and self-reliance.

According to participants, there was a sense during the war that only the defence of Innu sovereignty (*Innu tipenitamun*) might allow continuous self-determination (*uetshit takuaimatishun*) and guarantee the continuity of modes of auto-subsistence that knowledge of *innu-aitun* makes possible.[49] This food self-sufficiency, in particular, remains at the core of Essipiunnuat self-conception, even among some individuals in their thirties, and remains a central theme of intergenerational dealings.[50]

48 'I knew my grandfather. It wasn't the same vision [as many people understand it today]. No. It was "their rights", they were keeping to their rights. They wouldn't have sold it … They used to tell us stories. Even my father, Uncle Ludger, and my Uncle Joseph Moreau, they used to go all around in canoes. They used to go to Pessamit by canoe, so they were travelling a lot. So, "rights", you won't have them anymore, in other words; if we forget that, you won't have any soon.' (Mestenapeo, ch. 1, ref. 5)

49 The term Innu-aitun refers to an 'act, action; custom, way of doing things; culture' (Innu online dictionary: http://www.innu-aimun.ca/english/dictionary/). In the bureaucratic context of treaty negotiation, the term is used in the limited sense of hunting, fishing and trapping skills. But as mentioned by the late Elder Eli Mestokosho (personal conversation, Ekuanitshit, 2016), 'Innu-aitun is generally not understood properly'. It would, in fact, be more appropriate to speak of 'Innu science', which would include all knowledge, from hunting techniques to old stories, that are central to Innu traditional way of life.

50 'Yes, my father, and the old ones, were saying all the time "We have rights!" For the ancestors, that was it. I had learned it. That is how it was. As I said in court once: "That is what is in my head. That is where my own subsistence is; my life is there. When time has come, time has come; it is needed. If I want to eat moose, I go, I take it, or if I want to eat trout."' (Édouard, ch. 1, ref. 3).

Intergenerational transmission of knowledge about *Innu tipenitamun* was invoked as a source for action. Indeed, collective memory of past agency,[51] non-submissiveness and resistance to attempts to extinguish their rights were noticeably actualised at the moment of engaging in the struggle.[52] This is well illustrated, for example, by a story of resistance to the Crown that many people recalled. It concerns the manner in which their great grandfathers had prevented government intrusion into the reserve in order to protect their grandchildren from being recruited and enrolled in the Canadian army.[53] Resistance to authority is thus portrayed as a part of the Essipiunnuat's inventory of experience that was in people's minds at the time of the war.

Some older people argue that the 1980s uprising was no more than a continuation of the resistance carried out over several generations.[54] Such a position tends to assume that resistance and rebellion is now inherent in the group's self-concept and that there is an association between identifying as 'Indian' or Essipiunnuat and experiencing aggression. Personal accounts contain manifold allusions to incidences of aggression by authorities that narrators from all age groups witnessed in their childhood.[55] These aspects of individual

---

'We had also been told … that before, the Indians, it was them who where there, fishing in this area." (Ernest, ch. 1, ref. 1)

'When I was young, my grandfather [Joseph Ross], he always had a communitarian net … In ancient times, Indians fished there for sure. But the Boulianne acquired rights there, so they fished there too. I always used to go with my grandfather and Uncle Pierre. But it was not only my grandfather who fished there; it was the whole community. So, at the time of the negotiations, before the war, I remembered that, and I said, "Christ! We have the right." But we, we were young, and we were saying: "Fuck off! They won't crush us any longer."' (Sam, ch. 1, ref. 3)

51 See Bosi (1987, pp. 332–3): 'A collective memory develops from the bonds of family life, school, work, and so on. These bind to the memory of its members, add, unite, differentiate, and begin to fix clean. Living within a group, they suffer the vicissitudes of evolution and depend on its members and their interaction.'

52 'Oh no, we have never let them do that! No, the Indian has never consented to his abuse, no. No. No. Essipiunnuat have never let them do that. Except the sages, when there were quibbles, they left. It wasn't more than that. Because they thought they were idiots.' (Pierre, ch. 1, ref. 5)

53 'Before, there was a barrier at the entrances to the reserve. Nobody used to come in … I've seen the army retrace its steps right here. Oh yes! The barrier, they wouldn't go through it. Grandfather used to be on the gallery … and would stay there … it was ours.' (Mestenapeo, ch. 1, ref. 5)

54 'Young people watched what we did and they started to make claims too. That is where it started.' (Pishimnapeo, ch. 1, ref. 5)

55 Here is an example of stories of resistance and confrontation with authorities in relation to Essipiunnuat rights: 'I remember once upon a time, in Forestville. My dad, he respected wildlife agents, but he thought that they were not respecting First Peoples. So he had a bit less respect for them. You know, he used to travel by canoe all the time, with his gun and his fishing rod … He was exercising his rights, eating what he caught; he never poached, or sold anything. That's how he was taught and he liked it that way. So when altercations happened from time to time with wildlife agents, he thought they were very disrespectful. He was respecting everyone; he was not bothering anyone. So in Forestville, there was a barrier at

and common memories appear to have been central in the manifestations of collective subjectivity and social consciousness at the time of the war.

Older people's stories expose quite clearly the existence of a historical consciousness specific to the Essipiunnuat. The Salmon War, they maintain, remains an episode in a wider war. The events, and group agency, must be located within the wider framework of the historical indigenous people's struggles all over the continent. Their stories suggest that it was through contact with other indigenous groups that the historical consciousness of the Essipiunnuat was extended and kept intact.

Relations between First Peoples are important to interviewees. They are presented as having enriched the Essipiunnuat inventory of experience and enlarged their historical consciousness. For example, people frequently refer to the inspiring actions of Wendat, Jules Sioui, and Anishinaabe, William Commanda,[56] who met various members of the group in the early 20th century (and more intensively during the World War Two period) in his attempts to mobilise indigenous bands all over Canada in a liberation movement to assert their unceded sovereignty. The Essipiunnuat rebellion of 1980–1 is presented as a continuation of Sioui's militancy and his project.[57]

This contact with other First Peoples and personalities influenced people's image of their own group. Moreover, it fed the collective memory of the Essipiunnuat, particularly in relation to the nature and source of their ancestral sovereignty, but also to the legitimacy of that, and the obligation to defend it.

---

the ZEC, and it happened that there was a wildlife agent as we arrived. The guy was called the "Scar" by his peers. So he told my father "I wouldn't mind using my .38 for an Indian!" He was very straightforward, I can say; I was there and I remember. So my father replied, "Don't miss me with your .38," he said, "I'm capable of shooting a moose at 1000 feet, so I'm capable of shooting a wildlife agent." Apart from that, my father was not the kind of man to abuse his rights, but the wildlife agent had to respect his rights. It was as simple as that.' (Ivan, ch. 1, ref. 4)

56 For a complete description of Sioui's political stances and actions, see Shewell (1999) and Cyr (n.d.).

57 'I was aware of ... claims, I was very young, I was 13 or 14 years old then. Someone came here with my father ... They wanted to make claims over Canada. It was around 1945. There was a movement; my father witnessed these things. He was travelling at that time, he was going with his own money, and we were very poor. A man called Jules Sioui was working on that ... all over Canada. He even did a hunger strike ... I went to meet him at his place later on, before he died at 97 or 98 years old. He said "I attempted to give a start to the claim". Because it had been a while then that Indians had kept their mouths shut. And you never heard of Indians in this time. Some Indians wanted to speak and others were getting there, but meanwhile they [the governments] were scared of an Indian "renewal", as in fact was happening. We can say that it [the Salmon War] is rooted in this time, and that then, we entered into the Salmon War... The old man died poor, as did his wife, but others benefited from their actions, for the best. Last time I met him, when he was very old, he said: "I want to pass the torch to others." But the torch, as he said, others will benefit from it. Good, whatever!' (Pishimnapeo, ch. 1, ref. 1–3)

One person, for example, remembers feeling empowered when witnessing the radicalism of the Mohawks during meetings with the government.[58]

Collective and cultural memory at the confluence of the connections between First Peoples, and intergenerational transmission prior to the war, explain why the Salmon War was framed as part of *a wider war*. The intersection of autobiographical memories shows how the remembered past, or historical consciousness, had a galvanising effect on those taking part in terms of rebelling to safeguard their lives.

Innu tipenitamun: a movement for ancestral sovereignty

The existence of a movement among the Essipiunnuat is singled out in the interviews as a major factor in the group's interpretation of its circumstances. Specific social phenomena are suggested that favoured the emergence and growing influence of a movement within the community; a force that contributed extensively to the manifestation of collective agency and to the role of the group in helping to trigger the war. These observable trends principally concern a dynamic of radicalisation within the group, its internal organisation in preparation for conflict, the relatively spontaneous mobilisation of a majority of Essipiunnuat, and the perception of increased capacity for action and collective self-reliance (also called 'autodynamisation'). Together, these elements led to the birth and materialisation of a movement of assertion.

The 'true' warriors

The terms 'radicals', 'radicalism' and 'radicalisation' are used frequently in people's descriptions, either in self-portrayal, in presenting the psychological characteristics or ideologies of fellow Essipiunnuat, or simply to depict what they had observed going on within the group.[59] Interviewees report precise observations about a number of individuals who had become very intransigent in deciding to change the group's circumstances by attacking the root causes. There are particular mentions of a core of 'true warriors' who were ready to

58 Large gatherings of First Peoples' leaders have been, for all generations, important in meeting with other indigenous groups and learning from them. These meetings are often invoked in the stories and are seen as 'empowering'. For example, as Pishimnapeo recalls, the Mohawks by their radical stance provided an example to the other groups of resistance as opposed to submission: 'The Mohawks, they were very firm; I've seen it in meetings. When it was not to their convenience, they moved back. They were more protesting with authority, when the others accepted the little offered.' (Pishimnapeo, ch. 1, ref. 4)

59 'Radicals' are here defined as those being willing to tackle the problem facing their community at the 'root' (Latin 'radix'); they are people who 'support great social, economic or political change' ('Radical', Cambridge Dictionary) and are ready to act accordingly, even at the risk of their own lives.

adopt 'any means necessary', including the use of military devices and the possibility of self-annihilation, in defence of 'Indians' rights'.[60]

It is alleged that this cell of radicals was intergenerational and inter-familial (based on an alliance between the Ross and Moreau families). It was composed of four or five individuals in their early thirties, recently graduated from university, who decided to radicalise the whole group in order to establish (or reestablish, according to the point of view) a new 'indigenist-communitarian' system. They had grown up in the socioeconomic hardship of Essipit in the 1950s and '60s. Some of them had travelled internationally and encountered revolutionary ideas. Others had participated in Innu inter-band meetings and wider gatherings of First Peoples, had felt common grievances and were convinced that the time had come 'to strike' in order to 'wake the people up'.[61]

The other part of the cell was composed of 'old runners', men who were over 40, and psychologically profoundly repressed. They had 'hidden' their Innu self, and the ancestral practices associated with it, as a shameful illness. For many of them, the war was a first 'coming out' as 'Montagnais', with their decision to assume and assert their indigeneity. The occurrence of war transformed some of them into highly stubborn, radical and belligerent indigenist militants who had decided to honour their identity.[62] Indeed, they all shared grievances, as well as the assumption that the Canadian and Québécois governments were planning the extinguishment of inherent indigenous sovereignty in Essipit. They foresaw the occurrence of a new tragic episode in the history of displacement, dispossession and being lied to in order to obtain their surrender and consent to the cession of ancestral lands. These radicals therefore decided to ensure that

60 'Some of us would have taken up arms … They didn't need motivation. For them, that was it: "We will defend ourselves. If they come with guns, we will take our guns. Like them, we are able to use guns. We will not use arrows anymore. We are equal to them so we can shoot from near or far, as they do. Our rights, we will defend them and it will go this way. If we don't succeed, they just have to do as before, they just have to massacre us, it will end there." Yes, it was very radical.' (Riel, ch. 2, ref. 2)

61 'There was an awakening. I often went to the Attikamekw-Montagnais Council and saw things, I saw what was coming, and I became convinced that we needed to "strike" somehow to wake them up … and I'm not talking of the indigenous, but of the Whites … and say "Hey! This is enough, it's not possible anymore! You won't crush us this way anymore." All over the coast, rivers were the property domains of corporations and private clubs. "Indians, you don't have the right, you can't fish!" In Sept-Iles, settlers, they were aggressive, you can't imagine.' (Sam, ch. 1, ref. 12)

62 'It was repressed, they had so much frustration! He, Mestenapeo, he was enraged! It was inconceivable; for him, there was no possibility of negotiation. "They will move to the side!" We saw that on the [Euro]Québécois side, it was hardcore racism or mean jealousy … but for them, for Mestenapeo's generation (in their 40s and 50s), it was internal repression and there was no more negotiation: "Recede you bunch of jerks, it's finished! We assume who we are!" You see? It doesn't really work that way, but that's how they saw things, they were so frustrated and had experienced so many things … Imagine, they used to hide simply in order to assume their rights. Moose in winter, ducks in spring, all illegal. They were doing it secretly, as poachers! Whereas then, they were assuming it openly for the first time.' (Sam, ch. 1, ref. 6)

these past tragedies would not be repeated; they were engaged in protecting their collective rights, inseparable to the life of the group, and in peril of their lives. One warrior, for example, remembers being possessed by a fundamental motivation to refuse to see this history repeated.[63]

Increased coordination

The stories report increased efforts at in-group organisation, in coordinating militant activities and in channelling and directing emerging social forces through existing and new social orders. Leadership was apparently exercised by the band council and its main administrators at that time. It was done primarily through addressing the Essipiunnuat directly on the common issues at stake and preferred solutions, but also through stimulating reflection on strategies and tactics as well as encouraging participation.[64] It is suggested that members of the council and its administrators were ready to take a tough stance about their rights with the authorities, yet they wanted also to ensure that they had the support of members in order to move forward.[65]

To achieve its goal, the council, anticipating an imminent confrontation, wanted to unite the group. Those who took part remember the meetings vividly, reporting that they had a tremendous impact on the group's political unification, the dissemination of a revolutionary spirit and the creation of a nucleus of 'warriors'.[66]

63 'Back then they requested an interview, so I told the media: "They won't treat us as our ancestors ... buy us with small mirrors." So they asked me why I was saying that. I answered them: "Me, I'm indigenous and I have rights and I care for them. I don't want to lose them in exchanges for lies, and to experience what happened to my great-grandfather." They told us beautiful tales when they parked us on the reserve. The federal agents were there and said "step back, savage". Bastards! At some point, we saw that they were trying to displace us in Pessamit! ... These things happened. (Mestenapeo, ch. 1, ref. 3 and 5) As Édouard also recalls, 'I would have gone to great lengths, I would have allowed myself to get hurt ... for the respect of my rights.' (Édouard, Ch. 1, ref. 5). Mestenapeo, for his part, was enlivened by the conviction that their 'rights were part of life' (Mestenapeo, ch. 1, ref. 3).

64 'We had good "headmen". Good "brains" who talked to us, who organised the group by saying "Look guys, if we don't want to lose what we have, we need to try to keep it right now." So they said, "Wake up, let's all get together and move things!" They said "Some people outside want to bully us." You know our headmen ... they said "If we don't resist, we will lose everything. We don't want to enter into a war, but we have rights and we have to keep defending them in order to protect them. So if we don't wake up, if we don't participate, don't come complaining in 20 years from now saying we had the right but we didn't fight. It will be your own fault." It was very clear.' (Tshak, ch. 1, ref. 8)

65 'The council led the combat. It was composed of Ernest and Mestenapeo, who were councillors. You had Bernard who was band manager; and Redgi in the new position of education-economic development agent. But a great majority of the people were with us at that time; because without it, we would never have been through the war.' (Mesnak, ch. 1, ref. 5)

66 'The band council decided to set up a committee and the committee pulled the "trigger". It started as gunpowder, I would say. We started, we were several, we embarked with the band

The council and its newly created committee then turned to the general assembly of Essipiunnuat to get maximum support from all members. People recall being deeply moved at some of the meetings:

> When we had our first meeting in the community centre, I can tell you one thing, it was so strong in the room … there was such a level of emotion … When people heard people saying 'communitarian values, indigenous principles, our culture', people were crying … We didn't want the states to extinguish the principle we were defending. We were there, we wanted to have it, and were ready to use any means to have it. (Riel, chapter 1, ref. 9)

The importance of intergenerational cooperation in structuring collective action is also reported. Informal yet influential forms of 'coaching' were practised by the older fighters on the young. The younger leaders, for example, were constantly seeking advice from the older members, including those who were too old to physically engage directly in the struggle. Their support took the form of 'telling [leaders] stories from the past, often contradicting what the government was saying'.[67] Young adults also took part, old enough to engage in direct action but inexperienced; the intensity and unusual nature of the situation pushed them to rely on older fighters for guidance.[68] Those who were under 18, and only observers, reported being 'carried away by a collective wave'; the group 'swallowed' them.[69]

Mobilising members

As mentioned above, the leading faction wanted to ensure that they had members' maximum support and participation and, hence, they placed a great emphasis on mobilisation. Accordingly, various tactics were put into operation. These attempts to boost Essipiunnuat support are reported as being a 'propellant' of the movement towards contention. And it is said that these

council, we were 100 per cent with the band council, and the band council with us; "the captains are ready to sink with the boat". This was how it was for them. They were one with the people.' (Riel, ch. 1, ref. 6)

67 'Uncle David had told me stories; Uncle Arthur too. My father often told me, "Ask Arthur to tell you stories. Go and meet with him, he will tell you." Or "go and see David, he will tell you". Because we, the young people, we were wondering. They were our role models, including Toinon when he returned from the forest.' (Sam, ch. 1, ref. 13)

68 'We had never faced such things and bang! It happened. What do you do? You try to follow the older people, the seniors of the reserve; you try to follow in their footsteps a bit. You are 20 and you are in the boat, look! So somehow, I was relying on Marcel's reaction, he was older than me.' (Ivan, ch. 1, ref. 4)

69 'I didn't understand I was not catching the meaning of the event; for me it was all new. So, what marked me the most in the war was being the kid, the innocent child who did not understand what was going on but was going with the flow; I wasn't catching the dimension of the movement but what I did understand, I was getting from the people who were, if I can use the term, "coaching" us.' (Adam, ch. 1, ref. 1)

efforts did indeed receive spontaneous support from most members, but the hypothesis cannot be ignored that the cell wanted the war in order to gain authority and dominance.

Interviewees recall that they used to share a common perception that something deeply fundamental to them was going to be taken away: 'It was spontaneous, we defended what we had.' The analogy of being dispossessed of a cherished element of heritage was used: 'it was as if you are a child, that your great grandfather had given you a canoe and that is the only thing you received from him. And then, someone comes and says "that's not yours, it has never been yours."' Added to this perception of things being taken away is the reading that 'all your rights as Innu were in the balance', that their very existence as Innu was at stake and they were almost forced to resist.[70]

Accounts also mention that the perception of injustice in the present had awakened a sleeping volcano of emotions over past wrongs, a fury or overflow of rancour. This is where the leadership might have played a crucial role, in adopting a more confrontational attitude than previous generations and less tolerance of unfairness.[71] Attempts to mobilise the Essipiunnuat were, therefore, meeting with positive responses for various reasons. Interviews suggest that the racialisation of the conflict would have been fuelled by the Essipiunnuat increasingly identifying with their group while it was increasingly being stigmatised externally.[72]

Increased contention, for the Essipiunnuat, would make belonging simultaneously to the two reference groups ('Innu' and 'Euroquébécois'), instituted by years of assimilation and intermarriages, untenable. As individuals were confronted with abandoning one of their groups of reference, it forged the group closer to its Innu referents. Some individuals then engaged actively in the movement, or became 'warriors', in order to validate their cultural identity as Innu.[73] The complete lack of receptiveness of Euroquébécois to the

70 'This is because, if you let them take your rights, what will they do to you then? They will take your net and then say "You don't have any right to spread a net. You can't by the dock, you can't anywhere." So the only possible thing for us was to resist.' (Ivan, ch. 1, ref. 3)

71 'I had rage in my heart, especially when the [Euro]Québécois were speaking of our rights. I realised that they didn't care about us, they saw us as savages that they had succeeded in pushing into a small corner of land and that they had locked us away there. As they told our ancestors, they were telling us: "Don't cross the borders of your reserve. That's your place, we don't want to see you go out anymore; here is the fence, if you cross it, you will suffer." That's more or less what they were telling us Indians before and during the war. They really wanted us to stay on the reserve and shut up. Play the pacified Indian as before. Our parents were very pacifist, they were tolerant; we, we have been less tolerant.' (Tshak, ch. 1, ref. 2)

72 'Racists, as we say, were saying "Bastards of savages", you know. For some of them, we were all "stinky savages". Even if in our reserve, there were a lot of Indians married to non-Indians ... we were all the same.' (Tshak, ch. 1, ref. 3)

73 'I said to myself: "I will be hated, but hated for a good reason! They hate all Indians in any case. I'm an Indian so I'm as hated as the others anyway." So I participated in the Salmon War.'

Essipiunnuat claims resulted in a general impression in the group that they were facing a wall of negation that could only possibly be overcome by being willing to defend themselves and resist.[74]

Amplified collective autodynamisation

As already stated, the group had developed an embryonic sense of its own power in the late 1970s, symbolised by initiatives promoting socio-economic development. Contact with other First Peoples was also growing, in parallel with the idea that these were sovereign 'people' with a right to self-determination, with points of support both in the ancestral legal order and in international law. A generation of new graduates, recently re-engaged in their community, had also decided to bring about change. Even decades of colonialism, bureaucratic absolutism and economic marginalisation had not dampened the group's feeling that they could transform their condition.

These various elements contributed to a decline of the in-group sense of surplus powerlessness. Effectively, interviewees report a downturn in the acceptance of the status quo, of the belief that change cannot happen, of apathy and the unwillingness to struggle for greater control and influence. People recognised the increased internal autodynamisation[75] of the group already taking place in the years preceding the Salmon War.

Autodynamisation is a term closely related to what the Innu refer to as *uetshit takuaimatishun*, which can be translated as propelling and orienting/steering your own canoe, or doing things by yourself. In fact, stories clearly reveal the emergence of a conviction within the group that *Innu tipenitamun* (ancestral sovereignty) can only be auto-operationalised (*uetshit takuaimatishun*).

A direct link is identified between the uprising and a new perception propelled by a feeling that 'we were a big gang ... Well, we were starting to see ourselves as a big gang' (Édouard, chapter 1, ref. 1). The falling away of surplus powerlessness is well expressed in intense descriptions of affirmation and the declaration of an absence of fear:

(Tshak, ch. 1, ref. 8)

74 'My feeling was "why do you invade our land?" I also had a strong feeling of hatred ... How can it be, we are almost the only people who defend ourselves. Apart from us, the others, they don't defend themselves! Some of us had to defend the children, our goods and everything. So we stood up as warriors' (Pierre, ch. 1, ref. 1)

75 'Collective autodynamisation' corresponds to a 'therapeutic process ... that brings local people with common interests together in ways that strengthen their collective capacity to improve their socio-economic, political, and psychosocial conditions. It is a politically organising process that enables groups of people to mobilise their resources and take charge of defining their own community's strengths, weaknesses, strategic vision, and plan for action. It is a process that above all else fosters the conditions necessary for the autodynamisation *and* collective autodynamisation of individuals and communities to continue on an ever-widening scale. It embodies the power of believing in "*we* can"'. (Petersen, 2001)

> Pierre was alone on the yellow line, on the 138 road, with his gun, and he stopped the car in which the wildlife agents were travelling. He said 'Damn! We are at home here. You won't prevent us from fishing salmon in the river; the river doesn't just belong to the whites; we have rights'. It was the first time we affirmed ourselves as Indians, as Innu. (Adam, chapter 1, ref. 1)

The group's self-esteem would thus have resulted in what was previously called the 'end of toleration' towards any forms of abuse or symbolic domination. Elements of past abuse (forced sedentarisation, residential schooling, and so on) were very vivid in people's memories and resulted in spontaneous assertions that 'we won't be displaced anymore, we are at home here'. Individuals were marked by their strong embracing of indigeneity, especially the youngest:

> There was a lot of intimidation and it was really intense. I still see my Uncle Arthur, with his stick and Julien … Ti-Nours … and Pierre … they were all ready to go to war and were saying: 'Damn! We have rights and it's done! We won't bend down anymore, we affirm ourselves! No! We won't be abused anymore!' I was young and I didn't know all the reasons then. But what I was hearing the most was 'Christ! We have rights and our consent to being disrespected ends here! We will be respected!' (Adam, chapter 1, ref. 3)

Overall, people perceived the emergence of a movement of affirmation as the main current propelling the Essipiunnuat into war and revolt. This movement, with its own identified and converging sources and dynamics, would result in a multidimensional resistance and collective self-assertion of Innu sovereignty opposing multilateral attempts to extinguish it.

Unity of purpose

If the very composition of the group and its internal dynamics were instrumental in causing the war, the existence of clear and commonly consented to objectives reportedly played a major role in leading the group towards resistance and war; these common objectives are considered to be a primary source of the uprising. People often reflect on the purpose of the group's involvement in the war and on their interpretations of what they were pursuing. They indicate common objectives, understood in the military sense of clearly defined, decisive and attainable goals towards which their actions were directed.[76]

These common grounds for action are acknowledged as the third significant component that contributed to the making of the war. These objectives were recognised as widely shared and mainly self-defined, as well as based on a common perception of the collective condition and needs in a sociohistorical context on the eve of the Salmon War. Some discussion of these intentions

76 See the definition of 'Objective' in the *DOD Dictionary of Military and Associated Terms.*

helps to shed light on the development of group agency, and helps to clarify the group's interpretation of its role and actions in the unfolding of events.

Self-conservation

The conservation of Innu sovereignty (*Innu tipenitamun*) as responsibility towards the Innu ancestral domain is widely described as a principal objective and the motivation for people becoming involved in the war. To defend the year-round freedom to fish and hunt for subsistence, which is deeply related to people's identity, is presented as an imperative in preserving the group and its symbolic ability to sustain itself.

One interviewee, for example, maintained that 'we understood at that time that we were fighting ardently to conserve an existing right; a right to subsistence' (Esther, chapter 1, ref. 1). For another, these rights were deeply related to the 'indigeneity' of the group: 'for me it was clear. I was defending my rights as indigenous; above all, the net.' (Ivan, chapter 1, ref. 1). The salmon net was, in fact, the symbol of this entitlement to fish for subsistence. Effectively, ancestral activities related to food and nourishment remain at the heart of Innu claims, a core objective of the movement. The right that was being defended, and the underlying potential subsistence that it entailed, was widely perceived as profoundly inalienable.[77]

One of the fundamental objectives was to resist further reduction of the group's inherent collective rights and any attempts to extinguish *Innu tipenitamun*; it was about the responsibility to preserve the traditional base of the group's self-conservation and its very life for future generations. The issues at stake in getting involved in the movement went beyond the mere issue of salmon and ancestral fishing rights on the Esh Shipu; it was about resisting attempts to ultimately extinguish *Innu tipenitamun* on Innu Assi or the ancestral domain through the long-term processes of dispossession, deterritorialisation and therefore, programmed strangulation.[78] Yet stories

77 'I believed that as Indians, it is essential for us … Because even if they would give us millions, if you can't fish and hunt, what do you really get at the end? For me, not much. So we kept fighting day after day.' (Ernest, ch. 1, ref. 6)

78 'They wanted to take it from us! [*Innu tipenitamun*] It is as if I'm your father and I give you a small canoe. Three months later, someone comes and takes it away from you. It is not yours anymore and they say "it is ours, you can't use it anymore". And it is your father who gave you the canoe and it's the neighbours who came to take it. "It is not yours anymore, it has never been yours!" That's what was happening to us, they came to take away what was ours, things that belong to us, our ancestral territories, hunting grounds, trap lines and everything. It's the same thing. And then, it's only someone else who can fish, hunt and go there! Can you imagine? It had happened and it was happening again at the moment of the war. Transmission is done, but on their side, on the side of the most powerful. And because you're weaker, you have to shut your mouth: "If you don't want to get hurt, shut up!" You see? "We are stronger than you, you are 10 and we are 1,000." So who wins? That's how it worked back then. So as time went by, they took more and more, again and again. Then, instead of 75 per cent, they

told by interviewees also imply that people's actions were interpreted as going beyond the simple defence of Essipiunnuat interests and embracing a greater struggle for the protection of principles shared by all First Peoples; they were defending at a local level a principle common to all.[79]

Self-respect

As demonstrated earlier, it was difficult to assume an Innu identity in the years preceding the Salmon War. Various factors were involved in this harsh fact, and the situation had persisted for a long time. It is best expressed by the absence of the Innu language's transmission due to its general devalorisation, as summed up by, 'If you want to speak Indian, if you want to be an Indian, go to Pessamit!' So this collective self-assertion was implying the fact of assuming indigeneity, and, therefore, the reversibility of elements of self-image in order to gain self-respect:

> The Salmon War, the objective was to assert our rights but in the sense that 'we shouldn't hide anymore, we assume being Innu in broad daylight. We assume our indigenous identity for god's sake! We are Innu and we declare it. It's over.' This was the objective. (Sam, chapter 1, ref. 7)

This experience of internalising negative representations was widely shared among other indigenous groups disturbed by the effects of colonialism. The assertion of sovereignty and self-determination clearly transcended Essipit's border and was conceived as a pan-indigenist requirement of collective dignity; the movement of affirmation 'was pertinent to almost everything; it was a means of getting value, to assert ourselves as human, as a people' (Raoul, chapter 1, ref. 6).

Recognition

The stories are full of references to the experience of harassment during the practice of ancestral activities of hunting and fishing. Québec had been pressuring 'Indians' to cease their ancestral activities, particularly in the years preceding the war. The state wanted them to comply with regulations pertaining to hunting, fishing and trapping, and therefore to restrict and\or

required 100 per cent. It wasn't fair at all. So the objective before and during the war was to fight for what had always belonged to us.' (Tshak, ch. 1, ref. 8)

79 'We received support from other indigenous people … from outside; they came here. It was very powerful. A lot of people from other communities came to support us. We received support from Pessamit; they set up blockades on the main road for us but also to Restigouche. So it wasn't just about salmon … For the people, for us, all Innu, it was about more than salmon. I would say it meant "everything", it was about our lives. We were claiming our rights, but it meant the very reason why we wanted to fight, and also why we were ready to give our lives for the cause … So it wasn't just for a little piece of salmon, it was for much more. It meant "everything."' (Raoul, ch. 1, ref. 2)

abandon their traditional practices. Many Essipiunnuat were brought to court by wildlife agents for illegal hunting activities, had their equipment (guns, canoe, engines, and so on) seized, and were often ordered to pay significant penalties. Many Essipiunnuat hunters traced the cause of these disagreements back to the absence of any recognition of inherent Innu rights.[80]

To not be harassed in their ancestral domain and to have their rights recognised were thus important objectives for many people in the context of a group whose traditional practices were significantly repressed. For the older generation especially, 'it was mainly to confirm that we had rights, to have confirmed rights that we considered ours.' The goal was to have their rights, if not their legal order, recognised and respected in order to avoid further uncertainty and the fear of being repressed in their traditional activities.[81] This contextualisation helps in part to understand the post-Salmon War reception for state recognition and internal quarrels about an Innu evaluation of signed agreements.[82]

Reterritorialisation

From the mid 19th century, the Essipiunnuat had been continuously marginalised. This resulted in their sedentarisation and the creation of a reserve in 1892, in which they were restricted to occupying a mere 0.5 km^2. They allegedly no longer had any rights over their ancestral domain, which cover an area of approximately 5,000 km^2 located between the Saguenay and the Porneuf Rivers. This forced deterritorialisation had a tremendous impact on the Essipiunnuat way of life. Among other impacts, economic marginalisation was far-reaching due to their greatly restricted access to ancestral territories and their wealth, as well as an intense 'discomfort' while practising ancestral subsistence activities. The leaders soon realised that 0.5 km^2 was too tiny a space for their group and its growing aspirations for economic autonomy.

Reterritorialisation, then, became a group objective, meaning its people could reconnect with the lands, asserting Innu sovereignty over the ancestral

80 'We basically didn't have any right to fish and hunt. To be frank, we were constantly harassed at that period by wildlife agents. The Québec ministry of leisure, hunting and fishing was administrated by Mr Lessard ... who exerted a lot of pressure on indigenous people to stop hunting and fishing; really a lot of pressure. There was harassment for all the communities, in all seasons.' (Mesnak, ch. 1, ref. 1 and 2)

81 'The objective, I knew it. It was to get our rights, for our rights to be recognised. That was it. For sure, at first we were also a bit fearful since we didn't know whether we had the right or not. I had this in mind when I went to apply to hunt moose in winter. We went there three times. Three times, and it was for three days; they were condemning us to $12,000 penalties. So you remain apprehensive when you see that amount. Do we have a right or not? Back then, I was saying "Take a side!" If we have a right, we have a right. If we don't have a right, we don't have a right. And we will be done with that. It would be all set, all concluded.' (Édouard, ch. 1, ref. 6)

82 See also ch. 5 for the Innu reception of state recognition as genesiac or a stratagem.

domain, and enjoy the freedom to practise ancestral activities and ways of being. This small group perceived the need to achieve the goal of reoccupying a territory that had never been ceded and on which the ancient Innu normativity, inseparable from the land itself, still existed. The movement's claim was that it had a say, if not the power 'to give consent', in any significant projects on the ancestral domain. It is important to remember that at that time, the Québec government and local Euroquébécois were not considering any rights for the Innu outside of the reserve's borders.[83]

In the context of First Peoples' claims that were rising in parallel to Québec's involvement in major industrial projects on indigenous ancestral lands (hydro, mining, forestry and so on), the Québec government was greatly interested in seeing these claims extinguished. It was therefore developing a rhetorical response to indigenous claims saying that Indians did not have any rights regarding the Québec domain. For the leading group in Essipit, 'it was to demonstrate that indigenous rights existed outside the reserve, on all our homeland'.[84]

A succinct examination of people's subjectivity gives clear insights into the deeply rooted reasons for their involvement, and why they wanted to fight, and were ready to give their lives for the cause. The assertion and defence of the ancient Innu normative order or sovereignty comes to the fore as the unifying factor behind their diverse objectives. Despite some variances, mainly in relation to participants' situations and postures during the war (gender, past experiences, current needs, role in the movement, generation, and so on), stories report a unity of purpose in the clearly defined, decisive and attainable goal of defending indigenous freedom and its symbols.

From strategies to direct action

Those who took part discuss at length the practices or strategies designed before and during the war to achieve the above-mentioned objectives. They consider the thought processes, planning of actions and preferred means of realising their objectives as a central manifestation of group agency and an essential motivation for the war. The term 'strategy', in its etymological sense, implies leadership and command; its study also reveals information about its multifaceted agents and how they are interrelated. Strategy can be defined as 'a comprehensive way to try to pursue political ends, including the threat or actual use of force, in a dialectic of wills' (Heuser, 2010, p. 39). Since conflicts involve

83 In a radio interview during the Salmon War, the mayor of Les Escoumins declared that the Innu had no rights outside of the reserve borders. The same rhetoric was voiced by Minister Lessard, see Obomsawin (1984).

84 As Justin remembers, 'they would have been much less bothered if we had spread the net the other side [on the reserve land], but for us, it was a question of principle and to demonstrate our rights.' (Justin, ch. 1, ref. 3)

Figure 10. March of First Peoples in support of Essipiunnuat during the Salmon War. CBC/Radio-Canada Archives, 1981.

at least two interacting sides, strategy is thus characterised by its adaptability in the deployment of means.

Four main themes concerning strategies are predominant in the interviewees' accounts of the war. Mainly, they concern the steps taken to unite the wills of indigenous groups, the multilateral attempts to pressure the state/s, direct action or the unilateral assertion of *Innu tipenitamun*, and the use of the salmon as a symbol.

The unification of indigenous wills

A priority for the council was to get maximum support among the Essipiunnuat. The council's guiding idea was 'to have a strong majority ... before going ahead ... since if you don't have it, you go nowhere' (Sam, chapter 1, ref. 6). Group communication and participatory decision-making appear to have been a favoured approach to internal unification. Some leaders were going from door to door to encourage members to engage actively in the uprising.[85] There is a clear perception among interviewees of having been involved at every level of the decision-making process before and during the Salmon War.

In order to get maximum internal support, the council organised a number of general assemblies of all the Essipiunnuat, to whom it was firmly asserted that

85 '"Let's keep going!" people were saying. How come? It was by talking, communicating all together, organising meetings and talking and talking; discussing and asking ourselves "where do we go?"' (Sam, ch. 1, ref. 10)

'everybody must attend'. So a strategy was also employed which implied at the very least that absence or non-participation regarding the council's objectives would have negative consequences for those involved. Eliminating dissent was the aim (Sam, chapter 1, ref. 2). A central cause of dissidence identified was the fear of disrupting relations with white friends or relatives. For the leaders, Essipiunnuat collaboration with the external rival was, then, a fact to counter.[86]

In parallel with efforts to rally all Essipiunnuat to the cause, another endeavour was to obtain maximum support from as many indigenous groups as possible through diplomacy. As one individual says, the potential for support was huge, since Essipit's battle was about the defence of a wider, shared inherent legal order.[87]

However, before the war began, Essipit had also been involved in the Conseil Attikamekw-Montagnais (CAM), a tribal council that included a dozen communities. It was responsible for negotiating directly with Québec and Canada on issues pertaining to indigenous sovereignty and the modalities of implementing their self-determination. CAM meetings offered opportunities for leaders and individuals from diverse communities to meet for exchanges and to develop platforms on common grievances and needs. In particular, it allowed a new generation of Essipiunnuat leaders to establish a network and extend diplomacy. The role of indigenous diplomacy in the Essipiunnuat strategy during the Salmon War was well planned.[88] Leaders strategised to get trans-indigenous support specifically in order to reinforce Essipit positions towards the Euroquébécois and the authorities.[89]

86 'Some of us did not come … some of them were too friendly with the "whites" so they couldn't embark in our boat. It hurt us a lot when we saw that'. (Ernest, ch. 1, ref. 2)

87 'We were defending *Innu tipenitamun*, not just "our" little rights. All the reserves were concerned, Pessamit, Mashteuiastsh, and others. We were claiming the very same rights that all indigenous peoples are claiming today.' (Mestenapeo, ch. 1, ref. 4)

88 'We were in the CAM and we had a lot of contacts, a lot of exchanges with other communities; relations were strengthening. We were already in negotiation with governments, so we had developed solidarities. Before the Salmon War, we had been speaking of the defence of all our hunting and fishing rights. Do you see? So that we were feeling less and less lonely in our struggles, more able to conduct our own wars … In the negotiation [with CAM], we felt like a group, stronger. And then when the Salmon War happened in Essipit … we received a lot of support from other communities. People from all bands, including all the chiefs came … and we had a good strategy. We invited them to conduct an indigenous demonstration, of all the bands and all the chiefs. It was well done, well thought through. And we received a lot of backup from the CAM.' (Sam, ch. 1, ref. 5)

89 'We want to sensitise people and demonstrate to them that we are supported; that it's not just Essipit that will be conducting the action. So we decided to make a big show so our opponent would calm down and say "Hey … they are supported by all communities! Wait a minute … They are not alone in their small world, they are not just dreamers … they are really moving forward!"' (Sam, ch. 1, ref. 14)

Pressuring the states

Essipit had been in negotiation with governments through the CAM; it wanted to carry maximum weight at the negotiation table in order to exert pressure. The council adopted a strategy to force the governments to recognise the existence of *Innu tipenitamun* by auto-operationalising through asserting ancestral sovereignty and practising collective self-determination. The idea was to compel Québec to sit at the negotiation table with Essipit and accept its position. The leaders had been strategising, waiting for the best time to act.[90]

An element of their strategy remained the bringing of their cause to the attention of the media. They planned to catch the public's attention and to focus it upon the situation at Essipit, and then influence the interpretation of it. The idea was to alert other indigenous groups to the situation, but also to communicate their position to the Essipiunnuat and to the Québec government, through the media. This coverage would also facilitate internal mobilisation. Above all, the strategy aimed to give a clear message to the government about the seriousness of their claims.[91]

Direct action

Direct action was allegedly the key strategy in preparations for the war. The aim was to defend inherent sovereignty, achieve self-determination and force governments and local populations to respect them. This approach highlights the philosophy behind the movement at that time, which was that a right to self-determination can only be directly self-operationalised.[92] This is illustrated, for example, by the widely remembered episode of the ferry blockade as an automatic response to Québec's unilateral decision to seize the Essipiunnuat's nets. The council and its special war committee then decided to block the ferry

90 'There had been confrontations on the Moisie and Mingan Rivers. The minister had started buying back rivers to solve the problems [with the Innu]. And here we started some negotiation with the municipality. So the timing was good for action to make things move. So we decided to affirm our rights on the territory so the government would be obliged to move.' (Mesnak, ch. 1, ref. 6)

91 'The principle in that [the use of media] was just to demonstrate that we, the Montagnais of Escoumins, in Essipit, we were proud of being Montagnais; that we were in that state of mind and that we wanted to show that nobody would trample over our bodies, on our principles and values, on our indigenous culture … And the government understood. It was a means of appearing on the "map" and from then everything unfolded. The government said, "Essipit, they are serious". So it wasn't Essipit, the "quiet" reserve, it was Essipit "they are holding on to their ancestral rights, to their culture, and they want the right to fish salmon". It accelerated negotiations with governments.' (Riel, ch. 1, ref. 1 and 5)

92 'It was "Right now!" We do it right away, we don't wait, that's it. It's our rights, we protect our rights, and we defend our rights. As long as the government won't give us a positive response, we stay here and we don't move and we block the roads; and if they attack us, we will simply fight back.' (Tshak, ch. 1, ref. 1)

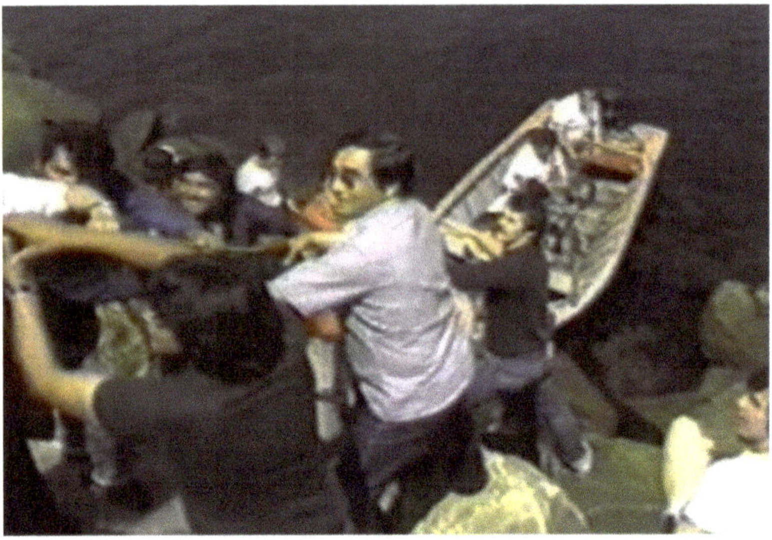

Figure 11. Indigenous leaders pulling Essipit's 'symbolic net'. CBC/Radio-Canada Archives, 1981.

dock in order to exercise maximum pressure on the Québec government.[93] The first blockade, with the tension it generated, is reported as the beginning of the 'true' war.[94]

This episode was the first to gain media attention for Essipit. A closer look at the unfolding of events suggests that the Essipiunnuat's acts of rebellion influenced and had a mimetic effect on other communities, especially the Innu groups of the northern shore (Pessamit, Ekuanitshit, Nutashkuan, the people of Listuguj, and others). The Essipiunnuat insurrection spread. Those involved at that time and the media all mention a Montagnais revolt or the beginning of a national insurrection.[95]

Salmon as a symbol

Another key strategic element was the use of the salmon as a symbol. As the group wanted to force the Québec government to negotiate directly with them, the leaders conceived a stratagem of transferring a private net, belonging to an

93 'The band council, to increase pressure on governments, decided to set up a blockade … It lasted for three days, day and night. So the ferry came but had to return with all the passengers. They came and we didn't let them cross, they went back on the ferry and the ferry left.' (Riel, ch. 1, ref. 1)

94 'The true war started when we blocked the road, when we set up blockades at the entry of the reserve and at the dock. The ferry couldn't dock anymore … we cut people's access to the ferry. So it really degenerated, there were brawls.' (Tshak, ch. 1, ref. 1)

95 'The sequence … Pessamit was putting pressure on, Restigouche also … it was reaching the front pages of the newspapers: "Essipit' and 'the Montagnais" are in revolt.' (Riel, ch. 1, ref. 2)

Essipiunnu (Ernest), and spreading it outside the border of the reserve land, at the tip of the dock. The Québec wildlife department, on behalf of the state, would then intervene to confiscate the net. The decision was carefully made to set it in a fishing area they had originally occupied, but from which they had been dispossessed with the creation of the reserve. A Euroquébécois family had a licence to fish in this area but their patriarch had died and his sons did not fish anymore. Essipiunnuat leaders saw a window of opportunity to reassert inherent Innu rights beyond the borders of the 0.5 km^2 of the reserve. A set up was therefore put in place to allow the net to be seized.[96]

Indeed, older people had been told by their grandparents since childhood that 'Essipiunnuat used to fish there before'. Stories therefore suggest a greater role for Essipiunnuat subjectivity in the causes of the Salmon War – or the intention to provoke and create a major event. One person clearly remembers that they 'wanted to piss them off; wake them up!' In parallel to this, the tactic was to ensure that government intervention would face strong resistance. One individual summarises how that opposition was achieved:

> At first, the strategy was simple: a net that belonged to all, the salmon are caught together and the fish distributed equally among families. If it belongs to all, you reach out to everybody. If the net belongs to everybody and you want to take the net, then you've just attacked the whole community. Then people will say 'Hey, they are attacking us!' You see? 'We are under attack!' Then we were meeting and saying 'Let's go! What are we doing now, what is the strategy, how do we negotiate?' (Sam, chapter 1, ref. 5)

In fact, each Essipiunnuat family did receive salmon from the community net, sometimes up to five times in the subsequent seasons. Such a practice was perceived as being deep-seatedly Innu and communitarian. These simple actions were not only concretising the auto-operationalisation process but were also introducing the communitarian principle directly into their daily life. More than anything, it boosted the understanding that the net belonged to everybody, and that the distribution of the salmon that had been collectively fished opened doors to direct encounters between leaders and members.[97]

96 'At first, we wanted to have the net seized by the Québec wildlife department. That was what indigenous people wanted. So we wanted them to come and cut the net so that the media would present a complete report, with journalists, the media; Essipit would then be in a position to give its point of view, what was pertaining to their rights.' (Maxence, ch. 1, ref. 2 and 3)

97 'It was communitarian in the sense of "for everybody". The principle is that it is for all the family, in other words, for all the community; I speak of family because Essipit is a small family.' (Mestenapeo, ch. 1, ref. 4)
'We distributed the salmon to everybody; it wasn't the council doing the job. Two people caught the salmon; there was a list and "oop! It's your turn; here are your two pounds of salmon." It was really communitarian.' (Napeo, ch. 1, ref. 1)

Beyond a common resistance to colonialism and external attempts to extinguish their rights, people were keen to stress a core difference between their actions and those of the Mi'gmaq of Listuguj who had entered into a conflict with the Québec state in 1981.[98] The Québec provincial police had intervened violently to stop their salmon fishing activities, but in contrast to the Mi'gmaq fisherman of Listuguj, who were 'taking the salmon and selling them' (Mestenapeo, chapter 1, ref. 4), the Essipiunnuat had chosen to distribute the catches in accordance with the communitarian principle that these actions served to nurture the base of a wider 'communitarian system'.[99]

The choice of using salmon as a symbol was made deliberately; salmon had had great significance in Innu culture over thousands of years, from the very beginning. The largest summertime gatherings and trans-band meetings and ceremonies were organised at the time of the return of the salmon to the river in July. Interviewees suggest that salmon were still, in the late 1970s, a cornerstone of Essipiunnuat culture and way of life. It was a food of great nutritional value but it was also redolent of fond childhood memories and associated with a sense of family sharing and celebration. Salmon thus runs very deep in the group memory; accounts of the war contain invocations of the salmon's beauty, its taste, its smell. People relate salmon to their childhood, to their fathers coming back with catches, to taking care of the net during the short fishing season from around mid July to the beginning of August.

The salmon symbolism also echoes the dispossession the Innu have experienced through the usurpation of the freedom to fish, culminating in complete prohibition by the eve of the Salmon War. In a way, for the Innu, the history of the abduction and negation of the right to fish salmon is the quintessence of their colonisation, the usurpation of their sovereignty and self-determination, and the decline of their capacity for self-sufficiency. In this context, the action of the Québec government with its response to the Essipiunnuat direct action touched a nerve, even in the late 1970s, 'It was our

'Everybody was very happy to eat good fresh salmon. It was really tasty. And it was then, I remember, that we would cut pieces and distribute them to each house.' (Ernest, ch. 1, ref. 2)

98 See Obomsawin (1984).

99 'There were people against this system. I can give you an example. There was a commercial fisherman who said "Let me fish salmon; I will take the commercial salmon fishing, I will take the salmon." But we told him "No! You are fishing crab! We will not give you everything because you are a commercial fisherman." We wouldn't have got very far with this approach. Nobody would have fought for that. So we were becoming aware of being "communitarian indigenists", I would say ... Because the fishing was really communitarian and we distributed the catch. Everybody was involved. Imagine a commercial fisherman saying "come and defend my fishing rights!" It would have all collapsed; it would have faded away, all forgotten: "This is your problem!!" But we were touching on something profoundly communitarian.' (Sam, ch. 1, ref. 2)

childhood they were taking away from us. You don't have it anymore; it takes away memories from your childhood. And there is no continuity.'[100]

The stories therefore evidence how people see the roles of designing and operationalising strategies as central to the making of that major event; it highlights the intentionality, as collective agents, of creating situations and opportunities for transforming internal and external circumstances.

Conclusion

The purpose of this chapter has been to assess the causes of the Salmon War according to Essipiunnuat memories, and to identify and reclaim self-perceptions of the group's condition and agency, mainly through using the concept of the 'event' as a crystallisation of historical determinants. The method of divining this consisted of disentangling from the story exogenous sociohistorical determinants versus the group itself and its agency as a determinant of the event. The scheme consisted of accessing elements of the group's reading of its condition at the moment the war began, together with the role it attributed to itself in contributing to its development. Colonialism, the politics of the Québec government, the social imaginary of the local Euroquébécois, as well as organised anti-Indian militancy, have been identified as the four main external determinants of the Salmon War. The confluence of these elements would have imposed on the group the dilemma of self-annihilation or war. The group's historical consciousness, its internal dynamics characterised by the emergence within it of a sovereignty movement, together with a clear collective objective and the operationalisation of strategies, have been identified as the four main significant internal determinants. The uniting of these internal and external phenomena and circumstances would nurture the group agency in the context of a growing perception of a stifling hegemony; which is to say, its commitment to war. This, at least, is how the origins of the war are related today and how that major event is mainly remembered.

100 Jeanne, ch, 1, ref. 2–4. Interviewees had eaten salmon almost from when they were born. They have a clear memory of its smell while cooking and the different ways of preparing it for eating. With the different ways of preserving it, they were eating salmon all year round. The culinary dimension of salmon is particularly vivid in the memories of the women, maybe since they did not participate in the actual fishing as their husbands, brothers and fathers did.

3. Capturing who we were: heroic postures in tragic circumstances

> To rebel requires that elusive virtue – moral courage. The person with moral courage defies the crowd, stands up as a solitary individual, shuns the intoxicating embrace of comradeship, and is disobedient to authority, even at the risk of his own life, for a higher principle – and with moral courage comes persecution.
>
> Chris Hedges (2015, p. 59)

> When it comes your time to die, be not like those whose hearts are filled with the fear of death, so that when their time comes they weep and pray for a little more time to live their lives over again in a different way. Sing your death song and die like a hero going home.
>
> Tecumseh

The role of subjective Essipiunnuat action during the Salmon War is explicated through autobiographical stories that clearly suggest collective agency, conscious and organised resistance, and a consolidated pledge to transform imposed situations and norms perceived as leading to group annihilation. Yet, what characterises the memories of those who were involved as the war progressed? What are the overriding images, representations and ethical components?

This chapter reports on the group's past-self associated with the course of war as revealed in autobiographical memories. Stories are abundant in resources that display self and identity (Markus and Nurius, 1986), and have the potential to disclose dimensions of the storytellers' agentive and epistemic selves; how they create positions and exhibit their social identities (Schiffrin, 1996). People's self-representations from the war thus offer a great opportunity to capture their self-images at different stages.

The 'self' remains fundamentally one's *memory* of oneself (Klein, 2001). The conception of individual as well as collective past-self consists, then, of 'who we believe we were' (Greer, 1999). Markus and Nurius have defined the concept of the 'past-self' as a subset of the universe of a 'group-self' associated with an experience, event or situation, and what emerged from it at the time. This past-self thus remains highly normative in the present, and explicit of current circumstances. Their research (1986) shows how it represents the agent's enduring concerns and perceptions, and the actions that gave rise to these concerns. Since self-narrative feeds into cultural memory and information is received through stories, we are somehow the stories we were told and that we tell.

A central characteristic of these past-self conceptions as reproduced is, however, that they are modelled by a deep-seated care for the maintenance of a positive sense of self-integrity. This desire is presented as the overall modelling factor of autobiographical memories (Fein and Spencer, 1997). In fact, previous research confirms a good/bad duality within the self; the good self/selves tend to be remembered warmly, while the bad self/selves tend to be just as soon overlooked and forgotten (Markus and Nurius, 1986). Self-representations in stories allow the exhumation of the subjacent and the social modes of production of these images, including the core component of social order and control that fed their manufacture and determined the formations of collective identity (Klapp, 1969).

As Kappeler explains in *The Pornography of Representation* (1986), modes of self-representation are inseparable from social forms of control. Representations have a continued existence in reality as objects of exchange; and moreover, they have a genesis in material production. Self-representations are, then, not only insightful about their producer but also of the past and current symbolic territories and social environments of their genitors. She suggests that self-representations in memory stories offer opportunities to grapple with their mode of production, including internalised orders and regulations institutionalising their fabrication (p. 3).

Foucault (1973) has highlighted how the mechanisms of social control and the operation of internalised norms determine one's self-perceptions of 'what one can, is able or prone to do, or is likely to do'. Yet, collective action and shared behaviours often aim at the transformation of such standards and are thus located beyond existing norms and ordered social relations. Consequently, group actions, especially in the context of rebellion and uprising, must also be considered as a materialisation of new rules, and represent attempts to transform existing norms (Della Porta and Diani, 2006, pp. 12–13).

Collective actions involve the surfacing of emergent norms very specific to the moment of action; they often grow out of the sociohistorical circumstances generated by social movement and a commitment to normative changes. These observable occurrences engender perceptions of unanimity of purpose and uniformity of behaviour, one of their functions being to enhance micro-mobilisation, solidarity, commitment and the solidification of collective identity (Scott and Marshall, 2005, p. 186; Hunt and Benford, 2008, p. 433).

Any investigation of earlier self-conceptions cannot ignore the fact that opposition to past social orders tends to fall into oblivion. This is also relevant for the current order, which is another powerful filter (Markus and Nurius, 1986; Conway, 2000). The potent effects of any command to forget emanating from figures of authority should never be underestimated. Current normative order tends to leave in the shadow dimensions of the past that are opposed to it or that question its legitimacy. The social order and its main agents are thus also inhabited by entrenched concerns, with the need to uphold a positive self-image involving an arsenal of psychological mechanisms used. These are also deployed in order to maintain them as figures of authority (D'Argembeau and Vanderlinden, 2008). In this sense, remembrance, and particularly that which counters a desire to forget, can be perceived as subversive, a source of uncertainty and an issue of power; it reactivates representations and sets of norms that have the potential to re-evaluate the current order and demonstrate discontinuities and inconsistencies. Significantly, it tends meanwhile to produce parrhesia, in the sense of speaking truth to power. Situating stories in the context of their social production provides access to shadowed figures and elements that have been forgotten.

Figures of the Essipiunnuat's past-self associated with the Salmon War, and aspects of its fabric, are here portrayed through three main modes of self-representation in autobiographical stories from the course of the war: the evocative dimensions of individual self-portraits, the dominant and normative characters contained in inter-individual depictions and in-group imageries and representations of the collective.

Self-portraits: narrating one's performance

A person's self-identity, as composed of unique traits and chiefly achieved through inter-individual differentiation and motives of protecting or enhancing the person psychologically, is central to autobiographical memories (Brewer and Gardner, 1996). Individuals' self-portraits are thus crucial material for accessing a group's past-self. This section exposes the most valued traits of individual past depictions during the main episodes of the war, including the linkages between elements of personal role descriptions, residues of social location contained in the background of self-portraits, and the self-narration of emotions.

Configurations of commitment

Autobiographical stories are generally characterised by one's self-depictions as the action develops (Conway, 2000, p. 25). A distinguishing feature of self-role descriptions is their evaluation and ordering in function of measures of commitment as an emergent norm specific to the course of war. Four main posturings emerge from the self-role depictions: commanders, warriors, supporters and the uncommitted. These roles vary according to the degree of involvement in and commitment to the war. Commitment consists of

> a person's identification that collectively orientates him or her to instrumental, affective, and moral attachments that lead to investments in movement lines of activity ... The salience and central theme of a movement's identity is imperative to understanding the degree to which an individual is committed to a collective. (Hunt and Benford, 2008, p. 400)

The concept of commitment refers to a person's willingness to carry out the requirements of a pattern of social action because he or she sees it as stemming from his or her fundamental nature as a person. The specific context of war would be exceptionally fertile for the generation of normative reflux from repressed referential and emergent norms, which are unique and sharply contrast with general societal standards (Kanter, 1972). In addition, these norms exert a powerful influence on behaviours. They create a momentary conformity to unique normative standards that develop spontaneously in this context (Forsyth, 2010). Such circumstances of collective action, contention and rebellion favour the eruption of re-identification dynamics and the rewriting of social roles (Friedman, 2004).

The centrality of participation and commitment is patent in recollections of the Salmon War. An understanding of individual commitment can be gained through considering the importance of the sovereignty movement's existence, particularly during the uprising when standards of behaviours were clearly being transformed. Stories report commitment as an emerging norm that shaped people's self-representations. This is understandable since the movement's nucleus of power in time of rebellion remains the larger function of the individual's dispositions, interests and worldview. These become linked to the goals, ideology and internal requirements of the movement as an organised collective; it was entirely dependent on whether people would leave or remain with the cause and commit to its aims.

Commanders and the promise of commitment

The command to commit and members' receptivity to it, as a prerequisite for the movement's success, dominated the self-portraits. This is particularly true of self-defined commanders, and testimonies illustrate well that the leaders' decisions, actions and self-confidence in wartime were inextricably linked to people's trust and support.[1]

Stories also reveal an 'us' that explicitly represents a category of actors whose primary function is associated with obeying group requirements, as well as promoting a similar hierarchy among followers.[2] This role includes self-representation as an agent within the movement, as an initiator of the event. It

1 'Such a strong sentiment that people are proud of your actions as leader, it is in wartime and at difficult moments that you feel it. And then we needed to feel, we, the council, that we had the people behind us. Otherwise, you don't go alone on that path. Above all, in the course of war, I felt that people were behind us in the battle and the movement. The guys, the people, were saying "Go ahead, we are behind you, do what you must do, we support you." Listen: when everybody is behind you, it undoubtedly helps you to stand and say "Let's go!" Whatever happens, we are there, and we have our people behind us' (Mesnak, ch. 2, ref. 9)

2 'We had warned people on the reserve. We did not want them to drink even a drop of alcohol. They were allowed to be there, yes, but they must control themselves, and try to control everybody.' (Mesnak, ch. 2, ref. 2)

includes self-attributed access to ancient knowledge about *sui generis* collective rights and obligations inherited from direct encounters with Essipiunnuat Elders, including a particular awareness of inherent Innu ancestral rights and historical consciousness justifying the transgression of the state order, despite its momentous consequences.[3]

Those self-portraying as leaders in the war are connected to images of direct confrontation with state agents and resistance to alleged illegitimate state intervention. This involved taking direct responsibility to protect collective interests and rights and being at the forefront of resistance through self-directed action at the risk of their lives.[4]

Self-confidence is also associated with this role, explained through deep connections with an indigeneity that would render them exceptionally impermeable to Euroquébécois intimidation.[5] The commander is a source of authority in war, able to turn situations to the advantage of the group and to influence his enemies. To be a leader would require being psychologically decolonised and freed from internalised negative self-conceptions as an 'Indian'. The commander is, then, in a position to escort his group towards its own liberation, his self-knowledge allowing him to closely understand what is going on with his fellows and to model accomplished forms of agency. Leaders tend to present themselves as the masterminds of the war, endowed with maximum self-control based on greater self-knowledge. Only some forms of disgrace allegedly justified their expression of rage, anger and revenge, as the performance of a 'higher duty'.

Self-control is a core element of being a good commander; the capacity to put the *self* at the service of the highest collective interest. This self-attributed 'highest reason' is used in some narrations to internally justify the exclusion of 'extremist' elements and those leaders who were not flexible enough in negotiation with governments. In fact, the stories told also show that power struggles were raging among some leaders of the group.

It is mainly people who were in positions of power during the war who paint self-portraits of themselves as 'commanders' – such as, for example, the

3 'It started this way. We had always been told that before, we, the Indians, we were here, before Charles Bélanger and the other settlers. So I said: "We will spread the net, and if we are arrested, we will be arrested … Do you understand?" Therefore, Marcel and I spread the net.' (Ernest, ch. 2, ref. 1)

4 'I did not wait. I jumped in a boat and went immediately to the agent's boat. And I told them right away: "you won't steal our net". I started to turn around them with my boat. An agent was pointing his gun at me. I told him: "Just dare to land at the wharf without your gun! Jump in my boat, you chicken-heart. I will settle your case!"' (Mestenapeo, ch. 2, ref. 7)

5 'During the Salmon War, I continued to have a drink in Escoumins township. Nobody bothered me. One guy tried to hassle me. I told him upfront: "Come outside and we will solve this". Nobody bothered me thereafter. I continued to go dancing when nobody from the community was going.' (Sam, ch. 2, ref. 1)

chief, the councillors, or band council administrators. Their role is described as a function of a collective purpose that requires the people's constant assent. They describe a self that must be mastered in order to accomplish its highest social obligations and display unsurpassable degrees of commitment. On the other hand, they require the same level of commitment from others. They call for mimesis and conformity of all selves with the imperative of respecting internal order. Cultural self-awareness, a sense of the deep-seated ancestral normative, as well as the highest consciousness of collective ends to be pursued, are presented in stories as being a precondition to captain. Above all, to be a commander implies a capacity to act upon this knowledge to carry out direct, authoritative, rebellious and perilous actions, often in transgression of exogenous orders. Indeed, they are expected to have the competence to direct other members of the movement as well as maintaining consistency among the cell of commanders.

Warriors: the art of self-sacrifice

Another category concerns people's self-identification as 'warriors'. They portray themselves in fusion with the group and their accomplishments as central to the making of the rebellion. Their depictions generally comprise joint actions in perilous circumstances leading to serious physical wounds.[6] They also pose as defenders of the Essipiunnuat in circumstances where, for example, they look after the elderly who might be mistreated, or when there are vulnerable children who need protection.

Eager claims of making the greatest sacrifices to defend the symbolic and 'sacred net' are predominant in the stories of self-identified warriors. They describe their actions as being free of the constraints of death. Their behaviours are presented in contrast with the attitude of the colonised and 'pacified Indian', allegedly characterising the past generation. Stories report the temperament of warriors as distinguished by a renewed volition for violent self-sacrifice.[7]

Warriors also portray themselves as acting as a decision-making nucleus. In perilous circumstances, those who were less experienced claim to have modelled their behaviour on that of the commanders 'at whatever cost' (Ivan, chapter 2, ref.5; Karl, chapter. 2, ref. 6). They manifest intractable recalcitrance towards exogenous control and symbols of authority. This spirit of revolt

6 'Our net was spread. I was with the gang … we were all holding the net. Then at some point a squad of whites got there. There were hostile people all around us, all kinds of things were being thrown at us … I still remember the last words of Georges when he said: "Let the net go!" Man! My fingers, the muscles were cut … I was all bleeding ... And then, I received a couple of punches as well.' (Karl, ch. 2, ref. 1)

7 'We had something to defend. From very deep inside, we were ready to go as far as was needed for that purpose. Everything happened very quickly. You did not do it to prove yourself or just to be a hero. In your head, it was an intrinsic response … It happens quickly. You do what you consider to be for the best, ultimately.' (Ivan, ch. 2, ref. 3)

often translated into insurrectionist acts, such as a spontaneous assault on the government agents or their vehicle.[8]

Descriptions of non-compliance with exogenous forces does indeed prove their disobedience, but also the absence of influence of these potencies over their interiority. Such rebelliousness is well illustrated by someone who was in his early 20s at the time. Wildlife agents captured him and tried to push him to the edge in an attempt to get him to talk. As he says: 'They were shouting at me to obey; I decided I would not.' In the story of his action at sea, for example, he stresses his absolute 'rebellion' towards the 'authorities' and his faithfulness in being a 'free hunter'.[9]

Warriors' self-portraits are overwhelmingly typified by joint actions in hazardous circumstances. These measures generally incurred physical suffering to protect 'sanctified' objects. The performances they describe exemplify complete loyalty to inner regulations and a break with the exogenous order.

Supporters

Some interviewees were supportive of the movement, yet in their descriptions of their situations, it is clear they could not do more or do it openly. This group manifests a degree of commitment but its members do not present themselves as warriors, mainly because of their age, gender, position or status in the community. Instead, their stories come under a 'supporters' category.

One self-narration, for example, visibly illustrates a strong desire to self-identify and to be perceived as a warrior. It looks like an attempt to justify why this was not the case. In a sense, this testimony clarifies the frontiers between being a warrior and a supporter. Because of his innocence and self-ignorance, mainly attributable to his young age, this individual lacked one of

8 'My wife came to me and said "there are police agents in our car park". I stood up and went out. There were wildlife agents with their cars. It provoked me so deeply … When these things happen, don't you think of protecting your kids? I went out and it was not funny at all. The guys looked down on us … as if we were criminals. They had probably received orders … I went to them and picked up a rock from the soil. I went to smash their truck'. (Pierre, ch. 2, ref. 1)

9 'We were trying to protect the net as much as possible. And … they charged us with their boat to scare us so that we would release the net. Except that Marcel and I, we resisted … [The agent's boat engine got trapped in the net, close to their boat] I told Marcel to puncture their dinghy but he did not understand. So I said "Pass me the knife, I will untangle the net." But the agent in front of me understood my trick. He caught me by the hair and pulled me on to their boat. I was trying to catch the agent who had pulled me by the hair and I put his head on the side of the boat. But then the other agent came with his machete, meaning "If you don't release him, I will strike your head with it …" So finally, they brought me further away from the edge. They requested from me all kinds of information. Yet I did not answer. They said, "We don't mind, we will stay here all day if you don't answer". But I said, "Soon you will get too hungry … and you're too cowardly anyway." So they said "You really think so?" We stayed on the sea one more hour or so, but not more. They brought me to the wharf; I disembarked from the boat and returned to my people.' (Ivan, ch. 2, ref. 1)

the core characteristics of a warrior – that is, the ability to commit entirely through conscious self-sacrifice. Interestingly, he then tries to compensate for the impracticality of being an integral warrior through diverse techniques such as embellishing his only significant action during the war, and overstressing the dramatic context of war in parallel with his own vulnerability, and his undeniable courage despite his young age (Neal, ch. 2, ref. 6). Thirty years after the event, people will still tend to conform to their past-self from the time of the war.

In addition, the individual in question demonstrates how his actions in the war stemmed from undeviating compliance to an order given by the commanders. In his attempt to absorb the qualities of a warrior, he describes meticulously the significance of his actions in maintaining the group integrity. He speaks profusely about the sacredness of the net, but also portrays himself in detail in relation to it. Significantly, he attests that his actions are the quintessence of a supporter's commitment.

According to the stories, women were confined to the role of supporters. First of all, salmon fishing was 'a guy thing'. Then, as one woman mentioned, 'We, the wives, we did not go to the front. It was too dangerous for us and anyway we had to stay with the kids. That being said, we were taking care of our warriors and were very supportive of the whole movement' (Esther, Ch.4, ref. 5). Newly married, Esther constructed her role as the model wife supporting her husband, totally embracing his struggle – the highest form of commitment for a woman during a war.

Another person could only be a supporter due to his job. As described at length, his position in the community prevented him from engaging as much as he wished as a warrior in contentious initiatives. As he explains, his role already had 'its utility for the community, in particular to maintain control and prevent homicide' (Maxence, chapter 2, ref. 2) His demonstration of commitment thus also meant he had to accept not being a warrior but taking the role the group requested of him.

In another interesting case the commanders supposedly asked a supporter, clandestinely, to play the role of external informant for the movement.[10] This person infiltrated the anti-Indian movement in order to influence and moderate 'the most extremist agents among the Euroquébécois' (Maxence, chapter 2, ref. 3). As a non-member of the group at that time, or a non-status Indian in accordance with the Indian Act, he was more of a secret supporter. He used his non-membership, and the distrust it produced, for the benefit of the

10 'I had news from the indigenous side from a person. And for the other side, I has ideas to moderate the non-indigenous who were aggressive, who were very resentful and who wanted to cut the net. So I made myself the intermediary. I knew which side I was going to take in case of any degeneration.' (Maxence, ch. 2, ref. 2 and 3)

movement. His support was useful because it was secret and his commitment went as far as it could.

Supporters' self-portraits are characterised by a strong and unquestioned inner commitment to the movement, albeit a restricted one. Their self-perception translates into stories of compensation, of mythologising one's actions, an over-identification with warriors' deeds and commitment, as well as diverse rhetorical strategies to maintain a positive self-image and to prove allegiance.

Uncommitted

People conspicuously comment on non-participatory members at the fringe of the group who 'stayed at home, not supporting us directly' (Ernest, chapter 2, ref. 13). The stories portray non-engagement in the context of the war as transgressive, if not a betrayal. As autobiographical stories tend to be strongly self-advantageous, self-perceptions of these non-participatory interviewees often feature justifications or silence. One, for instance, said he 'remembered nothing'; others flatly refused to be interviewed or accepted uneasily. The reasons behind these refusals and silences can contribute to contextualising forgetfulness.

Among those who agreed to be interviewed, Alyha, for example, affirmed that the unfolding of events is for her a memory blank: 'maybe it was more striking for others … But in my case, this event means *absolutely* nothing to me … I've never heard of the Salmon War' (chapter 2, ref. 1). Justin, who was in a position of power at the time of the interview, was in his early 20s during the war. At first he claimed not to 'remember much about the war' because of his age (Justin, chapter 2, ref. 2 and 3). Off the record, he shamefacedly admitted to having partied a lot with his friends, including many Euroquébécois, during this period of his life. As he subsequently confessed, he spent all his spare time at the tavern and furtively justified not participating because of his drug and alcohol use. He now identifies himself as a radical indigenist. Yet his memories do not chime with this image. He said at the end of the interview that the Salmon War is something that should be forgotten.

Tshak's testimony also helps our understanding of aspects of non-commitment. At first, he did not participate but then became a warrior, which allows him to speak more freely about his period of neutrality. He remembers that at first he was afraid that engaging directly would mean automatically losing his job; he was already suffering from the stigma of being an Indian at work (chapter 2, ref. 5).[11] After being mistreated at work, despite his neutrality,

11 'Me, I was more remote at first because of the job I had, which was as a gas attendant in Escoumins … I could not take one side more than the other. I was not allowed much to go to *the other side*. I had to be neutral. Even if nobody was neutral, man! When they [the anti militants] come when I was working, that was it … So I kept my mouth shut because my boss

and understanding that as an Indian he was 'never right anyway', he decided to engage completely in the war. After embracing his indigeneity, he left his job, came back to Essipit and was involved in the movement:

> Whatever I do, I'm looked down on. As an Indian, I'm at war anyway. So I will do it well … We are all considered dirty savages. We are accused of stealing everything from everyone. We are stigmatised, all put in one box. So I will accept it. I will exhibit myself to the world as I am and fight with my band. (chapter 2, ref. 5)

Social pressures weighed on people, discouraging them from identifying as Indian, and conditioning them not to engage with their group. There was a price to be paid if they supported the group and were perceived as Indian. For many, engaging in war meant jeopardising their only source of income. As the experience of Pishimnapeo illuminates, apparent non-participation in the war sometimes masked less apparent engagement, such as fulfilling the responsibility of feeding one's extended family (Pishimnapeo, chapter 2, ref. 5).

That said, not participating in the war remains something the self-portraits tend to gloss over. Non-participation therefore clearly broke a *command to commit,* was considered conduct that endangered the staying power of the movement and needed to be outlawed. It is presented as seditious, condemnable or shameful. Explanations and justifications for non-participation consist mostly of invoking social positions that heavily *contextualise* the role, some being perceived as more acceptable than others (sustaining the family, for example, as opposed to alcoholism, fear or the shame of being identified as Indian). Clearly, the emerging norm of commitment, and the conformity of individual self-portraits with it, are pivotal in any discussion of the remembrance and forgetting of the event.

Staging oneself: the social backdrops

The normative predominance of commitment in the specific context of war is evident in the self-portraits; characters are shaped in accordance with the potential for commitment that they represent. Moreover, characters commonly come from positions that are used to contextualise self-roles, or from social backgrounds from which they construct positions (Schiffrin, 1996). But what do people's self-portraits display about the social determinants of their production?

As commitment concerns the attachment of the self to the requirement of social relations (Kanter, 1968, p. 502), the comprehension of attachments to and identification with a group would then be crucial in understanding individual dedication to group purposes. In this sense, the social backgrounds

was saying "Shut up Tshak, shut up! Don't reply to them!" But you know how, sometimes, when it is too much? And it happened one night, it blew up!' (Tshak, ch. 2, ref. 5) of the self-portraits offer rich insights for contextualising narrators' constraints and the social settings of their actions. Noticeably, two social centrifugal forces to commitment emerge in the self-narrations: an ideological component about dual cultural identification, and an economic dimension concerning the group's dependency on external subsidies.

Dual referentiality

Self-portraits reveal a phenomenon of dual referentiality through an explicit relationship with the worlds of 'Indians' and 'Euroquébécois/whites'. A group of reference, one whose perspective is assumed by the actor, is activated by agents when evaluating their own qualities, circumstances, attitudes, values and behaviours (Shibutani, 1954; Thompson and Hickey, 2005). Stories clearly report the existence of two of these sources of reference among those involved as the war ran its course.

Until 1984, Canada's assimilation policy required that if an Innu woman married a Euroquébécois and had children with them she and the children would have their Indian status taken away.[12] Conversely, when a Euroquébécois woman married an Innu man, she would be given Indian status. Esther, for example, had just acquired Indian status through her marriage at the start of the Salmon War (Esther, chapter 2, ref. 9). Since 1945, almost all Innu men had married Euroquébécois women, and most of the time these men were away from the reserve for economic reasons. Yet all the Innu women who had married Euroquébécois men from surrounding villages had had to leave the reserve. As a consequence, the women from the reserve were anchored within a Euroquébécois referential and were apparently transmitting their conceptions to their children. During the war, in 1980–1, all Essipiunnuat families were, therefore, significantly related in one way or another to Euroquébécois families, especially to those in Les Escoumins but in the surrounding villages as well.

Situations of war generally imply in-group crystallisation of common societal and cultural attributes and the emergence of inter-group polarisations and antinomies (Hamilton, 1991, p. 12; Bhatt, 1999). Indeed, the event engendered a series of inner micro-fragmentations. For example, the intensification of inter-group feuds deeply affected the relationships Innu people had with family members by marriage:

> My boss understood my feelings and what I was going through since I talked a lot with him. But with my other brother-in-law was not the same. He saw that I was talking with my boss, his brother, and he did not like it at all. It was very rough … It is the brother, the business. Do you see? The brother-in-law is in the gang, but not in the right gang because he is

12 For more information, see the Canadian justice department website at: http://laws-lois.justice.gc.ca/eng/acts/I-5/page-3.html. For further discussions on the issue pertaining to discrimination against indigenous women in the Indian Act, see Palmater (2011).

Indian ... It caused tension. (Tshak, chapter 2, ref. 5).

As links with the people of Escoumins were significant for all of those taking part, these associations appear frequently in self-portraits as a background to individual action. If these landscapes are closely examined, two main ways of belonging to the group are revealed: cultural and legal. One person, for example, as a '*status Indian*', was a member of the group. Yet, as he says, culturally he was mostly tied to the other side. With his Innu father being away for work, since 'there was nothing on the reserve', his mother had sent him to his grandmother in a surrounding township (Adam, chapter 2, ref. 3–4). In essence, the Salmon War was, for him, an introduction to a reference group to which he legally belonged, but did not rely on culturally.

In contrast to this, some who did not have Indian status felt this double referentiality intensely as they did not '*legally*' belong to the group, yet had grown up on the reserve and felt culturally Innu. They were well aware of the tensions.[13] Karl, for example, defined himself as a member of the reserve and engaged in the war, despite the fact that his mother (and he himself) did not legally belong to the group. Maxence's[14] self-portrait also has this dual belonging as a preponderant background.[15]

The existence of two groups of reference among the Essipiunnuat during the war is a dominant feature that surfaces as a background in almost all the self-portraits. As for other bands that have been subject to Canadian assimilation policies, the Essipiunnuat's absorption of Euroquébécois cultural referents must be regarded as correlating with the circumstances created to prepare their planned 'assimilation into the dominant, non-Indian society' (Tobias, 1976). If the residential school was one of the devices that propelled this absorption,

13 'I was off-reserve, but all the time on the reserve ... We were living on Les Oblats Street. We were living right by the reserve. But my mother lost her rights when she married my dad. I was raised on the reserve with my cousin Eddy, Daniel, Ralph and all of them. We were all the time all together with the sons of Uncle David and Laurent Ross. We grew up together ... you see ... So that when the event happened, we defended our rights.' (Karl, ch. 2, ref. 8) See also Maxence, ch. 2. ref. 1.

14 Maxence was 28 at the start of the war. He was working, as was the case with many other people at that time, for a lumber company exploiting the surrounding forests. He was not a member of the band at the time, although he regained Indian status in 1985. His mother lost her status when she married a non-Indian person. Yet, even without Indian status, Maxence, and his brother Karl, had strong family and cultural ties with Essipit. In fact, his grandmother was Élise Ross, daughter of Paul Ross II, who was married to Joseph Pierre Moreau. Karl, Maxence's young brother, describes himself as 'a non-recognised Indian'.

15 'At this time, I was non-indigenous. I was not Indian. I was not recognised as such and I did not know that I would become a member one day. I had been raised on the reserve itself since I spent most of the time at my grandmother Élise and Uncle Arthur's houses. For sure my choice was somehow already made. But I wanted to be transparent in these situations since I was not Indian, despite the fact that I had family members who were and that the majority of my friends were on the indigenous side. There were people that I respected, however, on the other side.' (Maxence, ch. 2, ref. 1–3, 4–7)

state regulation of intermarriages was another. It consisted mainly of the use of Euroquébécois women as assimilative devices, and the destruction of the intergenerational and cultural bridges that Innu women had built.

This dual referentiality, as a result of advanced absorption of the Euroquébécois social imaginary, the antinomies it entails, and the existence of the settler society as a point of reference, definitively increased the price of committing to one group. It placed narrators in front of heartbreaking dilemmas, which demanded that they be in tandem with or choose between a dual attachment that became problematic as the war raged, and amplified the internal demand for allegiance.

Economic dependencies: 'We had large families to feed'

Other aspects of the social background, often associated with cultural alienation and dualism, concern the economic condition of the group, its poverty and dependence on external subsidies. More than half of the people interviewed, who were old enough to work at the outbreak of the war, were working for either a lumber company in the forest, a mining company in the north or a local business or institution in a nearby Euroquébécois village.

In all their self-portraits, identifying as being 'on the Indian side' had implications for them at their places of work. Maxence's story, for instance, expresses the intense discomfort people faced at work when they identified as Indian during the war.[16] Ernest relays how people had to go back to their workplace day after day, even when the conflict was going on, since there was 'no way to earn a living' on their reserve (Ernest, chapter 2, ref. 6).

Life on the reserve was inherently precarious and the need to go elsewhere for work resulted in the majority of the men being away all the time, and, hence, relatively disconnected from local affairs (Pishimnapeo, chapter 2, ref. 1–3). Since the early 20th century, the group had effectively been economically marginalised (Mailhot, 1996). Other indigenous groups throughout the region also shared this situation. As early as the 1940s, indigenist militants such as Jules Sioui and William Commanda had denounced the disastrous impact on local groups of authorities having intensified assimilative strategies, which consisted of 'treating the Indian in such manner that all the Indians abandon their reserves or gradually become extinct due to the impossibility of earning a living' (Sioui, n.d., quoted in Shewell, 1999). It could be said therefore that the Crown had effectively designed this dependency in addition to having specifically conceived the reserve and the band council to subsequently dissolve

16 'I was chopping wood. I was with Mestenapeo, Marcel Ross, Ernest, Ti-Nours, Pierre and Édouard. Up there, the war continued. Some people came to tell us that they would break our machines … They ordered us to stay in our rooms, not to move from them. They said they would break our timberjack tyres; that they would do other things such as burn our equipment, that all the Indians would lose their jobs.' (Maxence, ch. 2, ref. 14)

into the surrounding municipalities (Ross-Tremblay and Hamidi, 2019, p. 265).

The economic social background on the reserve in the 1980s, revealed in the stories, illustrates the ultimate consequences of such procedures. Broadly, economic marginalisation resulted in dependence on Euroquébécois society and fostered assimilation. In the context of war, this dependence meant the primary group of reference paid a greater price for their loyalty, since it jeopardised people's only source of income. Being forced to integrate into Euroquébécois society meant that these men had to face the stigma of identifying and being identified as Indian. Their absence from home also decreased their influence within their families and in the community in general, engendering ruptures in transmission that resulted in even greater absorption into Euroquébécois culture and its representations of 'Indians'.

The self-portraits that emerge from the stories suggest that the sense of commitment, as a requirement of social relations in war, faced two centrifugal forces. These constraints, apparently inherent in the group's social settings, emerge simultaneously as a colonial legacy and a sociohistorical determinant of group life. Yet, they also appear as the main elements against which the most committed fought. As the movement rebelled against the state's attempts to extinguish Innu rights and the historical state policy of 'effect[ing] assimilation through coercive and dogmatic means' (Shewell 1999, p. 234), it was also struggling within itself with forces discouraging self-identification as Indian, thus increasing the sacrifice involved in commitment and subtly normalising collective self-annihilation. Underlying the collective rejection of a colonial status, an internal struggle was raging against the admission, to use Fanon's (1959) words, that the group's 'misfortunes proceeded directly from its racial and cultural characteristics' – the insidious and underlying colonial myth that Indians as an 'inferior and decadent race' should vanish (pp. 42–5).

Emotional undertow

In the autobiographical stories, people paint their characters and the social landscape within which they were functioning but they also present their emotions quite openly. Since there is a clear emotional dimension, together with a legal, political and economic basis, to cultural domination, should be a routine aspect of analysing social movements (Howard, 1995). Greater attention to emotion builds 'thicker descriptions of social movements' and better understanding of their *micro-foundations* (Goodwin, Jasper and Polleta, 2008, p. 424).

The study of emotions illuminates key facets of the deployment of collective identities, including advances and setbacks of mobilisation and commitment as well as in-group impacts of counter responses from the movement's opponents

(Duperré, 2008; Hunt and Benford, 2008, p. 449). Previous research hints at the existence of vital yet 'tricky to catch' figures of collective agency that can only be assessed by considering a wide scope of emotions, including embarrassment, humiliation and other related feelings, such as shame linked to rejection or a sense of failure or inadequacy (Scheff, 1988, p. 96). The relationship between emotions and self-identity remains crucial; the emotional aspects of life stories link past experiences to the continuously developing sense of self (Fivush, 1994).

Yet autobiographical accounts tend to be self-advantageous, and as a result are likely to leave out any feelings of shame (Scheff, 1988, p. 96). Shame tends to be slyly forgotten. As a primary social emotion, mainly fed by threats to the social bond, it remains, however, a barometer of social order, control and perceived transgressions to collective identity. The consideration and contrasting of positive emotions ('that tend to be remembered vividly') and negative emotions ('soon to be forgotten') contained in personal accounts is essential to a fuller understanding of the representation of oneself in the past and of areas of shared experiences.

The thrill of an uprising

Personal accounts contain positive feelings; yet these tend to be shared only among the most committed actors. Positive feelings are associated with collective agency and impulses of rebellion, together with assertion of indigeneity. People also report feeling astonished and surprised to witness such a collective uprising. In general, contributors were profoundly affected by the great sense of self-respect expressed in the unfolding of events, in particular by some people's readiness to make sacrifices when resisting. Stories also report the experience of an aesthetic sense of beauty in observing 'the development of the whole movement, the unification of the people, the incredible extent to which people were coming together, the warriors' readiness to die for the cause and to see things through to the end' (Raoul, chapter 2, ref. 1 and 17). Sensations of 'joy and pride' are coupled with an awareness of the deployment of resistance, that the group they belonged to was 'standing up to their oppressors' (Pierre, chapter 2, ref. 8).

Various speakers fondly remembered the highly positive feelings arising from the intensification of comradeship in the course of war. They felt the strong spirit of camaraderie and the 'one for all and all for one' mentality was 'the most positive feeling they have ever experienced in their lives' (Raoul, chapter 2, ref. 24). People acknowledged an unusual feeling of solidarity and in-group complicity. This is also related to the exhilarating perception of the immense power and sense of potency associated with being in the movement, and with observing the defiant and brave attitude of the older warriors in tragic circumstances (Adam, chapter 2, ref. 4). This sense of empowerment was even more intense among the leaders; one remembers experiencing a distinctive and unrivalled feeling of power when he became aware that people were mobilised and were validating his authority as a leader (Mesnak, chapter 2, ref. 9).

Another set of emotions pertains to the transcendence of fear. It is well known that such a phenomenon is observable in the context of normative reemergence (Riis, 1998). During certain episodes, when their lives were in danger, various people said they felt a sense of release from the fear of death, or had witnessed others do so in similar situations. Riel, for example, heard bullets whistling through the air near him. Yet he recalls not thinking of his own death. As he says, 'they could have shot me with a 12-calibre rifle and I would not have bothered. It would not have meant anything to me … absolutely nothing. No, I was ready to die right there, on the wharf' (Riel, chapter 2, ref. 2).

This is not all. Interviewees report the experience of a zealous desire to sacrifice, to 'do whatever it takes' for the 'benefit of the entire group'. Karl explains his pleasure at offering one's life in simple compliance, as a warrior, with an implicit ethical code among the Essipiunnuat according to which 'one never bows his head in front of a threat, never obeys fear'. Instead, one must 'give everything [one] can' (Karl, chapter 2, ref. 7).

However, people do also report the awareness that this feeling of omnipotence was shaped by exceptional circumstances and situations. Édouard, for example, thinks it was essential to balance the fact that 'we effectively felt very strong' with the one that 'we thought we were strong' (chapter 2, ref. 3). He suggests that the specific context of the Salmon War led the group to overestimate its force and to underestimate the painful backlash that was to follow.

The miseries of reaction

The pleasures of collective agency were shared chiefly among a very small number of actors, particularly the most committed characters and, beyond that circle, those who most asserted their indigeneity. The emotions of those who identified less with the indigenous movement are closer to uneasiness, and they share feelings of insecurity, rejection and shame. However, the personal accounts do reveal the importance of negative emotions such as insecurity, terror, humiliation, rage, hatred and stress, felt by all. As these feelings were widely shared, they are, for the most part, associated with the effects of reaction. They highlight the hostile responses to the movement, the backlash following indigenous resistance and the self-assertion of sovereignty.

As in the case of similar resistance movements, the deployment of collective identity generated a counter response from opponents to the movement (Hunt and Benford, 2008, p. 448). Effectively, the Essipiunnuat uprising immediately encountered renewed attempts from the Québec state, as well as from local villagers, to reassert their power and to institute control. When not silenced or forgotten, the painful miseries of these reactions loom larger than the pleasures invoked previously in the memory of all interviewees and group members.

The Salmon War is connected in local memory with more negative than positive emotions; the memories contain some good moments, but these were entwined in episodes that were 'very hard to live through' (Mesnak, chapter 2, ref. 3), and the people who experienced them 'have been trying to forget the whole thing since' (Ernest, chapter 2, ref. 8). For many, the experience of the war was traumatic. The indigenous side was the most deeply wounded, 'inside themselves, for each individual. Some of them were deeply injured' (Maxence, chapter 2, ref. 17). Esther shares this evaluation. 'It happened 30 years ago and I can still smell it', she says. In her view, the emotional cost of the event was devastatingly high, and it marked people's lives forever. Even in the memory of those who were most committed, the event brings back negative feelings such as terror, fear, stress and tiredness (Esther, chapter 2, ref. 1–7).

Participants correlated their gloomy feelings with being repressed by the state and the locals, and the violence and intimidation that came from the Euroquébécois in general (Adam, chapter 2, ref. 3). As one example out of many, Pierre vividly recalls the emotional situations produced by the provincial police force's unexpected and massive intervention on the reserve:

> It was hell. There were kids on the grass. People cried. Women were fearful for their children, and we were afraid too … as if it was war … The bombs they were launching, it was hell! It was too much for me. You do not go mad but there is too much happening at once. Because when it has never happened to you and such a thing occurs … you think it is very dangerous … especially for the kids (Pierre, chapter 1, ref. 1).

Likewise, Ivan's memories of the event are dominated by the terror he felt when the Québec agents kidnapped him. They pulled him by the hair onto their boats and took him away to sea. At the mercy of three wildlife agents, he thought they were going to beat him to death (Ivan, chapter 2, ref. 3). Moreover, the magnitude of the state response to their resistance left a deep impression. In some episodes, the small group faced a Québec government helicopter that descended to within 15 to 20 feet above them. In other situations, large and well-equipped government boats charged at Essipiunnuat fishing boats. 'It was very imposing', remembers Ivan (Ivan, chapter 2, ref. 1).

These moments of confrontation with the authorities provoked feelings of terror, particularly among the women whose husbands were at risk. As soon as the men left home, the women felt great anxiety. As Esther recalls, 'each time the phone rang, we thought something had happened'. She says she will never forget her feelings in the war, especially when she was convinced that a homicide was close to taking place (chapter 2, ref. 2 and 9). Some also recall their terror when they heard gunshots. They knew that their husbands, or fathers in the case of the children, were out there. Elizabeth, who was a child during the war, remembers clearly hearing the sounds of gunshots, terrified, while sitting on her mother's knee. 'I remember the smells of that exact moment', she says (Elisabeth, chapter 2, ref. 2).

However, it is the intimidation, racism and aggressiveness of the local Euroquébécois that appears to be the greatest source of negative feeling. One of the most emotionally charged episodes remains the attempts, by the people of Escoumins, to assist the state and repress the 'Indian uprising'. People present at the wharf remember 'as if it was yesterday' their apprehension at seeing the 'white' population arriving to 'settle the Indian case'. As Ernest says, 'it was a huge thing for us. For my part, I never want to live through such an experience again' (chapter 2, ref. 2). Karl was reduced to tears during his interview, 30 years after the event, when he recalled the episode during which he was mistreated.[17]

Intimidation in the workplace looms large in many recollections. These highly emotional episodes clearly forged the collective memory of the group. Those who experienced it were afraid that 'terrible things happened' (Pierre, chapter 2, ref. 4). Tshak, for example, says 'It was hell for me', as he was working as an attendant at his brother-in-law's gas station. He was harassed and hustled at his workplace for more than three weeks. In expectation of a 'real attack', he carried a weapon in his pocket in order to defend himself (chapters 2–8, ref. 1). The rhetoric of the reaction consisted of disseminating the idea that 'since they are savages, they should be forbidden to earn a living from white companies' (Tshak, chapter 2, ref. 8).

The experiences of lumbermen, who continued working despite the war, are compelling in this respect. For them, the situation was especially tough. They were a small group of Essipiunnuat, isolated far off in the forest with an overwhelming majority of hostile Euroquébécois. The war continued in the workers' camp.[18] Broadly, all those who were identified as Indians, or their allies, were subjected to intimidation and associated feelings of tension. In this climate, people who were identified as Indians, regardless of whether they were

17 'The whites arrived from behind us. I remember that very well. I became exceedingly nervous. I was even weeping. We were not old you know … and we had to go through such things! It was serious … I asked myself "why such a war with the village?" I'm still affected … It was my first big experience in life … the Salmon War … when you held the net …' (Karl, ch. 2, ref. 2–6)

18 'Right upon our arrival, they began to assault us … We were forced to return, to leave. We were not respected anymore. We were treated … not as dogs, they were much better treated. They were showing us that we had nothing there … We had to come back. We were unable to be heard. At night times, they would arrive in the camps and start to shout "the damned Indians are here" … all the time. We were just three, Marcel, Ti-Nours and me, and they were 200. There were about 30 of them who used to shout at night and at lunchtime. There were just three of us, you know … not many. Damn, we were hassled. It affected me a lot at that time.' (Édouard, ch. 2, ref. 1 and 2)

committed to the cause or not, were all stigmatised and held responsible for the actions of the movement. Some remain scarred to this day by these degradations. According to Tshak, at least 25 per cent of the Euroquébécois were openly racist and supportive of the reactionary faction and its discriminatory views (chapter 2, ref. 2).

All those 'going outside the reserve' thus repeatedly faced their fears generated by wickedness, sadism, humiliation, threats and bullying, especially in Escoumins. They had to be constantly 'on guard' (Raoul, chapter 2, ref. 25). What interviewees state was harder to bear remains the collective stigmatisation of the Indians and their direct experience with racism. As Ernest says, 'to be called savage the way we were … it hurts' (chapter 2, ref. 12). 'We swallowed a lot of foolish words, all the Indians were "a bunch of profiteers",' remembers one person who was still a teenager at the time (Adam, chapter 2, ref. 10). This racial humiliation was indiscriminately and routinely directed towards people of all ages, including children.[19]

People were torn as they were under a lot of pressure to take a side, and even families were severely divided (Maxence, chapter 2, ref. 7). The reaction reverberated within the group. From the moment they decided to assert their rights, there was a lot of pressure, even within the reserve, and from their own families: 'there was racism everywhere. We faced racism daily, even within the reserve' (Mestenapeo, chapter 2, ref. 4 and 5). It was a great challenge encountering overwhelming racism outside the reserve, but it 'was ... hardest of all' within it (Ernest, chapter 2, ref. 5).

People associate their experiences of humiliation and intimidation, or being made to feel it was 'shameful to be Indian', and being punished for it, with the explosions of rage and fury that followed. This intimate relationship between emotion and violence, and the infernal 'spiral of shame and rage', is a well-known dynamic in destructive conflicts (Scheff and Retzinger, 1991). One interviewee, for example, associates his greatest moment of wrath and loss of control with a racist attack on his elderly uncle (Sam, chapter 2, ref. 7). Another recalls how the intervention of the Québec authorities by merely stepping on to reserve territory provoked in him a 'blast of hatred'; it was perceived as a symbolic offence that revived reminiscences of collective abuses and historical wounds (Pierre, chapter 2, ref. 2). Tshak asserts that as the war progressed it generated 'a deep and lasting rage' in him. He traces his feelings

19 'They called us "fucking savages"; they belittled us. "You're not people! You're less than nothing! You destroy everything!" Yes, yes, yes. "Dirty little Indian". You know, they were not just swearing at adults, they were offending even the kids. Oh yes, they were really cruel, and gave us such looks; it was astonishing. You know, if they had had guns, they would have killed us. It would have been like during the conquest of the far west of America, they would have killed us all, oh yes.' (Napeo, ch. 2, ref. 3 and 4)

back to the Euroquébécois' denial[20] of their rights and the wilful blindness of the historical injustices committed against them.[21]

Analysis of the most significant emotions highlights two fundamental phenomena that occurred in the war. These give access to the social sources of their production – an uprising and a reaction, respectively. In the end, if the positive emotions,[22] primarily related to the process of uprising, appear to be restricted to only a fraction of the members, the negative ones[23] tend to be shared by a greater number. Such emotions were experienced by all interviewees and were shared not only by those who identified themselves as Indians in the war, but also by those whom others identified as Indians or of being on the Indians' side. The course of the war, among the great majority of people who experienced it, is predominantly associated with negative emotions; these conclusively overwhelm the positive ones. Thus, the self-narration of emotions reveals that the process of uprising, of collective agency and assertion were the source of intense and positive feelings in the group, but this was principally among those who were most committed. The negative emotions are all related to the reactions to Innu resistance, self-assertion and the commitment to

20 This question of denial was significantly documented in Cohen (2001).

21 'That our grandfathers and great grandfathers used to fish, nobody can contradict such evidence. We have been here forever, us Indians. We are speaking of rights that have always been there ... So how come we have lost these rights? We don't have rights anymore because some Euroquébécois, from a tiny village, don't want us to catch salmon in the river with a net? They had already constrained us to a minuscule 0.5 km^2. It is not big for a reserve. That is where the source of all our rancour lies.' (Tshak, ch. 2, ref. 8)

22 The family of *positive* emotions mentioned in the stories is composed, among others, of pride, self-love, beauty, power and dignity. To contemplate collective mobilisation, solidarity among the group, self-sacrifice and revolt, together with an indomitable spirit of camaraderie, gave people a new sense of beauty and a pride in belonging to the group. As their identification with the group was boosted, they felt increased power. In turn, at times, they were released from their fear of death with the feeling of an acceptance of self-annihilation for group purposes, which, ultimately, provided them with the sense of being free and indomitable. These *positive* emotions are thus linked principally to their participation in the movement, the experience of camaraderie, the direct defence of indigenous principles, the assertion of their indigeneity, the confrontations with authorities, and the contemplation of the uprising itself.

23 The family of *negative* feelings, or *suffering*, is composed of intense stress, terror, humiliation and shame, as well as internal rage and hatred. These negative feelings are mainly associated with situations related to the reaction from the state and its agents, but also, and more significantly, with the actions of the local Euroquébécois. The deeds narrated range through all kinds of intimidation, humiliation and punishment. They include racial violence and threats. Terrorisation in the workplace is remembered particularly painfully, especially when interviewees were captives of hostile and racist crowds. Ultimately, if the experience of racism is remembered with great sadness, narrators admit that the most hurtful was to face *anti-Indian* discourse within the reserve, especially among family members and in-laws. Inter-group fragmentation has left a bitter taste in everybody's mouths. Indeed, regardless of whether this came from the authorities or popular reaction, humiliations and the abasement of indigeneity often resulted, for narrators, in uncontrollable outbreaks of wrath, rage and a loss of control.

indigeneity; the emotional traumas were shared extensively among all group members.

Finally, when characters, social backgrounds and emotions in self-portraits are studied, a group past-self is revealed, characterised by a profound commitment to and assertion of indigeneity, which resists the historical and actualised forces seeking its complete destruction. Furthermore, a collective consciousness is born out of the knowledge that uprising and assertion of indigeneity brings with severe punishment, and that, ultimately, being indigenous can be tragically painful. This is a determinant of cultural oblivion and a barrier to remembrance and intergenerational transmission.

Inter-individual depictions: narrating others' gestures

Interviewees' representation of others in their accounts is also essential in investigating the group's past-self. Released from the strict bonds of maintaining a positive self-image, these representations offer crucial complementary information; one's social identity remains, in fact, attached to the constellation of its composing relational and collective self.

It is assumed here that the individual self is composed of dyadic relationships and that it is chiefly manufactured by assimilating with others (Brewer and Gardner, 1996). Individuals are not only inclined to conform to others' behaviours, but also to copying their interiority (Readopt, 2003). Social representations have an immense impact on individual lives and provide first-hand material for exhuming collective past-self conceptions. Even a cursory glance at these representations in the stories illustrates the central place that is given to heroic actions.

Heroic characters become symbolic representations in people's stories. As Chatterji (1986) proposes, the concept of the hero-as-self can make visible how speakers, who cannot narrate their experiences from their own point of view, recite heroic gestures in order to absorb heroism. The identification between the narrator and his narration of *heroism* allows him to share it and its typical qualities of protection, bravery and self-sacrifice in unique circumstances. Inter-individual depictions in descriptions of the course of war are predominantly characterised, in their contents and forms, by the exaltation of heroic achievements.

An aesthetic approach helps to connect with 'more sensuous and perhaps more tangible, yet equally important forms of insights' (Bleiker, 2009) that might give access to the social composition of the Essipiunnuat representations and the social fabric of their memory. Halbwachs highlighted long ago how a set of images that is transmitted, received, absorbed and widely shared within a given group echo the presence of a collective memory (Halbwachs, 1950, p. 54; Rimé and Christophe, 2001, p. 131). Communalities in these inter-individual representations are therefore rich material; they provide access to elements of a past and shared sense of 'we'-ness in order to disinter, from the collective drama of the course of the war, commonly remembered figures of heroes and villains, shared contexts and stages of their actions, and the normative quintessence of these myths (Klapp, 1969, quoted in Hunt and Benford, 2008, p. 437).

Heroism

Inter-individual representations are dominated by descriptions of outstanding acts of courage and sacrifice in perilous circumstances, for the defence of the whole group and, at times, of all First Peoples. The presence of icons is reported, and actors and actions are commonly remembered and valued. Accordingly, heroism, and tributes to it, constitute the overriding scheme of inter-individual accounts; and reallocations towards the perception of self as an interchangeable exemplar of heroism are clearly observed (Turner et al., 1987, p. 50). Heroism thus remains a critical attribute of the group's past-self in war.

Perilous circumstances

As demonstrated earlier, people interpret the Salmon War uprising as a collective resistance to government attempts to annihilate them. They interpret it as a battle in a war that has been raging for more than a century against the Crown and its project to assimilate them through uprooting their Innu sovereignty (*Innu tipenitamun*) and undermining their self-determination (*uetshit takuaimatishun*).

Individually, the unfolding of war often put people in catastrophic situations where they were forced to flee or to act from positions of extreme weakness. The principle scenes in the background of inter-individual depictions are mainly related, but not limited to, the following hazardous episodes:

Main episodes of the Salmon War in autobiographical memories	
14 June 1980	Clashes at sea during the first intervention by wildlife agents in order to seize the net.
16 June 1980	A crowd of hostile Euroquébécois threatens a small number of Essipiunnuat workers.
10 July 1980	Direct confrontation on the road with armed officers during the interception of agents by Essipiunnuat after a second attempt to seize their net.

19 July 1980	An air–land–sea initiative is launched jointly by the wildlife agents and the provincial police. Violent confrontations with Essipiunnuat occur and shots of firearms sound; Québec agents push back and the Essipiunnuat end their fishing season.
7 July 1981	The Essipiunnuat spread their nets again and between 200 and 400 Euroquébécois from Escoumins township, according to the different testimonies, decide to seize the net. Violent confrontations occur with the Essipiunnuat on the Escoumins wharf.

The course of events, with contention at its heart, was described as like being condemned to fight enemies both externally (Mesnak, chapter 3, ref. 4) and internally (Mestenapeo, chapter 2, ref. 9). The unfolding of war was represented as hell (Tshak, chapter 2, ref. 7), as a place where there was nothing joyful (Karl, chapter 2, ref. 2), where there was only sorrow and disappointment on every side (Maxence, chapter 2, ref. 4 and 12). The course of war is described overall as a collective drama, with people forced to face overwhelming hostility (Adam, chapter 2, ref. 5), be involved in many clashes, and be prey to one of 'two lions grumbling and near to pouncing' (Raoul, chapter 2, ref. 3). Representations of individuals and of their actions are impregnated with sorrow, with hazardous settings and circumstances, and a sense of danger affecting each individual and the whole group.

Longing for sacrifice

Stories strongly emphasise the warriors in action portraying their behaviours as transcending fear, embodying courage and a sense of self-sacrifice that translates to self-annihilation as a conscious choice. Approximately 25 to 30 of those who were engaged in the uprising were allegedly ready to put their lives on the line as they faced some two hundred Euroquébécois (Karl, chapter 2, ref. 9).[24] Resolved to resist hostilities fearlessly (Riel, chapter 2, ref. 3), the most steadfast warriors preferred 'to die in the waters of the sea'[25] than surrender and consent to the extinguishment of their rights (Raoul, chapter 2, ref. 3). All the interviewees fondly remember the sense of sacrifice displayed by the most committed.[26]

24 The numbers vary according to different sources (from 200 to 400 people).

25 What Raoul calls 'waters' is considered locally as essentially a synonym for death. Water in the St Lawrence River, near Essipit, is slightly above freezing all year long. People falling into the water risk hypothermia if they are in it for more than a couple of minutes.

26 'When you see people in the street with guns who are strong and firm, and who are saying "Enough! If you pass, it will be over our dead bodies ... You and your little government truck, it is finished now. Go back to where you came from." I've seen people ready to go to war and ready to die. It was extreme but very powerful then. People were armed. It was serious. Everyone was shaking, people were ready to die, ready to fight to the bitter end.' (Adam, ch. 2,. ref. 3–6)

Those warriors are described as benefactors, not just to the group but also to the wider world. In the catastrophic context of the war, they are presented as the only people that could be relied on, since they 'feared absolutely nothing and were the first on the firing line' (Pierre, chapter 2, ref. 6). The most admired warriors are depicted as disregarding their physical safety, as if they had forgotten about their body and were ready to face anything (Raoul, chapter 2, ref. 22). The most fundamentalist, often called the 'old radicals' or those 'who did not budge', are described as having their rights tattooed on their hearts, armed with weapons and ready for self-annihilation (Esther, chapter 2, ref. 11; Riel, chapter 2, ref. 5). The discourse is presented as a categorical refusal, an absolute non-acceptance of any violation of their indigenous rights. They would rather die than allow such infringements:

> They will not come and shit on our community, and urinate on our ancestral rights. The time for compromise is over. Better to die. We are not using arrows anymore. We are now equal in arms. We are able to shoot from near or far. We will defend our rights and it will go that way. If it does not work, they will just have to deal [in the sense of 'to kill'], as they were doing before, with Indians. It will all end then. (Tshak, chapter 2, ref. 6).

The warriors' readiness for self-sacrifice, contextualised by the tragic circumstances and the at times death-defying situations, are highly valued in the stories. The purpose behind the warriors' actions also has a role to play in such admiration.

For the good of all

People's descriptions of the group's objectives have already been set out. In the case of stories pertaining to the course of the war, actors are portrayed as concretising these fundamental goals, which is to say deploying multi-faceted actions destined to protect the integrity of the group and its allies. Representations are mostly dominated by the actions in defence of the salmon net (Raoul, chapter 2, ref. 5 and 8). The net was a symbol that embodied the communitarian-indigenous principle – that is, the communitarian and indigenous axiology and culture of the group, and the collective capacity for self-sufficiency. External attempts to seize the net were perceived as an attack on the integrity of the group whose customs were 'ready to be extinguished' (Riel, chapters 2, 4 and 7, ref. 4). Fundamentally, the tireless, even desperate, defence of the net against the external interventions meant protecting the life of the group. All sacrificial actions are described as motivated by moral values 'deeply anchored in the head' (Raoul, chapter 2, ref. 16) and oriented towards the good of the community (Riel, chapter 2, ref. 3). The actors were reportedly overtly defending indigenous principles and presenting their rights as deeply connected with and even belonging to all First Peoples; they have come to define their struggle and uprising as global and on behalf of all indigenous groups (Mestenapeo, chapter 2, ref. 7 and 9).

Inter-individual depictions are clearly typified by heroism. Actors are repeatedly represented as possessing a sense of sacrifice in tragic circumstances, and deploying courageous actions for the good of all. These representations embody the quintessence of commitment, dedication and loyalty. The veneration of heroism and the glorification of warriors, present throughout the stories, are normatively charged and exceedingly informative of past 'we'-ness, including its manufacture. At their most fundamental, they echo a call for radical investments in a collective battle for the preservation of extended indigenous selfhood. A closer look at the shared memories of the significant actors best illustrates the central role played by heroism in memory stories; they constitute to some extent elements of an iconography of the Salmon War among the Essipiunnuat.

The theatre of revolt

In effect, the stories contain representations of personages, their actions and contexts being clearly remembered and valued by everyone interviewed. To some extent, each narrator describes and comments on these individuals, and evaluates their actions and contribution to the overall struggle. These images are icons in the sense that they correspond to sanctified personages that celebrate ethical attributes and postures in specific contexts. Their stories plainly express forms of veneration that generate identification, and reactivate tellers' indignation and a spirit of revolt when they recall them.

In this sense, crystallisations of collective memory and the existence of a certain aesthetic of rebellion are revealed; an exaltation of seditiousness with an explicit awareness of its tragic component. These images deserve a closer look as they are systems of communication and messages, and ingredients of social mythologisation (Barthes, 1957, p. 181). As entities that irrupted after an emotionally charged event, episode or situation, they are adapted to a given order or system and have the power to make visible arrangements (Baudrillard, 1968). Development of such images is essentially modulated by the social sharing of emotions; their spread serves the continuous interest of the group in distributing, extending and updating its database with new individual emotional scenarios. In that sense, they are memorised prototypes of behaviours and emotional scripts (Rimé and Christopher, 1997). As these narrated icons contain standards, their normative charge can be best assessed when put in contrast with their polarities – that is, undesirable behaviours and transgressions.

Icons of insurgence: the model to reproduce

Some representations are at the core of people's stories mainly through descriptions of actors, their actions and their contextualisation. These images, central to the collective memory, appear highly normative. They provide information about the group's past-self and how it standardised in the course of the Salmon War. These excerpts also help to counter the unified dimension that actors formerly and currently in authority tend to shape through a master narrative, giving them a preponderant role. Some shared elements of memory and common themes follow; they are derived entirely from individuals' own perspectives and stories. To make it easier for the reader they are presented here as short compositions, drawn from excerpts but with some minor stylistic adaptations.

Uncle Arthur

He was known affectionately as Uncle Arthur and he was in his late 80s during the war. He was disabled and in bad health; he walked with a cane. His age prevented him from getting involved in the hostilities and engaging in any fighting. Yet, he knew there were fights. At some point, people – those fighting at the wharf and others in the community – heard gunshots. Québec agents had just intervened and there were battles by the wharf. They heard gunshots and fled – that was because of Uncle Arthur. He was too handicapped and old to reach the wharf so he went out with his gun. He then took three shots with his high calibre rifle. He was upset and aggressive. For such an old man to shoot with a 12-calibre, he must have wanted to participate a lot. The scene astonished people. His message was clear: if he could have, he would have joined the fight. For the group, that was an awakening (Adam, chapter 2, ref. 9; Sam, chapter 2, ref. 9; Mesnak, chapter 2, ref. 6; Raoul, chapter 2, ref. 18; Maxence, chapter 2. ref. 5).

Mathias

A well-known episode of the Salmon War involved the Québec agents seizing the community net, leaving with it, and then being intercepted on Highway 138 on their way back to their headquarters in Forestville. This is when an altercation occurred between Mathias and a police agent named Leblanc. The net was in the back of the agents' truck. Mathias arrived. He told Leblanc (the policeman) to get out of the truck, that he was in the wrong and that they just wanted to get their net and go back to their community. Mathias told them it was not their net and that they should not touch it since it was sacred. Leblanc, however, refused. He was in the back of the truck. His arms were crossed. Then, Mathias came closer. He told him that, if he thinks he is God, then he would see that he can't do this. He told him he should get out. The agent put his hand on his gun. Mathias took the agent by his feet and threw him on the ground. Leblanc could not touch anything. The people took the net and went back to the reserve. Mathias is known to be as strong as a bear. When he got upset during the war, he was uncontrollable. He got so offended and aggressive during the war that it was in the interests of the group to restrain his involvement. Mathias had an indigenous consciousness. He is a hunter and a fisherman. He is in love with the land. He is devoted to nature. He was one of the first to decide not to hide and to claim his rights (Ivan, chapter 2, ref. 10; Sam, chapter 2, ref. 3–5; Esther, chapter 2, ref. 7 and 14).

Jean-Paul

One of the worst episodes of the war was when hundreds of people from Les Escoumins invaded the wharf in order to repress the Indian revolt. At some point, the situation degenerated. The Euroquébécois, much greater in number, became hostile and aggressive. There was an Amerindian police officer at the wharf. He was not from Essipit but was sent by a regional Amerindian police organisation to protect the Essipiunnuat in case of any violence. His name was Jean-Paul Nuatshish. He was a huge but calm man, 6 feet 5 inches and 350–400 pounds. He was muscular, afraid of nothing, and laughed all the time. Jean-Paul came with his car into the middle of the hostile crowd. People in the crowd decided to push him and his car into the sea. At some point, there were a dozen people around his car. They started to push it and succeeded in tilting it. Then, he took hold of his gun. His windows were open. He told them he did not mind, since he would float back. Everything calmed down. The Essipiunnuat were about 30 people, and the Euroquébécois about 250. To witness Jean-Paul's stoicism in the face of danger made people feel stronger than all their opponents. It showed their assailants that they would not give up, even if they were tiny in number. It showed them that the Indians were not going to obey them at any price but would instead spread their net repeatedly, whatever they did (Napeo, chapter 2, ref. 2; Raoul, chapter 2, ref. 5 and 6).

Pierre

Pierre was a formidable warrior in various episodes of the Salmon War. He was ready to die at any time. When the police taunted the Indians on the reserve, Pierre took a big rock and was ready to knock down the agents. When provoked, Pierre could be dangerous, especially when he had stones in his hands. The police then saw that the Indians were taking a stand. During the Highway 138 episode, it was Pierre who stopped the truck. He stood alone, on the yellow line, with his 12-calibre gun. He stopped the truck and told them that the Indians were in their homeland and that nobody would ever prevent them from fishing salmon in the river. He told them that this land did not belong *only* to the 'whites', that Indians had rights and that they would defend them with their lives. Then he took a piece of rock. He hit the hood of the truck and the windows with it. There were four police agents in it. He asked them to get out of the truck. He called them 'chicken-hearted'. He told them that their reign of terror was over. He was shouting '*We are Indians!*' Later, during the main episode at the wharf, Pierre arrived with his gun. It was dramatic. He was ready to shoot them. Pierre's radicalism, his bursts of anger and his fierce assertions ignited the consciousness of many who witnessed them (Mesnak, chapter 2, ref. 6; Mestenapeo, chapter 2, ref. 7; Sam, chapter 2, ref. 2; Adam, chapter 2, ref. 1 and 4; Esther, chapter 2, ref. 7; Raoul, chapter 2, ref. 8).

Mestenapeo

Some people at the wharf saw a boat on the sea. Mestenapeo was in it. There was also another boat with police agents in it. They had weapons. They were trying to cut a community net. Mestenapeo launched at them with the boat he used to hunt seal. The agents cut everything and left with the net. Then, alone with his boat, Mestenapeo went after them. After a lot of tracking, agents pulled out their guns and pointed them at him. Mestenapeo threatened them with his fists. Even unarmed, Mestenapeo scared them. Mestenapeo's attitude, in this episode, captures a mentality very specific to those days (Esther, chapter 2, ref. 4; Maxence, chapter 2, ref. 3; Raoul, chapter 2, ref. 7 and 25; Ivan, chapter 2, ref. 6).

Paul

Paul Ross Jr, alias Ti-Paul, was the kind of man whom nothing could scare. When the crowd of Euroquébécois arrived at the wharf, he was hit violently by a man called the 'Kiss-à-Bonhomme'. His assailant was a man of 6 feet 4 inches and 400 pounds. Ti-Paul was beaten with a crowbar. He was bleeding profusely. He had received a blow from the crowbar right in his face. He got up on his feet. He told people around him not to worry, to let him go. He would get his revenge one day or another. Ti-Paul was very upset over the Salmon War. If everybody had Ti-Paul's views, the Salmon War would have been bigger and more violent (Sam, chapter 2, ref. 6; Raoul, chapter 2, ref. 5 and 7; Napeo, chapter 2, ref. 2; Esther, chapter 2, ref. 13).

Marcel

Marcel, Paul's second son, was such an interesting character. He was always the first on the frontline. He was full of confidence and sure of his people's capacity to win. When something happened, he followed through. Whether upset or not, he was a comic, laughing and swearing all the time. In the course of the war, he was as brave as seven men. On the sea, he charged at the police agents with his boat and the agents charged back at him. He was fearless. Marcel was seen facing up to three officers, who were armed with guns and machetes, on the sea. He was threatening them with oars, challenging them to come closer (Pierre, chapter 2, ref. 5; Napeo, chapter 2, ref. 2; Ivan, chapter 2, ref. 4).

Romeo

Uncle Romeo, alias Meo, did great things during the Salmon War. Known as a pious man and a pacifist, he was firmly committed to the defence of the community. Romeo, who was not expected to engage in battle, was one of the first to commit. He faced adversity bravely. He shouted loudly. When he realised that his son had been captured by agents, pulling him by the hair onto their boat, he wanted to jump into the sea to go and save him. Then Meo searched for weapons in his truck; but fortunately, his gun was not behind the seat of his car as usual. He was a quiet and good man but if he was panicking, he could be dangerous (Sam, chapter 2, ref. 8 and 9; Ernest, chapter 2, ref. 12; Ivan, chapter 2, ref. 1).

Ti-Nours

André Ross, alias Ti-Nours (Little Bear), greatly asserted his Innu identity during the war. As an orator, he yelled and roared. He shouted at police officers. He commanded them to stop, said that they were not allowed to confiscate the net. At one point, he was seen in front of Uncle Arthur's house, where the community drugstore is currently located. It was raining heavily. He was with people from the community. They were all outside, standing by the road. Then, there was Ti-Nours, shirtless in the middle of the road. He was waving his arms. He was speaking intensively and excitedly; he was speaking to his people. He was telling them they are Indians. He was telling them they have rights. He was encouraging them to seize their highest duties as indigenous people. He incited them with all his heart to revolt (Édouard, chapter 2, ref. 2; Adam, chapter 2, ref. 1).

Ivan

Ivan was grabbed by police officers. While on the sea, as he tried to protect the net, the police boat was trapped in the net. Ivan was then kidnapped by the officers, who took him further out to sea. Watching the episode from the shore, people began to panic. The officers were armed. Ivan had tried to drill their boat. People were worried. They knew Ivan had a rebellious temperament (Ernest, chapter 2, ref. 2; Pierre, chapter 2, ref. 1; Pierre, chapter 2, ref. 6).[27]

27 This episode is described at length in Ivan's self-portrait.

Neal

Neal was a teenager during the war. He was there when the Euroquébécois attacked his people at the wharf. Since he was small, he was asked to take the net and go down under the wharf in order to hide it. The Euroquébécois, who came to destroy the net, couldn't get hold of it. That was risky. It was dark under the wharf. The sea was rising. Neal went down through a small hole between the rocks, under the wharf. He hid the net and neither the authorities nor the population could seize it (Esther, chapter 2, ref 5; Tshak, chapter 2, ref. 7).

Transgressions: the model to avoid

The story of the Salmon War also contains some villains. The behaviour of certain people was not described admiringly but instead openly perceived as reprehensible. Images of transgressions contribute even more towards locating the sanctum of the group-self associated with the course of the war. As mentioned above, self-portraits have a propensity to be self-advantageous (and show only one side of the story). Other stories, while also stressing more the circumstantial modalities of social norms, let slip images about what not to do.[28] Three main forms of transgressive behaviour emerged: irrationality, hypocrisy and, predictably, non-commitment and its justifications based on a rhetoric of shame, cowardice and longing for material benefits.

Irrationality

Some actors and their behaviour were depicted as too uncompromising, too radical, too uncontrollable, too emotional, too violent or insubordinate to any authority, or not acting in accordance with 'how things work' (Sam, chapter 2, ref. 8). Some conduct was described as counterproductive to the strategic interests of the group. Excesses of violence, of temerity and spontaneous displays of emotion are all characteristics associated with folly and exorbitance, endangering order within the group. In some cases, unreasonableness also justifies modes of control and domination.

Mestenapeo, for example, remembers meeting some partisans who were 'seeing red, had rocks in their hands that needed to be taken away' (chapter 2, ref. 6). Ivan recalls, when being kidnapped by officials out at sea, that his brother had to control his father who was panicking and therefore putting them in jeopardy: 'He wanted to jump into the cold water to get me back on shore. He was repeatedly asking "where is my gun? Where is my gun?"' According to Ivan, it was better that his father could not find his gun since it would have

28 In order to restrict the already wide scope of this research, it was decided to exclude the Essipiunnuat representations of the Euroquébécois. They were abundant in the stories, and far more often negative than positive. However, this would be relevant for future research.

done 'more harm than good' (Ivan, chapter 2, ref. 7). One person recounts that he did not take any chances at that moment and removed the guns from some people whom he could not rely on, those who 'were *too angry*' (Raoul, chapter 2, ref. 13). *Irrationality* and its *control* are thus presented as rooted in emotional distress and resulting in cognitive deficiency and inadequate conduct in the very specific context of the uprising. Interestingly, irrationality is at times used as a rhetorical strategy to demonstrate the highest reason, and as a tool for the disqualification of opponents within the context of the internal power struggles between leaders.

Hypokrisis and the simulation of indigeneity

Hypokrisis is another character trait represented negatively in stories. Etymologically, the term means 'acting on the stage, to pretend' (Harper, n.d.). Although it has a positive connotation when used in reference to theatrical acting, the term is pejorative when qualifying the action of a person in political contexts or in situations of leadership. Furthermore, to be two-faced, and to hide personal interests while advocating the public good, was interpreted in ancient Greece as unsuitable for politicians (Morwood and Taylor, 2002). In contemporary usage, it generally refers to insincerity and is concerned with 'people as they pretend to be' (Higgleton and Seaton, 1995, p. 54).

This conception of *hypokrisis* largely echoes what is denounced as a transgression in the Essipiunnuat stories; it matches a fundamental criticism of some leaders. One leader is accused, for example, in the stories, of speaking publicly of indigenous rights when being entirely ignorant of them. He is blamed for dishonesty, of 'playing the Indian' but 'not truly feeling it' (Mestenapeo, chapter 2, ref. 8). If this attitude allows him to cosy up to the state (Riel, chapter 2, ref. 4), his over-simulation of sameness[29] with the dominant culture is double-edged. One will ultimately lean more towards compromise on inherent indigenous freedoms if one doesn't value them or know *nutshimit* (life in the forest); or be more likely to sell these rights and, more significantly, to allow the commodification of the ancestral domain and Innu symbols.

This two-faced trait among some of the leaders is even identified as the greatest source of division within the group after the war. The devaluation of honesty was acknowledged, by some narrators, as the moment 'when our problems started' (Mestenapeo, chapter 2, ref. 4 and 5). Those who were traditionalists felt cheated, betrayed and used by some of the leaders and their acolytes. They accused them of having negotiated behind their backs, of changing what had already been negotiated and of playing the sameness card in order to reach an agreement and gain other advantages (concentration of their power, or accumulation of money, for example). Ultimately, these acts

29 On this phenomenon, see Samson's excellent article (2001).

were justified on the basis that some people were too honest to do politics, even regarding *Innu tipenitamun* on *Assi* which some of the older folk perceive as non-negotiable and sacred (Mestenapeo, chapter 2, ref. 4 and 5).[30]

Non-commitment: spectres of shame and fear

Predictably, non-commitment is depicted negatively in inter-individual representations, and it tends to be more severely condemned when it is known to be motivated by feelings of shame about being an Indian and justified by a neoliberal rationale. This primary social emotion is perceived as a sign of disloyalty and it was not expressed at all in any of the self-portraits. Some, who appeared 'ashamed of having been shameful', refused to participate in the research. Thus, shame is hard to access; it is concealed and, as previous research has confirmed, often mixed with guilt and embarrassment (Tangney et al., 1996; Wurmser, 1987). However, it remains a central emotion experienced by a fraction of the members and a powerful determinant of silence and oblivion that deserves a closer look.

Some people, who are now proud of being Essipiunnuat, were allegedly associating with racists at the time and were not willing to be identified as Indian. Cowardice or fear at losing friends or their jobs, or of being ostracised by their in-laws goes some way to explaining their attitudes. Some were heavily conditioned to not feel proud of their community, while others simply did not feel Indian inside (Sam, chapter 2, ref. 9). The feeling of shame remains, therefore, one of the greatest challenges that the movement had to overcome.[31]

Capitalism, antimonies and the erosion of Innu norms

'Capitalism', defined as the request by some that the means of production should remain privately owned and for the purpose of profit through the mastering and exploitation of Assi (Earth) and living beings, including the Innu (humans), is another trait that stands out from the representations for its negativity. The case of a commercial angler from the community, who was allegedly pushing for the commercialisation of salmon fishing, was noticed (Raoul, chapter 2, ref. 19). He is described as being strongly influenced by his

30 This is currently a core contentious issue in the community in terms of the interpretation of the federal government's 'comprehensive land claim process' and the effect of modern treaties on indigenous relationships with the land. The debate concentrates on the issue of extinguishment and the existence of a certainty clause within these contemporary agreements that would legitimise the cession of inherent indigenous sovereignty to the Crown. The Petapen Treaty (Essipit, Mastheuiatsh, Nutakuan), based on the Agreement in Principle of 2003, allegedly involves the extinction of *Innu tipenitamun* and represents a form of surrender.

31 'Once, there was a band councillor with us ... I won't tell you the name ... She was practically ashamed at being with us. So she just went and sat on the other side of the room when we got in there to start the negotiations. And she was an advisor for the reserve ... So ... that tells you something' (Mestenapeo, ch. 2, ref. 8)

wife, a Euroquébécois, who, like other members of her family, loved money more than anything else. She would tell her husband things like, 'they should give you all the salmon, it is not for them to fish, and it is you that should fish everything' (Sam, chapter 2, ref. 4). For her, it would only be about money, and she is presented as completely uncaring about the group's struggle. The woman and her husband saw the movement as 'removing the bread from their mouths' and that it 'did not suit his interests'. They were therefore not communitarians and that was allegedly the main reason for their non-participation (Raoul, chapter 2, ref. 19).

This attitude is presented as being a threat to the whole movement because there was a risk no one would fight for it. Supporting commercial fishing on the basis of collective indigenous rights was presented as antinomian to the *indigenous-communitarian* philosophy promoted by the movement and operationalised through the fishing activities and the distribution of the salmon. A predominance of capitalist ideology, including ideas of individual property and the commercialisation of animals, would accordingly have meant the crash of the movement and its fall into oblivion (Sam, chapter 2, ref. 4 and 10). Irrationality, hypocrisy and non-commitment (when motivated by shame or capitalism) are therefore the main elements of transgression that emerge from people's accounts.

Past-selves in war: aesthetics of uprising

Representations of people in the stories suggest an aesthetic of revolt and ethical attributes specific to the course of the Salmon War. The event, presented as a drama, has its own icons, heroes and collective idols, as well as its 'villains' who inform on transgressive behaviours. In this sense, an aesthetic approach to the Salmon War offers 'other types of insight and engenders new understandings' (Bleiker, 2009, p. 6). The access to greater genuineness requires the recognition of the 'philosophic importance of art, which asserts itself against all attempts to rationalise it away' (Gadamer, 1989, p. xiii). What, then, can we exhume from these commonly remembered icons, myths or representations? What do they tell us about an Essipiunnuat past-self in war?

People often explicitly express their admiration for the individuals they describe. They seem to venerate specific attitudes, behaviours, qualities and ethics, as deployed in precise circumstances. These images are not only emotionally charged and widely remembered, but also substantively normative. Stories are invaluable sources of norms and laws.[32] What is expressed in these descriptions are mainly the superior ways of performing in a context of

32 For more information on indigenous legal traditions, the power of stories and their value as sources of laws, see Friedland (2018); Borrows (2016); Episkenew (2009); Friedland and Napoleon (2016a), Friedland and Napoleon (2016b); McAdam (2015).

insurrection. Each in their manner – the people, their actions and contexts depicted – communicates crucial aspects of the group aesthetics and past-self in war.

Old Arthur's behaviour, for example, was frequently reported. Through his way of being, this elderly and disabled man seemed to capture, in people's memories, the whole condition of the group. Handicapped, vulnerable and worn by history and time, he demonstrated his indignation authoritatively by firing his weapon. He laid bare that power in circumstances where everything seemed finished and impossible.

Mestenapeo's recklessness on the sea, his direct actions and violent confrontation with the state officers evoke the group's unceded sovereignty and the illegitimacy of the provincial authority and laws over the Innu. His actions also evoke the certainty, inherited from generation to generation, that the Innu want their rights but know they need to be actively defended. The indignation of Matthias is a reminder that dignity exists; his uncontrollable rage signified that the dishonouring of Essipiunnuat sense of self would meet with wrath, but also total resistance. Pierre's fierce revolt expresses a sense of urgency and of being profoundly threatened by state intervention and racism, as well as the imperative to halt these aggressions. He symbolised the '*Indian*' who cannot be dominated, the uncontrollable one who will always prefer death to the absence of freedom. Jean-Paul reminds the group that they are part of a wider and strong people. If these groups have remained stoic, despite historical attempts at destabilisation, there is yet tremendous strength hidden beneath the apparent calm; the bear is still alive. Paul's situation, for his part, captures the violence of external aggression, the bloody repression following the assertion of indigeneity. He embodies the traumas of history but also a collective capacity for resilience. This shows that memory of humiliation, in spite of silence, can explain a profound longing for revenge over time.

Marcel embodies the hunter-warrior, the autonomous actor with an unfailing optimism in the most dramatic situations, who has a persistent *joie de vivre* that allows the warrior to keep his head above water and protects him from the temptations of fatalism. Young Ivan seems to embody pure rebellion, a radical opposition to authority and stubbornness in defending the collective at the risk of one's life. Romeo reminds the group to not be fooled by the appearance of the peaceful Indian. He teaches about not underestimating people's sentiments with regard to their rights and their willingness to defend them, especially when children are at risk. The spontaneity of Ti-Nours personifies the emergence of the collective, the uninhibited, irrepressible and integral assertion of indigeneity against all who seek its domination, repression, or association with shame and oblivion. Neal personifies how the future of the group and its integral defence rests on the commitment of the youth, on their respect for the Elders and a willingness to direct their actions in accordance with the most pressing needs of the group.

On the other side, in the recollections of the drama of war, transgressions appear to play the role of tricksters, of ways not to be. They should not be imitated but lessons should be learned from them. Irrational behaviours tend to be used by those in situations of power to justify modes of control. Hypocrisy for short-term gain tends to delegitimise power and leadership in the long run. Non-commitment is openly condemned, in particular when motivated not only by non-identification with the group and the shame of indigeneity but also by material accumulation. The representations of transgressive characters and behaviours, in interactions with situations and circumstances, clearly reveal the contours of a past-self associated with the course of war as well as the complex and less accessible determinants of oblivion.

These common scripts and judgements are highly normative since they reveal in the end intrinsic schemes of rationality, values and choices. They demonstrate internal modes of legitimating control over rationalism, 'true' Innu principles, and acceptable and unacceptable behaviours and their justification. The aesthetics of uprising is therefore characterised by a concern with demonstrating and articulating the revolt as rational, authentic, self-referential and universal. Such stories are inherently subversive; they offer testimony of a historical consciousness and an acute awareness of past wounds as well as exalting absolute rebelliousness against any forms of domination that can, when reactivated, help to formulate radical evaluations and critiques in the present.

Images of the group: gazing at ourselves

Essipiunnuat stories contain images and representations of the group as a whole, including in-group relationships, which contribute to illuminating other aspects of a collective past-self associated with the unfolding of the Salmon War. Images of society at a certain time can provide information about the social consciousness of individuals and commonly held worldviews. The collective self is mainly composed of group membership and implies contrasts between the group to which one belongs, that is, the in-group, and relevant out-groups. Indeed, a collective self would mainly be associated with the motive of protecting or enhancing the in-group; its priority over individual or interpersonal identities is very significant since it can 'alter spontaneous judgements of similarity and self-descriptions' (Brewer and Gardner, 1996). An inquiry into Essipiunnuat past-self in war requires a closer look at in-group/out-group differentiation as well as in-group members' bonds derived from common identification with the group (Sedikides and Brewer, 2001).

Three main elements surface in representations of the collective. The first concerns the existence of an in-group power dependent on the quality of the links maintained between members. The second pertains to the continuation of an authentic bond between the Essipiunnuat and other indigenous groups, resulting in it being characterised by indigeneity. A third image of the group associates the course of war with an intensification of inner conflict and, running parallel to the struggles with outsiders, an internal struggle for dignity within the group itself against internalised racism in particular.

All our relations: the power of solidarity

A recurring image of the group in war pertains to its inner power. This potency is represented as conditional on being bound to each other in some way. Such linkages and the power generated are remembered with a certain fondness and are widely referenced. It corresponds mainly to a spirit of camaraderie interposing itself into relationships, in diverse circumstances during the war, generating complementarity and producing a feeling of power. These emotions were particularly strong, for example, when people were meeting sporadically at campfires at all hours of the day and night, while taking it in turns to watch or conduct their vigil, or were involved in a battle (Tshak, chapter 2, ref. 5).

Interrelationships characterised by camaraderie in the war are described as secreting a synergy, a contagion that resulted in feelings of empowerment, as if a force was impregnating them all at once, making their individual wills stronger. This phenomenon was compared to a movement or a walk starting, continuing and not stopping (Adam, chapter 2, ref. 4). This cooperation was also observed among in-group categories. Women increasingly supported their husbands (Esther, chapter 2, ref. 12), the youngest intensified their support for the oldest (Ernest, chapter 2, ref. 8; Ivan, chapter 2, ref. 8; Adam, chapter 2, ref. 1), and the very old showed their support for the commanders by telling them ancient stories (Tshak, chapter 2, ref. 7).

The intensification of in-group cooperation in its diverse manifestations is associated with the *communitarisation* of the movement, or the increased mobilisation of members around the *communitarian-indigenist* principle.[33] This is the moment of the supposed realisation of the power of a collective principle to gather everyone around its defence. This is when really strong ties between individuals were generated, at the same time as a united community movement (Mesnak, chapter 2, ref. 3). The endurance of the social ties produced would therefore be the central element of micro-group strength: 'The density of the ties exceeds the strength of number. A tiny group can generate a terrific force. We then saw that it is possible for a dwarf to be really ready to fight to defeat a giant' (Raoul, chapter 2, ref. 1).

33 As will be shown in the next chapter, this corresponds to collective self-objectification.

People recall being caught up in the movement and the exceptional unity of wills that was generated (Adam, chapter 2. ref. 3; Mathias, personal communication; Ernest, chapter 2, ref. 9). This concord was reportedly translated into a generalised readiness to fight for the objectives of the movement and a willingness for sacrifice (Ivan, chapter 2, ref. 5; Mesnak, chapter 2, ref. 3). A revealing analogy was proposed between the net and the group's solidarity as the war developed; people were clinging to the net to prevent its seizure, and its symbolism also helped to keep people together (Adam, chapter 2, ref. 8).

From entrenched indigeneity to simulacrum

The course of the war is often related to a collective reconnection with cultural memory and conceptions, and the moment of identity renewal.[34] In fact, the evolution of events is linked to the reintegration of the Essipiunnuat within the scope of indigenous cultural parameters. The group is predominantly represented as Indian, Montagnais or Innu, and its actions are depicted within the wider framework of a combat embracing the indigenous cause as a whole.

The group was supposedly leading a global fight (Mestenapeo, chapter 2, ref. 7). The movement and its actions are explicitly defined as an expression of an indigenist philosophy. The receptivity of other indigenous groups to their actions, and their engagement with the discourse about communitarian principles and collective indigenous rights, was perceived as a validation of their own indigeneity. To receive increased external support from other First Peoples as well as international human rights organisations, and all the Innu chiefs, boosted the group's sense of belonging to, and its unity with, a wider indigenous grouping (Mesnak, chapter 2, ref. 4).

Eventually, the community came to the forefront of all these conflicts, brought together not just because of the salmon issue but also because of the need to affirm and defend matters around indigenous sovereignty and rights (Mesnak, chapter 2, ref. 5). This led to other indigenous groups and their representatives becoming involved in direct action in Essipit. The primary individuals taking part were greatly moved and remember this activity vividly. On one occasion, a walk took place that included people from outside the community, and which moved down to the wharf (see figure 10). People from the CAM, and outsiders from other reserves were among the supporters (Esther, chapter 2, ref. 9). Pessamit, a neighbouring Innu community, erected a barricade to block the only road that gave access to the region. Interestingly, descriptions of these episodes of inter-group solidarity contain a 'we' that is inclusive of all Innu and often of all indigenous peoples. The group agency

34 This will be analysed at greater length in the next chapter on the transformations associated with the Salmon War.

in war is therefore interpreted, overall, as a defence of 'all that it means to be indigenous' (Raoul, chapter 2, ref. 6).

The notion of 'us' took on a new internal dimension. Inter-group solidarity and contacts, among the Innu and other First Peoples, reinstated the value of referring to indigenous conceptions under the group self. It therefore visibly produced new self-definitions and reinterpretations of what it meant to be Essipiunnuat. People realised, for example, that to have the heart of a warrior, or a strong sense of team spirit, of one for all and all for one, are distinct aspects of their indigeneity (Raoul, chapter 2, ref. 21; Karl, chapter 2, ref. 4). Overall, the group agency is widely depicted in its outward orientation and its transcontinental resistance to exogenous imperial hostilities.

Inner struggles: the spectres of psychological colonialism

Stories do also report, however, internal division and tensions. Images of the group as united, unanimous and solid in war coexist with representations of it as deeply divided, internally fragmented and weakened by internal feuds. The group is presented as internally unbalanced by the war (Mestenapeo, chapter 2, ref. 6).

The beginning of the war is noticeably coupled with the irruption of the internal fragmentations inherent in collective action. As Sam says, 'you can't make an omelette without breaking eggs' (Sam, chapter 2, ref. 4). The assertion of indigeneity and the authority this generated was achieved in the face of great opposition. Within the group, for example, some were opposed to the communitarian net. An ideological conflict is recalled, polarised between communitarian-indigenist and capitalist ideologies, but also along intergenerational lines; others just stayed away from such disagreements. Commanders, warriors and supporters all remember relatives pressuring them to disengage from the movement.

In addition to the for and against divisions, a great in-group disagreement recalled by interviewees concerns the existence of an unbridgeable schism between leaders over the understanding of 'being Innu'. This particular phenomenon is even understood to be the origin of significant quarrels that surfaced years later in an internal war (Mestenapeo, chapter 2, ref. 2, 3–7).[35] It was also represented as an intergenerational conflict between the 'old radicals' and the more 'rational' and 'educated' youth, who were keener to negotiate an agreement with the state and to '[use] people' (Sam, chapter 2, ref. 2).

The Salmon War often took the form of a racial confrontation. It generated noticeable division over racial lines between 'Indians' and 'whites'. Racism against Indians was everywhere, even within the community itself. The group

35 This refers to a conflict that occurred in the early 1990s which will be covered in the final chapter.

is thus depicted as racially divided, a demarcation recalled as the most painful in-group fragmentation (Mestenapeo, chapter 2, ref. 5). The Essipiunnuat are also portrayed as not all having the same aims; some were genuinely engaged in preserving Essipiunnuat dignity as indigenous, while others were desperately eager to gain power by any possible means, including through identifying more as Euroquébécois at times than Innu. In this sense, a central image of the group as the war progressed is its struggle with itself not to reproduce colonial representations and forms of domination, thereby distancing itself from Innu values in order to please external actors and exogenous laws, and losing its dignity (Mestenapeo, chapter 2, ref. 4 and 7).

Conclusion

This examination of the Essipiunnuat's past-self as associated with the course of the war attempted to access rich stories, a sense of who those taking part believed they were at that time, and to arrive at an overall picture of the group's self-conception at that time. This was achieved through studying elements of self-representation as contained in the self-portraits and in inter-individual depictions, as well as through images of their group.

The study of self-portraits suggests a past-self characterised by a radical commitment to and assertion of indigeneity, in resistance to the historical and actualised forces seeking its complete destruction. A central emergent norm specific to the context of the war is thus the commitment to micro-group self-defence. Yet, it was also made clear that investments in indigenous self-consciousness, uprising and assertion come, almost inevitably, with severe retributions. The self-portraits ultimately help to demonstrate that committing to defend a distinctive Essipiunnuat identity had tragic consequences.

The analysis of inter-individual depictions proposes the existence of an aesthetic of uprising based on shared memories and articulated around the theme of heroism. Individuals in the war are portrayed as if in a drama, with its heroes and villains. This aesthetic communicates commonly remembered actors who embody, each in their own way, normative features presented as imperative to collective resilience. It also secretes an ethic of life and action, enrolled in a specific group ontology and rooted in an epistemology venerating immanence, the multilateral relationships between humans and all forms of life, as well as overcoming individuality and materiality in the context of revolt.

The examination of the main images of the group in the stories discovered collective heroism coupled with trans-indigenist identification within the wider drama of First People's experiences of colonialism on Turtle Island. The idea emerged that an integral and collective commitment to asserting indigeneity, and resisting attempts to invalidate inherent ancestral sovereignty (to counter genocide), especially among the Essipiunnuat, depends almost entirely on having the inner strength to fight hostile forces. Above all, in their view, survival seems to rely only on the group itself and on its members and the quality and consistency of the ties between them. Representations of the collective also voice a warning about power struggles and an appetite for authority among certain individuals inclined to duplicity, which could erode the group's dignity and freedom in the long run.

Finally, these elements combined are vital facets of the Essipiunnuat past-self during the Salmon War. The tragedy of this tiny micro-group in the war is highlighted by the very circumstances of its commitment. To commit and to resist were, in themselves, heroic for such a small entity. However, to be propelled to the forefront of a wider indigenous struggle affected the group in diverse ways. This past-self also contains the consciousness that colonialism, with its policies of divide and conquer, of extermination and institutionalised hatred, and its tragic effects, can only be vanquished by unity and the willingness of the oppressed, and their ability to assume their whole agency. Nobody else can help. Nobody will propel or steer their canoe for them.

The context of the war and its unfolding is essential if we are to explain why members were expected to give so much to it. Some were even willing to sacrifice their lives for the group. Others were ashamed to be identified as Indian or were more concerned with protecting their own income. We should not minimise the mimetic among the Essipiunnuat of Québec nationalist schemes, mythologies and conception of sovereignty, and the reproduction of its colonial imaginary within the group. The past-self we are trying to identify is not only tragic-heroic; it is also confused and awkward. A deep malaise reverberates through it; perhaps the restless demons of what is now called *America*. Yet, for the Essipiunnuat, this past-self in war echoes its greatest foe, the enemy within that nurtures shame and auto-genocidal tendencies, that identifies indigeneity as being a degenerated form of humanity, as an object and a simulacrum, and professes oblivion; the result of internal policies of erasure, purification and 'whitening' that have marked some group members within their families, sometimes from childhood and to varying degrees.

Interestingly, this tragic yet heroic past-self represents the most valued and normative trait of the Innu oral tradition (shared by the wider Algonquian family) that is several thousand years old, exemplified by the epic story of Tshakapesh. The Essipiunnuat past-self associated with the course of the war therefore remains highly normative and correlated to Innu referents despite being silenced, denied or ignored. A core element remains the knowledge that the decision not to forget, but rather to rebel, signifies being transformed, but also haunted, by what was buried and believed to be forgotten.

4. Stories on the transformative experience of war: from self-empowerment to a metaphysics of domination

The 20 interviewees associate their experience of the Salmon War with a range of outcomes, predominantly personal and collective self-transformations. There is a common assumption that the group emerged transformed from the episode. This chapter investigates the main theme of change in autobiographical memories as a result of participating in the uprising, and exposes the main figures and schemes of these stories of self-transformation.

The topics of collective action and uprising and their multifaceted and transformative effects have received growing attention in recent times, with revolt being identified as an accelerating global phenomenon. The study of uprisings provides fresh insights into the emergence of new social dynamics, movements, subjectivities, emerging rationalities, and the transformation of normative orders (Bertho, 2009; Drury and Reicher, 2000; Dupuis-Déri, 2016). Yet, the investigation of this intricate phenomenon, closely linked to the present, requires some new approaches and an ability to constantly renew our gaze.

Not surprisingly, the established order, including in micro-groups, tends to deny such occurrences, which threatens to undermine the foundations of their legitimacy. This is even truer for investigations of past revolts, stories about which have the normative power to modify the parameters for evaluating the current social order and generate historical reinterpretations, even decades after their occurrence.

The study of revolt thus requires a capacity for distancing oneself from actual categorisation and concepts, and a revalorisation of phenomenological approaches, embracing multidimentionality (Hamldi, 2019). It demands an epistemology that breaks with established orders to document episodes of their contestation. For investigators, it adds another challenge on top of the multiple forces producing oblivion. In fact, the investigation of uprisings should thereby comprise a greater consideration for their potentiality as a foundation, the subjective discontinuity they propose, and the alternative *episteme* it might suggest (Bertho 2009; Della Porta and Diani, 2006; Drury et al., 2005; Drury et al., 2003).

Involvement in collective action (such as protests, uprisings and riots) generates profound redefinitions of the boundaries of collective selfhood. Such experiences are coupled with radical changes in social identity, novel sets of social relations and the emergence of fresh social identities, as well as the actualisation of old ones and their celebration (Drury et al., 2000). Hence, the phenomenon of cultural re-emergence among marginalised groups can be significantly intensified in the context of political and cultural assertion (Chew, 2007).

Reemergence consists broadly of the return of the repressed normative order and the shared standards contained in cultural memory (Assmann, 2006). Uprising and revolt are thus associated with attempts to overthrow the related normative order, which is imposed and internalised. Identity politics must be considered in the light of a highly political, cultural fragmentation and the larger processes of hegemonic decline. That decline directly fosters the emergence of the dynamics of re-identification and carriers of a new discourse (Friedman, 2004).

New cultural forms were clearly generated out of the specific sociohistorical context of the Salmon War. Local subjectivities and epistemic mutations are directly linked in stories to wider global processes. In practice, the decline of external hegemony and definitions seems to be correlated with people divesting themselves from self-negating values and the emergence of new spaces for producing their own self-definitions (Black, 2007). Revolt as a concretisation of agency implies a rich form of self-design and symbolic mutations.

The experience of uprising has been associated with the phenomenon of collective self-objectivism (CSO), reinforcement and empowerment (Drury and Winter, 2003). The actualisation of people's social identity is central to the experience of rebellion against illegitimate orders, practices and systems. In research, this form of categorical rejection, and the parallel quest for reversibility, is inseparable from the salience of identity politics. It is also known that normative order remains one of the most powerful determinants for human activity (Turner and Killian, 1987, p. 37),[1] attitudes and actions. Also, technologies of social control can be expected to *change* according to the alteration of social standards. The experience of uprising, and its related transformations, is coupled with the emergence of new modes of social control and the production of new self-representations (Marger, 2009): essentialisation and its underlying tyrannies that often reappear and serve to legitimise monocratic behaviours and justify the internal erasure of dissidence.

The Essipiunnuat's experiences of the Salmon War in relation to their self-transformative dimensions are articulated around four main themes. The first concerns the remodelling of people's relational system, mainly comprising the breakdown and re-forming of relationships, associated with

1 According to Turner and Killian, normative orders include 'learned guidelines for socially approved ways of attaining these values, as well as rules for coordinating their everyday behaviour with that of other people'. These norms also include 'formal law and regulations, and informal customs, some with moral implications and others which might be called rules of convenience'.

a dynamic of reidentification and a switch of group reference. A second pertains to alterations in people's self-conceptions and group self-identity, if not epistemic mutations presenting the Salmon War as a founding event for a new incarnation of the group. Thirdly, people noticed a phenomenon relating to collective self-empowerment; the reinforcement of their social identity is seen as a main outcome of their participation. Lastly, in-group re-ordering and the establishment of a new regime are voiced in the narrations as the central schemes. Although highly controversial, the self-transformation undoubtedly led to nihilistic undercurrents, forms of tyranny and the internal reproduction of psychological colonialism. This is inseparable, in stories, from the interiority of new post-war dominant actors.

Ways of relating: relational system remodelling

Many aspects of the relationships between those involved were significantly impacted upon by the experience of the war. In this book, the redefinition of a 'collective self' is frequently highlighted as a major outcome of the uprising, associated with a double dynamic of the breakdown of relationships and the creation or reactivation of others. These changes apparently resulted in a double dynamic of dis-identification and re-identification in groups of reference. Ultimately, people notice a significant remodelling of their relational system, which would radically affect their social identity and the ways in which they related to Innu heritage.

Splintering

People link their experience of the war with breaks in relations and the emergence of new lines of demarcation. Their expressions of grief and forms of trauma correlate with the breaking down of their relationships and loom large in their stories.[2] These multi-levelled break-downs in relationships (with parents, friends, in-laws and so on) are often coupled with suffering as well as a desire to forget the whole event.

Following the war, relationships with the local populations and townships were very bitter. Those taking part report people no longer speaking to each other and animosity becoming the norm (Ernest, chapter 2, ref. 6). They remember their great disappointment at experiencing these drastic regressions in human relations. Connections perceived before the war as authentic friendships were suddenly transformed into enmity, distrust and perceptions of hypocrisy (Adam, chapter 2, ref. 4).

The loss of childhood friends is recalled as sad, if not painful. Uncertainty about the surrounding township population in general emerged, and hovered

2 This phenomenon is explained in Scheff (1988), p. 97.

over all levels of interaction between Essipiunnuat and Euroquébécois (Ernest, chapter 2, ref. 6). The severance from the friends of early childhood is said to have produced the deepest wounds of all (Tshak, chapter 3, ref. 3), and left the Essipiunnuat feeling miserable and rejected (Édouard, chapter 3, ref. 2). Disruptions in intergroup relationships were experienced even by young children and teenagers; some of the youngest individuals remember with great emotion losing all their out-group friends (Karl, chapter 3, ref. 1). For example, Napeo recalls catching sight of his good friends and their fathers among the hostile crowd. Their relations were never the same again:

> The link was cut for many years. After the war, they began calling us 'piggish savages'. We did not have friends anymore. We were only holding our small gang from the reserve together. We did not have friends in Les Escoumins. We still had friends in other villages. Yet, even with the people of Les Bergeronnes, Tadoussac and Sacré-Coeur, especially in the latter, our relations cooled. They belittled us. (chapter 3, ref. 3)

Relationships with in-laws were also affected. Stories reveal major wounds relating to out-group brothers-in-law who could not accept having a 'savage' in their family (Tshak, chapter 3, ref. 3). In some cases, nervous tension existed in families for decades after the war. For some, such anxiety continues to exist even to this day. At the time, many individuals did not speak to one another, while some were forced to make familial visits when others were not present. The discomfort endured, since no-one was able to forget; people were always aware of the effects of the Salmon War on their relationships (Tshak, chapter 3, ref. 3).

Divisions were also noticed within the group. These mainly concerned splits among the Essipiunnuat from those cooperating with people they considered to be 'racist'. As several interviewees recall, the war allowed Essipiunnuat to see the 'true faces' of their own people, as well as to identify those who were against their own group. Individuals fell into this category primarily because they were overly friendly with those who were viewed as racist, or because they were only considering the issue in terms of monetary gain. As has been mentioned, it was more painful to fight 'Indian' traitors than 'white' enemies. In the end, the grief experienced in the war was accompanied by the appearance of new truths about their own community (Ernest, chapter 3, ref. 5).

The experience also translated into changes pertaining to the Essipiunnuat's occupation of space. The most sociable in the group remember with sadness their exclusion from Euroquébécois social gatherings, and being prevented from going to places they used to frequent. After the war, they would have liked to do certain things but weren't able to. Instead of mingling, people felt uncomfortable and preferred to stay away (Édouard, chapter 3, ref. 3). Some young adults used to go out to bars regularly. However, after the war they stopped going to the Les Escoumins beer house, for example, and either went to other bars, or preferred to consume their alcohol at home. This lasted for many years, and some even retain this attitude today (Karl, chapter 3, ref. 5).

The impact of the Salmon War is therefore associated with a long-lasting severing of relations, with both in-group and out-group ramifications. The divisions did not spare friendships or family lines. Community members witnessed the development of new ties, predominately connected to those that were either 'for or against us'. These relationship-break were overwhelmingly observed along racial lines. Those who were racist were clearly identified and classified in a fixed category. It was now increasingly considered impractical to eliminate racism from people who defined themselves as racist. Self-defined 'whites' were henceforth synonymous with being anti-Indian, and as completely ignorant of, or at the very least, impervious to, Indigenous stories and the human condition (Raoul, chapter 3, ref. 5–8).

For this fringe of hardcore Euroquébécois 'white' supremacists, racism towards the Indians was deeply rooted, if not anchored permanently, so that no matter what an Indian did they despised him or her regardless once they had been identified as Indian (Édouard, chapter 3, ref. 3). It was as if these individuals had a wall in their heart; they had no respect for any Indian. And ultimately, the Essipiunnuat firmly believed that the racist's mind could not be changed through discussion (Tshak, chapter 3, ref. 2).

Therefore, the Essipiunnuat felt that the rise of anti-Indian racism rejected their existence as humans, and was coupled with grief and pain. The white–Indian recategorisation was internally translated into an inner group polarisation of being for or against. Loyalty to the group became an imperative for the maintenance of relations. The racial divide failed to spare any social component, affecting even the smallest of family units and close, old friendships. If a generalised dynamic of relationships splintering along racial lines was observed, this movement of relocation also followed in tandem with elements of solidification and diverse reconnections. As Pierre articulates, 'we did not only make enemies in the Salmon War, we also made a lot of friends' (chapter 3, ref. 5).

Associations and solidarities

New social associations and connections were reported. Experiencing the war is said to have produced, or reestablished, strong ties between individuals, families, generations and other groups, resulting in various forms of in-group complicity. Such new links, framed by the specific sociohistorical context of the war and still in place to the present day, suggest the existence of a generational unit (Karl, chapter 3, ref. 5). The Salmon War is said to have soldered together the group (Sam, chapter 3, ref. 8). It produced a rearrangement of social ties, resulting in unity or consistency, 'to be reactivated when required' (Mesnak, chapter 3, ref. 12).

This phenomenon of solidification was primarily felt and observed within and between in-group families. These relationships were the most profoundly impacted by the experience of the war. This perception of change is more comprehensible when it is contextualised. Pre-war Essipit had been plagued with old in-family and inter-family feuds. As Tshak explains, families lived next to each other who had not met for decades. For example, a brother did not speak to his brother; a sister did not speak to her sister. The father told his children not to visit some neighbouring cousins and that they would be severely punished if they did so. This resulted in children not socialising with one another, thereby leading to feelings of hatred and extreme disassociation over several decades (Tshak, chapter 3, ref. 5).

Inter-familial hostilities were allegedly being actively transmitted from generation to generation. These antagonisms had resulted in several Essipiunnuat, often neighbours and always with familial ties, not knowing each other at all. Members of the community – all related to each other in one way or another – were acutely aware of this situation. Yet, even if they knew of the existence of these deep-rooted conflicts, most members of the group did not know the reasons behind the silences (Tshak, chapter 3, ref. 5).

The Salmon War drastically transformed these circumstances, and it is said that it brought families closer together. Individuals who had never talked before were suddenly seen chatting and laughing together. Members of the community observed their own kin putting aside their issues, as if they had forgotten their entrenched conflicts. They seemed more interested in what was coming than in what was behind them. This observable fact had a tremendous in-group impact as it touched on a long-lasting fissure within this tiny group. These moments of reconciliation between families are remembered fondly:

> We started to chat. We had fun. We got to know each other. We loved it because we discovered relations that existed but that we didn't see. We discerned acquaintances that we hadn't known about, links that we hadn't felt. And then the ties developed. This was clearly generated by the Salmon War. It reconnected ties that had been severed decades before for the great-grandfather, the grandfather, the father, or whoever it was (Tshak, chapter 3, ref. 5).

The reunion and strengthening of links with other First Peoples, particularly other Innu, were also mentioned as a core outcome of the experience of the war. The circumstances of war it seems allowed people to experience feelings of proximity to other indigenous groups and the solidifying of links to these significant out-groups.

Indigenous rights were in the same state on all the rivers located on Innu ancestral domain, although they had different configurations.[3] Thus, the Essipiunnuat uprising resonated immensely for all indigenous groups; other out-groups perceived them thereafter as defenders of indigenous principles. This had a tremendous impact, as they obtained protection from all Innu while isolated and distressed. The direct support of each Innu chief, as well as those from various Anicinabe and Atikamekw groups, created a perpetuation of opportunities for contacts, visits and meetings, and the development of common views between groups. The Essipiunnuat had, then, increased opportunities to communicate with other Innu and they experienced new feelings of closeness. They received validation for their acts of resistance, which generated an observable solidarity among these entities. From this point onwards, the groups were increasingly united in defence of their freedoms as First Peoples. A positive outcome of the experience of the war for the Essipiunnuat was thus the reconfiguration of their relations with other indigenous out-groups (Mesnak, chapter 3, ref. 4).

The reconciliation of families within the group and the reconnection with indigenous out-groups were two of the most salient elements of solidarity associated with people's experience of the war. These perceptions of remarkable and memorable change can be traced back to pre-war conditions, justly characterised by in-groups and inter-familial gaps, as well as to the rising detachment from other indigenous out-groups in the period following World War Two.

Self-concept alterations: mutations and metamorphosis

People also associate their experience of the war with significant alterations to their self-perceptions and conceptions. The central point of these changes is noticeably the switch in reference group and an increase in self-identification as indigenous. This was nurtured by participating in the movement and is seen as a phenomenon that had remarkable consequences.

As involvement in collective action generally has a profound impact on self-identity (Drury and Reicher, 1999; 2000; Drury et al., 2003), metamorphoses in the self pertaining to perceptions, definitions, knowledge and value, are all potentially to be expected. People recall having experienced different types of epistemic and axiological mutations, as well as ontological changes, in their ways of being, acting and self-perceiving.

Above all, they perceive the labour of novel subjectivities inside themselves. Their perceptions of alterations and the metamorphosis of self-identity are

3 See 'Entrevue avec Pierre Lepage' (2010).

apparently inseparable from their experiences of the war. The descriptions and explanations pertaining to self-transformation stories are articulated around three elements, as outlined in the following sections, which all depict the Salmon War as a catalyst.

Sui nullius, or the burden of reciting one's own absence: war and social ontology

The first element pertains to the contextualisation of these changes, mainly narrations of the apparent non-existence of the group prior to the war. A dominant feature of these descriptions of the pre-war milieu concerns the presentation of the originality and indigeneity of the Essipiunnuat as dead and buried, corresponding to a collective state of absence; of *sui nullius*. What is known is that narrators tend to portray the reserve back then as a discrete district of Les Escoumins township, with no visible differences or distinctive traits between the two entities' representations of the group.

Knowledge of distinctiveness is, however, attributed to some individuals, such as a handful of older people who were initiated into their Innu heritage through indigenous militants, intergenerational contacts and experiences of *nutshimit* (living in the forest, on the land). Indeed, only this minority was allegedly informed of past inter-group conflict as well as of inter-group demarcations. Interestingly, interviewees generally assumed, and reproduced, the unified postulation that there was nothing on the reserve, as it was devoid of meaning before the war. The question of where this perception came from naturally arose. One hypothesis which could be formulated at this stage is that this unified dimension has to do with a certain rewriting and with the production of a new in-group master narrative generated by those in a situation of power who had monopolised public speech. It will be further explored how a metaphysics of domination may have arisen from the idea of an absence of self or *sui nullius*. This would have resulted in erasure of previous markers of Innu referents in order to valorise an entirely new self, structured in accordance with a chronology of specific actors' deeds, instead of a rebirth in continuity with the previous generations and ancient cultural memory.

Generational inventory of experience and perception

The assertion is also made that there were no differences, or only minor ones, between the two groups living in the area before the war. For the youngest in particular, and especially for those who had been less immersed in the group for various reasons, including familial ones, the people of Essipit and Les Escoumins not only did everything together but were also alike in their manners and ways of being (Adam, chapter 3, ref. 1–6). This led one person to wonder when interviewed whether he was in fact Innu or indigenous before the war:

> Was I Indian before the war? I did not even ask this question. In fact, I did not know. I was young and innocent. I worked for the reserve during the summertime. I was in charge of the newly built community centre. That was it. I have no memory before the war of my identity (Adam, chapter 3, ref. 3 and 8).

Perceptions of pre-war differences and of any distinct Essipiunnuat entity tend to increase according to how old individuals were at the time of the war. This was especially salient among people older than 30, as inter-group distinctions were already known. And yet, they remained silent. Their indigeneity was largely associated with their experiences at school and with racism, which resulted in their fear of asserting an 'Indian identity'. Attempts to hide this distinctiveness identity would be strongly remembered by all (Riel, chapter 3, ref. 5).

During the time of the war, those already in their 50s had previously experienced an epoch when any identification as Indian was buried. As with the older generation, such individuals lived in a time when the psychology consisted of hiding their indigeneity in order to avoid problems with other people and to prevent their offspring from being penalised. Silencing and dissimulating their Indian self was not only the norm but also a means of survival. According to their interpretation, to talk of being Indian used to signify the risk of being harmed or even killed, and this was an overwhelming part of their collective memory (Pishimnapeo, chapter 3, ref. 1). Thus, despite the overall richness of the Elders' inventory of experience and cultural memory, the notion of silencing indigeneity was a predominant part of their heritage due to a variety of sociohistorical circumstances. Under colonial rule, the Essipiunnuat have been collectively conditioned to not be Indian.

As a result, on the eve of the Salmon War, most Essipiunnuat simply hid their indigeneity, or were not even aware of it, and lacked awareness of the group to which they felt they belonged. Yet the sense of novelty they experienced depended greatly on their experiences and access to collective memory. For the younger generation, this perception of change was particularly acute, as many had never left Essipit and had experienced little, if any, social interaction with people from other indigenous groups (Sam, chapter 3, ref. 3).

Stories suggest that if some people were still self-defining as Indians on the eve of war, a certain number of Essipiunnuat appeared to have forsaken Innu referentiality in relation to themselves and the collective self. They had absorbed many aspects of Euroquébécois conceptions, including their colonial selective memory. Many probably self-identified as Euroquébécois and tended to look down on Innu identification and its referents. In this context, the hypothesis could be made that even those who knew the differences and elements of Essipiunnuat self identity might have been convinced of its fatal degeneration when others increasingly absorbed the idea that the group had no history. These elements should not be minimised as determinants of silence about war and cultural oblivion. The investigation starts then to sense the shadows of oblivion that loom large in the cultural condition of the pre-war generations. Produced by centuries of oppression, this oblivion made the Essipiunnuat particularly vulnerable to the idea of their non-existence, reinforced by the absorption of the Québec imaginary and colonial fictions as well as deep inner traumas. Were these fragilities going to be used for domination by the new leaders of the group and, if so, how?

These elements facilitate an explanation of generalised depictions of the Essipiunnuat cultural condition on the eve of the war, with the outward appearances of *sui nullius,* despite the long and rich history of the group. Significantly, discrepancies are observable between a person's discourse about continuity in their personal cultural indigeneity and their talk about others, and the group, which is represented as entirely de-indigenised. Yet it should be kept in mind that this central image of absence and its contextualisation are also related to contemporary discourse. A pre-war *sui nullius* significantly valorises subsequent changes and the new regime that was established, especially those that present themselves as either the creators, obstetricians of a commonly perceived collective self or as a 'father figure' .

The collective self is depicted in stories as either created, new, reborn, revived, or just emerging from hibernation; stories report the emergence or reemergence of a collective identity after the event. A sense of novelty was apparent among all the generations who took part in the war, but was more evident among the youngest, whose inventory of experience was less loaded. They possessed a greater sense of having made a new start, a collective birth, as if they were beginning to live, as if everything had begun with the occurrence of war (Adam, chapter 3, ref. 8).

This time marked the end of the silencing of their sense of being Innu, and the affirmation of a collective existence. Two different possible interpretations about the nature of the self emerge: that it came either before or after the experience of war. The Essipiunnuat's collective self-assertion of indigeneity appears to have been outside the field of the memory and experience of the vast majority of those involved.[4] Instead, they had generally experienced the

4 This was, in fact, remembered by only a few, such as, for example, Pishimnapeo. Similar to the awakening provoked among the previous generation by Jules Sioui's radical stance in the mid 1940s, the Salmon War awakened a consciousness among the current generation and an awareness of the power of unity among First Peoples. Governments and their officials, for their part, were forced to surrender to the evidence that they could not negate and extinguish indigenous rights without encountering a strong and extended resistance. (Pishimnapeo, ch. 3, ref. 1)

silencing of indigeneity, when it was not being hidden or totally denied. In this sense, the event is commonly presented as the beginning of a shared notification or awareness of a collective entity, as an act of assertiveness and radical self-definition.

As will be demonstrated later, the increased and overwhelming role that a new generation of leaders ('the cell') was to play in the public assertion of a collective self, and their power to define its substance and form, made inevitable over time the question of their own relationship to the past and Innu heritage. While this section may not solve the complex question of the genesis of the 'self', it will certainly ask difficult questions related to the essentialisation and subsequent use of this self, one that is successively asserted, contested, attacked and brought into being in alignment with increased acceptance of identifying with it.

Indeed, these actors (and consequently the group they directed), had to face their own paradoxes; their desire, perhaps, to essentialise the Essipiunnuat identity in order to instrumentalise and reproduce certain representations of the group for the strategic purpose of social control. These questions are inevitable within a group beset by profound policies of oblivion and plagued by intergenerational ruptures and collective discontinuities. Its absorption of Canadian and Québec colonial mythologies having resulted in epistemic schisms and antinomies, it is a group overwhelmed by its colonial surroundings, that has been forced again and again over the centuries to redefine the parameters of its collective self and escape the powerful claws of the *sui nullius*.

Traumas thus loom large in intergenerational cultural transmission. This phenomenon also affected the leaders, who, despite their good intentions, were to design new collective features without necessarily having adequate cultural resources to overcome the tendency for revolutionaries, seeking control, to feed off the very imaginary with which they have chosen to break. Their powerful desire to present themselves as 'genitors' rather than 'obstetricians' leaves the question open of how much the leaders reproduced discourse to the effect that 'we had no history'.

Cultural identity revitalisation

The mutation that people experienced due to their increasing identification with Innu culture and references is a second alteration in self-conception. As has already been stated, the circumstances of the war placed people in a dilemma about their sense of self. The Essipiunnuat had experienced accusations from other Innu of being 'white', allegedly because of their physical appearance and the fact that the language, Innu-aimun, had not been transmitted to the children in the period following World War Two. In turn, it was not only the surrounding Euroquébécois who had intensively discouraged identification as

Indian, but also Canadian colonial policies and institutions. In the Salmon War, every Essipiunnuat was confronted with the dilemma of whether to be Innu or not, with predictable, painful consequences. They were asking themselves some highly personal questions, such as:

> 'Are we Indians or not?' This choice of cultural identity implies the consciousness that you cannot have your cake and eat it; that you cannot only take the good side of being Indian and disregard the bad. People awoke to the fact that they were Innu, or that they were not (Sam, chapter 3, ref. 2–3).

The oldest, predominantly men married to Euroquébécois women, as well as a group of young and highly motivated students who self-identified as Indian, already knew which side they were on. The emergence of a local, collective indigeneity resonated with many. The leaders were asserting Essipiunnuat indigeneity and values in public spaces and community meetings, as well as in the media. For many, this was all new. Many members had become Indian by status (in accordance with the Indian Act), and often their children had not even been told about their indigenous background. Whether born or reborn, in the confusion of war, resistance and uprising, an embryonic Essipiunnuat sense of self provided opportunities for identification with and attachment to this rejuvenated social identity. Yet increasingly, this new self was to be fed from the discourse being produced by the new young leaders as the intergenerational power-shift took shape.

Conclusively, people associate the occurrence of war with a new cultural identification that has resulted in the revitalisation of their cultural identity, followed by a blooming of affirmation and the triggering of an individual and collective assertion of who they were. The circumstances of war provided new opportunities for self-definition (Adam, chapter 3, ref. 1–2, 6). The community's awakening to its own indigeneity, culture and freedoms, including the subsequent transformations following the war, can be traced back not only to the re-emergence of a collective Innu cultural identity but to the discourses of the leaders and to people's identification with it and its absorption (Sam, chapter 3, ref. 7).

Collective self-consciousness: 'The bear was not yet dead'[5]

Thirdly, people referred to their renewed self-knowledge and self-awareness as having been acquired through identification with an Innu cultural referential. The reinstating of Innu cultural values as a worthwhile point of reference is interpreted in the stories as a cause of successive major changes, one of which was an increased awareness of an Essipiunnuat collective self. The partial reabsorption of the Innu cultural imaginary and conceptions are directly

5 Raoul, ch.3, ref. 9.

correlated with a new sense of self-knowledge and subsequent alterations in self-perceptions, attitudes and behaviours.

It might be expected that individuals' switches in reference group would engender correlated modifications of attitudes and types of actions (Marger, 2009). A survey of associations between the local context of political and cultural assertion and the recognition of emerging new subjectivities in narration might also be affirmed (Chew, 2007). The combination of collective agency, in an environment of cultural hegemony, and the reemergence of a repressed normative contained in cultural memory, is also, then, a well-known phenomenon (Assmann, 1997).

Descriptions of self-transformation as a result of war clearly converge in identifying a correlation between the reinstatement of the Innu cultural referential as a valuable point of reference and a variety of ensuing observable facts. Epistemic mutations are coupled with types of action, experiences of cultural regeneration, and increased receptivity to re-emerging normative schemes.

Mutual aid and camaraderie as emerging norms

The increased in-group cooperation is the most observed and commented-on change in the testimonies. Stemming from the experience of resistance, people explicitly express the appearance of a collective consciousness whose central impact is the establishment of mutual aid as a dominant norm, during but also after the war. This new sense of mutual help is often interpreted as the direct result of the establishment of the 'indigenist-communitarian principle'.

This principle became the dominant ideology following the war. It became omnipresent, and the base and mode of legitimisation of the 'communitarian system' that was to be shaped thereafter. People's identification with this principle, but also its increased imposition to become the only acceptable philosophy, is considered the main determinant of the subsequent cultural renewal experienced by the group. As mentioned earlier, this ideology was a major tool in the movement's war strategy. As Sam says, 'Fishing was communitarian from the beginning to the end, from catching salmon to its equal distribution among all families. At this time, everybody was involved' (Sam, chapter 3, ref. 1).

The spread of a spirit of camaraderie in the group is also mentioned as one of the, if not the greatest, sources of pleasure in people's stories. It is this re-emergence of mutual aid as a normative scheme that is the decisive element in the development of self-awareness. This occurrence seems to have actualised a core element of the group's tradition. In addition to reconnecting people with a facet of their group's memory, it supposedly caused a breach in the dam separating them from their heritage (Sam, chapter 3, ref. 9).

Mutual aid is but one example, albeit a very significant and central one. Its praxis was presented and recognised as an actualisation of an ancient philosophy. The experience validated people's indigeneity, allowing them to feel Innu on a daily basis. It is mainly to this method of experience that people trace back the resurfacing of an Indigenous axiology and its absorption (Riel, chapter 3, ref. 4). It led individuals to be more receptive to an internal indigenous culture and external possibilities. They were also able to reminisce about previously unconsidered values and principles transmitted by their parents' generation, such as respect for their sense of being indigenous and defence of *Innu-aitun* as Innu worldview, knowledge and way of life.

It was clear that they linked the reevaluation of their previously disparaged indigenous cultural heritage with being radically committed to its defence. They spoke of having discovered the extent to which they belonged to the Essipit community, as well as their group's attachment to its culture and indigenous values. As formerly documented, the observation of cooperation and unity also expanded the possibilities of victories and triumphs (Riel, chapter 3, ref. 1).

Transformations between 1980–5

Community members also related reconnections with their indigenous cultural referential to observable changes in behaviour, in addition to more uniformity around certain issues. For example, when attacked because of their indigeneity, their responses were more targeted, affirmative and self-confident (Adam, chapter 3, ref. 3). These changes in behaviour sometimes took the form of a personality reversal. People known previously as quiet and pacifist, or as not participating, demonstrated extraordinary qualities radically different to their former behaviour (Adam, chapter 2, ref. 7). Emotionally, pride and self-confidence replaced fear and shame. People began to display their indigeneity in every possible way. The uneasiness of being 'Indian', coupled with the widespread reflex to hide their indigeneity, was replaced with direct eye contact and non-ambiguous statements; suddenly increased respect largely replaced bullying and racism (Riel, chapter 3, ref. 5).

This development of attitude was described in terms of everyone looking up at once and refusing to back down, despite the inherent inconveniences and dangers involved (Mesnak, chapter 3, ref. 9; Adam, chapter 3, ref. 6). It is to their experience of the Salmon War that narrators trace back the genesis of a subsequent Essipiunnuat collective pride:

> We were proud of ourselves. It was in the Salmon War that the *Indians of Les Escoumins* began to be proud of their race. We were called the *white Indians*. Whether we liked it or not, we didn't physically look like the Innu of Pessamit. However, we had the same heart or blood as them. Our pride in being Innu started with the Salmon War (Napeo, chapter 3, ref. 2).

People were undoubtedly witnesses to radical change in how they saw themselves in terms of the group to which they belonged. Their experience of war transformed their view. Their perception and evaluation of the group would henceforth be overwhelmingly effectuated through an indigenous-communitarian point of view, including new principles, values and cultural schemes. In other words, their worldview was now to be approached from a new *episteme*.

Listening deeply to the stories pertaining to transformations in self-identity associated with the experience of war, reveals the occurrence of significant individual as well as collective epistemic mutations. These metamorphoses are quite intricate and thus I do not intend to expose them exhaustively at this point. Nevertheless, people clearly portray the Salmon War as a founding event.

The Salmon War as a founding event

This new perspective following their experience would result in a deep awareness of the oppression of First Peoples in general, and, moreover, of the Essipiunnuat's profound dehumanisation throughout their history. As exhibited, the epistemic revolution encountered by the Essipiunnuat was coupled with a phenomenon of resacralisation, as opposed to the colonial heritage of dehumanisation and 'chosification' (Césaire, 1972): the colonial process of metamorphosing people into things, tools or objects. Fundamentally, this paradigm shift allowed individuals to recognise their struggle as inscribed in a larger project, shared by all oppressed people, to defend their dignity as human beings with definitive values and principles (Riel, chapter 3, ref. 2; Mesnak, chapter 3, ref. 4).

As a result, it was primarily as indigenous people that they conducted their subsequent struggle – 'indigenous' here interpreted in the sense of being human, with an inherent value that deserves integral respect and also urgent recognition (Napeo, chapter 3, ref. 5).

Meanwhile, the transformation of rationale allowed members to reconsider the potential of the group itself. It also led to a reinterpretation of history from an Innu perspective and a potential for rewriting and self-design, in addition to what occurred during the Salmon War. From this renewed point of view, the denial of Essipiunnuat ancestral sovereignty as a responsibility to the Earth and future generations, including fishing, was not only illegitimate and depreciating, but also a clear transgression of the sacredness of the Innu people as human beings. As such, these offences deserved to be stopped by all possible means.

This new episteme confirmed that 'the bear was not yet dead'. Furthermore, people increasingly recognised themselves as actors of history. They realised, in Raoul's words, that 'our history was not yet finished' (Raoul, chapter 3, ref. 9).

Fruits of uprising: the sweet and the sour

As shown, collective self-assertion had a great impact on internal self-definitions and the sense of a collective existence. This was not foreign to the project of collective assertion itself, which is to say the realisation of a collective identity. Experiences in the collective actions of war were explicitly associated with a panoply of outcomes, akin to the perception of collective self-empowerment.

In their study, entitled 'The phenomenology of empowerment in collective action', Drury et al. (2005) show that perceptions of self-empowerment are widely related in people's accounts of collective actions; empowerment remains a core outcome of action. In accordance with their phenomenological approach:

> The emergence of collective self-empowerment, as an outcome of collective action, is directly formed from actions that support participants' realisation of their social identity (and hence their definition of proper practice) over and against the power of dominant out-groups.

They call such a phenomenon 'collective self-objectification', or CSO (ibid., p. 312).[6] Its presence is the most determining element in the emergence of collective self-empowerment or the notification of an empowered self. In contrast, the failure of CSO would be featured in people's accounts of disempowerment. Out-group reassertion, success and hegemony reinstate self-perceptions of powerlessness. Defeat and the reimposition of out-group definitions of legitimate practices are experienced as disempowering (ibid., p. 312).

The collective actions of the Essipiunnuat were previously interpreted as self-assertiveness for the defence of indigeneity and freedoms against hostile attempts, by the out-group, to impose an illegitimate order and to foster the annihilation of indigeneity and inherent sovereignty. Also repeatedly mentioned is how the representation of an '*empowered self*' is crucial in people's depictions, the shared perception of immense in-group power, and potentialities conditional to unity and the consistency of in-group links. Descriptions of action reflect the sense

6 Drury et al. propose four main conceptual features of CSO: 1. Context change as self-change: in their view, identity derives from, and varies with, social relational context. An empowered self-concept is a function of participation in social relations defined in terms of power transformation – from the out-group to the in-group. 2. Novelty: empowering and inspiring acts are those which turn the existing world upside-down, the initiation of changes in ongoing unequal power relations. CSO refers to the actions of groups in resistance who challenge the status quo. 3. Action as realisation of legitimate practice: the experience of empowerment resulting from actions expressing the collective definition of legitimacy over and against that of dominant forces. To collectively self-objectify means to be a subject – and being a subject rather than an object of others' actions is a definition of empowerment or agency. 4. Provisionality: a) Since CSO is a cause of empowerment as an outcome of collective action, it should feature in people's accounts of empowered experiences, as unity and mutual aid; b) CSO is associated with increased participation in collective action; c) CSO is predictive of positive emotions and life-enhancing, joyful and positive feelings.

of self-legitimacy animating the actors. People directly associate their actions with the realisation of their identity as Indian, Essipiunnuat or Innu (Adam, chapter 2. ref. 3 and 8; Mathias, personal communication; Ernest, chapter 2, ref. 9; Ivan, chapter 2, ref. 5; Mesnak, chapter 2, ref. 3).

Furthermore, the most committed actors often describe their participation in collective action as the greatest source of pleasure in their entire lives. Accordingly, it could be stated that there has already been a demonstration of CSO in the light of previous analysis. However, since the event occurred in the 1980s, it is relevant now to consider more closely group members' interpretations of how the collective experience of participating in the war empowered the group, as well as the experiences and interpretations that may correspond to disempowerment in the longer run. It is also of relevance to look at how people described the empowering and disempowering effects of their uprising and the post-Salmon War era.

Collective self-empowerment

In-group power was presumably generated as a main outcome of the war. This new capacity played a major role in the collective actions that followed and in subsequent developments exercised by the group. Perceptions of collective self-empowerment are illustrated in the stories through four main points: collective self-care, a sense of self-legitimacy, effective self-determination and an upgraded group inventory of experience.

Caring for ourselves

The experience of the war is said to have generated an overall in-group self-benevolence or self-care, an enhanced concern and kindness towards oneself (Sam, chapter 3, ref. 3). The group would develop a renewed and higher sense of its value, a consideration for itself and its members. The collective uprising would generate an ethos of members looking after themselves, each other, and their community (Karl, chapter 3, ref. 8).

Together with increased social and cultural revitalisation, the practice of war resulted in new feelings of pride, and an increased sense of aesthetics and inner beauty (Mesnak, chapter 3, ref. 1; Adam, chapter 3, ref. 6). This amplified consideration for in-group affairs and for themselves includes the revalorisation of cultural heritage and practices; greater value was accorded to Innu science, including laws and practices. People immediately began to value being Innu and, as a consequence, were concerned with autonomising and producing new socioeconomic institutions and devices in order to be in a position to make their own decisions. According to Raoul, the concern for oneself can be traced back precisely to this experience of collective action (chapter 2, ref. 16).

A boost in members' participation in public affairs and learning at that time is reported, together with a real sense of belonging to the group, which as a result appeared to acquire a new and shared value. At that moment people would have discovered, felt and understood the real meaning of the communitarian-indigenous principle. As a group, they were metamorphosed. This new sense and respect for the collective was presented as the source of a fresh, extraordinary and lasting increase in strength (Raoul, chapter 2, ref. 16).

Self-legitimacy

The experience of war also generated a sense of self-legitimacy resulting in increased actions based on a new discernment of in-group power and strength. Before the war, for example, people would not resist the intervention of state agents during hunting episodes, which often included intimidation and the seizure of their equipment (Raoul, chapter 3, ref. 2). After the war, state agents were directly asked to move away so that Essipiunnuat could immediately hunt and fish before speaking to them. The insistence of agents would not only be met with a refusal to comply, but a categorical order to stay away (Sam, chapter 3, ref. 4).

Following the war, actions aimed at achieving greater autonomy and amplified in-group power, including the assertion of its symbols and re-inhabiting collectively ancestral territories, were augmented. Unlike the pre-war attitude, group members were now saluting defiant and assertive stances. The experience of the war thus significantly modified the definitions of legitimate practices. Members would from then on increasingly encourage, support and validate actions destined for a collective purpose, even the most radical ones. Community members encouraged this to defend what was right for the community, what was 'communitarian'. Assertions of indigeneity bloomed, as well as actions aimed at defending the community (Sam, chapter 3, ref. 8).

Stories suggest that the backlash which followed the collective uprising reinforced the group's conviction of being in the right. The aggression strengthened their collective sense of fairness and the legitimacy of their non-compliance. The evaluation of Québec authority and culture had been altered. Rather than diminishing their will to fight, the repression of the Essipiunnuat is said to have given authority to in-group figures and engendered greater validation for rebelling. The defence of indigenous freedoms and culture was thereafter not only recognised by some as necessary, but a majority confirmed it as primordial and considered it to be an important factor merging with the nature of the group identity (Raoul, chapter 3, ref. 1).

Effective self-determination: directing and propelling our own canoe

The collective experience of war is also portrayed as the source of diverse and unique developments in the community. This was supposedly the initial trigger of a wider process of collective autodynamisation, expansion, affirmation and reterritorialisation in various fields. It is said that the result was the whole group's greater self-determination. The Salmon War is, then, conceived as a manifestation of collective subjectivity but also as a catalyst for greater agency, mainly based on an aggregation of individuals around a common objective, including the capacity to engage in a chosen direction. The experience would generate unity and grounds for the group's development and would lead to an improvement in collective wellbeing (Adam, chapter 3, ref. 1 and 2). The formation of a new myth and its absorption can also be perceived here.

A metaphor often used by interviewees is that the salmon net was initially used to gather people, then produced in-group unity, and then reinforced the movement, rather than just being used to capture salmon. If perceptions converged in the recognition that the experience of war was at the origins of a new and shared community vision, they also identified with the emergence of a new way of putting it into operation.

The aftermath of the collective experience of war was linked to the new regime that resulted and new modes of social control being developed. The Salmon War was coupled in people's accounts with the communitarian system which then evolved, bringing socioeconomic in-group prosperity. This experience was correlated with a system resulting in a shared understanding that all actions conducted by individuals had the purpose of ameliorating the collective wellbeing of each and every one (Adam, chapter 2, ref. 6). Interpretation of the Salmon War then became foundational for the new local regime.

That said, the passage of war resulted in people feeling increasingly at home on the land, even if this was outside the reserve. The war was conclusively associated with the subsequent increased reconnection with ancestral lands outside the borders of the reserve (Adam, chapter 3, ref. 5).

Updated inventory of experience

Interviewees maintained that going through the war had increased their inventory of experience; it had increased in-group knowledge but also their capacity for evaluating present conditions. It provided new information for better discerning in-group potential. This enrichment of the group knowledge allows, then, for the possibility of reactivating the self-knowledge harvested in the war in situations when actions of resistance would be required.

In this sense, people thought of their individual and collective actions during the conflict as having released potentialities, as generating a new inner force and a new sense of self-value, but also a shared referential, a generational unit allowing for the projection of the self into the future, a vision of continuity. Several narrators report the emergence of a new consciousness in the power of unity, an almost limitless power of human capacity when amalgamated (Mesnak, chapter 3, ref. 7).

This new knowledge was presented as proof that a small but determined group could defeat a larger group, and that it could obtain what it wanted. In addition, it was realised that success depended entirely on the consistency of in-group social bonds, a unique and effective unity of will, including the consciousness that they were able to come together when necessary (Mesnak, chapter 3, ref. 12). This force of collective freedom also entered into the self-imagery of the group, the defence of these indigenous rights being directly related to the perception of the phenomenon of collective self-empowerment. People felt and realised that collective indigenous rights were stronger than individual and commercial approaches. These rights at their core asserted an actualised indigenous self. That assertion is therefore presented as a cause of greater unity among in-group members, but also of an increased solidarity with indigenous out-groups (Mesnak, chapter 3, ref. 6 and 11).

Indeed, in-group members were not afraid to charge and go to the front when these collective rights were at stake. In turn, they would then feel the strength of pride in themselves, and would receive admiration from other in-group members. As a result, they would be contributing to the success of all Essipiunnuat. Direct action was henceforth interpreted as a necessary condition for collective success (Tshak, chapter 2, ref. 1). The empowering effect for the group, as gained from experiences in the war, was presented by some as the cause of future victories in contentious circumstances with out-groups, such as during the conflict with the federal government during the 1990s employment crisis.

Resistance and out-group representations

Another aspect of upgrading the inventory of experience concerns the possibility of influencing the perceptions of out-groups. As people noted, out-groups were transformed by observing the resistance of the Essipiunnuat. Public opinion was changed significantly and the Innu communities vividly remember seeing transformations among their enemies. External respect, recognised after the war within a Euroquébécois fringe, is explained by the fact that the Essipiunnuat fought against their enemies primarily to defend their principles. This struggle, impregnated with self-respect, inspired recognition even from enemies (Riel, chapter 3, ref. 6).

On the opposing side, people confirmed that if the Essipiunnuat had not resisted, the Euroquébécois' representations of 'Indians as cowards' would have been validated. Thereafter, the inventory of experience of the 'enemy' was also modified, with new data showing that the Essipiunnuat would not accept intimidation and would stand up for their freedoms as long as it took, despite beatings and suffering, even to the point of endangering their own lives (Esther, chapter 3, ref. 2).

A memory of reversibility can be traced back to the fact that the Essipiunnuat elected to look directly into the eyes of their enemies. They firmly told their oppressors that they would not comply with their idea and representation of the Indian, and that they were fellow humans and thus deserving of the utmost respect. These facts also entered into the Essipiunnuat inventory of experience. Links were consequently made between resistance and transformation of out-group representations (Riel, chapter 3, ref. 3).

Essipiunnuat stories articulate an extended and lasting perception of collective self-empowerment or of an empowered self. The foremost characteristic of this mutation relies on increased collective intelligence, a self-knowledge that led the group to greater auto-dynamisation, empowerment and self-determination. But this new information seems to have exceeded the passage from surplus-powerlessness to auto-dynamisation, or from the perception that 'we cannot' to a firm belief that 'we can'. It included a more practical awareness of the potential of the collective self and how it can be used, of the strength it can release in certain circumstances; in other words, of the practical value of people who have engaged in actions against their enemies in order to realise their social identity.

As previously shown, evidence tends to the hypothesis that the younger actors engaged in the war already understood its potential, and to a certain extent it could have been planned and shaped to establish and legitimise a new regime of power; the extent to which participants in the war were 'used' became a subsequent and central object of controversy among Essipiunnuat.

Collective disempowerment: shadows of cultural oblivion

The experience of the Salmon War is widely referred to as a source of empowerment and increased collective agency. However, the stories also contain explicit evocations of disempowerment, of the reimposition of out-group conceptions and the state's definitions of legitimate practices, as well as the reproduction or continuity of exogenous representations inside the group. If the passage of war was characterised by a reconnection with an indigenous referential, which resulted in epistemic mutations, new subjectivities and indigenisation, the post-Salmon War disenchantment felt by many was also related to alleged dissociations from these self-conceptions.

Those who interpreted the results of the post-Salmon War negotiations as an intricate commodification of their cultural symbols[7] experienced disempowerment. As will be analysed later, this discourse focuses on changes in relational contexts with hostile out-groups, the purpose and legitimacy of the agreements signed with them, and inner differences in the receptivity of external recognition.

More significantly, it reflected an enduring in-group controversy over the nature of indigenous rights, laws, heritage and sovereignty and the interruptions of the decolonisation process. Yet it also refers to ways authority was exercised within the group, and the effects of that. A deeper understanding of features of disempowerment requires a study of post-Salmon War circumstances and the new modalities of Essipiunnuat reception to state recognition.

Conditions during the post-Salmon War period: perceptions of groups' interactions

Interviewees noticed significant changes in their relations with out-group actors as a result of their acts of defiance and self-assertion. One major impact was state authorities' recognition of Essipiunnuat rights, in addition to changes in public opinion, including relations with the local Euroquébécois population. These changes contrasted radically with pre-war and in-war representations.

René Lévesque's involvement: Québec's new approach

Following the war, external actors increasingly recognised Essipiunnuat collective rights. As early as the end of 1981, and partly as a result of the impact of the Salmon War, the Québec state modified somewhat its approach to Innu rights and territorial negotiations. One of the principal changes was that the government did not require, at least on the surface, the extinguishment of Innu rights and the renouncing of collective self-determination as a prerequisite for negotiation. Effectively, the Québec premier, René Lévesque, founder of the nationalist Parti Québécois, publicly recognised at this time that extinguishment was no longer a state imperative in its negotiations with the Innu (Girard, 1981). Lévesque openly recognised First Peoples as having similar rights that he was pursuing for his own people, a collective right to self-determination. The issue of Innu sovereignty and its sources, different from European conceptions, remains complex, however; furthermore, Lévesque's recognition of Innu ancestral sovereignty was most likely strategic and limited to European definitions. Yet this was a major change, particularly for the Essipiunnuat who were closely linked to the fate of Québec society and who

7 The term 'commodification' is used here in the sense of 'treated as mere commodities', which is to say the tendency to instrumentalise Innu heritage and symbols for the purposes of marketing and commerce, and using this as a stratagem for political ends.

Figure 12. Essipit 1980s, Institut culturel et éducatif montagnais (ICEM), 16440.

had suffered negative if not racist propaganda and stigmatisation as well as the manoeuvres of the minister Laurent Lessard. He had played a predominant role in calling for the repression of the Innu uprising, and so Lévesque effectively decided from then on to deal with the Innu people himself. This change in the Québec discourse would have resonated deeply among the Essipiunnuat.

State agents' attitude

Modifications to the Québec state's approach to relations with the Innu also translated in the field into radical changes in state agents' attitudes to ancient ancestral practices of hunting and fishing. This was striking. For example, state agents now simply asked the hunter to show his Indian card to prove his status. Rather than being antagonistic, the agents would now respond with 'all right, that's fine, thanks'. People related this change of attitude directly to the fact that they had resisted, that they had risen up and fought to defend themselves and their rights (Pierre, chapter 2, ref. 5). In general, then, the uprising was seen as having not only improved conditions for exercising indigenous rights, but also of having increased the respect of the state and its representatives towards them (Édouard, chapter 3, ref. 5).

Public opinion

This change had a great impact on public opinion and on the neighbouring townships and the people of Les Escoumins. Indeed, the latter were forced to recognise, whether they liked it or not, that the Indians, as well as their rights, existed outside the reserve's borders. An agreement on the co-management of the river that they had categorically rejected before the war – based on the fact that Indians did not have any rights and were not a distinct people –

was signed. Television and radio recordings from this period show the mayor of Les Escoumins denying any inherent right pertaining to land outside of the Essipit reserve's borders, known today as their ancestral territories or the homeland. These inherent rights, even if denounced and generally not appreciated by the Euroquébécois, were henceforth perceived to be facts that must be acknowledged. This was highly significant for the Essipiunnuat, who had faced the denial of their ancestral sovereignty and existence for centuries (Mesnak, chapter 3, ref. 2).

Unsubmissiveness: the Indian as resistant

Indeed, the Essipiunnuat struggle had somehow impressed on the Euroquébécois, or at least made them aware of, the indigenous determination to resist attacks, repression, and the symbolic and concrete denial and violation of their rights. They were used to facing behaviours that were generally more submissive or tolerant of their denial and racism. Now, in their own backyard, they had witnessed organised resistance to their actions and it was a novelty. For the first time they had seen directly, often with astonishment, the Essipiunnuat in-group solidarity, strength and determination to resist external aggression. These new images cut deeply into the Euroquébécois' previously widespread social representations of degenerating, invisible, weak and submissive Indians.

Apparent decline of conflict

According to those who took part, their resistance and new power brought respect. The integration of the Essipiunnuat into the management of the river was interpreted as recognition. Yet, the uprising also generated a crisis of legitimacy among local Euroquébécois. It questioned the validity of their discourses and hegemonic positioning as pioneers and returned a painful image of themselves as colonialists (Mesnak, chapter 3, ref. 6 and 11). The direct confrontation with the Innu, and the witnessing of the indigenous group's stubbornness, is said to have demotivated many hostile Euroquébécois who 'were not real warriors with a clear vision of their struggles' (Raoul, chapter 3, ref. 6). In fact, a softening of relations between the people of Les Escoumins and Essipit was observed thereafter (Ernest, chapter 3, ref. 5). People of Les Escoumins now possessed new information in their own inventory of experience. The inter-group dynamics had changed overall, and the Essipiunnuat were generally highly sensitive to these out-group changes and how their former enemies interacted with them.

Receptiveness to state recognition: genesis and stratagem

If the experience of the war altered Essipiunnuat self-evaluations, it also went some way towards transforming their perception of the Québec state and authorities. Negotiating directly with the state was a new experience for almost all of those who had participated in such activities. Most people now felt that state officials took them seriously, whereas previously they had denied their very existence and rights. The attraction of Québec nationalism for some of the younger leaders, and their relations with Québec officials, should not be underestimated as an influence favouring the rapprochement with the province.

As changes in the relational context with out-groups were observed, they were generally welcomed very positively considering the dramatic experience they had just been through.[8] In particular, the Essipiunnuat were now hearing a new discourse pertaining to their rights and recognition, accompanied by new positive attitudes towards them.

However, this external recognition was not received in the same way by everyone. In fact, two main polarities in this respect appeared in the stories, materialised around the notions of indigenous rights, their value, nature and sources. Fundamentally, an in-group crisis around a proper definition of indigeneity, or being Innu, was reported, and also its sacralisation or commodification as a major post-Salmon War determinant of disempowerment.

Recognition and the discomfort of indigenisation

For many, involvement in the Salmon War corresponded to the first and most significant connection to their cultural identity as indigenous or Innu. This was when they first defined themselves as indigenous, or consciously assumed their chosen group of reference. For this category of people, their primary identification as indigenous was apparently generated more by their participation in the war than from previously transmitted collective and cultural memory, stories, knowledge and culture, even if the war allowed for forms of transmission.

8 State recognition of aspects of Essipiunnuat ancestral rights, especially relating to practices such as fishing and hunting, also had side effects. It produced some ongoing jealousy in a Euroquébécois fringe. At times this took the form of 'white revenge'. It allegedly led some Euroquébécois poachers to go shooting moose in winter and ensure that the Indians would be publicly blamed. Some went as far as collecting moose foetuses and putting them on the steps of the church. They called the media and publicly accused the Indians of inhumanity and savage practices (Pierre, ch. 2, ref. 3 and 4). Another sad story concerns an Essipiunnuat woman. After the war, Essipit agreed to participate in the Québec national day. This consisted mainly of including some Essipiunnuat in a parade that went around the village and up to the tip of Pointe-à-la-Croix, by the big cross. For the occasion, an Essipiunnuat woman agreed to craft a traditional dress that she would wear in the parade. When the parade reached the cross, where a fire had been prepared as usual for the Québec national day, two men arrived and completely covered her with blue paint (the colour of the Québec flag) (Karen, personal communication, summer 2010).

Due to their age, acquired status through marriage, inter-generational ruptures in transmission, or simple self-denial, some people had not been in touch with any Innu cultural referents. Instead, they had widely absorbed Euroquébécois concepts and social imagery. Their new self appeared fragile and not deep rooted; they were simply speaking French while their access to any Innu cultural referential was limited to an extent. But the very particular circumstances of war, with its specific reconnections and emergent norms, led them to commit more radically to this group of reference. They found themselves immersed, individually and collectively, in a movement that had been propelled to the forefront of indigenous resistance.

Recognition that gives birth to the self

The testimonies suggest that for them, the perceptions of out-groups – external recognition from the authorities and its inherent representations – became a preponderant source of their self-image as Indian. The government's recognition of their rights corresponds to the birth of their rights. For them, this recognition was greatly empowering, almost constitutive of their empowered self, if not genesiac. The state was therefore identified as the major source of Innu normativity. This was not new, however, for it merely reproduced the century-old policies of the Crown that culminated with the 'Indian essence' or racialisation of indigeneity, as materialised in article 91(24) of the Canadian Constitution of 1867 and put into operation through the Savage, then Indian, Act; the entire state policy aimed, through sophisticated devices, to gradually make this 'essence' extinct through assimilation and the interpretation of Innu 'rights' as being rooted in state law.

The perception, by some, of state recognition of indigeneity and the rights associated with it as the genesis of the group, was an internal continuation of such policies. If the war fostered self-identification as indigenous among people, state recognition of indigenous rights ensured the exogeneity of their source and location outside an Innu self. This particular type of reception for external recognition revealed a particular in-group positioning. Some people observed that, for those who acquired Indian status through marriage, or those who had no access to Innu conceptions, for example, this overwhelming external recognition noticeably released them from the various discomforts of indigenisation.

This receptivity of recognition as genesiac, or having generated their own existence, led several people, including some of the new leaders, to perceive that the state had produced rights which had not previously existed, a posture revealing an internalised form of *terra nullius* – the successor to, and advancement of the term *sui nullius.* For these individuals, including some leaders, it was evident that '*Indians*' remain, fundamentally, *objects* produced by the Crown. It was therefore essential to maintain cooperation and negotiation with the state at all costs – alternately simulating indigeneity and sameness – in order to obtain more rights, in the name of realism, to progress and evolve in accordance with external standards.

From this perspective, indigenous rights are not only negotiable with the state, but must be agreed upon in order to exist. The collective freedoms of the Essipiunnuat are therefore entirely correlated to state representations and definitions of legitimacy, and ultimately form the basis of the band council's authority as created in accordance with the Indian Act. This authority is also therefore deeply rooted in the Canadian constitutional regime. For this category of receptors, culturally disconnected, the empowered self was born from the womb of the Crown. Increased access to its 'milk' is the best promise of empowerment. For them, continuous state recognition after the war resulted in a constant sense of empowerment (Mesnak, chapter 3, ref. 1). In this context, cultural oblivion, as the underlying strategy of policies towards First Peoples in Canada, systematically invalidates Innu's epistemology of ancestral sovereignties and laws, relation to *Assi*, and ways of governing themselves.

Recognition as a stratagem

A second type of receptivity to external recognition corresponds to the interpretation of state recognition as a mere stratagem, a ploy to take Indians into the trap of extinguishment through the subtle legitimisation of state conceptions and devices – stratagems of the Canadian state to obtain the Innu people's abandonment of their inherent obligations and the surrender of their *sui generis* ancestral sovereignty (*Innu tipenitamun*). Cultural disruptions and assimilation meet the interests of the Crown and the assertion of its absolute supremacy and sovereignty to the point of becoming the only legitimate source of indigenous law and rights. It is through inciting the Innu to sameness and cultural assimilation that the Crown eventually succeeds over time in making them accept the erasure and negation of their historical ancestral conception of sovereignty and their inalienable rights to self-determination (Samson, 2001), in patent violation of the international *jus cogens*.[9]

Some people were aware of these stratagems, especially that state recognition of their rights was a double-edged sword. This is reflected in their analyses of the post-Salmon War negotiations and agreements. Older people in particular were aware that the Essipiunnuat leaders were becoming increasingly trapped in the state stratagem in return for short-term gains. They correlated this abduction by state definitions of indigenous rights with a subsequent decline

9 *Jus cogens* comes from the Latin for 'compelling law' and refers, in contemporary international public law, to certain fundamental, overriding principles, from which no derogation, in domestic law or international law, is ever permitted. See Brownlie (1998).

in in-group participation and, ultimately, the reinterpretation of the Salmon War as a collective defeat. This discernment is particularly acute among these older individuals, the traditionalists, who have received ancestral teachings or have kept regularly in touch with other indigenous groups. They directly correlate their feelings and perceptions of disempowerment with the new leaders' multi-faceted post-Salmon War opportunism and their increased use, or commodification, of Innu symbols.

Some stories accuse leaders of having complied in a cowardly, unforgivable way with state definitions of proper traditional activities as indigenous, if not their Innu identity, because they could be bought and thought of the Innu ancestral domain (or more widely, Assi) as transferable. As will be demonstrated, this posture is very similar to the critique articulated around the comprehensive land claims negotiation process which disregarded indigenous conceptions, including inherent sovereignty. Following their experience in the war, people's expectations for integral respect of inherent indigenous sovereignty were high. State recognition merely validated their own Innu conceptions and released them increasingly from exogenous definitions; it gave the people human dignity, a dignity as Innu. But in their view, it was to alter nothing of their collective rights and duties, forever rooted in *Innu tipenitamun*, their ancient conception of sovereignty as responsibility. For them, there is no link between state recognition and the nature of their collective rights, for they had existed long before colonisation. If colonisation and settlement contributed to the usurpation of these rights, at no time did they alter their existence and nature. Their lands would remain unceded, and *Innu tipenitamun* would be integrally preserved, despite the mood of the dominant society and the Crown (Mestenapeo, chapter 3, ref. 4; Ernest, chapter 3, ref. 2; Pishimnapeo, chapter 3, ref. 7; Édouard, chapter 3, ref. 2; Pierre, chapter 3, ref. 8).

For people in this category, who already had access to Innu referentiality and philosophy of law, their experience of the war had not enhanced their knowledge of those rights, but only the extent to which they were recognised by the state. This was meaningful chiefly in relation to the practice of ancestral activities; this was the great difference. No longer would the state agents harass them. However, any compromise with state imposition of what legitimate indigenous practices are remained unacceptable.

Indeed, for these individuals, such recognition did not change the arbitrary nature of the actions of the state based on a specific conception of power and sovereignty. The state changed its manners, but kept its ability to command the Indians and to remove the rights they recognised (Édouard, chapter 3, ref. 1). For them, recognition had either much less value, no value at all, or it was a state strategy to take something from them. As such, Indians needed to be more vigilant than ever, as an older war was continuing, despite the end of the contentious battle over salmon fishing. Negotiations with the state with regards to indigenous rights capitalised on the founding principles of the group itself. It was an immoral and at the very least inadequate reification of indigeneity and a clear and unforgivable transgression that resulted, above all, in a dangerous form of disempowerment.

Legitimising the devices of the state

Several people afterwards felt they had been fooled, mainly by the government but also by their leaders who negotiated with the state. The Essipiunnuat eventually 'got caught in the Québec government net'. As Pierre describes extensively, somehow the Salmon War had been lost and they entered into a game by signing an agreement that the government needed more than they did. The state had a stratagem. The Innu had inherent rights; signing an agreement over these rights was serving the state and could only result in new delimitations of these rights. To spread a net by the wharf meant, for the government, the symbolic expansion of the Indians, their occupation of a land beyond the reserve. The government sought to stop this. The negotiations finally resulted in the issue of a licence being a requirement for Innu community fishing. Some saw this as a betrayal of the group's fundamental principles and a systematic legitimisation of state devices. To a certain extent the group had been forced back to its former position, as the state was subtly becoming the source of their sovereignty and 'rights' (Pierre, chapter 2, ref. 4).

Individual Essipiunnuat fishermen would now need to pay a provincial licence fee, as the Euroquébécois did, to fish in the Esh Shipu River. The problem with this was not about finance, but the fact that the Innu needed any licence at all, especially as one had never been required before for fishing and hunting. People felt that they were again being assimilated and their rights were being disregarded. This was firmly interpreted as unacceptable, and the leaders were accused of not truly believing in inherent indigenous rights. Even if the community was co-manager of the river, its members had fought the government at great peril to their lives and their leaders were now requiring them to obtain a permit to fish salmon from the river. This was viewed as absurd, and yet, to a certain extent, revealed the new leaders' thinking (Pierre, chapter 4, ref. 1).

Some of the older generation also felt they had returned to a time when the European Crowns were exchanging territories for 'a few small mirrors'.[10] With the Salmon War and the negotiation that followed, the Essipiunnuat had accepted the 'gift' of a right that they already possessed in accordance with

10 This expression comes from Europeans' fraudulent practice in the past of exchanging pieces of mirror for higher-value items. Another story describes the attempt to exchange a whole territory for a piece of mirror, an act that caused the First Peoples to laugh because territory cannot be exchanged.

their Innu legal tradition, and they were not comfortable with this idea (Pierre, chapter 3, ref. 2 and 3; Mestenapeo, chapter 3, ref. 9). Schedules and laws were imposed on the Essipiunnuat, which were understood to be more favourable to the settler population. This was an excessive self-restriction to their rights when the whole of the Innu homeland was in fact their ancestral domain (Napeo, chapter 3, ref. 5).

As previously documented, the upcoming leaders excluded some of the older leaders on the basis that they were too uncompromising in their approach towards indigenous rights, as well as too honest to play the ongoing political game. For those excluded, these negotiations and their results were to remain illegitimate to this day. Consenting to the usurpation of Essipiunnuat sovereignty and definitions was incredibly disempowering, if not a form of collective self-annihilation, and completely contradicted what they had resisted in the war.

Stories evidence that this dynamic of reification of indigeneity was, indeed, serving the interests of some individuals who were willing to legitimise their newly acquired authority over the group. Consequently, recognition was perceived as a state stratagem for imposing its own definitions and to legitimise practices in parallel to feeding an increased internal authoritarianism. The most disempowering aspect was perhaps awareness of internal attempts to legitimate power. The post-Salmon War era therefore left a range of Essipiunnuat with the bitter taste of having their extensive sacrifices in the war devalued. Their voices resonate with the disempowering sense of having been used for ends they had not consented to or stated during the war. One may wonder to what extent this disillusionment contributed to the non-transmission of stories about the war to the next generation and the production of cultural oblivion.

Internal reordination: the path to monocracy

> A state of war only serves as an excuse for domestic tyranny.
>
> Aleksandr Solzhenitsyn

A commonly perceived fruit of the uprising remains the emergence of an 'empowered self', a notion shared by almost everyone, despite the post-Salmon War reevaluations and experiences of disempowerment. This empowered self was to become critical to the post-Salmon War normative order. However, its value, contents and definitions also became an issue of power and control. An in-group re-ordering through bureaucratisation and the establishment of panoplies of institutional devices and modes of domination, all coupled with ideologies and representations, are reported in the stories as core results of the war.

The collective experience of war is commonly presented as the genesis of later community developments and actions, and as the moral foundation of an indigenous-communitarian regime. Stories often explicitly suggested a collective subject generated by the experience and an associated governing mechanism. This section explores extracts which refer to that 'subject', the local post-Salmon War regime, the normative order, and related modes of control that emerged as enduring outcomes of the event.

The production of this 'subject' appears, in a Foucauldian sense, as an object historically constituted on basic determinations that remain fundamentally exterior to it; it has a genesis, a formation and a history; it is not conceived as inherent. The analysis of this subject thus requires access to its genealogy through historical contextualisation and a form of history that reflects 'the constitution of its knowledge at the risk of being empty in its identity, all over history' (Foucault, 1997, quoted in Revel, 2009).

Changes in collective self-representations or group self-identity generally signify correlated modifications in terms of epistemic mutations, but also in normative ordering and modes of social control and their legitimisation (Kappeler, 1986). Effectively, the self-representations generated by the experience of the Salmon War are directly coupled with subsequent developments and the establishment of new social institutions. These social designs materialised in a communitarian system that claimed indigeneity as its moral foundation but also referred with some constancy, as will be shown later, to aspects of a socialist vision – socialist but with an authoritarian tone.

Nevertheless, interviewees also voiced perceived incompatibilities and contradictions between 'ideologies' and their interactions with the subject. For example, people frequently mentioned an inner racism as a core component of the group condition, and it is essential to reflect on what happened to these evaluations and their foundations in post-Salmon War Essipit. More dramatically, some discreetly set out – for fear of reprisals, expulsion from the reserve, job losses or psychological harassment – evidence of a despotic drift in the small community.

The inadequate consideration given in research to essentialisation in micro-group self-representations and ideologies, particularly among the most racially oppressed of these entities, is well known. As Bhatt (1999) argues, subjectivities emerging in resistance to racial oppression risk containing forms of 'absolutisms of the powerless' that would contradict the radical claim to equality of dignity among humans and groups that nourish their actions. Such inner antinomies would contribute, in the long run, to collective exhaustion. To break free from 'epistemic generalities' and access the 'material of identity', which is substantially contained in 'historical and social processes, institutions, networks, and associations' would, ultimately, be a promising way of discovering 'how progressive sensibilities can disavow the possibility of their appropriation by authoritarianism'.[11] Such criticism of the intimate links between the essentialisation of identity and authoritarianism, as lived by people, is more than ever necessary in order to comprehend the deeper effects of the reserve system.

The question is particularly relevant in a context where Indian status, based on a 'blood quantum' fiction and raciality as defined by the Crown, remains the only official valid definition of identity for Indians in Canada. In addition to the reserve, the band council, as a device of the Crown specifically designed for complete domination and assimilation, has absolute power over the Indians – one that can only be restrained by the Crown itself, which has the legal power to dismiss it at any time. Therefore, the constitutional regime of 91(24), materialized in the Indian Act, founded on an essentialist definition of Indian identity, and which takes its source of power from the authority of the Crown itself, is a system that favours authoritarian practices. It is also inseparable, and in a sense a continuity of, the residential schools' regime of power. Symptoms of internal tyranny on the reserve must be studied in accordance with the wider political environment; they can be traced back through the state's definitions and practices, which must be examined if we are to understand the magnitude of contemporary internal conflict and in-group discontinuities they generate.

As an outcome of the war, three main elements, pertaining to the post-Salmon War social order and modes of control, surfaced in the stories. The first concerns the concentration of power in the hands of a few. The second is about the emergence of a new and unique ideology, or communitarian-indigenist scheme, deeply related to the Salmon War as the foundation of a new interpretation for the group. A third element concerns manifestations of authoritarianism as perceived and articulated in stories.

Condensing of command

In the intervening years, it became apparent that the Salmon War was a founding event for the group and its subsequent reordering; a myth that looms large in the post-Salmon War Essipiunnuat imaginary and which has specific functions. It is often presented as a new beginning for the group, as a turning point in its history, and even as a successful rescue from nothingness. Allegedly, it is entirely to that period that the origin of the collective socioeconomic

11 Based on an analysis of Hindu ultra-nationalism, Bhatt (1999) asserts that essentialist self-conceptions would be easily reproduced in the contemporary world since 'one can actively choose to ignore the face of the other, and celebrate only the poetics of the self. In modernity, one need not be a member of an already described chosen people; one can choose oneself, and can manufacture mythical stories, folk genealogies, political symbols and histories; cultivation and nurturing of a metaphysical self that identifies both the archaic and futuristic with itself'. (pp. 2 and 82)

developments and actions of reterritorialisation, subsequent to the war, should be traced. Yet, if the Salmon War is linked to a collective decision to revitalise the reserve, to develop it and to work together for the group, paradoxically only four central actors relate that fact, one of whom reportedly openly expressed his wish to establish his full domination over the group (Mestenapeo, chapter 3, ref. 3; Pishimnapeo, chapter 3, ref. 8).

Four figures are in effect portrayed as the main if not the only decision-makers in post-Salmon War Essipit. Their discourse was said to be along the lines of 'Stop! This is what people want. This is what people will get. We will take things into our own hands. We will develop our community as we see it, with our own rules' (Napeo, chapter 3, ref. 4). Representations of their post-Salmon War actions tend to be polarised as legitimate and entirely based on the will of the people on the one hand, and illegitimate and increasingly forced on the people on the other. This paradox is inseparable from the contemporary state of affairs in the community, which was characterised for four decades until 2016 by the overwhelming control exercised by a small group and then only one person, its impact on what is perceived as legitimate or not in the public realm, and the space granted to critical and dissident views. The individuals concerned are all now retired from their administrative positions, but the questions over the type of influence some former leaders had on band council decisions, and whether or not some of them still pull the strings, remain open in the community.

These four actors are described as belonging to a new generation. In the beginning, at least, the stories report the merging of the will of this cell of newly positioned leaders with the interests, desires and will of the whole group. These militants are presented, in post-Salmon War Essipit, as the true defenders of the group's freedoms. Their actions are associated with the beginning of the authentic defence of the community. More specifically, the proper security of collective interest and life can be traced back to the moment when the council decided to be the only source of leadership (Mesnak, chapter 3, ref. 1).

The band council discourse was characterised by a call for direct action aiming at a radical socioeconomic autonomisation of the group. The goal, as presented in people's accounts, was mainly for the council to create a new economy, articulated around the central priority of job creation for members. Ending economic alienation and getting 'their people' working was therefore a priority. The link is widely made, for example, between the current socioeconomic situation of the group, characterised by the absence of unemployment for resident members, and the actions of the four leaders (Riel, chapter 3, ref. 4).

Whether or not presented as legitimate, the escalating concentration of decision-making in the hands of a new generation organised as a cell is commonly recognised. The cell was disseminating the idea, among others, that the ownership of the means of production should be placed in the hands of the members, through designing and operating a communitarian economy. The actions of the predominant cell are, indeed, linked with the emergence of a single party composed of their supporters, together with a unique ideology and a monopoly on public communication and economic development, as well as interpretations of Essipiunnuat history and norms.

This concentration of power is also said to have produced an intensification of in-group conflicts, coupled initially with the exclusion of the preceding generation of decision-makers and other dissidents. As one Elder described at length, those who felt this exclusion from the centre of power continue to denounce this elimination as a great injustice. But in their view, they were not the only ones to be excluded. In fact, all those not part of the '*gang*', or somehow dissident to the ruling party or not in agreement with the new '*pattern*' of the reserve, were cast aside. Exclusion was, and remains for some, the key instrument used against opponents of the council. If you were not part of the political approach of the cell, then you were outside it. Right after the war, people were classified as being either 'in' or 'out' of the group, and their dignity and individual rights were allegedly dependent on their allegiance to in-group authority. Loyalty was somehow determining individual belonging to the group and being recognised, or not, as a full member (Mestenapeo, chapter 3, ref.1). To what extent these practices are still effective, even after 2016, remains difficult to assess and is not the purpose of this research.

One technique for exerting control over members consisted of lending money. Since it was not possible for Indians to get loans from a bank, money was being loaned at astronomical interest rates, which could reach 35 per cent. As Mestenapeo maintains, it was harder then to get support at the assembly since many in the room were increasingly vulnerable and fearful of their new leaders (chapter 3, ref. 8).

We can therefore see how the stories reflect the concentration of decision-making that followed the war within a small cell. Those who were excluded from this restricted circle felt that they were witness to an abuse of power. The stories suggest that dissidence or opposition to leaders was not much tolerated in post-Salmon War Essipit.

Before us there was nothing: metaphysics of domination

The concentration of power, in parallel with the introduction of a new system, was accompanied by various strategies of legitimisation. The new leaders peddled their own discourse, conceptions, practices and interpretations of the past that were to profoundly mark the group and its relation to the past, and still do today. The more autocratic the regime was to become, the more the interiority of the leaders was to be projected on the whole group and to be a powerful determinant of its mnemonic practices.

We might wonder to what extent a strong desire to forget – among leaders, for example – translated into a drive for collective erasure and a desire to make everyone forget. It is fascinating to study on a micro-scale how the psychological condition of a dominant leader, characterised by a form of *mnemophobia*, became a determining feature of the group's relationship with the past and led to one individual having political and economic control and to a gradual unification of interpretation.

Legitimacy and legitimation

The new leaders were allegedly fuelled by a strong sense of self-legitimacy in taking command to benefit the whole group. Legitimacy was rooted in disseminating a discourse, recognised by most members, that these new leaders spoke 'the truth' about the group's shared grievances, having been oppressed and tortured, and would make it a priority to overcome this state of affairs. Presented as a continuation of pre-war ideology and struggles, the legitimacy of their actions would be grounded and reinforced in a common experience of the war. They claimed to have the support of the whole community, with people telling them that their deeds were justified and thus their authoritative attitude was valid (Sam, chapter 3, ref. 8). Indeed, evaluation of their actions was presumably based on their higher knowledge concerning, among other things, the financial aspects of management and investments. The new leadership 'knew where to put the money' (Édouard, chapter 3, ref. 2).

Another discourse emanating from the leading cell is the sociohistorical context of everything they did in terms of the repeated dogma, 'before us, there was nothing'. Everything that took place prior to their intervention tended to be portrayed negatively, and this dominant mantra was disseminated and steadily absorbed by Essipiunnuat.

The psychological reserve: mental barbells

This discourse evidences the establishment of a post-war in-group governmentality, characterised by a specific and unidimensional representation of the group's past. This new *leitmotif* echoes a well-known dynamic of the production of ignorance intrinsic to bureaucratic and institutional formations, which is a favoured tool of legitimisation (McGoey, 2007; 2012a; 2012b).[12] As McGoey has demonstrated, ignorance is a powerful resource that can serve, 'as a productive asset … to command resources, deny liability in the aftermath of crises and to assert expertise in the face of unpredictable outcomes'; it can

12 On the study of ignorance or agnotology, see Gross and McGoey (2015); Proctor and Schiebinger (2008).

be 'harnessed as a resource, enabling knowledge to be deflected, obscured, concealed or magnified in a way that increases the scope of what remains unintelligible' (2011a; 2011b). The new post-Salmon War 'Indian' would therefore be born from nothing if it did not come from its powerful leaders, and was at risk of steadily returning to nothingness, if opposition to the new plan and its operators was expressed. Obviously, such a new and far-reaching statement regarding the Essipiunnuat past, reminiscent of the assertion that 'before the creation of the reserve, there was nothing',[13] reaches the core of the matter regarding cultural oblivion and its production. Whether qualified as directed forgetting, erasure with a goal of dissimulating traumas, monocratic rewriting or the predominance of a certain revolutionary ideology that does not valorise references to the past, this posture would have consequences for the group.

In the stories, emphasis is often given to the communitarian system set up after the war. This was central to the internal reordering put in place by the cell, and was allegedly the main tool for the economic, cultural, social and political autonomisation of the group. The origins of this system, which is still in place but which has been governed by a new general manager since 2016 – as well as its philosophy and legitimacy – are related to the experience of the group during the Salmon War. The system remained rooted in and dependent on this story, which could explain a gradual and observable rewriting of the unfolding of events, characterised by the centrality of its contemporary leaders in the stories. The Salmon War became a founding event in collective memory, but it also became a useful myth, allowing for its reactivation in accordance with specific purposes, such as mobilisation, but also repression. This is illustrated by the assertions interviewees now make that they are ready to defend the whole system just as they were ready to die for the communitarian net 30 years earlier (Raoul, chapter 3, ref. 2). As subsequent events would illustrate, it only takes a mention of war for mobilisation and norms of commitment to be triggered among the Essipiunnuat, and leaders have used this at times to their advantage.

That said, if a growing mythologisation of memory seems to favour the maintenance of in-group unity, the stability of the system and the commitment of members, the hypothesis can be made that it serves, above all, to legitimate the central command unit, its authority and heritage. This would help to explain how the ownership of the memory of the Salmon War is so crucial, as well as controversial, for the community.

13 This quote comes from the interview with late Elder Elise Ross and the archives used for the Attikamekw-Montagnais Council's report. See Laforest (1983).

Perceptions of authoritarianism: unearthing tyrannies

> The self-reflective activity of an autonomous society depends essentially upon the self-reflective activity of the humans who form that society. A politics of autonomy, if one doesn't want to be naive, can exist only by taking into account the human being's psychical dimension; it therefore presupposes a high degree of understanding of this being.
>
> Cornelius Castoriadis (2007, p. 151)

> The greater the power, the more dangerous the abuse.
>
> Edmund Burke

A close study of the testimonies evidences significant disagreements over established authority following the war. If interviewees frequently mention post-Salmon War technologies of governance, interestingly they are correlated with a reading of despotic attitudes that was to increase over time.

First, the results of the negotiation with the government left some individuals perplexed. The manner in which the negotiations were conducted is deplored as well as the attitude of those who finally settled the deal. In fact it was during these negotiations that the major generational switch of power – or, according to others, the takeover of the group by a small cell – was put into operation (Mestenapeo, chapter 3, ref. 8).

This point leads to internal arguments and a polarisation between the new power and its opponents (Ernest, chapter 3, ref. 6). Ideological intolerance was noted, then a lack of respect for different points of view. Any freedom of expression was noticeably devalorised, and some people felt they were pushed into an 'opponent of the regime' category (Ernest, chapter 3, ref. 5). These conflicts, associated with a power struggle during the Salmon War, have already been mentioned as the source of subsequent conflict within the group, including the unemployment crisis[14] that arose when segments of the group were systematically stigmatised for seditious actions against the council's authority (Ernest, chapter 3, ref. 6). Those identified as traitors by the administration were subsequently given a job, on the condition that they ask for forgiveness in public – a ritual humiliation remembered bitterly by those subjected to it. There was also increased exclusion of community members because of their ideological orientations and beliefs. This exclusion was not only perceived as related to ideological issues, but also critically to indigeneity.

14 This episode from the early 1990s is described at length in chapter 5, in its first section, 'The weaving of forgetfulness'. It began with a band member denouncing to the federal police a system of fraud that had been developed over time by the band administration. The event resulted in the court condemning the band administrator but also to great division within the community.

The schism in perception of the legitimacy of power, and about what is sacred, was to be enduring and would affect how the whole system was viewed in the years that followed.

The central critique did not pertain so much to the results of the leaders' actions but to their authoritarianism in decision-making, an approach unrespecting of ancient consensual modes of governance. Some of the interviewees assert that not all of the leaders believed in their struggles during the war and that if the people of the reserve had known this from the beginning, they would not have so readily accepted exclusion from that circle of decision-makers. This is perceived as a crucial and unacceptable determinant of disempowerment and weakening of the group, particularly since this duplicity was also witnessed by the Euroquébécois out-group.

When those who fished as their ancestors had always done, and lived in accordance with *Innu-aitun,* ceremonies and ancient modes of government, saw others ignorant of such traditional practices rising to dominance, they interpreted this as dishonourable, embarrassing and tantamount to treason (Ernest, chapter 3, ref. 5). After the war, they could not recognise the legitimacy of those who were presuming to speak for the group, but who were in fact camouflaging their real motivations which were mainly directed by personal interest (Ernest, chapter 2, ref. 6).

The sense of being used

There was a sense among the group that the leaders were unifying and dividing at will in their own interest, and that other members were being used rather than being authentically defended. For community members to be defended and supported by the band council was not dependent on principles, but on the willingness and discretionary power of some of the leaders (Ernest, chapter 3, ref. 1). Interviewees felt their deeds in the war were not recognised for their intrinsic heroic and sacrificial value, but only as a tool for leaders to gain power and legitimate it (Ernest, chapter 3, ref. 1). Mestenapeo confirms this view about manipulation:

> It really happened and it is terrible. Politically, they were using you but as soon as they did not need you anymore, you were left to one side. They would find a way to kick you out of the reserve. People just arriving on the reserve do not see that, but we, the older folks, we know their tactics. (chapter 3, ref. 6)

'They used to call him God': micro-scale autocracy

Another phenomenon that was observed concerns the gradual concentration of power in the hands of only one individual. This was to culminate in this particular individual gaining complete control over the group. Georges was, until May 2016, the director general of the band council and the only decision-maker for the group, with a veto on everything. He began his career as an employee of the band council in 1980.

Apart from some of the older interviewees, few of those taking part dared to address the issue of Georges' power and practices, and even less to articulate any criticism. The statements that follow are based on personal communications and interviews with those who experienced abuses of power, and on testimonies given confidentially, as well as more than a decade of field observations. These statements do not aim to break reputations or put anyone on trial, but only to uncover the regime of power that has been at the core of Essipiunnuat politics for decades and the central role exercised by this one public figure. The shadows cast by his own relationship with the past on the whole group's mnemonic practices became increasingly central to the investigation, although it was not the initial intended focus.

Since such monocratic pathologies are experienced in numerous communities plagued by psychological colonialism and the effects of intergenerational trauma, the experiences of Essipit in this area deserve to be exposed and shared widely. Truth and being courageously honest about toxic masculinities and abuse, whether sexual or power-related, are a core remedy for healing our wounded groups, especially since silence tends to benefit any abusers. The importance of shedding light on the power relations within the community, for the sake of truth, was mentioned in conversations, especially with the Elders. Truth-telling is particularly important for healing relationships, restoring intergenerational trust and for a healthy local political culture.

It is still too soon to access all the components of Georges' legacy, positive or negative, as he has only recently left office. His collaborators should in fairness not face such future investigations since they also felt the impact, to a certain extent, of his control and quest for power. These circumstances are well known in this small community; the past exclusion of dissidents, a local culture of secrecy, the fear of retaliation and members' almost complete financial dependence on the administration are factors that help to explain the silence surrounding his reign.

'One day, I will be the only one in charge': the elation of power

According to Mestenapeo, the current internal regime can only be understood if we shed light on the psychology of Georges, and the role he played. Early in his career, he explicitly stated that one day he would be the only one in charge of the whole group. His studies of authoritarian models, including Stalinist Russia, and the application of his methods of domination to assert total control over the small reserve were mentioned by several different people, including Elders. Generally the comments were made off the record, but some interviewees were ready to talk about it publicly. They were interviewees who were profoundly angry and who, when not traumatised by his deeds, had been deeply wounded by harassment and humiliation. The end result of Georges' reign would be the slide of the regime towards a very particular form of ethno-bureaucratic authoritarianism and the operationalisation of sophisticated modes of psychological control.

Hated, feared or showered with adulation, Georges exercised his authority through a small cell of devoted followers that he called his 'dogs'. He was keen to play the father figure, in particular towards vulnerable individuals, whose complete loyalty he felt was his. According to a female Elder, 'he is a very intelligent and charismatic man, there is no doubt of that. The problem is that he uses his power for bad purposes' (Adèle, personal conversation, 2011). As he once told me in conversation, pointing to one of my fatherless, very young cousins: 'Become his father figure and he will do whatever you want him to do' (personal communication with Georges, 2008). All the events experienced by the community, from the Salmon War to the unemployment crisis, were an opportunity for him to get a better grip on the destiny of the small group.

Facets of micro-totalitarianism: from monopoly of interpretation to the praxis of psychological domination

Georges' system of political, economic and cultural domination was based, among other things, on the weakness of the members' general assembly, the seat of democracy in the community, which he controlled entirely. The climate at the assembly was characterised by an atmosphere that discouraged attendance, and meant that people were afraid to speak in opposition to the line taken by the administration. There was a shared feeling among the residents that they would not succeed in changing the course set by the administration once it had been decided.

Georges made sure that he controlled the band council, the chief and the councillors, and made them his pawns. He was a master of the 'divide and rule' precept, but at a micro-level. If the debility of the general assembly gave more power to the chief and councillors, the weakness of this very council ensured that decision-making powers remained entirely in the hands of the general manager, Georges himself. He appointed directors who were loyal to him and obeyed his every order so that he retained complete power over the group.

Another feature of his system was economic control. The small band administration hired more than 500 people through various community-owned enterprises. Despite the interesting features of this local economic system, the fact remains that the band administration is more or less the only employer of band members, who are therefore entirely under its economic control. There was a general perception that whether or not workers received their salary was down to Georges' whim.

Such situations favour submissiveness and compliance with power. Also, as the majority of the employees of the band administration and community-owned businesses were Euroquébécois, and not band members, they had no political power and tended to be completely submissive in order to keep their jobs, thus reinforcing the leader's political domination. Band members who criticised the administration would experience pressure from Euroquébécois employees who felt they were in unstable work. Assertion by band members, for example, that the epistemological approach and cultural practices of the leaders were more Euroquébécois than Innu would be met with disapproval and taken as a threat, if not an accusation of racism, towards the Euroquébécois. It was therefore difficult to produce any internal cultural critique.

One of Georges' techniques was to play the Indian–white racial divide to his advantage, between Essipit and Les Escoumins in particular, by speaking to 'Indians' against the 'whites', and vice versa. This resulted in a constant division that could be reactivated at any time in order to change public attention, create a diversion or galvanise the group when needed.

On the one hand, he presented himself as an Innu wise man, but on the other, he would not hesitate to criticise other Innu communities and present Essipit as superior to other groups. I myself witnessed him on various occasions making disrespectful comments about others, including close collaborators, using misogynist and humiliating terminology. This is common knowledge within the group.

Indeed, Georges would exploit the anomie and cultural amnesia experienced by the group to increase his dominion and institute his word as the only valuable source of indigenous knowledge. Conveying the myth of the group absence of history, and favouring an interpretation of the group history through the eyes of the Euroquébécois colonial discourse would make even more space for rewriting. Significantly, he restricted Essipiunnuat history to a chronology of his own actions, which he meticulously upgraded year by year.[15]

Georges did not hesitate to use his charisma to seduce vulnerable individuals and use them for his own ends. The less the group considered itself as Innu, the more his own authoritative words could mystify his interlocutors.

Personal communications with community members reveal his brutishness if he experienced any dissent. Other people, as previewed in the testimonies, confirmed the grave accusations that had been made about his exploitation of people's weaknesses and generosity. Public insults and degrading comments to his collaborators during meetings, including his own family members –

15 This chronology is accessible at http://innu-essipit.com/essipit/rappelez-vous.php (consulted Jan. 2019).

such as 'get your finger out of your arse', for example – were heard. And he publicly humiliated the former chief (a candid and caring man), whom he regularly called 'turkey's feather'. He was particularly keen on questioning the intelligence of others in order to be perceived as possessing superior intelligence himself, and to take credit for positive developments emanating from Essipit.

The doctrine of 'divide and conquer' was deliberately employed with in this small community. In particular he diminished others during conversations and was astute at making interlocutors feel more intelligent through being close to him. This was especially effective with the younger generation who were more likely to question his authority and overshadow his reign. Potentially subversive, all younger members who could exercise power in the small community and question his intellectual superiority were progressively put aside by different stratagems in favour of a tiny 'gang' of people who were under his control. For example, the most recent chief, Martin Dufour, was 'chosen' precisely because he was entirely under Georges' control and he would do 'what we want him to do' (anon., 2011).[16]

He would sow the seeds of discord, leading some band members to believe that other band members were against them; he would cause the breakdown in relations between individuals in the group, create paranoia and ensure a climate of distrust. A technique used against dissidents, or those who did not share his views, was to circulate false information in order to damage their reputations and psychologically put pressure on them. Such circumstances of pressure, denigration, harassment and treason generally meant that the people concerned had no choice but to leave the reserve. Over time, he succeeded in distancing people with political power, either through expelling them from the group or through giving jobs to partners who did not have 'Indian status'. The mass hiring of Euroquébécois, who did not have any political voice in Essipit enterprises, ensured that he had complete control over them, as he was their provider. He surrounded himself with family members or people who were submissive and obedient to his orders; he exercised total control over incomes, political life and the interpretation of the group, in a typically autocratic style.

As he mentioned in conversations, he meticulously analysed the psychology of his surroundings. Since he knew everyone in the community, of any generation, he was relaxed about controlling parent as well as child, bending them to his will or finding their weaknesses. His speech was often characterised by an imposing aggression and arrogance that created a climate of fear.

Stories report a slip of the 'indigenous-communitarian' system into bureaucratic absolutism and authoritarianism. This was justified by its orchestrators as being due to external racial threats or internal attempts to 'destabilise' power, something quite surprising given the small size of the

16 Personal communication with one of his advisors who prefers to remain anonymous.

community. This was to have serious repercussions for the small group and its already critical cultural condition. Is it reasonable to hypothesise, in light of the stories, that the desire for control and policies of oblivion imposed on the group was nourished by a deeper personal desire to forget which could be related, among other things, to the leaders' own family circumstances and traumas going back to childhood? The biographies of long-standing leaders remain of primary importance, and deserve closer attention.

This kind of personage, and their success, can also be observed in other reserves as a symptom of psychological colonialism, perhaps best evidenced by the tyrant archetype, incarnated by the chief Tooktoo, in the novel *Chronicles of Kitchike*, by the *wendat* writer Louis-Karl Picard-Sioui. Such an authoritarian spirit and ethnic absolutism is clearly favoured by the colonial regime of the 1867 Constitution Act 91(24) and the Indian Act itself, which is founded on essentialist definitions and a racial fiction. The unhealthy valorisation of the 'good Indian' as being dominant over the 'bad Indian', yet obedient to colonial state and church institutions, is directly related to the irruption of sadistic practices and the scourge of humiliation in reserves. This is why a contemporary critique of these internal, and often invisible oppressions, should not overshadow the root cause of its emergence, which is the Canadian constitutional regime and the history of its implementation, as well as the intergenerational effects of residential school which a generation of leaders attended.

The colonial rule of the Indian Act gives overwhelming power to the imposed band council system, while not valorising in-group power sharing, consensual democracy and the responsibility of the leaders towards band members. The power concentrated in the hands of the director general appears, therefore, as a continuation of the Indian Agent's domination and facilitates the reproduction of the '*Indian-object*' for the purpose of the Crown's prevalence over First Peoples and their ancestral territories and the weakening of internal resistance.

Commitment in the light of experience

Retrospectively, and as in many revolutionary experiences, some people wonder if they would participate again in the Salmon War knowing the demagogic manoeuvrings that were to follow and the use of its memory for the erection of an authoritarian regime. Whether or not interpreted as legitimate, whether good or bad for the group, it is commonly recognised that a new paradigm was established in the community that gave priority to the recent past and tended to silence and present as non-existent what had preceded the war. As time passed, the interpretation of the war itself became increasingly articulated in a way that valorised the role of those exerting authority within the group. As autocratic rule was gradually instituted, the community's relationship with its past was overshadowed by the interiority and interests of a ruler who projected his own internal politics of forgetting and propensity for narcissism onto the whole group. The major effects of this are still difficult to grasp. What is evident though, is a tendency to perpetuate colonial features which represent the Essipiunnuat as having no past before the Salmon War (in the same pattern as no history having existed before the creation of the reserve), and which commodify Innu principles while allowing a simulacrum of indigeneity (such as playing the good Indian, discourse about Essipit as role-model and the *innubliable* marketing campaign). The complex process of metamorphosis by which the Indian-object, at the heart of Canadian colonial rule, became a simulated-Indian, remains a central contemporary topic; the case of Essipit raises the question of how a new subject, coming out of collective resistance, can be transformed again into an object, but according to local modalities. With the Punchinello character, An Antan Kapesh seized, perhaps before everyone else, the fact that the simulation of indigeneity would take centre stage for local managers as colonialism advanced among Innu, and the psychological effects it would have.

The scholar Bruno Cornellier (2013) has shown how what he calls the 'Indian thing' remains central to the comprehension of the dynamics of control over representations in terms of First Peoples and domination in general. This 'thing' corresponds to 'that constantly deferred presence of the self, which emerges from the interstices of a racial-colonial relation of power each time Natives and non-Natives attempt to designate that which is truly Indian and that which is not.' Brought back to power relations within First Peoples' communities, his perspective offers a tool towards a better comprehension of the phenomena of reification and internal domination, as a result of psychological colonisation, but also encompasses how,

> making the Indian [his] 'thing' means, for example, that [he] can define a reality even while taking care not to express precisely what that reality is or to what bodies (or surfaces) it truly refers. This allows the speaker or the creator of images to maintain a measure of control over what is defined and named, insofar as this naming calls out something that ultimately refers to nothing and no one ... the 'Indian thing' ... allows the subject to discriminate, exclude, or concretely identify the bodies that are presumed to be (or not to be) that 'thing' in virtue of a criterion of indeterminability which has as its only reference the will for power of the subject who says, represents, outlines, and authorises.

As this research unfolded, it gave rise to a strong awareness of the powerful determinant of oblivion that this autocratic rule represented. Georges once asked about the research: 'Are you sure you want to dig into our past? Abusers won't like it!' (Georges, 2009). If some understanding of the colonial system, and the individual traumatic experiences it generated, helps to contextualise the tyrannies experienced by Essipiunnuat, amnesty cannot be given to its dominant actors in spite of their age, traumas and wounds. Yet it would be healthy for the next generation to thoroughly investigate their deeds, which were exercised in the public realm, and to evaluate all dimensions of their heritage in order to avoid the reproduction of colonial patterns of domination among themselves; a return to the teachings, repeatedly evoked by Elders, to the effect that only the truth can help heal a person or family group.

There is evidence that the leaders, and then the leader, were inclined to use the group identity, and control of its memory, in order to legitimate personal power and authority. Testimonies, personal communications and direct observations illustrate, despite widespread insecurity at making such claims, intense in-group polarities over the legitimacy of the current internal regime, a schism that increased until it became unbridgeable under an autocratic rule that did not tolerate any interpretation beyond its own reach. It is one of the roles of oral history, and the sociology of mnemonic practices, to break those unified dimensions and to re-establish silenced voices as a critical evaluation of the group's condition and its internal order. There is also a confluence here with *Innu aitun* and philosophy, which tends to affirm that memory is in a sense integral, that the truth will out, that it flows inevitably to the present.

Conclusion

This chapter has examined the multilateral and complex transformative experience of the Salmon War for the Essipiunnuat. Collective self-experience of uprising took the form of remodelling the Essipiunnuat relational system through the breakdown of some relationships and the forging of new associations, which culminated in a dynamic of reidentification. Essipit was then reinstated as a prime and valuable group of reference for the great majority of those who took part, mainly in opposition to out-group racist and integrationist definitions.

A second theme concerns alterations of individual and collective self-identity and conceptions, mainly the narration of a passage from a state of collective non-existence, inherent in the pre-war period, to the perception of a collective self during and after the war which allowed increased identification with it, with associated impacts on norms, attitudes and behaviours.

Thirdly, the phenomenon of collective self-empowerment was identified as an outcome of the uprising. People's commitment to acts of asserting their *indigenous* social identity allegedly culminated in self-representations of an *empowered* self. Yet inversely, advancements of the out-groups' definitions of legitimate practices resulted in disempowerment, institutional illegitimacy, contestations and auto-critics, in the wake of actions some carried out in the name of the collective.

Fundamentally, stories on empowerment and disempowerment reveal a schism best illustrated by polarities in the reception of state recognition and in the interpretation of Essipiunnuat 'self' and the possibility of its commodification for the purpose of domination. Such divergence in conceptions of recognition reveals a deeper fracture concerning the identity of the group itself and its sources, and the power over their interpretations.

A final transformation concerns in-group reordering and the establishment of new modes of control, but also specific self-representations related to it. Significantly, this internal reorganisation includes the condensation of the decision-making process into the hands of a small cell of people, and the exclusion of older leaders who somehow became dissidents of the new regime, often in spite of themselves. It also reports the appropriation of power devices by a small group, and then by one individual. This person's supremacy appears to have been reinforced by the reproduction of pre-war *sui nullius*, culminating in a metaphysic of self-control ensuring total legitimacy for all subsequent actions.

Autocrats naturally project their own relationship with the past onto the group; a strong desire to forget can then become a 'command to forget', with its subsequent result of controlling access to the past, and then the modalities of collective identity for total control. Was the new Essipiunnuat 'subject', born out of people's response to sociohistorical perils, threatened, then, with becoming an object or sinking into nothingness in the future in not respecting the new normative order and its sole guardian?

There is clear evidence in the stories that the group has experienced a gradual shift towards an advanced form of authoritarianism, in transgressions with ancestral conceptions. The post-Salmon War dominant discourse is contested on the basis that it is a mere reproduction of essential colonial images of the '*Indian*' aiming at its continuous control and annihilation, mainly manufactured through the Indian Act and its definitions of legitimate 'Indianness', translated in bureaucratic terms. The question of how much the Essipiunnuat freed themselves, or not, from the colonial representation of indigeneity as 'disease' and 'something to heal' remains open.

Inevitably, the promises of a post-Salmon War collective self were to confront the requirements of a developing new order, in particular the attractions of essentialisation for the very purpose of legitimation. Its shape was evidently influenced, if not mostly determined, by the designers who took over the responsibility of collective development and management. Pre-war Essipiunnuat self-representations were imbued with Crown representations of the '*Indian*', as well as the Euroquébécois social imaginary and complexes.

In the light of people's stories, it appears that these representations, deeply related to a system of power and colonial domination, were not extirpated by decolonisation efforts, especially along psychological lines; they were, on the contrary, reproduced and refined for purposes of political domination and internal control. The *Indian-as-object*, at the core of the Crown imagery, was to be re-framed as *simulated-Indian* as a tool of social control.

The idea that these images were widely and explicitly reproduced in the new system, is validated by older people who have a better view of the whole process, from before the war to the present day. The cohabitation of *indigenist* and *essentialist* representations was to generate significant cultural antinomies and a crisis of auto-referentiality. Essipiunnuat self-representation, post-Salmon War, appeared widely modelled in accordance with the requirements of the new normative order, including its legitimisation, but dependent on their 'controllers' and their highly personal conception and interpretation of being Essipiunnuat. The concentration of power inevitably resulted in increased dependence on leaders' representations of the group, including their version of the war, but also on their interiorities and inner knowledge, and their respect or denial of indigenous epistemologies. A deep desire to forget can become a drive to erase, a command to forget, and an act of rewriting in accordance with a self-centred chronology.

If cultural crisis is an attribute of the pre-war Essipiunnuat condition, it remains central to their experience of the Salmon War and presumably as important to their current condition and actuality. It echoes forms of nostalgia and regret, but above all a suspicion regarding the past and an obvious propensity to forget it in the present that deserves close attention.

5. The Essipiunnuat's actuality in light of the past

And we forgot because we must
And not because we will.
Matthew Arnold, 'Absence' (1857)

When you look long into an abyss, the abyss looks into you.
Nietzsche

Despite our wars, we will always have to make peace again.
Essipiunnu Elder (2009)

How can stories we tell about the past inform us about our current condition, our actuality?[1] This chapter will examine mnemonic practices in the stories, in order to exhume elements of the Essipiunnuat's current condition in the light of people's ways of relating to the Salmon War and their past. The first section outlines the main forces identified in the testimonies as favouring oblivion of the Salmon War, including interferences in remembrance, the social as well as the historical determinants of forgetting, and the normative charge contained in the memories of those who took part. The second section describes what accounts of the past reveal about the group's current condition or contemporary realities, including nostalgia, social criticism and views on its current needs and cultural condition. The final section concerns elements of the stories pertaining to intergenerational transmission, including contents and means, as perspectives on collective self-design and reversibility.

The weaving of forgetfulness

Elements acknowledged as fostering the oblivion of the Salmon War are clearly identifiable in the stories. First, specific episodes that occurred between its ending and the moment people told their stories (mainly 2009–11). Second, there is logic to forgetting the war, ranging from the automatic oblivion of trauma, the will to forget as a consequence of cultural assimilation, to features of a desire to forget; and finally, reminiscences of the Salmon War reveal the non-absoluteness of forgetting and its high normative charge as a major event.

1 In this chapter, 'actuality' refers to what is considered as 'real' or 'facts' about the group's actual cultural conditions according to the stories.

Interferences in remembering (1981–2011)

In recalling the Salmon War, people often refer to events that occurred after it. For example, in some cases, they systematically conflate the war with another event that occurred ten years later, the unemployment crisis. In different ways, such interferences in remembrance influence people's relationship with the past. These in-between memories, confused with the Salmon War, operate as a veil over the past in general and as 'dams' preventing the return to dimensions of the past-self. They are significant since they inhabit the group imaginary and are part of its current condition; obstacles people stumble over when on the path of remembrance. These incidents provide elements that are now included in people's cultural inventory and their conception of their past and are therefore inherent in their present.

The following incidents often arise in conversations about the war and it is necessary to describe them in order to grasp their implications for memory. They are, respectively, the agreement of 1982 that officially ended the war; the reintegration of new members (for example, women who had married Euroquébécois men, and their children) following the 1985 partial redefinition of Indian status pertaining to women as contained in the Indian Act; and, finally, the internal crisis of 1990, remembered as the 'unemployment benefit' crisis that led to intense tension and violence within the group. This followed internal denunciations of fraud and allegations of attempts to oust leaders established for a decade.

Post-Salmon War agreements on fishing (1982–)

In July 1981, after a violent intervention by the people of Les Escoumins to counter Innu resistance, the Essipiunnuat ended their salmon fishing season. The following year, Québec and Essipit reached an agreement. The government recognised the group's right to spread a community net west of Escoumins wharf, and to distribute the catches among members. The group was 'granted' a Québec licence on this basis. In parallel, Essipit agreed to participate in a study conducted by the Canadian government on the impact of their fishing activity. The study did not lead to any conclusive findings.

Subsequent negotiations led to the Essipit–Les Escoumins co-management of salmon fishing on the river, and strategies of development for sport fishing in the early 1990s, well documented by Paul Charest (2009; 2012). Community fishing and the distribution of salmon were abandoned thereafter, allegedly because the amount of salmon in the river decreased. Salmon were only caught for the annual summer community gathering (in the sea on the coast of the reserve, and not in the Esh Shipu River). As with any other sport fishermen, Essipiunnuat were allowed to fly fish on the river if they bought the same Québec state licence required by other Euroquébécois.

These negotiations and agreements on salmon fishing, and the constraints they created for the Essipiunnuat, were received with much scepticism. As documented previously, the requirement to pay the Québec government for a licence was viewed as illogical and humiliating. If some people accepted the idea of paying fishing fees in order to support salmon conservation activities, they categorically refused to buy a licence from the state. They argued that, as Innu, they did not need any state permission for hunting or fishing; for them, this was the core issue. It was interpreted as an invalid and unacceptable concession, a violation of the principles they stood for and for which they had been ready to die during the war (Ernest, chapter 4, ref. 18). The requirement was seen as a symbolic surrender of their inherent sovereignty. Some inhabitants categorically refused to get the licence and preferred not to fish at all:

> The Québec government will not receive a penny from me. They will not get this compromise. I have always said the same thing: I will pay for the right to fish in the river, to support the river, but I will never buy a licence from the Québec state, even if it cost almost nothing. For me, it is a question of principle. Why? If we don't respect this principle, everything collapses. Agreement, agreement, agreement ... there are things that we must protect, that we must keep ... When I think of the Salmon War, it also reminds me that I must now pay a licence to Québec if I want to fish ... and that I don't go to fish for that very reason. And I won't go, as long as I have to pay for that licence. Perhaps I will be so old that I will not have the urge to go ... not as a poacher, but as an Innu. (Raoul, chapter 4, ref. 7)

Fundamentally, these concessions were interpreted as the group being caught in the government's game. The latter was primarily interested in preventing the expansion of Innu assertion of ancestral sovereignty. The spreading of a net by the wharf meant the assertion of inherent rights outside the mere borders of the reserve, and the *Innu tipenitamun* clash with Euroquébécois and Crown claims to sovereignty. Granting a licence for communitarian fishing was therefore the preferred means of stopping this growth and reaffirming that Innu rights flow from the sovereignty of the Crown (Raoul, chapter 4, ref. 7).

Similarly to the first explorers' strategy of awarding small mirrors to chiefs in exchange for ancestral territories to which 'they belonged as humans', and from which they could not be alienated, it seemed incoherent to be 'granted' a right when they already had that right (Pierre, chapter 4, ref. 30). Older people therefore interpreted the agreements that followed the war as governments playing tricks in order to extinguish Innu sovereignty, a treason, in their eyes, against the spirit of the Salmon War (Pierre, chapter 4, ref. 5).

Less than a decade after the rebellion, the council decided to stop community activities so that members could not fish salmon together any more; a situation that those who took part in the study lamented and which provoked lasting rancour:

> They spread the net at the pow wow, when ministers and the deputy minister were visiting. They 'must' eat salmon. But we, on the reserve, we do not eat salmon anymore. I and many others cannot accept that. You do not even taste it today. After ten years of scientific research, it is enough; you must also give some to your community. Before, each family received a bit of salmon, a couple of pounds per family. It was not a lot, but at least everybody could eat salmon. (Tshak, chapter 4, ref. 2)

Bill C-31 (1985)

Until 1985, in accordance with the Indian Act, women with Indian status who married non-Indian men lost that status. They were required to leave their community, and their children lost their rights as well. Thus, according to federal legislation, they were not considered Indian anymore. But non-Indian women who married Indian men obtained the status and were legally considered 'Indian'. In the mid 1980s, this legislation was judged as discriminatory against women, and the situation changed partly in 1985 when the Canadian parliament passed Bill C-31 modifying the Indian Act. Some of the discriminatory provisions pertaining to the status of women were ended. A number of women and their children who had been denied or lost status and/or band membership in the past had that membership suddenly reinstated (Canada – Department of Indian Affairs and Northern Development, 1985).

In Essipit, this resulted in a significant increase in the number of band members. The return of the women to the community was allegedly opposed by some of the leaders (Mestenapeo, personal communication, December 2011). Some of these new members had been living outside the reserve in Les Escoumins. Consequently, some individuals who were against Essipit in the Salmon War, and had been enemies, became members (*membre apparenté* in French, or 'related member') of the band, a situation that was to cause tension for a long time (Raoul, chapter 2, ref. 23). Some confess to having had images in their mind of these people as individuals who had been ready to fight against Essipit, and felt aggrieved that they now belonged to the group (Adam, chapter 2. ref. 3).

Individuals who acquired their status in 1985 were called the '6.2'. The arrival of those among them who had fought against the group in the Salmon War resulted in direct confrontations (Mestenapeo, chapter 4, ref. 3). This return of the women and their children with reinstated membership came with a phenomenon unique in the history of the group: an increase in non-members resident in the community. These mostly comprised the Euroquébécois husbands (who were not band members) of these women, often self-reliant individuals who were unlikely to be submissive.

Thirty years after the Salmon War, some of the most committed warriors still felt sad when observing people who were against the reserve, or who were not at all committed to its defence. They felt pushed aside. A direct link is made between this situation of former enemies in positions of authority, and a form of collective amnesia of the war, including a disregard for the actions of the most committed warriors (Mestenapeo, chapter 4, ref. 3). Some of these former enemies, including family members of Georges, were recruited and placed in key positions in the band administration. Now in a position of power, they would have no interest in remembering the war or the actions of those who committed to it; they would, instead, do everything they could to prove their allegiance to the council:

> What is our place [the former warriors and commanders of the Salmon War] in this community today? We are forgotten. I see some members today who entered the reserve in 1985, and would never have wanted to defend the reserve in 1985. I still see them, they were up the hill, in front of the wharf, watching us struggling ... And I see them today, they are band councillors ... So it makes us wonder ... (Mestenapeo, chapter 4, ref. 8)

The unemployment benefit crisis (1989–90)

In 1989 a member of the band contacted the Royal Canadian Mounted Police (RCMP) in order to expose fraud in Essipit. The band council and its managers were accused of defrauding the Canadian federal system of unemployment insurance. The RCMP opened up a communication channel with one of their liaison officers and initial meetings were organised in the parking lot of a shopping centre (Sam, chapter 4, ref. 6).

Soon after, the RCMP set up a tactical squad that entered Essipit in the summer of 1989. Helicopters and police surrounded the community. Roads were blocked. The administrative offices were occupied. All computers and community archives were seized. In an attempt to resist the intervention, a barricade of cars parked in the middle of the road was quickly formed. But the size of the RCMP squad rapidly outnumbered the rioters, who were taken by surprise by the sudden use of tear gas (Sam, chapter 4, ref. 6).

All employees of the band council were questioned, and many of them were blackmailed and threatened with more than $30,000 in penalties if they were found guilty of fraud and of non-cooperation (Sam, chapter 4, ref. 6). But if they did cooperate with the investigation, they could be rewarded with full protection and a reduced sentence. Band managers pressured those requesting their silence to avoid the risk of retaliation. A growing climate of mistrust arose in the community, and violence broke out between supporters and opponents of the regime. Dubious information was circulating. Serious doubts possessed certain individuals who had shared information with the federal authorities under pressure.

Leaders maintain that band managers and council members were not benefiting personally from the fraud, as some informants had claimed. They defend the idea that the community used the federal unemployment insurance to create jobs. The system set up by the managers consisted of giving employees with seasonal jobs higher wages than they would normally receive, so that they could receive higher unemployment benefits. Thereafter, they gave back a portion of their wage so that more jobs could be created. This procedure was well established and all employees were aware of it. It was not necessarily illegal or in violation of federal law.

The council's official discourse is that the system developed was legitimate, and that the actions were based on an integral Innu right to self-government. From this perspective, the actions of the council that led to the crisis in 1990 were a continuation of the principles defended in the Salmon War. The difference was the type of rights being defended (Mesnak, chapter 4, ref. 3). However, a court case resulted in the conviction of four members of the band administration. The council decided not to appeal the decision, allegedly to facilitate reconciliation in the community. The leaders decided not to have members of the council's political branch condemned, in order to demonstrate their enduring trust in them. An agreement was reached, and the community had to pay more than $750,000 back to the government. But the greatest cost remains the internal divisions in the group.[2]

The general assembly blamed the informants and cast suspicion on employees. Some families were excluded from the distribution of salmon. All political opponents were described as being behind an attempted coup and were publicly accused of being enemies of the group. There were divisions in all families between supporters and opponents, and the community experienced its darkest hours. The council identified a community member as the mastermind and the individual mainly responsible for the government's attack on the community. He was judged a traitor by the general assembly, especially because of his higher education and his role in the mobilisation of members against the council. Despite objections from the League of Rights and Freedom, he was condemned to leaving the reserve. Stones were thrown at the front windows of his house (Sam, chapter 4, ref. 6).

Employees identified as informants could resume their positions only if they asked publicly for forgiveness before the assembled members. Some submitted to this public humiliation, but others did not. In 2000, the band council decided to draw a line under the episode; no one need henceforth apologise or request forgiveness. In this way, the council implicitly recognised

2 'It cost the community a lot, but it is not the money that hurts. It is the human cost that was enormous. It is the human relations that have been hit hard. Yes, and in all families. There are no exceptions. We are a very small community.' (Adam, ch. 4, ref. 10)

that responsibility for what happened was shared, something that would facilitate in-group reconciliation (Adam, chapter 4, ref. 10).

The new members had arrived (following Bill C-31) in the midst of this crisis. They were caught between two in-group clans at war and were under pressure to take sides (Karl, chapter 4, ref. 3). However, some of the new members had been ambivalent in the Salmon War, and had sometimes been the enemy. Some were eagerly looking for opportunities to show allegiance to their new group, and the unemployment crisis helped them to demonstrate loyalty, to quickly integrate and erase their previous shameful deeds (Justin, chapter 2, ref. 3). However, this resulted in collaborators being zealously condemned and informants being stigmatised (Pishimnapeo, chapter 4, ref. 1). Those who did not live on the reserve during the conflict and did not directly experience it are the ones who tended to be the most intolerant and did not accept the amnesty (Adam, chapter 4, ref. 10).

Unlike the Salmon War, which is associated with the solidarity of the group, the 1990 crisis concerns deep and unhealed collective wounds resulting from contention and polarisation. Those who experienced the episode still suffer from it privately even though it occurred three decades ago. Mourning is not over and the resentment is toxic (Ernest, chapter 2, ref. 7). Many questions remain unanswered and there is a lack of information pertaining to the events of 1990 that contributes to the perpetuation of a general uneasiness about it (Adam, chapter 4, ref. 10). Some people still feel that they were victims of an injustice. They cannot explain or forgive their treatment to this day:

> The crisis of 1990 was the worst experience in my life. We were suddenly excluded from the community. It was hard. I don't think I will ever be able to forgive council members. Because the employees, the workers, they had the right to have unemployment benefit, but they had no choice but to deal with the system established by the administration if they wanted to have it. They were trapped in the system. But the leaders, the bureaucrats, they were not trapped ... It was the workers. So they did not know what the workers were facing while dealing with the RCMP agents. The employees were simply struggling with RCMP threats, trying to avoid paying as much of the penalty as possible ... This episode was very painful, I found it terrible. I personally never want to speak about it anymore. (Ernest, chapter 4, ref. 3)

Consequently, the stories frequently express the belief that this episode in their history 'should be forgotten all together' (Ernest, chapter 2, ref. 7). The conflicts generated by the Salmon War wound down much more rapidly than those from 1990, about which there is palpable tension to this day (Ernest, chapter 4, ref. 10). Crueller than the Salmon War in its impact on families and relations, the 1990 episode generally induces silence and a strong willingness among members to forget (Adam, chapter 4, ref. 2).

In the stories, interviewees often conflate the episodes of 1980 and 1990. This confusion usually comprises the elements of the unemployment crisis being inserted into Salmon War and accounts range from asserting that the RCMP had a role in 1980 to stating that people were attacked with tear gas. Some people completely confused the two events while others' memory of the Salmon War disappeared beneath their recollections of the unemployment crisis. It is also noticeable that some statements, which need closer examination, simulated forgetfulness or complete amnesia (Ivan, chapter 4, ref. 1; Karl, chapter 4, ref, 3; Alyha, chapter 4, ref. 1). Indeed, entire memory blanks, real or simulated, were often invoked as a reason for refusing to be interviewed. The occurrence of the 1990 episode would reinforce a collective propensity to forget the past, including memories of the Salmon War (Ernest, chapter 4, ref. 16).

References to events that occurred between the Salmon War and the present day are significant; they are clearly linked with the Salmon War and interfere in the rememorisation or oblivion of it in different ways. Therefore, these past events have a direct impact on the remembrance of the Salmon War. They institute, each in their own ways, dams or negative conditioning favouring disconnection with the past and the forgetting of preceding episodes.

The logic of forgetting: a microsociology of oblivion

What are the main elements contributing to the forgetting of the Salmon War, as exposed in the stories? What are the 'dams', the centrifugal forces or elements mentioned as obstacles to rememorising and to reconnecting with its imaginary? Identifying those forces that are favourable to the oblivion of the event, its silencing or denial, taking into account the deep rupture in intergenerational transmission that comes with it, could facilitate a better understanding of the group's cultural condition, or, to use an expression coined by the artist Jimmie Durham, of 'what we know about ourselves and what we want to be' (quoted in Lippard, 1993).

The study of amnesia in its most subjective forms offers insights into the shadowed side of the self, what we don't what to know about ourselves and don't want to be. It is assumed here that forgetting is not given fair value in research as a decisive dimension of cultural memory. Forgetfulness relates to what we don't want to know anymore, including that which we don't want to be and don't want to reproduce through transmission to the next generation. It is shadowy yet potent, as it intensely affects cultural investment and shapes the future self. The study of oblivion as a produced and subjective outcome deserves closer attention.

Whether unintentional, intentional, or more social in nature, the phenomenon of forgetting has severe normative implications. In all cases, forgetting and its causes shape an individual's access to the collective inventory of experience, and therefore the capacity for evaluation. It also has consequences for the imagination. Loss of memory can be automatic, as in the case of childhood trauma. It can also be more densely subjective, as a manifestation of a willingness or desire to forget and erase something judged irrelevant, embarrassing, unbalancing for the self-image, or worthy of desacralisation through silencing. Forgetting can also be social in nature; for example, the absorption of a dominant selective memory, through 'antinomic' elements and images, can result in self-denial. In addition to those already discussed, four other determinants of forgetting the Salmon War surfaced in the stories: traumas, the protection of relationships, interests in denial, and a bureaucratic will to ignorance through erasure and rewriting.

Traumas and mnemophobia

The Salmon War was deeply associated with negative feelings of fear, sadness, suffering and shame. For many, whether they participated directly in the war or not, it was a traumatic experience in which they faced violence, humiliation and aggression. The automatic forgetting of negative and traumatic experiences is well known (Widom and Morris, 1997; Sheflin and Brown, 1996), and is particularly intense when it concerns the experience of abuse as a child, or of military combat. The experience of being abused significantly affects the recalling of an episode and the circumstances surrounding its occurrence (Van der Kolk, 1997).

People describe how the intensity of their feelings of stress, fear and diverse suffering effectively explains why they forgot episodes of the war. Paradoxically, the wish not to relive such an episode, related to remembrance and the ability to resist, remains a mainstay of their desire to forget. The worst times, those associated with intense feelings of stress, for example, are more or less forgotten automatically, and people express disconnections with memories of the war together with a desire not to relive such situations and emotional states (Ernest, chapter 2, ref. 2).[3]

One individual was a teenager during the war. He was beaten and slapped in the face on one occasion but had completely forgotten about it, although he remembered it while being interviewed. As he was wondering if anyone had taken pictures during the Salmon War, he suddenly remembered that he had himself been doing so. As his memories returned, he recalled that he had been asked to take photographs and that it was because he was taking photographs of Euroquébécois who were trying to beat up Innu that he had been attacked.

Karl began crying during his recounting of certain episodes of the war as he remembered the times when he suffered. He confessed that forgetting had

3 Various elements of post-traumatic syndromes were identified.

brought him internal peace, but that such inner calm came only with the passing of time (chapter 4, ref. 1).

Another type of forgetting of the war pertains to individuals' life circumstances. Each person has a particular relationship with her or his own past. For some, events that occurred before the war made their relationship with their past highly problematic, and that was also true of the Salmon War. For example, one Essipiunnu had experienced a traumatic situation during his childhood – the loss of a friend in tragic circumstances. This seems to explain why a form of mnemophobia had overtaken him and led to a desire to turn away entirely from the past.

For others the Salmon War happened to coincide with a difficult period in their lives. One older woman, for example, did not want to recall anything about that exact time because she had been in the process of getting divorced and being thrown out of her house. Another person preferred not to speak about the war because she had almost died in a car accident during that period. Mention of the Salmon War reminded someone else that he had been dependent on drugs at the time. In almost all of these cases, the desire not to talk about the war, or the past in general, was accompanied by visible discomfort, suffering and manifestations of shame.

Protection of relations

Forgetfulness as a means of being able to 'co-exist' is described as a core element contributing to the forgetting of the war. Unlike other movements of decolonisation, the Essipiunnuat had to remain alongside the 'colonisers', or be symbiotic with them. This highly particular situation must be given careful consideration if we are to comprehend the importance of silencing memories of the war in order to recreate links and find stability in relationships. As opposed to various decolonisation processes around the world, Innu individuals and families, largely outnumbered over time by the settler population, must exist side by side with the local Euroquébécois population in perpetuity

In many cases, the silence surrounding the events of the war was a prerequisite to maintaining relationships. Former enemies linked by family ties would speak with each other again, but never of the Salmon War (Karl, chapter 4, ref. 1). The impact of the war on the group's social relations was long-lasting and some divisions persist to the present day. In order to re-establish relations with the people of Les Escoumins, especially former friends, some people decided to put aside the bitterness associated with the memory of war. To a certain extent, this became a social necessity (Karl, chapter 3, ref. 5).

Despite being hidden and harder to detect, racism directed towards the Innu still exists in Les Escoumins – extending to within the group itself and among employees of the band – and has existed for as long as people can remember. Yet, since the Essipiunnuat must live closely tied to this village, they have developed a thick skin so that they can talk to their colleagues, clients or neighbours, despite being conscious of the racist attitudes held by some of them (Raoul, chapter 2, ref. 25). But there remain open wounds, despite the passage of time (Raoul, chapter 2, ref. 25). The impact of such silence on Essipiunnuat self-conception now needs to be investigated.

Certain interviewees now work in pubic-facing careers and are forced to serve ex-enemies. One individual explains that when former foes speak to him, he answers because he is obliged to. Yet, were it not for his position, he would act differently:

> If I could, I would tell them 'Hey you! Go away! I have not forgotten. The Salmon War … if you forgot it, I haven't. I have many small scars on my heart, so go away; I do not want anything to do with you.' But we do not really have the choice. We do not forget, but we must close the lid. This is how it is. (Tshak, chapter 3, ref. 2 and 5)

The main reason invoked to explain why 'moving on' is imperative is that not doing so would only penalise those who constantly remember the war. They live day-by-day with their former enemies and meet them each time they go out into any public spaces outside the reserve. Therefore, cultivating the memory of the war and remembering the injustice suffered results in self-exclusion from local networks of relationships, and also leads to self-penalisation. The forgetting and silence are, therefore, ways of complying with the requirements of living together, coupled with an inability to forgive. In Tshak's words, 'If the smoke evaporated, the burn scars would still be vivid' (Tshak, chapter 4, ref. 2 and 3).

This leads some people to maintain that the primary function of the Essipiunnuat's silence and lack of assertiveness is to please the Euroquébécois. The episode then becomes a negative moment to be forgotten altogether (Justin, chapter 4, ref. 2). Everyone taking part acknowledges that they did not talk about the war afterwards. They kept it inside, mainly to stop the intergenerational transmission of their inner hatred and resentment towards the other Les Escoumins community:

> I believe that people of Essipit did not want to hate people of Les Escoumins as much as they did. Because we will both stay here and we will live a long time. My children and grandchildren will also live with them. So we kept a silence about the war with the thought in mind to stop the haemorrhage; our children will not be hated, and they will not hate the other children (Napeo, chapter 4, ref. 8).

As for others involved in the study, Pishimnapeo, for example, maintains that it is better not to mention names of past opponents in remembering the war because it could hurt people needlessly, and could be used to attack those who do not deserve it. In his view, opponents were more guided by their ignorance than being really opposed to Essipiunnuat claims and inherent rights. Many of them would now realise their foolishness (Pishimnapeo, chapter 4, ref. 1).

Interests in denial

The role each person played in the war has a central impact on remembrance or non-remembrance, as demonstrated earlier. It is a pivotal determinant of forgetfulness. Some members who were not committed at the time now have a certain social status in the community. Some were not previously members of the group but became so in 1985. Some Euroquébécois, whose parents were openly enemies of the 'Indians', are now married to Essipiunnuat and/or are employed by the community, either by its administration or in its enterprises. The evaluation of these past-selves and the roles played in the war directly determine a willingness to forget the event in order to maintain a positive self-image and/or to protect their integration within the group. These elements help to explain this willingness to forget, to silence, to erase, and, in some cases, to effect a simulation of forgetfulness.

One individual, for example, was a band council member at the time of the interview. In 1980, he was in his mid 20s. He was reluctant to give an interview about the Salmon War and, during it, he admitted that he had been partying and drinking a lot at that time. He had not been committed to the war at all and did not participate. He was also working outside the community in lumber camps. He dates his integration into and commitment to the community to 1986. He was keen to discuss his role as a warrior in the unemployment crisis but preferred not to talk of the Salmon War and to forget all about it. Therefore, it seems that he does not remember it because of his activities at that time, which appear to be a source of shame for him; this results in a willingness to forget the whole event (Justin, Chapter 4, ref. 1). Members' friendships with Euroquébécois, and their choice not to commit in order to protect these relationships, were also mentioned as a central cause of non-participation. Today, such an attitude is, for many, a source of embarrassment (Ernest, chapter 4, ref. 5).

As mentioned above, certain individuals who were formerly hostile to Indians, not only became members of the group in 1985 but became influential in decision-making processes. A former councillor, for example, whose role in 1980 was allegedly hostile to Essipit, is known to have been a fierce protector of the leaders under attack in 1990. This role earned him great recognition from Georges, who presented him as his 'saviour' and included him in the decision-making circle (he became a band councillor as well). Other individuals' parents were anti-Innu leaders but they now have family ties with Essipit and influential positions in the band administration (Maxence, chapter 2, ref. 5).

There are other examples of willingness to put the Essipiunnuat's past, and more specifically the Salmon War, aside. Deep inside, these negative self-perceptions or bad-selves 'to be soon forgotten' remain correlated with assertive indigeneity and a cultural memory specific to Innu norms and their defence. Also observable is not only the will to forget their past 'anti-Indian' role, but the image of the rebellious Innu from which it was built. The cultural assimilation of the Essipiunnuat has already been widely discussed. However, this dynamic of assimilation has not stopped with the Salmon War. Essipiunnuat absorption of the Euroquébécois imaginary continued after the war in often subtle ways.

The arrival of new members and their families in the wake of Bill C-31 after 1985 clearly had an impact on remembrance of the Salmon War. The subsequent economic developments of the community, and the extensive employment of Euroquébécois within the organisation, reinforced the predominance, and therefore the absorption, of their social imaginary. Intermarriage with Euroquébécois remains common. Euroquébécois dependent on Essipit for their incomes tend to distance themselves from the hostile, if not racist, postures of their parents during the war, and from the event in general.

But this phenomenon of forgetfulness and silence about the war appears to surpass the need to maintain relationships and friendships or income security. Québec's colonial selective memory and national narrative shouldn't be underestimated as a fertile soil for oblivion among Essipiunnuat, and for the erasure of indigenous postures and rewriting in accordance with Euroquébécois collective identity needs. Commenting on a stage play called *Invention,* University of San Diego professor Julie Burelle (2014) testifies to a long-standing cultural dynamic of rewriting in Québec, pertaining to this society's relationship with First Peoples:

> When Québec celebrates these early alliances as a sign of a more benevolent form of encounter with First Peoples, it fails to account for the long history of betrayal that followed these alliances and that eventually left First People[s] on the margin of their own territory. While Canada's role in betraying since the creation of the country is undeniable, Québec demonstrates here a form of selective memory that supports its own identity politics and *Invention* does little to disrupt this idealized narrative of the past. (p. 32)

The absorption of the Euroquébécois imaginary, which is characterised by a deep-seated psycho-cultural denial of the existence of the Innu, is a powerful determinant of amnesia. Once internalised through assimilation, it appears as a core element of cultural oblivion and self-denial among the Innu themselves. In the case of Essipiunnuat, the effect of being overwhelmed with Québécois' nationalist discourse and interpretations not only marginalises the Innu referential but also other dimensions of the group memory. It includes, for example, the particular case of the Ross family, whose Eeyou as well as

Gaelic legacies, especially the non-French and non-Catholic aspects, are not valued; indeed, they have been almost entirely erased. One might question the links between the Euroquébécois cultural hegemony and the Essipiunnuat, and the mutilation of significant sections of the group and families' diversity of inheritances. They have led to the marginalisation of a major proportion of the Essipiunnuat inventory of experiences. Stories thus report complex linkages between systemic directed forgetting, assimilation, breaks in the transmission of cultural memory, and the advancement of collective amnesia.

The power of ignorance: institutional oblivion

Forgetting the Salmon War is likely to be, above all, linked to the current circumstances of the social order. According to band council statistics, more than 55 per cent of Essipit's hundreds of employees (in public administration and band council-owned enterprises) are Euroquébécois.[4] Most of the clients of the community enterprises, which have a turnover of more than $10 million, positioning Essipit as the fifth largest employer in the Upper North Shore region, are also Euroquébécois. While speaking of the war, a former band administrator said, 'make sure you do not kill the goose that lays the golden egg that is recreational tourism'. Economic development and financial advantages are the first priority of many; the belief that cultural oblivion is a condition of stability looms large within the group, particularly among the Euroquébécois community's employees. For example, there were conversations to the effect that racist Euroquébécois employees are tolerated within Essipit's enterprises.

Memory of the war clearly has the power to destabilise the established economic system, which is not only based on Euroquébécois investment in Essipit, but on employees' psychological stability and fragile Innu–Euroquébécois relationships. These circumstances tend to favour the use of 'Innu' symbols, illustrated by the *Innubliable* marketing campaign, as a varnishing over and simulacrum of indigeneity, feeding *sui nullius.* Picard-Sioui (2017) perceptively illustrates the paradoxical attitude of Euroquébécois (those who live near First Peoples communities), in a chapter entitled 'During this time, in the neighboring city' (p. 49); a mindset often characterised by a mixture of racism, opportunism and duplicity. Indeed, as the event that propelled the new generation of leaders to the forefront of local politics, the Salmon War and its memory remains the founding myth of the new regime. As time passes, the story tends to be rewritten around the unified idea that the leaders stood and succeeded in repelling the enemies and held the fort.

4 For more information, see the Essipit band council website: http://www.innu-essipit.com/index2.php?rubrique=lesessipiunnuat. It should also be noted that a number of these Euroquébécois employees tend to self-identify as 'eastern métis'; this phenomenon, widespread in Québec, afflicts the Essipiunnuat with a new form of cultural colonialism whose harmful effects of erasure are now known (Leroux, 2019).

The Salmon War remains the basis on which the legitimacy of the regime, and the communitarian principle, is based; and the same regime must control the interpretations and representations of the event and of the group's past. The contemporary parameters of remembrance, at least up to 2016, tended to be configured for the purpose of enhancing the aura and the cult of a leader.

As the former chief who took office in 1979 and left in 2012 maintains, 99 per cent of the population was supportive. He clearly over-stresses the unity of the group. He depicts the war as the genesis of collective pride and unity, but also of the beginning of the defence of indigenous rights. It is presented as the moment when the community took charge of itself, but also when the council decided to be the leader and sole source of authority within the group. A link is clearly made between the leadership in the war and the results of their actions three decades later. It is no exaggeration to say that, based on the evidence, the interpretations of the past by the former chief and Georges serve to depict them as the 'creators' of everything that the group did.

Stories report an interest in remembrance to the extent that it serves those who benefit from it; it reinforces their heroism, their virtues and legitimates their power. Memories of the Salmon War are, therefore, a power issue that affects the very foundations of the system's legitimacy, as well as being threatening to several members of the group. It is not surprising, then, that my research became increasingly represented, and to a certain extent perceived, as a threat to the leadership. However, the gradually polarising effect of research, as a space where people's stories and interpretations were released, has made it possible to see clear lines of demarcation and new data concerning those supporting the principal leader and those who have opposed him.

At the other end of the spectrum stand those who felt cheated and humiliated after the war (see the previous section 'Commitment in the light of experience'). The perception exists that people's spontaneous participation and enthusiasm were, in fact, used to serve the new leaders and the establishment of self serving power devices. This feeling of being instrumentalised is revealing. For these individuals, speaking of the Salmon War has a potential to delegitimise the contemporary regime of power by revising its mythology; it breaks the unified dimension, but also potentially positions them as dissident. It might explain, in part, why some individuals did not want to speak of the Salmon War, or said 'Don't you think that we've had enough of it?' (Jeanne, chapter 3, ref. 5). The current bureaucratic and social order in the community appears, therefore, to be another filter encouraging the production of a kind of self-knowledge that fits with the established forms of control. More dramatically, this selective memory includes a specific representation of the 'Indian', impregnated with both Canadian and Euroquébécois representations, superimposed onto existing inner phenomena of *sui nullius* and mnemophobia.

The small community of 729 members, with 215 living on-reserve and 514 off-reserve (Indigenous and Northern Affairs Canada, n.d.)[5] has a huge bureaucracy considering its size, and includes Essipiunnuat and non-Essipiunnuat. The administration and its enterprises employ hundreds of people, for a population of 215 resident members.[6] As McGoey (2007) demonstrates, regulatory bureaucracies imply a will to ignorance, which works 'to circumvent a regulator's ability to carry out its explicit aims and goals'. The creative use of ignorance is often key to a regulator's survival. It enables entities to maintain relations with other entities, such as industries. It is essential, therefore, to look carefully at how ignorance can be a strategic resource within 'regulatory and bureaucratic structures' (McGoey, 2007; 2012). As the case of Essipit suggests, selective memory and strategic forms of forgetfulness are key to facilitating increased relations and joint ventures with external corporations, and ensuring the psychological comfort and cultural safety of the majority of Euroquébécois employees. They also contribute to close links being forged with governments and to the concentration of power.

Essipiunnuat who live on-reserve, especially those who work for the band administration and the band administration as a whole, are dependant on just two sources of income: governmental monetary transfers and capital from community-owned enterprises. The relationship with the state became more cooperative, and the financial transfer flow increased. Indeed, the Essipiunnuat have developed significant band council-owned businesses that have evolved in the capitalist realm; the band and its administration is the fifth largest employer in the region. The Salmon War, with its normative charge, thus tends to actualise past-selves and norms that have the potential to destabilise these relationships; it speaks of decolonisation through revolt, of solidarity and the defence of principles at all costs, including *Innu tipenitamun*, that tends to be antinomian to neoliberal paradigms of domination and alienability pertaining to the relation to the Earth.

Whether effected through erasure, selection or silence, forgetfulness seems to play a role of desacralisation or to promote 'abandonment' of what would otherwise be sacred; and favours some sets of norms to the detriment of others. In any case, such practices help to better understand the past and contemporary experience of anomie. Silence surfaces as the preferred medium

5 The band administration makes a rigid differentiation between on- and off-reserve members. Off-reserve members cannot access the general assembly, vote in elections or access some programmes reserved for the residents only. This is an important issue in the group, especially in 2019, since there is a long-term strategy of forging consent for the signature of a modern treaty by trying to control as far as possible the political power of the members and the general assembly.

6 Non-resident members have no political rights; they cannot run for, vote in or attend the assembly.

in the production of forgetfulness. It perhaps best illustrates the fragility of oblivion, and how forgetfulness is hardly absolute.

Reminiscences and the fragility of oblivion

What is mysterious about oblivion is that it is never really achieved[7]
P.L. Assoun (1997, p.155)

When truth is buried underground it grows, it chokes, it gathers such an explosive force that on the day it bursts out, it blows up everything with it.
É. Zola

Forgetfulness, especially in its subjective forms, is by no means total. The act of forgetting, whether automatic, or as a manifestation of willingness or generated by particular social circumstances, remains inextricably linked to the forces and contexts that shaped its nascence. Each in their own way, people reported the presence of the Salmon War in their individual present and the resilience of memory against the forces favouring forgetfulness. They also pointed to the great silence surrounding the event. Curiously, those who had lived through it, and who recognise its importance in their lives, have not generally spoken about it again. Yet, behind this silence hiding lasting reminiscences, there were emotions and values valiantly defended. For the majority of those involved, in their consciousness at least, it is as if the Salmon War happened yesterday.

The medium of silence

Élisabeth, aged five at the time of the war, never spoke of it again – with her mother, father or anyone else (chapter 4, ref. 1), even though her father was one its main protagonists. As with others of her generation, she knew the war was about fishing, a community salmon net and external opposition to indigenous fishing rights. Her memory of the use of guns was that of a small child (chapter 4, ref. 3). She remembers the sensations she had at the time, including the smells, and yet has no idea of the causes of the event. She recognises that the Salmon War has no meaning for her now, but that it did have an impact on her life. She feels a need, above all, to know (chapter 4, ref. 2).

In fact, even the warriors, it seems, avoided discussing the war once it was over. The post-Salmon War attitude was principally characterised by silence (Raoul, chapter 2, ref. 7), presented as the preferred medium of forgetfulness. On the other hand, silence is also depicted as a strategy to avoid reliving an emotionally traumatic experience (Ernest, chapter 4, ref. 8). The Essipiunnuat were noticeably more calm and submissive after the war. The undeclared reason

7 Ce qui est mystérieux avec l'oubli, c'est qu'il n'est jamais réellement réussi (my translation).

behind this silent obedience was the deep fear of having to experience such events again and a terror about them ever being repeated (Pierre, chapter 4, ref. 3).

The paradoxes of emotional reflux

Memories of the Salmon War are frequently presented as open wounds. Enemies are remembered clearly and many have not been forgiven; the passing of time 'has not healed us' (Tshak, chapter 3, ref. 3). Despite forces favouring forgetfulness, the stories suggest difficulty in forgiving but also in forgetting. The feeling of having been persecuted in a moment of great weakness left indelible emotional traces in people's memories. People swear never to forget acts of cowardice of which they were the victims, such as those who took advantage of their weak position to inflict pain on them and attempt to make their situation even more difficult (Pierre, chapter 4, ref. 1).

This deep resentment is coupled with fear. Stress and racism also remain central to interviewees' emotional memories. Some confess that their life was marked forever by what they saw, and that their emotions are so vivid they remember even the smells when episodes occurred (Esther, chapter 4, ref. 1). Whenever people speak about the war, it is as if 'they ripped off a plaster and re-opened the wound' (Esther, chapter 4, ref. 5). To this day, rage erupts when unpleasant episodes from the Salmon War are mentioned (Maxence, chapter 4, ref. 1 and 2).

The normative burden of memory

As revealed in the previous chapter, the Salmon War is linked to past-selves with specific normative components. To speak today of the war plunges those who were involved into the struggles of the time. It refers to indigenous unity and power, *Innu tipenitamun* and thorough resistance to its usurpation as well as acts of sedition. It brings to the table the condition of the Essipiunnuat as a colonised people belonging to a wider indigenist movement, with their own particularities and a specific set of norms. People remember having defended their link to Assi at all costs, but also the extent to which they had to stand up for themselves (Karl, chapter 4, ref. 2 and 6).

To invoke the Salmon War signifies the reanimation of the awareness of the Innu's defence and reappropriation but also government and colonial society's constant attempts to tear them away, not only from the Earth, but from the epistemological foundations of their thought, rooted and inseparable from the ancestral domain. Talking about the Salmon War reanimates forms of historical consciousness too – that ancestral territories and ecosystems were destroyed by governments and corporations, for example, including the extermination of the salmon in the Esh Shipu River, and that Essipiunnuat fishing practices were blamed for harming the river's salmon population. These memories are linked to the historical lies and myths that were constructed at the expense of an Innu perspective and which aim to legitimise the occupation of the Innu homeland and the legal domination of First Peoples in the region.

Therefore, the Salmon War was not only about the salmon but the whole Innu way of life and strategies for reinstating its integral value. Stories of the war refers to forms of assertion, as a people, and the means to collectively render things sacred. Stories of the war are a form of sacralisation (Raoul, chapter 4, ref. 2). Reactivating the memory of the Salmon War reminds us that people acted in line with their ancestors' conceptions of their ancestral sovereignty and freedoms, for their defence, and in recognition of the fact that this way of being remains possible (Ernest, chapter 4, ref. 12).

Memory as a loaded gun

During the conversations, people were explicitly concerned with the impact of narrating their experience of war. They understood that the history of one generates and reproduces the history of all. They reported that one must be careful of what one says and does in relation to the Salmon War; providing people with more facts could bring back increased spite and resentment (Maxence, chapter 4, ref. 1–2; Esther, chapter 4, ref. 4).

More than three decades on, the Salmon War, a central aspect of the group's inventory of experience, has the potential to be reactivated at any time, with an outburst of emotion and normative stances. As one collective identity can be reactivated through access to new information and transmission, narrators perceive that the past memories of the war can re-enter public spaces and dynamise the present at any time. As Raoul says, 'it was very powerful; you felt that it was very strong. There are things that were not done, some would have done them and would do it again today. I am certain' (chapter 4, ref. 3).

Reporting their experiences repeatedly brings people back to the present, resulting in forms of evaluations of the present as a function of the normative content identified in their past-self in the war. The past appears as an evaluative tool of the present, involving critiques of the contemporary social order. For example, remembering the behaviour of the government towards the Innu reminds them that they face the same issues today, and that the same long-standing objective of their extinguishment still remains. Accordingly, resistance is still necessary, if not more so today since the state has even greater means to usurp, transgress and annihilate First Peoples' cultural memory and inherent sovereignty:

> Today, we are still able, but it seems we let things go … But if we agreed to take action, there would be people behind the blockades, and in front … and beyond … such action seems necessary … today, it is

> about negotiating, negotiating, negotiating … I do not believe in these negotiations. We bend and bend. (Raoul, chapter 4, ref. 2 and 7)

In Essipit, remembering the Salmon War, and talking about how it developed, is therefore a defiant act in many respects. It recalls, for example, how things work when dealing with governments. Remembrance reactivates the knowledge that uprising and rebelling can trigger internal forces, which result in increased external respect and recognition, as well as internal self-empowerment and auto-development (Riel, chapter 4, ref. 1). But this spirit of rebellion is twofold and could also become instrumentalised by internal agents to generate feelings of cohesion and fictions of collective consent. Interestingly, since Essipit is more economically self-reliant today, there is a perception that if the same conflict occurred now, the potential for violence would be greater. Indeed, the Essipiunnuat are today self-confident and materially secure. Greater numbers of Euroquébécois work for them than in the past. In any war, there would be direct as well as covert action. According to Raoul, people remember the extent to which the group can gather together and fight and they would do so again (Raoul, chapter 2, ref. 15).

It is principally the consequences of forgetting their real condition as a colonised people and its continuity over time that would lead the Essipiunnuat to enter a war again for the purposes of survival, if the consciousness of their collective condition is not translated into daily acts of resistance. On the one hand, forgetfulness would worsen their condition, produce forms of relaxation that would make more likely a desperate fight to avoid the tragic gap of nothingness, and also lead to greater alienation at the hands of an all-powerful bureaucracy and the devices of the Crown. On the other, remembrance carries a whole set of norms associated with people's struggles, including the purpose of their sacrifices. These memories are patent vectors of Essipiunnuat norms, inherent sovereignty and a historical consciousness of colonisation. The collective experience of war entered the collective inventory of experience, making *anamnesis* to past-selves, in the sense of reminiscence, a constant possibility. Thus, the study of stories suggests that the group memories of the Salmon War are a loaded gun, waiting for the right moment to revolt against the forces aiming at genocide and collective annihilation, and working internally to marginalise Innu views and interpretations. In this sense, narrating the past has direct implications for the present.

Contemporaneities: the mirror of memory

Illusion is heeded to disguise the emptiness within.
Arthur Erickson

It is a promise of oral history that stories about the past are always produced from the present and can mirror it (Thompson, 2000). The act of narrating the past is modelled by current social circumstances, including the social order and evaluations of the value of the past for the present. In their stories, Essipiunnuat included views on their present condition with variable degrees of intentionality.

As a subjective act and manifestation of agency, narrating consists of the reproduction of norms, of stories that invoke what has value and what has not. Narrating implies norming, and the production of representations and signs with ethical charges. When it implies memory of the past, the narrator makes selections and choices that increase the possibilities for sacralising components of individual and collective past-selves. Discourses about the past are therefore nets to *contemporise* past elements in people's current condition.

Three main characteristics of Essipiunnuat relations to their present existences surface in the stories. One of these is nostalgia; another concerns elements of social criticism and the evaluation of the current social order and governance. The last pertains to the perception of collective needs for norms, and features of the current cultural condition. These trends in memory offer rich insights about the group's actuality.[8]

Nostalgia

'Yearning for yesterday', is a key characteristic of nostalgia (Davis, 1979). This reflects the etymology of the term from the Greek *nostos* and *algia,* literally a 'painful yearning to return home', or homesickness (ibid.). Nostalgia reveals contexts of 'present fears, discontents, anxieties, or uncertainties even though those may not be in the forefront of the person's awareness' (Davis, 1977, p. 420). Feelings of nostalgia can express dissatisfaction with the present, when not actual melancholia, and of past selves. It reports a temporal and spacial dimension, mainly regrets about past times and ageing, and the disappearance of certain elements of the natural (ecological grief) or social landscapes associated with pleasant ways of being. It therefore encompasses recognition of an exceptional past, 'imbued with special qualities, which, moreover, acquires its significance from the particular way we juxtapose it to certain features of our present lives' (Davis, 1979, p. 13).

8 The term 'actuality' is used in the sense of people's perceptions of Essipiunnuat's reality and actual conditions.

As Fred Davis proposes, sociologically nostalgia often erupts out of a people's isolation. It is used strategically to boost their sentiment of belonging and participation in social life. Nostalgia involves both idealisation of the past and a distancing from the present. The violation of sacred items may reveal particular aspects of a group's vulnerabilities and contortions, as in the case of mythologising its origins. But what are the main examples of people's nostalgia that have emerged along with their stories of the war?

Gatherings and the spirit of unity

People express nostalgia for past gatherings that used to occur throughout the year. These include celebrations in winter (mainly New Year's Eve and Christmas) and inclusive meetings that were organised in the home of each head-of-family; these were gatherings characterised by exchanges and visits between all families in the community, all related to each other. During these events, 'houses were filled all the time with people from other families who were visiting' (Mestenapeo, chapter 4, ref. 14).

In addition, the traditional duck-hunting trips took place in the spring, during which groups of hunters would gather at Pointe-Sauvage. These events are remembered as day-long feasts, a celebration of the new season (Pierre, chapter 4, ref. 6). Another was the ancestral summer gathering, now commonly called *pow wow*.[9] People would make campfires at home of the head of the family. Everyone would join in. They would sing, and everything would be shared. What people loved most was feeling at home, playing simple games and being together (Esther, chapter 4, ref. 4).

For those who said they missed these gatherings, it was the family or community spirit of solidarity and reciprocity that they remembered and which they most regretted losing. If there were some chicaneries in winter gatherings, a wider family spirit existed. Today, this has been replaced by each family staying in their home and not visiting other families, resulting in isolation and solitude, especially for the elderly (Mestenapeo, chapter 4, ref. 14). The *pow wow* has also collapsed alongside this unity felt at gatherings, and it has proved almost impossible to revive it (Esther, chapter 4, ref. 4). This collective spirit that is perceived as having been lost was a way to live one's life with others, and to support each other (Édouard, chapter 5, ref. 1; Karl, chapter 4, ref. 2). It

9 The use of the term 'pow wow' has generated controversies in recent years, in Essipit and in wider Québec society. [See Cassidi's interview with Natasha Kanapé-Fontaine (2016), an article on the use of 'pow wow' as a title of a TV show in Québec.] The term refers originally to a form of collective ceremony among First Peoples. In Essipit, it is currently used to name a form of annual festival that includes social activities, music shows and consumption of alcohol, but that has little to do with its original meaning. In some communities, the choice was made to conduct two gatherings, one closer to the original *pow wow* and its ceremonies, with spiritual and symbolic meanings, and another more public and commercial and more like a festival.

leads one Elder to say that 'we call ourselves communitarian all the time but I feel that we have become the Innu community with the least solidarity' (Paula, personal communication, December 2015).

Innu vision and way of life

There is also nostalgia for the way of life of parents and grandparents that interviewees remember from childhood and early adult life. For example, they recall hearing their grandparents conversing in Innu-aimun. They fondly remember other Innu arriving from Pessamit or elsewhere and being welcomed and respected. They remember everybody being hunters and trappers (Mestenapeo, chapter 4, ref. 14).

They remember receiving teachings from the older people, mornings by the sea, being told stories from Essipiunnuat history and way of life (Tshak, chapter 4, ref. 5). They also reminisce about the taste of traditional food, and in particular of fresh salmon, which they present as a condensed symbol of their whole childhood (Jeanne, chapter 4, ref. 1). Others are nostalgic for their grandfathers' vision of Essipiunnuat ancestral sovereignty, the supreme value they gave it and a dread of losing that sense of worth (Mestenapeo, chapter 4, ref. 8).

Collective commitment and resistance

Essipiunnuat expressed a need for more information about the war – pictures or film of the events, for example. One individual recounted how he returned regularly to the wharf trying to find the net he had concealed under the dock decades ago; he confessed that this net was an *obsession* for him and regretted not having found it. He still thinks about it often (Adam, chapter 4, ref. 1, 3 and 9).

This individual's fixation, shared by others, illustrates the nostalgia felt by the older generations, including the Salmon War generation. It concerns the experience of being committed to the community, and being engaged in resisting the external violation of their inherent rights. This nostalgia is associated with their observations of the post-Salmon War generation. They are sceptical about the new generation's ways of identifying with the group and the likelihood of their commitment in any future war of resistance. They tend, instead, to see misidentification and a lack of interest in public affairs. Their assessment is that there would be fewer warriors among the young, and lower levels of engagement in the community among young women especially, for example. In general they believe few individuals from the current generation would be ready to go to the same lengths they went to for Innu sovereignty (Esther, chapter 2, ref. 9 and 12).

Nostalgia thus looms large in the stories. Those involved in the research explicitly relate the nostalgic issues mentioned to the group's present dimension. They overtly denounce, often with a sense of powerlessness, the increased fragmentation within the group, and the disappearance of their cherished communitarian spirit, its values and practices. They observe rapid changes in the group's way of life, and the dissociation with ancestral conceptions and perspectives. They also note the lack of engagement of the post-Salmon War generation in resisting external oppression, and they are doubtful of this generation's readiness to face any future war. Overall, the present generation seems disconnected with the spirit that animated those involved in the Salmon War. That said, the fact that the event is not spoken of goes a long way to explaining this dissociation from the recent past.

Social criticism: voicing incoherence

In their recollections, people often turned their gaze on the present and there was a trend towards using reconnection with the Salmon War as a springboard for articulating a collective self-critique. This suggests the use of memory as an evaluative tool for the present. Interviewees draw parallels between the past and present. As a result, their stories contain critiques of the group's current social order and highlight the normative base from which they are built: the standards, values and concepts specific to the generations that participated in the war. All together, these views offer insightful reflections on the present, in particular the perceptions of legitimate relations with states, conceptions of indigeneity, the sources of indigenous laws and internal modes of governance – central themes of the war that continue to resonate to this day.

Relations with states

One issue raised in the wake of recollecting the war concerns contemporary leaders' ways of relating to other states.[10] The current process of negotiating treaties, for example, comes in for heavy criticism, especially from the eldest involved. Negotiations that occurred during the Salmon War are compared to those of today. A distance is perceived between the values defended then and now, and compared with past negotiations, the contemporary ones are seen severely lacking (Raoul, chapter 2, ref. 16).

A perception exists that the indigenous heritage, laws and inherent rights that were defended so perilously in the Salmon War are no longer the touchstone they once were for the leaders. With agreement after agreement, interviewees say, the fundamental right to live free, feed oneself and be self-reliant – 'the

10 Although some of these criticisms could, to a certain extent, also be applied to managers and representatives, leaders and\or band administrators here refers primarily to those who were in place at the time of the main interviews in 2008–9 and until 2016.

first right that must be defended as Innu', – is gradually being eroded. There is a feeling that compromises are being made over these rights and that such compromises should not be accepted (Raoul, chapter 3, ref. 1).

The negotiation process, which has been ongoing for forty years, is interpreted by its main critics as a strategy of the government to reduce First Peoples to the point of accepting the abandonment of their ancestral sovereignty and inalienable responsibility, as Innu, to protect *Assi* for future generations (Mestenapeo, chapter 4, ref. 5). The state is succeeding in achieving the fundamental goal of its policy, which is the abandonment of inherent indigenous rights 'in exchange for a few crumbs from the table' (ibid., ref. 6). The Essipiunnuat will then be forced to accept that they are 'just Canadian citizens like any others'. The signature on a 'treaty' would then result in illegal annulments of *Innu tipenitamun*, a cession of ancestral lands and ultimately the consented extinguishment of indigenous sovereignty, which other Innu groups would regard as treasonable. One individual says he was opposed to the treaty negotiation process from the beginning:

> I have always been against negotiation because I can see that we are going round and round in circles. I have spent a lot of time in negotiation meetings. I tell people, 'We are wasting our time and our energy.' For example, once, the Nordic ZEC did not want to open their fence to let us go on our territories. I said, 'If you do not open this fence, I will smash it.' And that is what we did. Then there were negotiations and we got small agreements ... But I know very well as an Innu in the forest that I have the right to enter it whenever I want to. (Sam, chapter 4, ref. 4)

Negotiations with governments over 'land rights' and treaties are therefore seen as a waste of time and money and of no benefit to the community (Sam, chapter 4, ref. 6). There is the perception that the administration and propagandists hired by the administration emphasise only selected aspects, deliberately hiding consequences of signing a treaty, such as new payment obligations, taxes and the state being released from its fiduciary obligations.

Indeed, the 'autonomous self government' promised by successive Canadian administrations is tantamount to a lie told in order to obtain surrender. Since the real cost of signing for the group remains unknown (no member to date has been allowed to see or analyse the treaty) individuals' consent would not be fully informed (Ernest, chapter 4, ref. 18). Indeed, as things stand, the costs of administration would increase, and local members would be forced to pay income and other taxes for the benefit of the bureaucracy (Ernest, chapter 4, ref. 6). Others denounce the tendency of the leaders to impose self-restrictions on Essipiunnuat's traditional hunting and fishing practices in order to endlessly accommodate Euroquébécois society (Napeo, chapter 4, ref. 3).

The idea that there is such thing as a 'granted autonomy' would be a simple lure, the best illustration of the leaders' loss of the true meaning of the group's freedom. This approach would be rather counterproductive since it incites individuals to minimise their concerns with self-determination. To promote this illusion is seen as contributing to the colonisation and exploitation of one's own people (Sam, chapter 4, ref. 6).[11]

As an Elder recalls, 'we asked them at the meeting if we could see the treaty before its ratification. They told us that we wouldn't understand its language anyway. Indeed, they send non-Innu employees of the band to inform us about the treaty and our rights as Innu' (Paula, personal communication, 2016).[12] Indeed, various band employees are paid with funds coming from agreements with federal government and loans to the band. Problematically, these actors can hardly be critical of the modern treaty process and its implications for the Innu since they are, in fact often not Innu while being paid to advance and ratify it. Discourse pressuring members to consent to the treaty are particularly observable among Euroquébécois employees of the band, often nationalists who have no political power in the community and tend to be highly complacent in their dealings with band authorities as well as the Québec provincial state.

Innu tipenitamun: the inalienability of Assi and the untradability of Innu obligations

Former leaders allegedly set financial gain above principles such as inherent ancestral rights and *Innu tipenitamun.* These, it is asserted, 'they were ready to sell out' (Mestenapeo, chapter 4, ref. 5). This is antinomian for fundamental Innu principles since, as Ernest argues, 'even if you are a millionaire, it will not free you from being indigenous. You cannot eat money.' A scathing critique holds that those who love money tend to be more respected in the community than those for whom ancestral principles are sacred. Those leaders who could most easily be bought would, therefore, comply readily with external authorities, and behave with members of the group as if they were 'a God ... for whom your opinion has no value' (Ernest, chapter 4, ref. 8 and 9).[13]

There is fierce opposition to the idea of any commodification of indigenous ancestral sovereignty, which is seen as sacred (Mestenapeo, chapter 4, ref. 1). Yet there are people in the community, and among the decision-makers, who want to be indigenous and have rights but who do not want to stand up for any of these rights, since they fear a confrontation. This attitude is seen as being a danger to the community:

11 Consultants and law firms working for the band are natural defenders of the process of negotiation and its outcomes. Opponents to the process are demonised, further reducing the space for criticism to be heard. Overall, the negotiation process has become an 'economic activity'.

12 The then chief Martin Dufour sent letters to some of the Elders asking them not to criticise the council in public.

13 This is a reference to the former general manager, Georges.

> If you do not defend yourself today, you will not have much tomorrow. You have to leave those who have nothing to do with your rights outside the management of your business. If you do not defend your rights and you do not claim them, you will have no rights in the end. Yet where will this interminable race to economic development lead you? You will sign any kind of agreement and then what will you do inside your community? Where will your rights be? You will have no more rights. There will be an extinguishment of your ancestral rights, and many other things that will have been negotiated at the expense of the people. I have nothing against economic development; it is alright to create jobs for First People who are able to work. But that's not what's happening anymore. I can tell you that if it weren't for us, there would be no reserve [14] (Mestenapeo, chapter 4, ref. 8).

As an Elder mentions, there are two sides to economic development. It can enrich the community, but it can also be a veiled way to commit blackmail. Once a community has enjoyed material comforts it will be reluctant to lose them, and this can make it more dependent and obedient to the hand that feeds. Development is therefore accompanied by a sort of fear, and a likelihood that members of the community will compromise on principles and be easier to control. It can also erode their sense of the sacredness of their indigenous rights (Sam, chapter 4, ref. 6).

'They try to make you believe things': perspectives on power and recolonisation from within

As previously described, another aspect of criticism pertains to in-group modes of decision-making in the name of the 'collective', namely that the views of members are not taken into account. This sense of exclusion was shared by interviewees of all ages. There is also the perception that current decision-making does not reflect what is in the communal interest, in spite of the council's constant statements that its actions are for the people. This is seen as one of the greatest problems the community faces today: a permanent democratic deficit (Mestenapeo, chapter 2, ref. 5). It gives the impression that 'they try to make you believe things, that they invent things' (Ernest, chapter 4, ref. 4). The overwhelming role of the former director of communication was also denounced as monopolising public discourse about the group and framing a story uniquely in accordance with the perspective of the administration. There is also the feeling, mentioned by many in the study, of being included 'only when it suits them' (Ernest, chapter 4, ref. 7).

Interviewees confessed to losing interest in meetings, since 'in their hearts', they did not believe in practices opposed to ancestral modes of deliberation (Ernest, chapter 4, ref. 19). Moreover, they felt that they would be excluded

14 In the sense that 'it would have all been sold.'

from decision-making circles again once they were no longer needed (Mestenapeo, chapter 4, ref. 8). These attitudes would serve to explain the decline in motivation to participate in community affairs, the shared sense of powerlessness experienced by ordinary members and the perception that it is one tiny cell that makes all the decisions.

Secondly, a sentiment exists that there is a 'gang' mentality. As another Elder describes, you are in the 'gang' if you comply with the decision-makers, and out of it if you contest their authority. If you're not in the gang, you will not receive the benefits of being a member and of belonging to the community. Therefore, one 'must know how to get into the gang', sometimes 'keeping silent about what is going on against one's conscience and the truth'. Speaking your mind freely can result in fierce exclusion. To express disagreement with decision makers can result in not being listened to again. One needs to 'be there but lower the head, listen and say "yes". And if you are an elected member of the council and you are against "them", then they make sure you will not be there for long' (Mestenapeo, chapter 4, ref. 5 and 10). This is mentioned as the second greatest political weakness inside the community.

A third element of governance inspiring strong criticism concerns the exclusion of the majority of members from assisting the general assembly, voting in elections, and benefiting from some of the other advantages arising out of belonging to the group. This exclusion touches around 580 'off-reserve' members who live outside the reserve.[15] This situation, contrary to a recent Supreme Court decision, is known within the administration but perpetuated, most likely as a way to maintain political power and influence, and collective consent, through a small and weakened general assembly. Some critics maintain that this exclusion mainly serves a small minority in retaining power and control over community affairs. Their main opponents and dissidents, who were forced to leave the community, are then left with no voice. Indeed, the managers would instead prefer an increase in the number of those without rights, such as Euroquébécois workers and affiliated members through marriage (but without status), since they are easier to control.

Those who are off-reserve would be excluded, mainly as a strategy of control and monopoly. This treatment is perceived as unjust and as delegitimising the local system. It also compromises the land claim process on which those who live off-reserve will ultimately be called to vote but without having been efficiently involved in the negotiation beyond cosmetic initiatives for political marketing purposes. This also weakens the community, as there will certainly be other 'wars' to face in the future. Those who are off-reserve are sidelined, and the community is deprived of their support. Since they are uninformed

15 Indigenous and Northern Affairs Canada, http://fnp-ppn.aandc-aadnc.gc.ca/fnp/Main/Search/FNRegPopulation.aspx?BAND_NUMBER=86&lang=fra (consulted 10 Jan. 2019).

and may feel excluded, they cannot play their potential role as a supporter and as ambassadors for their community and culture (Sam, chapter 4, ref. 5 and 6).

Meanwhile, there are flaws in the argument that those who are off-reserve did not participate in the development of Essipit, and therefore should not benefit from it. Indeed, they should have the 'same access to the common wealth' (Sam, chapter 4, ref. 6). The community cannot provide them with a living since they already have work elsewhere. Offering them increased knowledge about local situations would transform them into ambassadors. Finally, their exclusion from the decision-making process increases dramatically the risk that any community initiative would collapse as their number grows (Ibid). Discrimination inside the reserve, including racism and the stigmatisation of indigenists, as well as impunity, is the best guarantee that things will crumble in the long run and that members will move away from each other (Mestenapeo, chapter 2, ref. 5).

As best described by Elders, some of whom have been observing political life on the reserve for more than six decades, the denunciations of discrimination come with the observation that justice inside the reserve is not the same for all, that there are inequalities. Dissidence results in not being considered as an equal. This possibility of being identified as unorthodox and then excluded is a sword of Damocles hanging over every member on a daily basis. Until recently, this decision would be made by one person in particular, who controlled the council. It is said that the chief was only his puppet. Elements of autocracy result in a decline in honesty,[16] and consequently the impossibility of obtaining consensus among the group (Mestenapeo, chapter 4, ref. 9 and 10). Manifestations of authoritarianism, coupled with bureaucracy, would engender an erosion of individual liberties and the density of social interactions. This is seen to result from some leaders being too enamoured with power:

> You know the dictum 'Feed a pig, it will shit on your porch'? The power! The power! It is a bitter pill to take, very hard. It is the assembly and the senior management. I'm not sure if they are free themselves … but they do not think of the freedom of the indigenous people, all the peoples. (Pierre, chapter 5, ref. 8)

Therefore, stories of the Salmon War generate explicit critiques of the current social order, its legitimacy and the practices of those ensuring its maintenance. Such criticism reveals the perception of a distancing from Innu values and conceptions, and a need to return to a set of normative values on which these critiques are based. It demonstrates a need to return to ancestral norms, including the spirit of resistance to that which threatens them, as was manifested in the Salmon War, in order to preserve social cohesion, and to ensure self-defence and a continued existence. If the rationality of power sees

16 For an extensive study of truth-speaking (*parrêsia)* and its implications, see Foucault (1984).

short-term gain in engineering fragmentation, its logic amputates and weakens the group in the long term, particularly in its future struggle with external actors.

As shown, stories of the war are normatively charged and include radical critiques of the present. They echo the intimate links between modes of social control, the decline in social interactions and their succeeding effects on collective erasure and anomie engendered by and benefiting both the colonial regime and the internal bureaucratic monocracy. A major effect of such recolonisation through cultural oblivion guarantees detachment from Innu conceptions of inherent and ancestral sovereignty; this facilitates transgressions and more importantly the weakening and decline of resistance to extinguishment. The production of cultural oblivion is thus the core ingredient in the manufacture of Innu consent through the accelerated absorption of colonial definitions and interpretations; it allows an implicit abandonment of the epistemological foundations of their ancestral sovereignty as inferior sources of knowledge and laws.

Cultural condition: tracking the present

As Mol (1977) demonstrates, demand for identity remains a fundamental need of human societies. In fact, this need is a requirement for establishing norms as it identifies what is sacred and what is not. Group identity is, then, shaped by tendencies towards sameness and integration of traits for stability and the maintenance of wholeness. The strengthening of boundaries around the unit enables it to remain well functioning in its environment. In engaging with bolstering their wholeness, humans succeed in achieving health rather than death and reacting effectively to sources of change and danger. However, groups are *sui generis* and come to exist as entities independent of their individual members. As a result, the greater efficiency of mutual support (in facing attack, in defence or in hunting) is the main explanation of these aggregations, which allow complementarities to better fulfil deficiencies in each unit. For Mol, the search for identity is fundamentally a sociopsychological need for symbols and norms for self-conservation (Mol, 1979).

Langenberg (2005) sustains that sacralisation, through group narration in particular, and as a manufacturer of norms, has a function of social standardisation for the maximisation of in-group capacities, forces, strengths, and their coordination towards a unified willingness to solve common problems. It uncovers a search for mutually consistent decisions. As Andrew Russell (2005) suggests, standards can emerge 'as a consequence of consensus, the imposition of authority, or a combination of both'. Social standardisation appears, therefore, as the process of 'articulating and implementing technical knowledge' pertaining to the praxis of unification and coordination (ibid.).

In their descriptions, Essipiunnuat consistently evoke the current condition of the group and its needs. Their discourse includes perceptions of their own needs, as the Salmon War generation, but also their observations about the post-Salmon War generations, including an overall concern about intergenerational dealings. Anxiety about the future and deep concerns about the cultural continuity of the Essipiunnuat are commonly voiced. The focal point of these accounts is the discernment of an accelerated phenomenon of cultural oblivion, coupled with a need for identity, which exposes the complex interactions between collective oblivion and anomie. Furthermore, there is a deeper collective requirement for norms and rooted self-design to move beyond the crisis of auto-referentiality inherent in psychological colonialism.

Surfacing epistemologies: perspectives on uneasy truths

(i) Collapse of the collective

The stories contain a range of observations filled with perspectives on the state of mind of the post-Salmon War generations. The perceived disappearance of an *esprit de corps* is a main characteristic. This spirit of solidarity and enthusiasm for the common good has faded away, giving way to a small-minded, egocentric individualism and an obsession with a superficial materialism and consumption. The Essipiunnuat are, it is claimed, more concerned with intimacy ('their own back yard'), and less attracted by public spaces when not plagued by social phobia. A decline of indigenous heritage and perspectives is a phenomenon observed among all generations, together with the fading away of their representations in the public sphere (Mestenapeo, chapter 4, ref. 11).

(ii) Dissociations and the politics of abandonment

Collective alienation from indigeneity appears more patently, however, among the post-Salmon War generations. Younger people tend to distance themselves from the dominant ideology of the band council and, instead, construct identities considered as more 'real'. This may suggest a phenomenon of misidentification (Costa and Fleming, 2009), which is to say a survival strategy that the minority subject practises 'in order to negotiate a phobic majoritarian public sphere that continuously elides or punishes the existence of subjects who do not conform to the phantasm of normative citizenship' (Munoz, 1999, p. 4).

According to Mestenapeo, this phenomenon of dissociation with an indigenous self has to do with the politics inside the community, tinged as it is with autocratic practices and neoliberal ideology. If the definition of Indian status is clear in a reserve according to federal law, members' recognition and identification with Innu philosophy would be weakened in several members.

Generally, Innu identity is only asserted when it is in one's interest, and denied when perceived as a burden. The dominant mind-set, for example, is characterised by opportunism. It consists of using the 'Indian status card' only when it suits one's interest, such as not paying tax. The state's definition of 'indigeneity', embodied in the Indian Act and profoundly antinomian with ancestral conceptions of kinship and citizenship, has now come to the fore. Colonial law is therefore overwhelmingly identified as the only source of indigeneity. When a section of members abandon Essipiunnuat's ancestral conception of inherent rights, these are greatly threatened. This is partly because 'the customs of the group have been long devalued and relegated to last place', in favour of cultural erosion and 'assimilation' with Euroquébécois society (Mestenapeo, chapter 4, ref. 13). In other words, not knowing that you are indigenous and that you have your own set of laws is the last stage before ceding them. Interestingly, the Essipit experience has the potential to highlight the ultimate and often unseen stages of colonialism in its psychological and legal forms, and to be of great relevance to other Innu and First Peoples.[17]

Ultimately, this posture makes the member 'a single individual among other individuals'; it generates the erasure of cultural identity. The post-Salmon War generations have become the victims of a community in which there are legally First People, but they are unaware of what that means (Mestenapeo, chapter 4, ref. 13). In this context, neoliberal ideology and its epistemological foundations tends to replace Innu philosophy and the humanitarian values and love for the Earth that it embodies. This opportunism is also noticeable among Euroquébécois, who have changed their minds about Essipit and want to be closer to it now there are potential financial advantages (Édouard, chapter 4, ref. 2). Psychological and symbolic needs are boosted by additional absorption and internalisation of neoliberal ideology, as well as the colonial selective memory. The group's assimilation to neoliberal paradigms, widely antinomian to Innu axiology and a powerful force in determining cultural oblivion, is presented as generating self-ignorance and psychological needs commodified and compensated for by material consumption. These phenomena, present in the dominant society, are likely to be more acute in a community already fragile in its connection with indigenous heritage and which has a heavy story of oppression and submission to a long-ranging cultural hegemony.

Stories report that a significant proportion of the younger generations is experiencing a profound crisis of identity. They often take refuge in a Euroquébécois self, the deep crisis of the latter adding to their own psychological coloniality. In some cases, indigenous identity can even be seen as a foreign one, inspiring uneasiness if not actual shame. Prejudice against First Peoples,

17 For further reflections on the discursive construction of Indigenous identity under the conditions of colonization on Turtle Island, see Coburn, 2019).

as a manifestation of self-ignorance, is an existing phenomenon among these generations (Mestenapeo, chapter 4, ref. 11). Recent conversations on social media involving Essipiunnuat in their mid 30s have explicitly shown the existence of racist rhetoric towards other Innu. The issues surrounding racism and xenophobia, as much towards other Innu as towards other groups (in particular Muslims), are a taboo subject in the community.

The cultural amnesia experienced by the youngest generation has been previously described, and furthermore the Elders observe a generational gap between conceptions of collective identity and values. This gap is said to have produced forms of amnesia but also a sense of anomie, felt deeply among the youngest. People see the decline in self-identification as Innu as a great, perhaps the greatest, challenge for the group, and a source of its weakening. Ignorance of one's own past among the post-Salmon War generations was clearly voiced, both by the Salmon War generation and the next.

In addition to the social criticism previously reported, there is the perception of a feeling of distance, an anxiety for the disaggregation of the current social order among interviewees, and the perception of a collective difficulty to assess the value of things. This dissociation from what are seen as valuable collective norms exposes, in its breach, a rising demand for identity and a clarification of collective standards.

There is an underlying and shared awareness of the intimacies between amnesia and anomie, their threat to collective maintenance and as a path towards cultural annihilation in a complex and multifaceted dynamic of auto-genocide. There are clear voices, especially those of Elders, which are calling for wakefulness to the imperatives of remembrance, self-defence, uprisings and war, if necessary. The post-Salmon War generations are generally depicted as less committed, and doubts were expressed about their ability to engage and fight in future wars for the group. In Esther's view, for example,

> The sense of community is less present among the younger people, the idea that if we unite and fight, we can make it; and that in adversity we must take, not give up, and go for it. I think that's what most young people lack today. They are clearly less attached to our values that we had in the time of the Salmon War. (chapter 4, ref. 3 and 4)

(iii) 'We did not show them': effects of intergenerational communication breakdowns

If a conflict similar to the Salmon War were declared today, some warriors doubt that there would be many people on the dock, apart from those who were there in 1980–1. Above all, it is this identification with the community and the readiness to mobilise that has been lost (Napeo, chapter 4, ref. 5), a capacity widely based on members' absorption of common standards.

Younger generations would also be keener to transgress Innu norms because of intergenerational ruptures in the transmission of *Innu-aitun*. For example, imprudence in practising traditional activities is a good example of the younger generation's lack of expertise. As an Elder maintains, the decline of ancestral hunting and fishing practices should be laid at the door of the previous generation, not the youngest one – the children: 'They were not taught. If they had been shown adequately, they would be practising it. If our young people are imprudent [on the sea], it is because they were not accompanied by adults and shown.' (chapter 4, ref. 2).

However, this task of communicating ancestral knowledge is hard when dealing with the 'generation of child prodigies, those who know everything before learning it' (Jeanne, chapter 4, ref. 2). These young people would be less receptive to ancient teachings, less inclined to listen than to speak. Before, the boys would listen carefully to their fathers during fishing and hunting expeditions; they knew that it was a question of living, of having food to eat, but also of preventing accidents. This type of knowledge inspires no respect in the young, who do what they want to when they want to. Consequently, if they 'do not return by themselves towards traditional knowledge and practices, they will not learn anything and do nothing'. One needs to be with someone who knows and has experience in order to learn, and to listen to that person, 'as in life' (Jeanne, chapter 4, ref. 2).

(iv) Psychological condition of the youth

Young people are presented as disoriented, and generally unsure about norms and what has value and what does not. They have a hard time assessing their own needs, their capacity for self-evaluation decreased by their disconnection from oral traditions and veiled by amnesia. According to Pishimnapeo, it is essential to take a psychological approach in order to understand the current generation. Only an understanding of their psychological needs would allow intergenerational transmission and cultural continuity to be reanimated. He gives as an example one of his nephews, aged 23, the father of two children, who was seeing a psychologist because of suicidal thoughts. The old man remembers being struck by what he saw, the inability of this young man to take responsibility for himself and figure out his own way in life, despite the means available to him (Pishimnapeo, chapter 4, ref. 2).

(v) Symptoms of cultural oblivion

Pishimnapeo identifies an alarming psychological need for norms among the youth. He sees this absence of a sense of what has value in life as a major determinant of a rampant desire among the youth to die. In his view, this need could best be met by favouring a move 'back to basics, to Innu philosophy and way of life'. Yet, internal feelings of emptiness and nihilism among the youth must be put in the context of a generalised material wealth among the new generation, a situation completely opposite to the previous one when 'work for survival was the only thing we had in mind' (Pishimnapeo, chapter 4, ref. 2). He stresses that the generation that preceded his own gave them an increasing strength in the face of challenges. As he says, 'Kids today have everything easy, which might explain why their problems appear so insurmountable and why they kill themselves so easily.' If he does not wish them to return to his time, since it was too hard and full of suffering, he believes that knowing about their hardship and 'being told their truths' may make them wiser and stronger, that being bluntly honest, despite the discomfort it entails, is part of the remedy. Although it may shock them at first, in the long run it would reinforce intergenerational relationships, since they would know that the Elders can be trusted.

(vi) Marginalisation of Elders

Memory and ancestral teachings are vectors of subversion, since they offer a platform for reassessing the present time. In many aspects, the authority of Elders and the power of their experience and stories were transferred to new out-group and in-group actors such as bureaucrats, communications consultants, and especially lawyers, trained and educated within the dominant institutions and not brought up absorbing Innu perspectives and practices. It is not surprising, then, that younger members do not identify as Indigenous in a community that distances itself, explicitly or not, from these values. In this context, an epistemological revolution would be the least that would be needed to reinstate Innu philosophy, not as the only source of reference but at least as a valuable one. It would offer a cultural environment that effectively valorised Innu culture and respected ancestral teaching and laws in all aspects of community life. The intergenerational transmission of cultural memory is useless if the social environments in which the young evolve do not reinforce these values, but instead devalorise them for, among other reasons, the purposes of political domination and trade.

In such cases, ensuring that young people identify as Innu could be an impossible task and an insurmountable challenge; they would be less likely to take this path if their parents and community leaders refused to take it. With the community having moved away from *esprit de corps,* and with the prevalence of a rather negative perception of indigeneity, they have few windows through which to absorb and live in accordance with Innu standards (Mestenapeo, chapter 4, ref. 14).

A double-edged search of standards: the reserve as fertile soil for monocracy and resistance

While it is generally assumed that memory has a large normative load, it is as important to consider the effects of collective memory loss, a direct one being the production of anomie. It is not surprising that in parallel with observing the advancement of cultural oblivion, stories also report a common search for standards and norms. The need for identity acknowledged among the youngest members echoes a wider concern with normativity and the cultural continuity of the group. Stories suggest that the community recurrently faces situations of war, during which it must stand and resist and defend its dignity. Each time, the community is obliged to specify what is sacred for it and adapt its internal order accordingly. An example of a potential future situation would be a confrontation with the federal government over the recognition of First People and their ongoing sovereignty (Mesnak, chapter 4, ref. 3).

The continuous struggle for recognition and respect would always require, for Innu, a movement that includes other First Peoples. The defence of *Innu tipenitamun*, the fundamental collective right to self-determination and the imperative of indigenous auto-governance, concerns all First Peoples. The upcoming struggle will need to be translated, as for others in the past, into affirmative action at the grassroots level. The result of this war will depend on First Peoples unification and their ability to stand together. According to Sam, if members are 'to mobilise to defend the common good, common norms must be clearly asserted, known and shared' (chapter 4, ref. 6).

The multifaceted need for norms and their internal reassertion, beyond mere administration and political marketing, is presented as a way of preventing their transgression. In relation to the government, one's consciousness of what is sacred and has value is a protection against attempts to 'buy' and reduce inherent indigenous rights. The auto-definition of internal norms increases the capacity to evaluate external offers, and to remember their sources and historical context in order to prevent the repetition of past mistakes, such as being fooled by government into being 'parked in a reserve' (Mestenapeo, chapter 4, ref. 14).

(i) Demobilisation

It is often suggested in the stories that the historical condition of the Essipiunnuat requires a permanent readiness to engage in resistance, and there is therefore a need for warriors. Indigenous rights are the subject of intense jealousy among the Euroquébécois population. Since the idea of ancestral sovereignty encounters hostility, courageous people are needed to assert it. As Pierre remarks, 'this is what is terribly missed in the reserve these days' (chapter 4, ref. 6). A politics of exclusion, mainly a matter of internal domination that was underway in the community at the time of the interviews, would seem to undermine the group's capacity to quickly mobilise and become stronger in a situation of war. The current decision-makers tend to withdraw into a closed circle, which is seen as 'not good at all for the community' (Sam, chapter 4, ref. 6).

(ii) 'It cut us off from memory': overcoming intergenerational silences

Among the youngest, there is a persistent and unsatisfied need to know more about the Salmon War; they recognise that their knowledge of it lacks central elements. One person mentions his urge to know the circumstances of the community before the war, in the hope that he would be better informed about why he was suddenly involved in such strife (Adam, chapter 5, ref. 10). Élisabeth maintains that people of her generation need to know why this event occurred, and to hear it from the mouths of those who took part themselves. In her view, the fundamentals of the war, the reasons for it, and why it became so confrontational must be uncovered, to give some of the younger people in the study the chance to understand their strong, unexplained emotions:

> We have an emotional memory. We have resented what the adults experienced during the war. There were transmissions of emotion. It helps to explain how the current generations are feeling about the community, there is a lot of emotion but not the information and knowledge about what happened exactly. And since some of these emotions resented by the kids were negative, we tend to put them aside. Negative emotions associated with the war were felt and transmitted by the adults, but not any explanation of their sources and contexts. It cuts us off from memory. But there is something important to get hold of there. (Élisabeth, chapter 4, ref. 4)

Thus, explaining the Salmon War to the youngest generation would open a direct window onto the history of the community and its memory, and give them access to a wider inventory of experience. It would foster a better understanding of the genesis of the contemporary Essipiunnuat and of the current internal system and its normative foundations. Ultimately, Élisabeth believes that it would boost younger members' sense of inclusion. It would show them how participating in an event to defend the common good can increase the consistency of the group, including the pleasure of belonging to a group that defends itself and 'what is sacred' (chapter 4, ref. 4).

Conclusively, intergenerational rupture not only concerns the transmission of the inventory of experience pertaining to the Salmon War but the indigenous memory of the group and the norms at its foundations. It results in a rather gloomy perception of the post-Salmon War generations and their ability to ensure the cultural continuity of the group. But this dissociation with Innu philosophy of law is related to the wider social context and the societal condition of the group, characterised by its dissociation with customary principles, authoritarianism and the integration of a neoliberal ideology and being submerged in the bath of the wider North American society. The heavy effects of the Euroquébécois colonial erasure should also never be minimised. The Essipiunnuat would seem to be facing the weakening of indigenous values inside the group and a reduced access to its heritage.

(iii) Psychological recolonisation and the new dams of silence

For the youngest generations of Essipiunnuat, especially the most marginalised, this weakening of indigenous values is voiced as a form of psychological distress and disorientation – the feeling that nothing has value. Interviewees make a direct link between self-ignorance and the transgression of Innu norms, as well as between amnesia and anomie. They also notice a dynamic of misidentification with indigenous referents among the youth, a far-reaching decrease in commitment and a low receptivity to Innu philosophy and values. As opposed to the Salmon War generation, the post-Salmon War one has always known material security, but it is now plagued with an intense psychological and symbolic need for identity. At its most basic, this reveals the inherent burden of belonging to a group steadily reorganised in accordance with the colonial reserve and 'Indian' status as a conceptual foundation, alongside a persistent demand for sacredness, the transcendence of materiality, and the experience of immanence while living on the land (*nutshimit*).

Linked to the observed collapse of the group's *esprit de corps* is a need for collective standards, something felt by everyone interviewed for the research. Without a clear sense of what is good or bad for the group, there is no possibility of identifying transgressions of the group's dignity or freedoms, or of mobilising members for their defence. They would otherwise be condemned to negotiate the modalities of their own burial as Innu. Only a wider understanding of their community and its background will lead the post-Salmon War generation to overcome its disorientation, find explanations for its ambivalent feelings towards the community and be able to engage in defending its continuity beyond the unified dimensions and monopoly of public discourse inherent in monocratic rule.

Does the feeling of emptiness, absence and melancholia in the post-Salmon War generation reflect a form of the collective's agony? Either way, the post-war generation's desire to know deserves close attention since it is calling for intergenerational investment in collective self-conservation. The intergenerational gap felt in relation to the Salmon War is perceptibly related to a disconnection from cultural memory, which, as Assmann and Hölscher have shown, affects capacities for the 'concretion of identity' ('we are this and not that'). They rightly point out that the capacity to reconstruct a concept of the self and actualise it within a contemporary frame of reference, to access collectively shared knowledge through transmission and the cultivation of values among the current generations, is a prerequisite for individuals' sense of obligation towards the group (Assmann and Hölscher, 1988). Consequently, it could eventually mobilise the new generation of Essipiunnuat in forms of collective resistance. How can it be ensured that the younger generation's desire to hear and to know will meet the older generation's desire to talk and transmit?

This would help to deal with a heavy, if not unbearable, colonial heritage that has swallowed and crushed whole peoples over centuries; the type of overwhelming sociohistorical processes with no transformative outcomes and apparent reversibility.

Figures of continuation: from planned annihilation to self-designs

> After thinking well and having once taken, I an Indian, the decision to write, here is what I understood: anyone who thinks to accomplish something will encounter difficulties but despite this, she should never get discouraged.
>
> An Antane Kapesh (1979, preface)

Essipiunnuat have expressed their views on the past and the present, but they have also reflected on a possible continuation for the group. As cultural oblivion is produced, it can be countered through communication and stories. Interviewees spoke a great deal about what should be transmitted to the youngest generation and how it should be done. What they wish to transmit of their experience and essipiunnu cultural memory clearly evidences their interpretation of current needs, the group cultural values and what should be normative and cherished for the benefit of future generations.

Intergenerational transmission concerns making investments in order to determine future choices; it attempts to shape a future collective self. As a subjective act of sacralisation, transmission can be defined as a performance of self-design composed of strategies aiming to find what has value and ways of relating as well as defining commonalities. Such strategies also aim to identify what is shared and what deserves to be defended. Based on information contained in the inventory of experiences, it carves out a model that should be reproduced rather than avoided.

Transmission, based on the imagination of a possible self, relies and feeds on the pre-existing data of a group, on feelings, and on signs as well as images. This type of communication, as practised by the older generation, through narration but also through silence about the past, is a powerful determinant for the sense of self of the next generations. In this last section, the *contents* of what people think should be transmitted to a future generation, about the Salmon War, will be looked at as well as the *means* for achieving this transmission.

What to transmit: a confluence of stories

Take care of yourself.
Paul Ross Jr.

Three main themes emerge from people's stories in terms of the content that 'should be transmitted' to current and future Essipiunnuat generations. They correspond to the cultural memory of the group, its experience of the Salmon War and fundamentals of the group's cultural laws and practices.

Essipiunnuat oral tradition and memory

Interviewees mentioned four main components of the group's experience that should be transmitted. The wider stories of all First Peoples of Turtle Island, prioritising those who have a historical relationship with the Essipiunnuat, such as other Innu communities: the Eeyou, Atikamekw, Anishinaabeg, Wendat and Mohawk etc., is one component. Younger people need 'a global view of indigenous communities'. They will then be in a better position to reflect on the presence of all First Peoples on the continent, and more easily recognise and appreciate the existence of their own group, its history, way of life and historical condition (Riel, chapter 4, ref.3).

The younger generation needs to be told about the ancient way of life of their ancestors. They should be aware of the Innu way of life that moves in accordance with seasonal displacement. They might then appreciate the historical significance of the mouth of the Esh Shipu River as a meeting place, as well as a central dimension of ancestral custom, which consists of always returning to the location of your birth in summertime, as the salmon do (Sam, chapter 4, ref. 6). They should be told that life on the reserve has not always been as it is now; until quite recently (the early 20th century) there were, for example, few houses, surrounded by 'beautiful landscapes, looking like a paradise, not polluted'. Indeed, it has been requested that the agricultural experience of the group should not be hidden away after being sedentarised on the reserve. Agricultural practices were complementary to fishing, hunting and trapping activities. It should be clear that since sedentarisation, agricultural practices 'were also necessary to survive when living in the reserve' so that 'everybody had a garden and a cow, horses, chickens and pigs; farm animals'. The idea is that agriculture, as a component of autarky, is also part of the collective experience of the group (Pierre, chapter 4, ref. 6).

The collective experience of colonialism, this sinister dimension of memory, should not be 'neglected since it is central to the history of the community'

(Maxence, chapter 4, ref. 4 and 5). Understanding the colonial history of the Essipiunnuat will provide them with keys to decode the actual issues facing the group. Among other elements, children and young people should be aware of the racism that their ancestors have endured, including the discrimination encountered at school and the mistreatment to which 'savages' were submitted (Maxence, chapter 4, ref. 3 and 4). They should be able to see the links between the problems we face as First People today, the history of our colonisation and the catastrophe of the residential school system. It must be made clear that dimensions of our current human condition are related to children being forcibly removed from their family at an early age by the authorities, the type of violence they experienced, and how they were widely abused by priests and nuns. They need to know that First Peoples never gave their consent and the authorities never asked permission. The lives of these children, as with today's young people, were with their parents. Back then, Innu life was on the land. In the residential schools, they were not learning anything 'Innu'; they did not feel good, and they were missing their parents terribly so it was hard to concentrate and learn. That was their culture, they were proud of being indigenous, but they were kidnapped; they wanted to return to be with their parents but could not. The residential school system deeply traumatised our societies, and the effects are felt to this day (Riel, chapter 4, ref. 3).

Figure 13. Essipiunnuat, members of the Ross family c.1940 *(family archives).*

An alternative Canadian history is needed, other than the one in the books that indigenous children were forced to study at school, in order to show how this country's goal has been to undermine indigenous sovereignty (Édouard, chapter 4, ref. 4). It needs to be emphasised that the history of Canada is about oppression based on colonialism and attempts to extinguish indigenous cultures and rights. The history of the Essipiunnuat that children will hear and read should be clear about the fact that their ancestors always resisted usurpation (Raoul, chapter 4, ref. 2).

A pedagogy of the Salmon War

The Essipiunnuat who witnessed the Salmon War view it as 'the most important chapter in the history of the community; and it should be always remembered' (Karl, chapter 4, ref. 7). Since the war was a core event for the group, it is essential that younger Essipiunnuat place it in its historical context. They may then be more able to understand the issues at stake for the community – the importance of the movement as well as the symbolic importance of the salmon net. They will be better armed to 'decipher and read the actual condition of the community, realise where we started, what was done, and that everything has not always been easy as today, that some people fought for what they have today' (Adam, chapter 5, ref. 6).

For the Salmon War to be a whole chapter in the history of the community, it is not the people who fought, or their enemies who should receive attention, but the objectives pursued at the time (Adam, chapter 5, ref. 6). It should be known that the Salmon War was waged 'to defend our rights, to have them recognised by the dominant society; we were requesting respect for our dignity as First People' (Édouard, chapter 4, ref. 4). The Salmon War should be presented as the reason why the community still exists today; it was a struggle for collective survival in the face of renewed attempts to extinguish inherent Innu rights and annihilate Innu cultural identity (Sam, chapter 4, ref. 1).

The praxis of resistance is central to the experience of the Salmon War and it is a core component of transmission. Memories of the war contain a panoply of examples of good practice and of role models who resisted oppression and the extinguishment of inherent collective rights and rebelled against illegitimate authorities (Mestenapeo, chapter 4, ref. 8). The experience of war also comprises lessons on how to succeed in resistance and war. For example, if the decision is made to go to war:

> make sure that you are not alone, that the community is behind you. Do not go to war for your personal interest – you will not succeed. Go to war for collective interests and people will go with you. Success in waging war also requires communication and leadership. All members must take responsibility collective success in a battle, especially when you are a tiny group. It is ultimately a collective effort. As a leader, you must absolutely

> ensure that you have community support: it is essential. (Sam, chapter 4, ref. 1 and 4)

The power of unity and the conditions for an optimisation of collective potentialities is certainly a central theme of the Essipiunnuat experience of resistance. Transmission should therefore include information about the fact that though small, if you are determined, you can fight a bigger group; that 'when you want something essential for you, you can get it as long as you unite, and you are not afraid to charge' (Tshak, chapter 4, ref. 1). Future generations should remember how the whole community came together and reached a relative unity of will, but also why it arrived at this decision to fight to protect the rights bequeathed by the ancestors for future generations. 'They should be informed about what is primordial and what is not, and that we defended something that was really sacred for us' (Raoul, chapter 4, ref. 6).

The results of resistance, cultural assertion, uprising and waging war should be presented (Adam, chapter 5, ref. 6). The outcome of the movement of resistance has to be understood, as should the 'truth about interethnic relations, and above all the increased respect towards the Innu following the war; that resisting oppression can bring more respect from enemies' (Maxence, chapter 4, ref. 3). It is imperative they know 'where they come from; that if they are here today, it is because wars were waged, and that there were moments of assertion resulting in external recognition' (Adam, chapter 5, ref. 6 and 8). They must be informed that resistance 'triggered the assertion of who you are' and that 'it allowed us to pass from a state of shame at being Indian to reclaim, and even be proud of, being Essipiunnuat today with its advantages and disadvantages.'

They should also know about the positive consequences of standing up for one's identity: among these being the rise of community auto-development, the emergence of the communitarian system, and the unity of will around the objective of acting together for the wellbeing of everyone (Adam, chapter 4, ref. 3). A recurring theme in the stories is that the coming generation should be made aware that the group is always at risk if it does not defend itself and is blindly obedient to the state:

> If the community had not awakened, it would have disappeared. Kids must know that you are Innu or you are not Innu. Self-definition is central, the last rampart against extinguishment. The kids must know that it is not because we do not obey Québec laws that we are outlaws. Also, if you self-define as Innu, it includes strict internal norms which require discipline and respect. It means that you are not alone, that you belong to a group but also that you must share with others. (Sam, chapter 4, ref. 1)

A fundamental teaching is that if you stop standing up for your rights as an indigenous person or group, you will lose them. Indeed, to renounce your rights means to renounce your Innu heritage, and vice versa. Stories suggest that knowledge of one's indigeneity is the cornerstone of resistance; if one does not feel Innu, it is highly unlikely that attempts at extinguishment will be resisted. Children and young people's introduction to the defence of their inherent rights can only be translated into practice if it is based on the transmission of a cultural identity and values (Mestenapeo, chapter 4, ref. 12). Receptivity to an ancestral conception of sovereignty and vision, such as *Innu tipenitamun*, ultimately depends on identification with Innu values and cultural identification remains a prerequisite for any successful initiative of resistance (Raoul, chapter 4, ref. 2).

Essipiunnuat cultural heritage: from respect to the art of consensus

The last theme for transmission to the next generation, concerns the intergenerational communication of norms and core components of Essipiunnuat heritage and stories.

Transmission of a specific ethic of respect for all life is central. This core element of cultural identity is translated, for example, in the common disapproval of selling meat from animals that have been hunted and the assertion that 'moose should be killed only for our subsistence' (Édouard, chapter 5, ref. 5), although in some cases, ducks can be exchanged for bullets (Pierre, chapter 5, ref. 4). The guiding principle that an Innu must only collect what he really needs, and not 'cause harm' while hunting, fishing or trapping, includes the obligation to disapprove of practices that are disrespectful of these codes. The ancestors teach that you should not shoot a duck, for example, if you might not be able to retrieve it. It must be transmitted that the act of not wasting is not only 'a respect for the environment but above all a respect for your pantry and for yourself' (Jeanne, chapter 4, ref. 4). For someone to be able to say 'That is enough, I've killed one or two moose, and that is enough for my people, I can stop' is a sign that they have acquired an essential element of 'being' Innu (Raoul, chapter 4, ref. 7). It is also a 'sense of sharing' and 'to leave food for others'. This is perceived as a fundamental truth, that 'if one does not respect nature, one lacks respect for one's own rights and for oneself as human, but also for future generations who will suffer from such deeds.' (Mestenapeo, chapter 4, ref. 12).

A 'good' Innu is careful and prudent in conducting his or her traditional activities and life in general. They do not jeopardise their own or others' security needlessly. Yet, prudence is something that has to be learned, as 'any animal that will teach his baby to take care and watch out'. It has to be taught to children as part of their cultural heritage to survive in their environment. This is why 'there needs to be an older person accompanying the young person, until the young person is able to do it alone' (Jeanne, chapter 4, ref. 3). Prudence is central since it prevents accidents, and helps younger people 'not to get lost' (Jeanne, chapter 4, ref. 4).

Transmission of the sense of dignity in indigeneity is seen as crucial. It implies a sense that your culture is valuable, that the indigenous point of view is valid and deserves consideration and respect. Pride in being indigenous reduces tolerance of attacks on indigenous human dignity. Yet, this sense of indigenous honour also includes appreciation of past generations and consideration for the ancestors and their wisdom. Only a sense of dignity and honour can lead children and young people to be assertive in front of enmity, looking directly and confidently into their opponents' eyes:

> I am Innu. I am proud of being indigenous. We are human, we are equal and sacred. It is also the pride of being a people different and apart. Kids should be told to be proud of their parents, of their great grandparents; it is because of them that you are a community, that you are Essipiunnuat. Everything you have now, it comes from them (Riel, chapter 4, ref. 2).

It is seen as imperative for children and young people to overcome the colonial representations of Innu society as deficient and degenerate, condemning people identified with it to failure, dependence and despair. The new generations should be aware that being Innu is 'something very positive in our lives' and 'a treasure of knowledge and wisdom that you hold' (Napeo, chapter 4, ref. 4). Not adopting this attitude is to dishonour your own heritage; not recognising and honouring the deeds of preceding generations and our

Figure 14. A present-day traditional site (personal archives, 2010).

ancestors is an unacceptable sign of ingratitude (ibid.). We have to remember that some people fought for the rights we have now, that sacrifices were made in confrontation and war (Karl, chapter 4, ref. 8). Young people need to know that to fight for your dignity is the greatest source of pride (Ivan, chapter 4, ref. 3), but also that it is not by being disrespectful that you gain respect. On the contrary, that 'respect is best acquired by offering it to others, especially to those who do not know it and cannot give it to you' (Riel, chapter 4, ref. 1).

An Essipiunnu does not receive orders from anyone. He needs no licence from any authority, either indigenous or from Québec. No government has authority over an Essipiunnu (Pierre, chapter 5, ref. 4). It is his own consciousness and mind that guide him. Accepting rules over Innu activities signifies obedience and submission to external control. That is how freedoms are lost (Mestenapeo, chapter 4, ref. 12). When the Québec and Canadian authorities do not respect Innu rights, there needs to be an automatic response, since 'if you give them an inch they take a mile' (Sam, chapter 4, ref. 5). In the group, freedom of speech is a core value. When there is a problem, ideas should be suggested fearlessly, and solutions proposed (Pierre, chapter 5, ref. 9). Young people have to be taught not to expect things to fall into their lap, but instead to take steps to realise them:

> Kids should not expect things to fall from the sky. If you believe in something, you must strive to reach your goal. Also, work with the people who believe in you. You must do it for the right reasons, always having in mind the interests of future generations. Implement things by yourself. It must be clear to them that if you flinch in the face of adversity, you will never reach your goal (Mesnak, chapter 4, ref. 3).

What has been lost, and should be reinstated, is intrinsic resistance to any form of usurpation (Pierre, chapter 4, ref. 7): 'Do not let anybody oppress you' (Ivan, chapter 4, ref. 1). Young people should be taught that they have rights, but also that these rights should be protected, even if it means waging war. Young Innu must understand that,

> If they do not fight for [their rights], nobody else will, that there is nobody else who has their back. It is a question of respect for the sacrifice of your ancestors to protect, at least, what they fought for. It was done for you. If you let your rights be negated and extinguished, it means that we fought for nothing. Assert yourself, fight! (Tshak, chapter 4, ref. 8)

The young should be taught never to accept the withdrawal of their inherent sovereignty. They need to have instilled in them 'the strong feeling that nobody will take away what I have' (Pierre, chapter 4, ref. 6). In waging war for one's rights, it is not enough to be persuaded about the worthiness of the cause, one must also persuade others. But it should be clear from the first that these rights are sacred and non-negotiable, and are not redeemable for money. They cannot be put on the negotiation table (Ernest, chapter 4, ref. 17). It is essential that future generations can always return to the source of their rights, and reassert them.

First Peoples should never play the government's game. When governments come forward with proposals, Innu members should ask 'Do we really need that to live? Is it essential for us?', so that 'before selling our rights, there are many other things to do' (Sam, chapter 4, ref. 7). Young people should be able to discern between legitimate and illegitimate authority, respect the first and revolt against the second. 'We should train them to judge what is fair and what is not. But they should be able to accept just a "no". This is part of living together in a community' (Pishimnapeo, chapter 4, ref. 3). A central element of transmission remains communitarian spirit and values. The young should learn to be communitarian, which also signifies resisting that which goes against the interests of the group (Napeo, chapter 4, ref. 5).

In the stories, elements that should not be transmitted were also mentioned, such as enemies' personal names. Certain vulnerable individuals or their descendants could be harmed by being named (Maxence, chapter 4, ref. 4). Indeed, interviewees offered 'gentler' versions of certain episodes, removing images of violence. Some felt that the younger generation should be told as little as possible about the use of violence, because it causes more harm than good. When being related to the young, accounts of the war should also emphasise the importance of dialogue and negotiation (Riel, chapter 4, ref. 2). However, there are debates among participants about what should or should not be transmitted; some pleaded for the integral transmission of information, including the fact that participants in the war had been inclined to solve problems with their fists (Maxence, chapter 4, ref. 4). One Elder, however, suggested that the younger generation should be told little of the Salmon War. The emphasis on the past should instead focus on the ancient way of life of their ancestors, including the virtues and care required to achieve success. The mythologising of the Salmon War, serving a specific role of legitimation, tends to overshadow other more fundamental components of the Essipiunnuat's past, such as ancestral teachings and concerns with intergroup harmony (Jeanne, chapter 4, ref. 2).

The praxis of cultural continuity

People identified specific tools, devices and means by which the content is to be transmitted. These techniques define even more precisely conceptions of Essipiunnuat heritage and its continuity. They propose a range of tactics for intergenerational communication and transmission, but direct encounters, contacts and community projects are prioritised.

Direct encounters: meetings, reflections and actions

An increase in intergenerational encounters is imperative to improved transmission. Meetings between young and older people should be organised regularly to discuss issues pertaining to hunting, fishing, customs and rights (Mestenapeo, chapter 4, ref. 11). Honesty should guide the intergenerational exchanges. Children should be told the naked truth, and the *parrêsía* might 'catch their attention and make them think, even if they ... get upset at first' (Pishimnapeo, chapter 4, ref. 2).

In Napeo's view, emblematic communitarian actions should be launched in the same spirit as the symbolic net that was spread to catch salmon for everyone during the war. It was considered crucial for older people and the young to taste the fresh salmon. Children should be involved at every stage, gathering salmon with their fathers and uncles, cleaning it, sharing it around the houses and offering it into the hands of the older community members. Such actions facilitate intergenerational connections, producing pleasure and joy for everybody. The quantity is not as important as the fact that you took it yourself to someone else in the community, and they are happy to be given something that is precious to them. But this could also be done with partridges, moose and seals. This is investment in your community, increasing your greatest treasure: communitarian values and spirit (chapter 4, ref. 5).

Community gatherings and empowerment

An increase in meetings and other encounters between members of the group was seen as important, as communal celebrations are an essential point of exchange and transmission. However, these meetings should be more inclusive, since off-reserve members tend to be left out. Many have never lived in the community, so they often do not know about their group and have had no access to its traditions. This results in non-identification with the community, and in hostility as well as idealisation. One proposal is to organise a communitarian hunting trip in the spring. A small camp could be set up. That would create space to be together and to participate in exchange. Those who had not grown up on the reserve would learn more about their community, and some would go on to become ambassadors for it. After the community hunt, a celebration and dinner could be organised. It would facilitate exchange between those living in the reserve and those living away from it, and therefore reinforce the community's inner peace. There would be a general invitation sent to all members (Sam, chapter 4, ref. 5).

Remember together: memory projects

As well as the wish to learn more about the experience of others, some participants in the war expressed a desire to tell their own story. These life stories are perceived as the most important material to be included in an oral history of the Essipiunnuat. There is a wish to participate in community oral history initiatives such as requesting that a circle be set up to ensure that as much information as possible is documented and potentially transmitted. Although it is better to cover some subjects through individual interviews, 'we remember better in a group, together', says Ivan (chapter 4, ref. 6). The meetings between individuals would enhance their memories, find complementarities, and a higher level of remembrance would be reached.

The importance of producing a document for future generations was identified; a book they can refer to forever, with references to the past and the time of their ancestors. It would make a link between past and future generations:

> It is crucial. It will be a tool and a landmark. It is essential to consider and valorise those who have this knowledge first, and then it will be possible to show the values of our ancestors. (Jeanne, chapter 4, ref. 5)

The history of the community should be conducted among the general public, house by house, person by person, and be based on a community oral history project. The information will then be complete. There is nothing better than consulting the community directly (Tshak, chapter 4, ref. 4). A book is identified as the best tool for memory; it is less expensive than a film and it should include many pictures (Sam, chapter 4, ref. 2 and 3). A document specific to the Salmon War was requested and a more general one on the history of Essipit, with a focus on purpose and results (Édouard, chapter 4, ref. 4). Such documentation will prove to future generations that this war was really waged, and it would include the names of those who were involved and their actions (Ernest, chapter 4, ref. 15).

The production of a well-made and attractive documentary, able to capture young people's attention, was proposed, in order to show future generations the strength and power of a community that is united. It would be used as a tool for intergenerational communication. The film could put the Salmon War in the wider context of the extermination of First Peoples on Turtle Island or the Americas, and especially in the United States. The Salmon War could, in this context, be presented as an awakening. Raoul recommends calling the film *The Awakening of a Force*, which refers to a power that was 'buried, a force that was more individual but that merged, that became a kind of terrific communitarian might' (chapter 4, ref. 8).

The necessity of establishing a community strategy in order to empower young people and give them opportunities to connect with Essipiunnuat ancestral knowledge was pointed out. Priority should be given to reinforcing their relationship with the land and the community, but also with other parts of the world. First, training for young people should be organised, while they are 'not too old, because at 16–17 they are often already spoilt to a certain degree'. During the weekend, for example, a small group of people could go into the forest. Pierre suggests 'not to put too much pressure on them, let them go ... you will see which ones are the best, those who like it the most. Some of them might become trappers' (chapter 4, ref. 7). The idea is to return to the basics. It should be part of their education to taste 'the real life, freedom. Your identity, as indigenous, is based on freedom.' The young must 'experience their freedom and learn to be free' (Pierre, chapter 4, ref. 6).

Young people should be involved in concrete initiatives for the autonomy of the community, such as a community garden. It was also mentioned that a conference should be organised for schoolchildren with a speaker accompanied by someone who took part in the war, who could begin by saying, 'It is the pride of being indigenous, of being Innu, and above all of being from the community of Essipit, that brings me in front of you today' (Riel, chapter 4, ref. 5). They should also be given more opportunities to travel and have exchanges with other communities around the world. Children should be told, 'go and explore beyond your community; travel, but come back to reinforce, enlarge your community, improve it and pass on all the wealth and knowledge obtained outside of your community and the children' (Napeo, chapter 4, ref. 4).

The establishment of a small museum on Essipiunnuat heritage and memory was proposed; a house of cultural memory. There would be lots of visual elements, photographs and images, as well as an illustrated chronology of the history of the community to orientate the visitor. One section should be dedicated to the ancestral hunting territories, with a special focus on family ancestral territories. All of this should be illustrated with geographical maps. There should also be information about how these territories were usurped. The benefit of such a space would be particularly important for the youngest generations who could find out about their family lines, their ancestors. They would visually see their ancestors in relation to *Assi*. There should also be information on the ancestors' way of life, their tools, how they travelled (with their dogs, for example). This would be an excellent tool for introducing the community to foreigners. The young people would be proud of that. It would give them the feeling that the community is old, that their ancestors were indigenous. Tools (snowshoes, arrows, clothes and so on) could be exhibited, alongside explanations of how they were made. It would empower them to be reminded that their ancestors were First Peoples. The museum could be started from material that already exists in the community. People would say, 'Some have blonde or red hair, some have blue eyes, but there was cultural transmission, and they are still indigenous.' There would be stories about the Ross and Moreau families, but also the Dominique, Bacon, Aglée, Nicolas, Denis, Napentie families and so on (Tshak, chapter 4, ref. 4).

The power of research and materials for transmission

People reported the need to ensure that the results of the investigation would be accessible to members as well as transferred to future generations. The present book (originally a community-based PhD research project) was seen as a device for gathering cultural information, for facilitating intergenerational communication and also conserving cultural knowledge for future generations (Napeo, chapter 4, ref. 9).

The research was seen as a tool to give younger people access to the experience of those who lived through the Salmon War. Their experience and testimony could help younger people to understand many things concerning their own background:

> It will allow me, with my childhood memories, to go and answer my old question 'What really happened during that war?' Because I was too young to be conscious and aware of exactly what was happening. It is precious for me to know how people experienced it, those who were directly involved. It will help me to explain many things (Élisabeth, chapter 4. ref. 3).

The information gathered could be transmitted in different forms, according to the community's needs (Karl, chapter 4, ref. 8). People who took part in the project could gather and listen to the results of the investigation, although some of them asked that access such gatherings be restricted, since 'remembering the Salmon War is very likely to awaken old demons among our neighbours [meaning people of Les Escoumins]' (Esther, chapter 4, ref. 6). Younger members of the community would attend as well as leaders. At the end of the presentation, intergenerational exchanges would be encouraged (Mesnak, chapter 4, ref. 3). The young people could ask questions and the older people could answer (Napeo, chapter 4, ref. 9). The presentation should be accompanied by a booklet or a short film. It would refresh memories (Ivan, Chapter 4, ref. 6). Many stressed the importance of incorporating pictures and images (Pierre, chapter 4, ref. 7).

Some people asked that this investigation be used for a book or even a documentary, since it would illustrate how the Innu have always fished in the mouth of the river, and that between 30 and 40 families came each summer to do so. A history of salmon fishing in the river would make visible to younger people the symbolism of the changes imposed on the Essipiunnuat way of life over time. Young people need to understand the transformations that have led up to today; especially how changes in their way of life were determined by the arrival of the lumber companies and how the Innu were displaced. There could even be a permanent exhibition which would include pictures of our past warriors, as a way of honouring them with pictures and texts (Mesnak, chapter 4, ref. 3).

Beyond dams and masks: the hard work of truth

Stories about the Salmon War inform the present time and condition of the group in different ways. They report on social determinants that contribute to keeping the memories of the war in the past, when not pushing them into oblivion. They mirror sentiments of nostalgia, social criticism and direct observations about present circumstances. They reveal the hardship of seizing the present, what it means to speak under colonial rule, and the profound effect exerted by the barbells of psychological colonialism on the group's relationship with the past, and therefore its own truths. Essipiunnuat's stories expose the imperative for group continuity, mainly through considerations of what should be transmitted to the youngest generations, but also by examining how this might take place.

Traversing these rich perspectives highlights how silence has not erased the Salmon War from the group's memory. Deeply entrenched as it is in people's life-stories, its evocation generates a strong emotional and normative charge. Because of this, the Salmon War has a quasi-incendiary potential to destabilise social relations and the established orders, outside as much as inside the group. Reconnecting with the memory of war provoked interviewees' reimmersion in their past-self schemas, generating the actualisation of their past postures. It is by understanding the normative power of the memories of war, in the minds of the participants, that this research has revealed the fine architecture of its forgetfulness.

The post-Salmon War generations live in a community, or are linked to a community (in the case of those living off-reserve), they often know little about. They live with the social and emotional heritage of the past and the shadows of intergenerational trauma, but without much knowledge of what preceded their time. In this context, it is natural for these younger generations to ignore, disregard or even deny an indigenous heritage that the society into which they are now, to different degrees, deeply related perceives as negative, degenerative and deficient. But wasn't this *sui nullius* and the production of the Indian-as-object empty of an Innu subjectivity the endgame of an entire Canadian regime's strategy in respect of First Peoples up to now? Isn't Essipit a 'success', and the recognition it has received from mainstream society, including the government, a mark of its epistemological collapse?

In his book *The Imaginary Indian* (1992), Daniel Francis reported eloquently on the 'Indian' as the 'creation of the European' (what I've called in this book the 'Indian-as-object'). As he explicitly states, 'while Indians are the subject of this book, Native people are not', and he adds that his investigation is not about 'native cultural history' but 'the images of Native people that White Canadians manufactured, believed in, feared, despised, admired, taught their children.' (p. 21)

But what happens when a leader or people 'representing' First Peoples wear the costume of the 'imaginary Indian'? When the exogenous images produced are internalised or used for marketing purposes, political control or simply to conceal an ignorance or ambivalence about their heritage as First Peoples, what then?

Our interest thus lies in the way by which Innu, especially those in positions of power, reproduce and use these images, generating a simulacrum of indigeneity (the 'simulated-Indian'). To borrow an image from An Kapesh, what are the consequences of putting on Punchinello's coat? Perhaps as Francis asserts, 'it is part of the legacy of the Imaginary Indian that we lack a vocabulary with which to speak about these issues clearly.' (Francis, 1997, p. 9.)

The fact remains that the post-Salmon War generations are facing an impressive number of dams which prevent the intergenerational flow of stories. One is the intensive channelling of local voices through various, often highly sophisticated, methods of communication that has helped to dissolve Innu critics and perspectives, as well as to shape the idea of collective consent to modern treaty processes. These practices have had a mutilating effect on the diversity of internal perspectives in favour of a single official story serving the purposes of band council authority and colonial governments' interests.

The post-war generations do indeed witness the overuse of the term 'Innu', for it is used in superficial and decontextualised ways, either about political strategies and negotiations with municipalities and states, or as a term exploited and commodified for the purposes of marketing. The existence of the simulated Indian is inseparable from financial and corporate interests, even if they have a community base. This reinforces already existing feelings of inner emptiness associated with indigeneity: the fear of death, the amnesia, lack of self-knowledge, psychological distress, and dependence that come with living on a colonial reserve. Such places were purposedly designed to generate an 'absence' of the Innu; the only allowed subjectivity being the desire to forget and disappear. It must be stressed that this perception of emptiness and distance is particularly experienced by off-reserve members who now compose the majority of Essipiunnuat but have no political rights.

The post-Salmon War generations (at least up to 2016) voice a need for identity and belonging within a group that is struggling with the forces of forgetfulness and a constant fear of cultural annihilation, which favours a metaphysic of complete domination. It will take yet more time to assess the impact of the internal regime of power, with its growing authoritarian features. Neither jobs, bank accounts, real estate, cars nor recognition or approval from colonial society can heal the psychological scourges of colonial violence; it is only a superficial bandage for the soul. If Essipit's experience with socioeconomic development over the last four decades is important and rich, the Essipiunnuat's experience in psychological recolonisation is equally if not more so; it is an extraordinary window, which may benefit other First Peoples, onto the fact that 'playing the good Indian' is not without consequences.

But at this point, there is clear evidence in the stories that autocracy has progressively made the entire group captive to the projected interiority of one individual, psychologically, at the very least. Though a fascinating topic, the study of the relationship between an individual leader and his own past goes beyond the scope of this investigation. Nevertheless, it remains highly relevant for future research within the wider context of the phenomenon of rewriting under autocratic rules, such as has been happening in the United States since 2017.

Conclusion

> There is an ancient Indian saying that something lives as long as the last person who remembers it. My people have come to trust memory over history. Memory, like fire, is radiant and immutable while history serves only those who seek to control it, those who douse the flame of memory in order to put out the dangerous fire of truth. Beware these men for they are dangerous themselves and unwise. Their false history is written in the blood of those who might remember and of those who seek truth.
>
> Floyd Red Crow Westerman

> It is in societies where social memory is primarily oral, or where they are in the process of collating a collective written memory, that the struggle for the control of recollection and tradition, effectively a manipulation of memory, can best be understood.
>
> Jacques LeGoff (1986)

Over the past century, the Essipiunnuat have experienced a series of events, from genocide to permanent colonisation. This has produced intergenerational wounds and resulted in cultural disconnections, large-scale marginalisation and the obliteration of core features of the cultural heritage. Over many generations, and intensifying in the last decade, large portions of the Essipiunnuat collective cultural memory has not been transmitted. Today, the current youngest generation is widely unaware of a pivotal event in their parents' lives that happened just three decades ago: the Salmon War. People aged under 35 at the time of the war were never told about the episode and those who participated in it had never talked about it; the younger generations knew that something significant had happened but had no idea of the details. The stories weren't told, but why?

This book is the result of a decade-long investigation, tracing back the genealogy of cultural oblivion as experienced by the author's family and community, and identifying the lineage of an intergenerational silence about a historic event in order to determine the factors that have led to the contemporary outcome. For this researcher, going up the river of memory would result in having to face the complex dams of silence that had formed over the centuries – obstacles preventing the group from accessing deep and sometimes erased or mutilated sources of knowledge and alternative perspectives on 'truth'.

What we heard and saw

Stories of the Salmon War suggest at first a clear demarcation between external determinants (colonialism, Québec politics, Euroquébécois representations, anti-Indian militancy) and internal ones; the latter showing, by contrast, the importance that those involved in the project attach to their own subjectivity and that of their group, and the predominant role leaders play in using contentious issues for strategic reasons. The rationale for this seminal collective agency is based on explicit descriptions of mnemonic practices and references to a common inventory of experience on the eve of war, and on the emergence of a sovereignty movement born from the womb of the group, as well as shared objectives operationalised mutually through specific and chosen strategies.

Representations of this agency in the course of war, through images arising from the stories, offer glimpses of the community's past self. Self-portraits are characterised by defined roles in war articulated around commitment as an emergent norm. The background to these self-portraits, used by participants in the war to contextualise their actions, illustrates the group's identification with dual, and often antinomian reference points, as well as its advanced economic marginalisation, dependence on external subsidies and the heavy burden placed upon it by material and psychological colonialism. Frequent depictions of emotions reveal shared pleasures associated with commitment and participation in the rebellion, as well as the most commonly distributed feelings of suffering and pain linked with the subsequent reaction to and aftermath of war.

Representations of others in autobiographical memories gave access to the group's past-self in war. They contain images dominated by an aesthetic of revolt and common descriptions of idols or specific actors, mostly represented in heroic postures with common ethical attributes placed in contrast with images of transgressions. Overall, the images confirm features of a group past-self whose aesthetics display all the characteristics of strength, revolt and an irrepressible rebelliousness – yet also the danger of a nihilistic self-giving attitude being used by leaders and diverted for the purpose of strengthening internal power. These representations of a past-self suggest a powerful normative charge specific to the Salmon War and its connection with wider indigenous worldviews and the conception of life, sovereignty and self-determination it carries within itself.

Testimonies relating to the outbreak of war centred on themes of change: the remodelling of people's relational system, deep alterations in their self-identity, collective empowerment, and the establishment of new forms of in-group management characterised by a metaphysic of domination, and a progressive insertion of a monocratic chronology in public discourse, with lasting consequences for mnemonic practices to the present day.

Presented as a major event that marked profoundly the group's memory and generated forms of collective revival and empowerment, participants testified to a subsequent growing remoteness from the normative model connected with their experience of the war. The events of the war culminated in the establishment of a regime which reproduced the useful imagery of the

'Indian-as-object' to conform to the Crown representation, which legitimated a monocracy. Furthermore, in an advanced stage of recolonisation, using this simulated-Indian imagery for the purposes of legitimation and marketing, a new collective narrative was generated by a tiny leading unit, increasingly eclipsing the contribution of everyone who took part to enhance the reputation of but a few. The predominance of a paradoxical public discourse about the absence of the Essipiunnuat before the war, added to representations of Essipiunnuat produced through a Euroquébécois lens, reveals erasures that have benefited the dominant internal actors and resulted in a significant historical reinterpretation of the group experience.

Mnemonic practices contained in the testimonies reflect the times and the group's cultural condition. Forces favouring the oblivion of the Salmon War, and the general tendency towards forgetting and disconnecting from cultural memory, were described with astonishing precision as 'dams' preventing remembrance. These 'dams' included subsequent events that interfered with remembrance and social phenomena that countered rememoration and reinforced a logic of forgetting and cultural oblivion. They comprised the multiple traumas participants experienced, which they associated with the course of the war and which they were afraid to relive; 'truth', having a deep effect on community relations; the destabilising and unpredictable power of past narratives; and the constellation of interests favouring denial and erasure within the group, including the omnipresence of Québec's selective memory, partially absorbed by the Essipiunnuat. The dynamics of internal psychological erasure and recolonisation were also linked, among other things, to the dual logic of monocratisation-bureaucratisation of political power, accompanied by the reiteration of Innu symbolism for the purposes of marketing and legitimation. Reminiscences and elements of resistance to the vectors of oblivion, such as emotional reflux and the normative charge contained in memories linked to people's cultural identity, were also recognised. Not envisaged when the research began more than a decade ago, the current social order was reported as the most important element determining oblivion, as well as the interiority of leaders who tended to project their relationship with the past on to the whole group.

Ultimately, remembrance of the Salmon War is highly controversial due to its normative charge which offers standards for evaluating the current social order and its modes of control, countering the unified front shaped by the post-war regime over four decades as a continuation of colonial definitions and institutions. The study of mnemonic practices revealed nostalgia, articulated social criticism and participants' views on the current cultural condition. The concerns of different respondents coincided in terms of their views on cultural continuity and specific contents and means of intergenerational transmission.

The group is presented as being on the brink; in spite of its material achievements and economic self-reliance, its continuity can only be ensured by a radical epistemological shift aiming to revitalise its self-knowledge. Specifically, a reinstatement of Innu ethics, laws and modes of governance is seen as needed to form the foundation of a self-defined social order in opposition to racist and colonial definitions, essentialised concepts that can bring short-term political and financial gains but that favour assimilation, cultural discontinuity and decreased self-referentiality in the long run.

This challenge of self-definition is faced by all First Peoples living under the Canadian constitutional regime of Article 91(24) and the Indian Act. In the long term, complying with exogenous categories favours the absorption of the representations at its roots. Cultural oblivion, as a complex phenomenon produced from specific determinants, is not irremediable if its manufacture is understood and the major mechanism and devices of its production are disclosed and uprooted.

What we learned

Memories of the Salmon War are emblematic of a genuine subjectivity – a collective agency favouring resistance in response to multilateral efforts to undermine the normative foundations of a micro-group. Interviewees report acts of sovereignty, self-determination and resistance based on a historical consciousness and endogenously defined notions of Innu laws (including obligations of guardianship to Assi and future generations), that have survived colonialism in its advanced forms.

The normative charge of respondents recalling their stories during the war reveals the cultural identity of the group and the fundamental ways people relate to the Earth. Remembrance of the event thus reactivates these standards, often highlighting their antinomies with the established orders and their essentialised representations of the Indian as object. The struggle to counter this colonial logic, especially in its psychological forms, is played out primarily within the group itself, where the Eurocanadian and Euroquébécois colonial myths and representations, progressively reabsorbed and internalised after the war, clashed with the ancestral Essipiunnuat definitions revived by the actualisation of memory in the present.

The command to forget that the Crown imposed on First Peoples remains the key to understanding the architecture of cultural oblivion afflicting Canada. The Canadian Crown's objective, for its part, from the very beginning and through its Indian policies for the last 150 years, has been to establish its absolute supremacy over Innu ancestral territories and people, to ensure ease of access to them, and to exploit them. The preferred way to achieve this, as expressed in the official commissions from the mid 19th century, was through a material and cultural deterritorialisation: to disconnect the '*Indians*' physically from their ancestral lands and way of life (and symbolically from their own cultural referential), in order to foster their complete assimilation and drain them of their symbolic resources. As it was for other First Peoples in Canada, this systemic and implacable approach appears to be a central cause of Essipiunnuat cultural disempowerment.

When people are categorised along racial lines by colonial powers, it can result in them perceiving themselves as deficient and decadent. This sense of inferiority tends to legitimate submissiveness and auto-repression, and quash any form of resurgent subjectivity. The 'Indian-as-object', a representation which is rooted in the Canadian constitution itself, became the 'simulated-Indian' over time. It is, above all, the corollary of a policy designed to obtain absolute domination over indigenous ancestral territories and their wealth. In this sense, cultural oblivion is the ultimate means of achieving total domination and appropriation, of eradicating Innu stories and laws, and of getting people to consent to the surrender of *Assi* and to abandoning their inherent ancestral sovereignty – this act of cession being explicitly represented by the Crown as the core of their contemporary approach to reconciliation.[1] Once erased from memory, Essipiunnuat treasure can be traded for crumbs and people may still perceive that they have gained something.

As policies of oblivion underlie all the structures imposed on First Peoples in Canada over time, the role of memory remains crucial in the construction of individual and collective identity; cultural oblivion reduces capacity for self-definition, generates anomie, opens doors for all possible self-mutilations and ensures docility and loss of imagination. In its latter stages, internalised negative representations of indigeneity constitute a standard of the group's sense of self, or 'identity polysemism'. A politics of the collective self that does not involve an increased rooting in cultural resources is flawed, as it leads to anomie and forms of nihilism that favour the instrumentalisation of wills and self-serving tendencies and the reproduction of categories that were initially contested. Once voided of its own normativity and epistemological foundations, and the sense of what is sacred, the group more easily absorbs exogenous definitions, until auto-referentiality is definitively altered.

The experience of the Essipiunnuat demonstrates the ultimate logic of the constitutional regime of Article 91(24) of the Constitution of 1867 and the Indian Act, and how the doctrine of *terra nullius* becomes, once internalised, the phenomenon of *sui nullius*. This supremacist and racist Crown definition

1 A group of Innu hunters sent a letter to Carolyn Bennett, the minister of indigenous affairs, to denounce the land claims negotiation process and the extinguishment of their sovereignty. In her response, the minister states that this process and the 'modern treaties' aim to generate an important step towards reconciliation (Ministère des affaires Autochtones et du Nord Canada, 2017).

of the 'Indian' has another characteristic: it is based on underestimating real people's capacity for agency, resilience, cultural continuity and their own definition of civilisation and progress. This fundamental blindness at the heart of colonial institutions, imbued with 19th-century representations, explains the architecture of colonial structures. This is best symbolised by the continued existence of the Department of Indian Affairs, which was supposed to be temporary, only set up to put the 'reserve' system into operation. In this context, collective efforts aiming at self-determination – which does not engender the replacement of the imposed structure of governance and its founding definitions – entail the gradual absorption of colonial imagery of indigenous citizenship (status, racial fiction), conceptions of the earth and the ancestral domain (the reserve, borders, alienability of lands), self-determination, decision-making and diplomacy (the band council, authority, obedience) as well as the relationship with the past and truth (command to forget, *sui nullius*).

The investigation presented in this book found evidence of a dominant in-group ideology displaying a mix of absolutism and racism. These elements are necessary to a system designed for the purpose of producing auto-genocide, as they generate a will (in particular through the residential school system) to replace the 'bad Indian' with a good one, following the logic deeply ingrained in the constitutional regime that indigeneity is an 'illness that needs to be cured'. Canadian colonialism added up to a partly interiorised Québec nationalist soaked with discourses of race and genetics. The experience of the Essipiunnuat should inform other indigenous groups in Canada and elsewhere about what awaits them if they rely on a system designed to assimilate them entirely, and also what happens when nationalist ideology (Québec nationalism, in the case of Essipiunnuat) becomes predominant among the leaders. In the words of a young Essipiunnuat interviewee who shared his vision of the group's current condition: 'It changes or we die' (personal communication, May 2010). This sounds similar to what was heard in Essipit almost 40 years ago, on the eve of the Salmon War.

If cultural oblivion generates anomie, it also produces inertia and the idea that things have always been this way and always will be: it paralyses and numbs. Forgetting paves the way for the absorption of negative representations, surplus powerlessness and renunciation if not self-abandonment. In contrast, cultural memory and stories are the basis of cultural identity, the capacity for self-definition and access to humanity – as a core source of the 'self' – in accordance with ancient philosophy.[2] A group's knowledge of its own

2 As an example, former grand chief Derek Nepiak says regarding the definition of belonging to the group: 'I've been to kinship and adoption ceremonies in our Anishinabek tradition. I've seen the power of our ceremonies and it has nothing to do with blood quantum or being "white" or the Indian Act. The Elders say we will move to a nationhood of humanity. In time, this will be more common. I only hope that the Anishinabekweg [women] and grandmothers

history is unavoidably dependent on intergenerational exchanges, sharing and reciprocity. Cultural memory and the referential it carries remain, after all, the material from which imagination is exercised. Past experiences bestow the ability to judge and a capacity for evaluation, but also increase the capability of anticipating the future and carving out a collective self, culturally deep-rooted, with the symbolic resources to avoid the pitfalls of internal recolonisation.

How the past illuminates the present

In a country intoxicated with discourses on reconciliation, inseparable from underlying interests such as industrial developments on ancestral territories, extractive projects, pipelines and the formatting of collective consent to modern treaties, the Essipiunnuat memory of the Salmon War remains highly seditious and a threat to all those actors, whether external or internal, wanting to increase their control over the First Peoples and their ancestral domains. In this context of a programmed extinguishment – or what Russell Diabo has called the 'termination plan' – the control over cultural memories, interpretations and references to inherent sovereignty and the exercise of self-determination, but also of an inventory of experience containing resistance and rebellious stances, is of utmost importance to local, provincial and federal authorities. The legitimation of these agents' endeavours depends greatly on their capacity to influence what should be remembered and forgotten. Cultural oblivion is, then, key to forging consent and getting people to surrender as they start to believe that what is on offer is a gain, mainly because the treasure they are asked to trade has become invisible to them over time.

However, the widespread assumption that forgetfulness, as silence, is absolute and can be produced indefinitely is inaccurate; it can, in fact, be undermined at any time by dreams, a confessional voice, reminiscences or an unexplained desire to go up the river of memory to the place of one's own birth, resulting in a kind of rebirth, breaching the dams of silence in one's own story. The power of a deep desire to know should not be underestimated. Wherever we go and whatever we do, we ultimately remain connected to the circumstances of our own birth, as individuals and as part of a group. The 'New France' and the 'Canadian confederation' are founded on the weak belief and imperial fantasy that previous civilisations did not exist or will soon vanish. Thus what has been 'forgotten' will one day be of interest to those who choose to go back up stream, swimming against the current of silence and the forces seeking oblivion.

take this responsibility back because it is beyond the political/spokesperson roles of chiefs and councils to perform this task.'

Katshikauashtet: gazing into the abyss of oblivion

For vulnerable microgroups, especially First Peoples, a clear need for further academic research exists, involving their members in every way possible, and resulting in concrete solutions being put into practice to benefit those who need it most: an indigenous public that the academic world in Canada and Québec often pretends to serve. Listening to people carefully remains a prerequisite for relevant research. Elders should be listened to particularly closely since they are the fount of knowledge, an invaluable source for younger indigenous researchers to draw on and bring out into the open. As the stories have shown, the constant questioning about the authority and legitimacy of those who claim to embody it remains at the heart of Innu political culture. We should also look at those in charge and other representatives, in parallel with criticising colonial institutions, in order to operate a radical cultural critique of the views they espouse; the more power they have, the more their blind spots threaten the group they lead. Studies of amnesia, forgetfulness and oblivion have a great future in Canada; the spectre of what we try to forget often remains closer to us than we tend to believe.

Analysis of the remembrance and forgetting of the Salmon War crystallises around what 'should' be transmitted to coming generations. When individuals or groups choose to forget, this constitutes a judgement over their own experiences, the ambiguous emotions associated with asserting indigeneity, and rebelling against authority and questioning the dominant culture into which they have at times integrated. It also testifies to the absence of transmission, the reasons people fell silent, and the strength of their feelings about what happened three decades earlier.

Indeed, the assertion of indigeneity, often in racialist terms, also engendered profound individual and group antinomies and internal toxicities. This is highly complex, yet their evaluation of what should be known about this event becomes more than a consideration of the intrinsic moral value of their experience. There is an echo of their grandparents' dilemma in their wondering whether or not to speak *Innu-aimun* to their children, embodying an appraisal of whether or not it is beneficial to reproduce such radical postures in the society their children inhabit. They understand that the actualisation of norms in the stories of the Salmon War is not without consequences; it has the potential to activate historical consciousness, anger and rebellion, but also to be a benchmark for assessing, and eventually contesting, the current institutions that they are destined to face and on which they often depend.

More than ever, and beyond the 'status card', Essipiunnuat heritage is heavy to bear and assume responsibility for. Memories of the Salmon War tie in with a wider indigenous historical consciousness and a range of ethics. This provides an insight into the benefits of defending one's group's collective dignity but also the pitfalls of radical movements and the risk that they be appropriated by those who might not have the group's original interests at heart. 'Remembering' can come to be perceived as a challenge to authority, or a dangerous 'contamination' of the present with the past, so that the young people who assert their indigeneity can become marginalised within their own community. This suppression of dissent within reserves has a long history that deserves special attention; being stigmatised as the 'bad Indian' has had, and can still have, serious consequences.

This part of the story, one that often eludes academics, is perhaps best investigated by indigenous researchers themselves. It is a task that requires great caution; among other things it demands the capacity to face one's demons without being consumed by them and having the strength to delve deeper to uncover what produced them. This book provides evidence that revolutionaries – if not 'faithful to [their] first noble promise', to use Camus' warning – can become oppressors, a fact that has been observed in various decolonisation processes around the world. The weapons that enable liberation can be turned against those they once liberated. The struggle for decolonisation, especially in its psychological dimensions, is never entirely won.

Intergenerational healing and transmission

How can the existing yet fragile will to transmit cultural knowledge and the memories of the Elders meet the will of the young to know and learn about the stories of the Salmon War? This is what I set out to investigate by starting a community project aimed at increasing the opportunities for the young to learn from the best of the groups' cultural inventory of experiences, and, through this, to enrich or reactivate their cultural identity (for it was clear that the latter was perceived as being in decline and fragile, if not entirely buried). My intention was to use oral history as a way of freeing people's voices to recreate a community of memory and words, to produce a common narrative that would counter the monopolisation of memory by public discourse, both externally and inside the reserve.

However, few people, especially those who were older, seemed to believe in the possibility of cultural renewal among the Essipiunnuat. For them, such a revolution in self-knowledge, and the willingness to take an Innu referential as a valuable model for the group, would imply the overthrow of the constitutional regime. It would imply its uprooting after having reached the heart of communities. The Essipiunnuat experience therefore, illustrates how potent political memory is, and how excavating memories and looking deep into oblivion can destabilise the status quo; it paradoxically shows how much what is 'remembered' can be inseparable from a deeper will to forget in monocratic regimes soaked with coloniality.

This research demonstrates how the memory of the Salmon War played a specific role in legitimising the 'communitarian system' and the regime established in the decades that followed. It reveals a prevailing narrative about the war, and representations correlated with identifiable in-group modes of control. By investigating the relationship between the group and its past, this research absorbed as primary data the obstacles it met and the barriers to remembrance.

Cultural oblivion as a human rights issue

Forgetting and the production of cultural oblivion has been a central mode of domination over First Peoples in Canada from the very beginning, and of a long-term strategy of permanent dispossession. The power to define access to cultural memory – what is remembered or forgotten – brings with it the capacity to control modalities of collective identity and provides access to its sources. The 'command to forget' remains a powerful determinant of 'cultural oblivion'. The widely absorbed mantra in Essipit that the group has 'no past' and 'was nothing' before the war resulted, for example, in asserting that the current internal regime was the only possible and legitimate model – a fascinating absorption of the 'reserve' concept. Beyond the official discourse and the voices which conformed to the social order, existed voices of a past, and of tradition and cultural continuity, that were silenced after the war. There were discrepancies between the individual stories and the monolithic script that had been written over four decades.

A few actors increasingly monopolised public speech until they became the only valued source of knowledge and reason. The cultural continuity of the group became almost entirely coupled with the conservation of the local 'system'. It was also linked to the crucial loyalty given to its designers and managers; actors who also have control over financial resources and transfers from colonial institutions as well as a monopoly on asserting collective consent. The will to remember, to give voice to interpretations of the past and to empower the willingness to know, directly attacks the foundations of the regime and the monopoly on collective identity that is held by a tiny minority and legitimated by colonial institutions and representations. The multiplicity of voices and of memories relativises a unified dimension, questions monocratic rule and allows for more critiques of power. This is one of the greatest strengths of people's stories and Essipiunnuat epistemologies, oral history, microsociology and mnemohistory.

This research studies the group's relationship with its past, bringing to a wider audience internal perspectives on the challenges to Innu cultural continuity. By questioning dominant discourses pertaining to the past, and investigating the patent oblivion of current generations while reinterpreting the stories of the

Salmon War, this book offers new tools with which to tackle the narratives of colonial rule and its imaginary, and links with local despotism and abuses of power. It shows the power and value of Innu storytelling and the stories' normative charge as cultural resources for increased self-referentiality and democratisation in the production of memory as an antidote to psychological colonialism. Research can provide the knowledge for resistance as well as for healing.

The project modestly contributes to reestablishing the value of people's stories, voices and experiences in order to offer alternative perspectives on Essipiunnuat self-knowledge and what it could become. Such endeavours give a sense of the importance of academic freedom by opening up spaces where the dogma that legitimises power can be fiercely questioned and deconstructed. The researcher's subjectivity is a limited but useful device for questioning the objectivity and 'superior rationality' associated with the monopoly of speech that representatives of the established order enjoy, and the rejection of such investigations only reinforces the conviction that it is vital. The concern of conventional researchers to maintain a distance from their object of research has been replaced here by a constant preoccupation with remaining 'close' to the stories shared by participants. This research has allowed for the confluence of individual stories (including my own), family and community, uniting them in a new collective framework. This may be somewhat expected, but it has allowed us to know ourselves better, and to understand more clearly what we collectively wish to avoid and reproduce.

The cultural oblivion experienced by the Essipiunnuat, even if on a micro scale, expresses a fundamental similarity with the experience of physical and cultural deterritorialisation of other First Peoples in the Americas and elsewhere. Their common subjection to imposed standards and ways of life to which they never consented, now some 500 years later, has resulted in the dramatic invalidation of their own ancient conceptions and normative order.

These common and tragic experiences of genocide, even if not well documented, and when not silenced due to their painful nature, remain more than ever relevant and real. This is about the marginalisation of an ancient wisdom and alternative conception of freedom in 'America', its continuation today, and the possibility it will be reactivated as a heritage of humanity to counter planned 'nothingness'.

The desire to forget, subjective amnesia and the tendency to bury our own truths, deserves further study. Elders repeatedly affirm, in Essipit and elsewhere, how truth-telling and a strict ethic of honesty are the guarantors of healing, justice, greater collective intelligence, powerful intergenerational relations and a healthier political life. The ways in which we invalidate ourselves, and contribute to our own annihilation as a result of psychological colonialism and the belief that we do not exist, cannot be silenced any more. At some point, it becomes necessary to change the system imposed on you, or submit and disappear through having relied on the hands that strangle you. The choice of obedience or resistance will determine your life and the lives of those who follow as well as the ancestral domain for which you are responsible. Ultimately, a group which loses sight of the great treasure of its cultural memory and heritage finds its ability to see what is at stake in terms of its ancestral territories and human dignity jeopardised. It thus directly affects the permission it gave to alienate what was never alienable and to trade untradable obligations to the Earth and future generations. In this sense cultural oblivion, and its invalidating effects in the wake of genocide, on both capacities for collective consent and resistance, becomes a major human rights issue.

Postface | Heirs of oblivion: leaders' interiority as a public issue

Like other First Peoples in Canada, the Essipiunnuat have experienced the collective and intergenerational casualties of genocidal policies and of a regime that aims to eradicate them. Other policies, some of which are still in place today, have been successful in producing 'oblivion'. This must be stated upfront: the Essipiunnuat are collectively survivors of a genocide and, to varying degrees, are heirs to oblivion. This experience demands a fearless critique of power, and of the internal reproduction of colonialism, especially in its psychological forms, through external definitions and forced forgetting.

To what extent those policies of erasure and the command to forget have been internalised and become a desire to forget and make forget, remains a question that is as necessary as it is cruel. Here, as a corollary to the earlier discussion in this book, I present briefly, for pedagogical purposes, my experience as a researcher investigating psychological colonialism and forgetfulness within my own community over more than a decade.

Investigating one's own group and family requires a level of reflection that can be stretched to its limit at times. The issue of maintaining a distance, which preoccupied me at the beginning, was progressively replaced by a concern with maintaining proximity to people's words and thoughts, and to my own integrity as a truth-hunter. Without such strict ethics applied to all circumstances, I could not have persevered. It's the stories of people and their need to speak and listen that have carried me through. As a member of the community, it was neither possible, nor even desirable, to be objective. It was wiser to recognise my own bias and give it space and visibility in order to work on and with it, and ensure it overshadowed as little as possible other people's stories.

In the process of conducting this research I met a number of obstacles, a major one being people's fear of speaking their mind freely due to the consequences, sometimes immense, that might accompany the articulation of their truth. It led some of those I approached to decline my invitation to talk, or pretend they were unable to attend the meeting'. Those who accepted and who were employees of the administration (or their close relatives), chose their words carefully and often preferred to speak off the record. They would then be more critical and sometimes express dissent. Only a few dared to criticise the council, its former general manager and the current internal social order, directly. I found that the Elders, without whom this research could not have been completed, were the bravest. Their conviction was a source of motivation and inspiration to persevere, even during the most difficult moments. But given the circumstances of the community, and the potential consequences for those who spoke out, it was decided that anonymity ought to be preserved. But the price of this anonymity, unfortunately, is to sacrifice the recognition of the remarkable contribution of each individual.

As in other research conducted on contended political terrain, I was perceived at first either as an agent of the regime or as a potential dissident, which reduced the possibilities for communication and exchange and impacted upon the research. Let's be unequivocal: investigating oblivion and 'things we want to forget' is challenging, especially in a community that has experienced many kinds of trauma over centuries and where *mnemophobia* is a constant presence. I learned the hard way that we do not connect with the truths of the past, the treasures of memory and its sources, without facing the barriers that were erected to separate us from them. And these barriers can seem impenetrable. As I tell my students, half seriously: 'Don't try this at home without adult supervision'. Studying forgetting can be highly dangerous; it's like putting one's hand down a hole without knowing what is inside, but in the knowledge that it is the hiding place of something which is hidden for specific reasons, rarely for joyful ones. But it is precisely why research on memory is so interesting because it poses with such force, and sometimes with indecency, our relationship with the truth.

Inward as well as outward forms of hostility towards this research, and its explicit attempts from the very beginning to democratise the production of Essipiunnuat memory became crucial material towards gaining an understanding of an overreaching unified dimension which happened to be broadly shaped by the Band Council leadership. The notion of the predominant role of leaders in shaping the community's relationship with the past only came to me late, around 2011. This was presumably because I identified too much, as a young researcher returning to his community, with this power and with those who exercised it. Reflection on my own indoctrination and blindness, these 'psychological barbells', have also become central to my research. The attempt to give marginalised members a voice, allow multiple interpretations and search for the 'hard truths' behind oblivion, attracted hostility in the form of attempts to control my research and the parameters of its public reception, and prevent potential dissidence. In the words of a community adviser, my research became a 'risk prevention' issue, one of reducing in advance a potential threat.

Choosing to tell the leaders some home truths is certainly noble but not without consequences. I had to expect some spokes in my wheels. Indeed, a researcher can hardly escape the modalities of his agency and its epistemological foundations, especially when investigating his own social settings. After all, the researcher is related to the regimes of power, especially when studying a group to which he belongs and where he lives with his relatives, as well as within generally dense, extensive and complex family networks. The particular value of such research probably lies in the process by which, because of the very nature of the investigation, it becomes increasingly perceived as a threat, an approach that, because it goes against the grain, can give access to data about power that can only be assessed when in opposition to it. Faced with insecurity and lateral violence, the best a researcher can do is perhaps to recognise his limits and shed light on his own programming by being mindful to turn the gaze on himself. By this means he can foster his reflexivity, go deeper into himself, and avoid being betrayed by his own blind spots, staying true to the stories shared with him and continuing to honour the truths they contain. Experience of the field, and life experience, give keys to understanding his own indoctrination and intention, which can help in accessing a deeper reading of stories.

The fact of seeing oneself at times overwhelmed by the phenomenon one is studying (for example, finding oneself in thrall to the very 'oblivion' under scrutiny, and living with its effects), can be tackled by a strict ethic of honesty. This means being faithful to people's views and interpretations and presenting their stories as they are to the best of one's knowledge, and not in order to please the people in charge or through fear of being excluded or stigmatised. Such intellectual integrity is made harder by the fact of living in the community; the possible impact on relatives; the potential for blackmail; and being confronted daily with familial realities and the concrete social problems under investigation including deeply entrenched misogyny and internalized racism. If a researcher is not sufficiently grounded and surrounded by mentors, the work can be psychologically destabilising; the desire to please can make us overlook what motivated the investigation in the first place.

Oddly, I've learned that it is subjectivity that can save the researcher, allowing him or her to pursue the original vision and research objectives to their conclusion, and trust that the aims of the research have authentic value, not only for the researcher, but for the group. That said, it has never been easy for the intellectual to question colonial authorities and their heirs – leaders well-versed in sophisticated techniques of psychological control. But again the history of the intellectual's travails provides key data.

Only the passing of time has brought me insight into what I have experienced in the field of investigation. Even if the equation at stake is real and rooted in an enigmatic and shared phenomenon, the research will at some point be limited by my self-ignorance, prejudice, suffering and relationship with the group and its regime of power; relations being indeed impacted upon and transformed by the fact of looking for truth, thus producing uncertainty.

If the research pertains to elements of the group experience that tend to fall into oblivion, the researcher will naturally face the forces determining and producing the forgetting. In such cases, the researcher may be trapped in a posture of criticising those who exercise power, while in some cases remaining dependent upon them. This is far from easy. It leads to intense pressure, especially if the researcher lives in the community in question. The stakes become very high. If the experience of the researcher becomes richer, the psychological pressure also rises. This is perhaps when one's ability to interpret other people's testimonies reaches its peak; one's own unfolding life-experience can easily thereafter, especially if forms of suffering are being experienced, overshadow other people's stories.

At what moment should a researcher investigating his or her own community withdraw in order to make sense of his or her life and feelings, which form part of the results of the investigation? Shedding light on one's own experience will provide the key to what couldn't be perceived because of a lack of first-hand experience, particularly in regards to power and the leaders. It can also provide insights that will bring deeper understanding of peoples' stories and more accurate interpretations of their testimonies. Altogether, this new source of knowledge lays renewed epistemological foundations, including the cultural empowerment inherent in digging into one's own group and listening to Elders. Silences and abstentions are particularly difficult to decipher, and experience of living in the community itself and taking the time to listen carefully is the key to doing so.

A researcher who identifies as indigenous can be unpleasantly surprised by the reactions of the people in power, especially if the prior expectation had been that reclaiming ancestral culture would bring the group and its leaders closer together. Finding oneself confronted by internal racism and being branded the 'bad Indian' can cause a brutal awakening. This is again when one's own experience becomes central to an understanding of one's own group. It allows one to realise, among other things, how much the need to belong to one's group of origin, despite its cultural 'disconnects', can make one easy to indoctrinate and vulnerable to manipulation. Understanding our own process of and reasons for psychological indoctrination, as heirs of oblivion, is immensely important. Is it not the storm that shapes the captain?

Group internal tyrannies, as a deep legacy of colonialism, have their foundations in a web of omissions, silences, absences and complex emotions, such as suffering, shame and fear, that are not easily readable at first. An autocrat is generally a dissembler. By a progressive process of substitution the relationship a tyrant entertains with his own past, once projected on the group, becomes, as time goes by, the relationship the group entertains with itself. Through a complex chain of muteness and deafness, intergenerational ruptures and discontinuities – not foreign to deep traumas and rewriting – the leader's desire to forget his own past mutates into a desire to make everyone forget everything about the group memory; a command to forget, this time destined for the whole group, is then put into operation. It can lead to complete control of the parameters of a group's collective identity, and shape and normalise a shared desire to forget. Such a situation generates, among other things, the ongoing legitimation of power, the collective absorption of a new mythology articulated around the leader's role and chronologies in generating the group itself, and, more importantly, the strong belief in the absence of history and of a collective self before the domination of the group by the one in charge. His actions and realisations are represented as generating the very being of the group; any opposition to his authority is countered with the threat that the people will fall back into the nothingness of what they were before he 'gave birth' to them. History has unfortunately, and often tragically, produced a panoply of these 'fathers of the people'.

Whether it be on the scale of a small minority group or of an empire, the relationship practitioners of monocracy entertain towards their past and childhood should be at the heart of the public gaze. Their obsession with controlling their image, often hiding past humiliation and deep shame, and with acquiring the power to erase, in order to fulfil their desire to forget, may soon cast a heavy shadow on the public realm. Such a will to make people forget everything in order to ease the production of new myths to feed their glory, buries even further their deepest memories of their most secret vulnerability. Through an incessant quest for truth, the researcher runs the risk of subjecting the tyrant to an intolerable torment, the threat of showing his weaknesses, and how his thirst for power may in fact be based on a terrible affective deficit.

These are some of the reasons why investigating forgetfulness can be dangerous, in particular where colonialism has left open wounds. Once he has seen or heard the secrets concealed in the corpses, it is the researcher as truth holder that the leader may want to bury, in order to ensure that these burning truths are carried as far away as possible. It is crucial for the leader that the foundational silences on which his empire is erected remain strong.

The researcher, for his part, may learn from tyrants how power is intimately intertwined with the production of ignorance and oblivion, and how reflectiveness, honesty and care remain the last borders preventing the projection of their own interiority. The integrity of a researcher (especially when that person is operating under the shadows of colonialism) demands that he never lets his desire to be loved outweigh his desire for truth, regardless of the personal cost.

Bibliography

Acquelin, J. and J. Bacon (2011) *Nous Sommes Tous des Sauvages* (Montréal).

Agamben, G. (2008) *Qu'est Ce Que Le Contemporain?* (Paris).

Alfred, T. (1999) *Peace, Power, Righteousness: An Indigenous Manifesto* (Toronto).

— (2004) 'From sovereignty to freedom', in S. Greymorning (ed.), *A Will to Survive: Indigenous Essays on the Politics of Culture, Language, and Identity* (New York), pp. 111–25.

— (2005) *Wasase: Indigenous Pathways of Action and Freedom* (Toronto).

Amherst, J. (1763), 'Letter to Bouquet', http://www.nativeweb.org/pages/legal/amherst/34_41_114_fn.jpeg (accessed 10 May 2016).

Anderson, R. B. (1999) *Economic Development among the Indigenous People of Canada: A Hope for the Future* (Toronto).

Âpihtawikosisân (15 Feb. 2016) 'The myth of the corrupt chief and band council – part I', https://apihtawikosisan.com/2016/02/the-myth-of-the-corrupt-chief-and-band-council-part-i/ (accessed 5 Jan. 2019).

Assmann, J. (1995) 'Collective memory and cultural identity', *New German Critique, Cultural History/Cultural Studies* 65 (Spring–Summer), pp. 125–33.

— (1997) *Moses the Egyptian: The Memory of Egypt in Western Monotheism* (Cambridge, MA. and London).

— (2006) *Religion and Cultural Memory: Ten Studies*, trans. R. Livingstone (Stanford, CA).

Assmann, J. and T. Hölscher (1988) *Kultur und Gedächtnis* (Frankfurt am Main).

Assoun, P. (1997) *Psychanalyse* (Paris).

Audet, V. (2012) *Innu Nikamu – L'Innu chante: pouvoir des chants, guérison et identité chez les Innus* (Laval, Québec).

Bacon, J. (2009) Bâton à message – Tshissinuatshitakana, Montréal.

Bacon-Hervieux, K. (2017) *Innu Nikamu – Chanter la résistance* (APTN/Canal D).

Bandura, A. (1999) 'Human agency in social cognitive theory', *American Psychologist*, 44 (9): 1175–84.

— (2001) 'Social cognitive theory: an agentic perspective', *Annual Review of Psychology*, 52: 1–26.

Bartlett, C., M. Marshall and A. Marshall (2012) 'Two-eyed seeing and other lessons learned within a colearning journey of bringing together Indigenous and mainstream knowledges and ways of knowing', *Journal of Environmental Studies and Sciences*, 2 (4): 331–40.

Bartlett, C., M. Marshall, A. Marshall and M. Iwama (2015) 'Integrative science and two-eyed seeing: enriching the discussion framework for healthy communities', in L. K. Hallstrom, N. Guehlstorf and M. Parkes (eds.) *Ecosystems, Society and Health: Pathways through Diversity, Convergence and Integration* (Montréal), pp. 280–326.

Barthes, R. (1957) *Mythologies* (Paris).

Baudrillard, J. (1968) *Le Système des Objets* (Paris).

Baumeister, R. F. and S. Hastings (1997) 'Distortions of collective memory: how groups flatter and deceive themselves', in J. W. Pennebaker, D. Paez and B. Rimé (eds.), *Collective Memory of Political Events: Social Psychological Perspective* (Mahwah, NJ), pp. 277–93.

Beaudoin, J., G. St-Georges and S. Wyatt (2012) 'Valeurs autochtones et modèles forestiers: le cas de la Première Nations des Innus d'Essipit', *Recherches Amérindiennes au Québec* 42 (2–3): 97–109.

Bélanger, R. (1946) *Les Escoumins* (Chicoutimi).

Bellefleur, C. A. (n.d.) 'Tales of Tshakapesh', in *Nametau Innu – Memory and Knowledge of Nitassinan*, Virtual Museum of Canada, http://www.nametauinnu.ca/en/culture/spirituality/tshakapesh (accessed 12 Sep. 2017).

Bernier, M.-C. (2003) 'Les autochtones d'Essipit: sans plume ni tipi', Panorama Québec.

Bertho, A. (2009) *Le Temps Des Émeutes* (Paris).

Bertman, S. (2001) 'America is suffering from cultural amnesia: American thought', *USA Today (Society for the Advancement of Education)*, November.

Bhatt, C. (1999) 'Ethnic absolutism and the authoritarian spirit', *Theory, Culture & Society* 16 (2): 65–85.

Black, M. (2007) 'Fanon and DuBoisian double consciousness', *Human Architecture: journal of the sociology of self-knowledge*, summer: 393–404.

Bleiker, R. (2009) *Aesthetics and World Politics* (London).

Blühdorn, I. (2006) 'Self-experience in the theme park of radical action? Social movements and political articulation in the late-modern condition', *European Journal of Social Theory*, 9 (1).

Borrows, J. (2016) *Freedom and Indigenous Constitutionalism* (Toronto).

— (2019) *Law's Indigenous Ethics* (Toronto)

Bosi, E. (1987) *Memória e sociedade. Lembranças de velhos* (São Paulo).

Bouchard, S. (1982) *Pour parler des Amérindiens et des Inuit: guide à l'usage des professeurs du secondaire, histoire et géographie* (Québec).

— (2004) *Récits de Mathieu Mestokosho, Chasseur Innu* (Montréal).

— (2015) 'The exchange between native and non-native cultures in time of crisis', Radio-Canada, 25 November, http://ici.radio-canada.ca/premiere/premiereplus/histoire/80534/serge-bouchard-la-necessaire-amitie-avec-les-autochtones (accessed 2 May 2018).

Bouchard, S. and M.-C. Lévesque (2017) *Le peuple rieur. Hommage à mes amis innus* (Montréal).

Boudreault, R. (1994) *Les Escoumins* (Wendake).

Boydston, J. A. (ed.) *The Collective Works of John Dewey, 1882–1953* (Carbondale, IL).

Brewer, M. B. and W. Gardner (1996) 'Who is this we? Levels of collective identity and self-representations', *Journal of Personality and Social Psychology*, 71 (1): 83–93.

Brownlie, I. (1998) *Principles of Public International Law* (5th edn, Oxford).

Burawoy, M. (2005) '2004 American Sociological Association presidential address: for public sociology', *American Sociological Review*, 70 (1): 4–28.

Burelle, J. (2014) 'Encounters on contested lands: First Nations performances of sovereignty and nationhood in Québec' (PhD thesis, University of California, San Diego).

— (2018) *Encounters on Contested Lands: Indigenous Performances of Sovereignty and Nationhood in Québec* (Chicago).

Canada (1857) *Gradual Civilization Act* (*Act to Encourage the Gradual Civilization of Indian Tribes in this Province, and to Amend the Laws Relating to Indians*, 20 Victoria, c. 26, sanctioned 10 June 1857.

Canada – Department of Indian Affairs and Northern Development (1985), 'First Nations, Bill C-31, Indian Act', Communications Branch.

Cancian, F. M. (1975) *What are Norms? A Study of Beliefs and Action in a Maya Community* (Cambridge).

Candida Smith, R. (1999) *Mallarmé's Children: Symbolism and the Renewal of Experience* (Berkeley, CA).

Cargo, M. G. (1998) 'Partnering with adults as a process of empowering youth in the community: a grounded theory study' (PhD thesis, University of British Columbia).

Carnagey, N. L., C. A. Anderson and B. J. Bushman (2007) 'The effect of video game violence on physiological desensitization to real-life violence', *Journal of Experimental Social Psychology*, 43 (3): 489–96.

Cassivi, M. (2016), 'Natasha Kanapé Fontaine: se tenir debout', *La Presse*, 4 May.

Castoriadis, C. (2007), *Figures of the Thinkable* (Stanford, CA).

Césaire, A. (1972) *Discourse on Colonialism*, trans. Joan Pinkham (New York and London).

Champlain, S. (1993 [1615]) *Des Sauvages* (Montréal).

Charest, P. (1973) 'Écologie culturelle de la Côte-Nord du golfe Saint-Laurent', in M.-A. Tremblay and G.L. Gold (eds.), *Communautés et culture. Éléments pour une ethnologie du Canada français* (Montréal), pp. 33–82.

— (1992) 'La prise en charge donne-t-elle du pouvoir? L'exemple des Atikamek^{w} et des Montagnais', *Anthropologie et Sociétés*, 16 (3): 55–76.

— (2003) 'Qui a peur des Innus? Réflexions sur les débats au sujet du projet d'entente de principe entre les Innus de Mashteuiastsh, Essipit, Betsiamites et Nutashkuan et les gouvernements du Québec et du Canada', *Anthropologie et Sociétés*, 27 (2): 185–206.

— (2005) 'Les assistants de recherche amérindiens en tant que médiateurs culturels: expériences en milieux innu et atikamekw du Québec', *Études Inuit/Studies*, 29: 1–2, pp. 115–29.

— (2009) *Le rôle des Innus dans l'exploitation et la gestion du saumon des rivières des Escoumins/Essipit et Natashquan* (Québec).

— (2012) 'La participation des Innus d'Essipit à l'exploitation et à la gestion du saumon de la rivière des Escoumins/ Essipit', in P. Charest, C. Girard and T. Rodon (eds.), *Les pêcheries des Premières nations dans l'est du Québec. Innu, Malécites et Micmacs* (Québec), pp. 81–107.

Chatterji, R. (1986) 'The voyage of the hero: the self and the other in one narrative tradition of Purulia', *Contributions to Indian Sociology*, 19: 95–114.

Chevrier, D. (1996) 'Les premières populations humaines: 8500 à 2000 ans AA', in P. Frenette (ed.) *Histoire de la Côte-Nord* (Québec), pp. 73–104.

Chew, M. (2007) 'Contemporary re-emergence of the qipao: political nationalism, cultural production and popular consumption of a traditional Chinese dress', *The China Quarterly*, 189 (March): 144–61.

Chrétien, Y., D. Delâge and S. Vincent (2009) *Au Croissement de nos Destins: Quand Eupishtikueiau Devint Québec* (Montréal).

Christopher, F. (2009) *Dead Reckoning: Champlain in America* (PBS).

Chu, J. A., L. M. Frey, B. L. Ganzel and J. A. Matthews (1999) 'Memories of childhood abuse: dissociation, amnesia, and corroboration', *American Journal of Psychiatry* 156 (May): 749–55.

Clément, D. (1995) *La Zoologie des Montagnais* (Paris).

Cobley, P. and L. Jansz (1997) *Introducing Semiotics* (London).

Coburn, V. (2019), 'A genealogy of contemporary Indianness: a Foucauldian analysis of identity and society in anti-colonization politics' (PhD thesis, Queen's University).

Cohen, Stanley (2001) *States of Denial: Knowing about Atrocities and Suffering* (Cambridge).

Connerton, Paul (2008) 'Seven types of forgetting', *Memory Studies*, 1(1): 59–71.

Conseil des Attikamekw et des Montagnais (1980) *Rapport de la prise en charge*, September.

Conseil des Attikamekw et des Montagnais (1993), *La négociation des revendications des Atikamekw et des Montagnais: un processus frustrant qu'il faut modifier*, Report for the Canadian Royal Commission on Aboriginal Peoples (Québec), September.

Conseil de la Première Nation des Innus Essipit (2007) 'Paroles de femmes: regret, fierté et espoir', *Tipatshimun* 4 (5): 4–6.

— (2009) 'Pour nos pères et nos enfants: occuper le territoire de la mémoire et du rêve', report for the directory of culture, May.

— (2010) *Rapport sur l'histoire d'Essipit,* unpublished document (prepared by Pierre Frenette).

Conseil des Innus Essipit (2016) *Rapport Annuel.*

Conseil des Montagnais des Escoumins (1994) *Essipit et son choix de société* (unpublished document).

Conway, M. (2000) 'Memory and identity', in C. Emdem and D. Midgley (eds.), *Cultural History and Literary Imagination* (Oxford).

Conway, M. and G. Cohen (2008) *Memory in the Real World* (London).

Corbiere, A. (2000) 'Reconciling epistemological orientations: toward a wholistic Nishhabe (Ojibwe/Odawa/Potowatomi) education', *Canadian Journal of Native Education*, 24 (2): 113–20.

Cornellier, B. (2013) 'The "Indian thing": on representation and reality in the liberal settler colony', *Settler Colonial Studies*, 3 (1): 49–64.

— (2015) *La chose indienne: cinéma et politiques de la représentation autochtone au Québec et au Canada* (Québec).

— (2016a) 'The struggle of others: Pierre Vallières, Québécois settler nationalism, and the N-word today', *Discourse: Journal for Theoretical Studies in Media and Culture*, 39 (1).

— (2016b) 'Extracting Inuit: the "of the North" controversy and the white possessive', *American Indian Culture and Research Journal*, 40 (4).

Costas, J. and P. Fleming (2009) 'Beyond dis-identification: a discursive approach to self-alienation in contemporary organizations', *Human Relations*, 62 (3): 353–78.

Cowan, J., M. Dembour and R. Wilson (eds.) (2001), *Culture and Rights: Anthropological Perspectives* (Cambridge).

Craft, A. (2013) *Breathing Life into the Stone Fort Treaty: An Anishinabe Understanding of Treaty One* (Saskatoon).

Cross, S. E. and H.R. Markus (1994) 'Self-schemas, possible selves, and competent performance', *Journal of Educational Psychology*, 86 (3): 423–38.

Cyr, M. 'Une nation Indienne en Amérique du Nord?', *Le Couac*, http://www.lecouac.org/spip.php?article204 (accessed 23 Oct. 2010).

D'Argembeau, A. and M. Vanderlinden (2008) 'Remembering pride and shame: self-enhancement and the phenomenology of autobiographical memory', *Memory*, 16 (5): 538–47.

Davis, F. (1977) 'Nostalgia, identity and the current nostalgia wave,' *Journal of Popular Culture*, 2: 414–24.

— (1979) *Yearning for Yesterday: A Sociology of Nostalgia* (New York).

Deleuze, G. and F. Guattari (1980) *Mille Plateaux* (Paris).

Della Porta, D. and M. Diani (2006) *Social Movements: An Introduction* (London).

Deloria, V. (1992) *God is Red: A Native View of Religion* (Golden, CO).

D'Errico, P. (n.d.) 'Jeffrey Amherst and smallpox blankets: Lord Jeffrey Amherst's letters discussing germ warfare against American Indians', http://people.umass.edu/derrico/amherst/lord_jeff.html (accessed 10 May 2016).

Dessi, R. (2008) 'Collective memory, cultural transmission and investments', *American Economic Review*, 98 (1): 534–60.

Diabo, R. (2012) 'Harper launches major First Nations termination plan: as negotiating tables legitimise Canada's colonialism', *First Nations Strategic Bulletin*, 10 (7–10).

— (2017) 'Trudeau cloaks continued attack on First Nations sovereignty with charm', https://ricochet.media/en/1154/trudeau-cloaks-continued-attack-on-first-nations-sovereignty-with-charm (accessed 28 February 2017).

Dickason, O.P. (1993) *Le Mythe du Sauvage* (Sillery).

DOD Dictionary of Military and Associated Terms (JP 1-02), http://www.dtic.mil/doctrine/dod_dictionary/ (accessed Oct. 2010).

Drury, J., C. Cocking, J. Beale, C. Hanson and F. Rapley (2005) 'The phenomenology of empowerment in collective action', *British Journal of Social Psychology* 44: 309–28.

Drury, J. and S. Reicher (1999) 'The intergroup dynamic of collective empowerment: substantiating the social identity model', *Group Processes and Intergroup Relations*, 2 (4): 381–402.

— (2000) 'Collective action and psychological change: the emergence of new social identities', *British Journal of Social Psychology*, 39 (4): 579–604.

Drury, J., S. Reicher and C. Stott (2003) 'Transforming the boundaries of collective identity: from the "local" anti-road campaign to "global" resistance?', *Social Movement Studies: Journal of Social, Cultural and Political Protest*, 2: 192–212.

Drury, J. and G. Winter (2003) 'Social identity as a source of strength in mass emergencies and other crowd events', *International Journal of Mental Health*, 32 (4): 77–93.

Duchesne, É. (2016) 'Compte-rendu: Nitassinan – Notre terre. Alliance et souveraineté partagée du peuple innu au Québec. Des premiers contacts à nos jours', *Recherche amérindiennes au Québec*, 46 (1): 126–7.

Dufour, P. (1996) 'De la Traite de Tadoussac aux King's Posts: 1650–1830', in P. Frenette (ed.) *Histoire de la Côte-Nord* (Québec).

Duperré, M. (2008) 'La rationalité des émotions dans les processus de mobilisation collective', *Service social*, 54 (1): 67–81.

Dupuis-Déri, F. (2016) *Les black blocs. La liberté et l'égalité se manifeste* (Montréal).

Episkenew, J.-A (2009) *Taking Back our Spirits: Myth, Policy and Healing* (Manitoba).

Erasmus, G. and R. Dussault (1996) *Report of the Royal Commission on Aboriginal Peoples* (Ottawa).

Essipit (2007) 'Paroles de femmes: regret, fierté et espoir', *Tipatshimun*, 6: 5–6.

Fanon, F. (1963 [1961]) *The Wretched of the Earth* (New York).

— (1965) *A Dying Colonialism* (New York).

— (1967) *Black Skin, White Mask* (New York).

— (1969 [1964]) *Toward the African Revolution* (New York).

Fein, S. and S. J. Spencer (1997) 'Prejudice as self-image maintenance: affirming the self through derogating others', *Journal of Personality and Social Psychology*, 73 (1): 31–44.

Fivush, R. (1994) 'Constructing narrative, emotion, and self in parent-child conversations about the past', in U. Neisser and R. Fivush (eds.), *The Remembering Self: Construction and Accuracy in the Self-Narrative* (Cambridge).

Foley, D. (2006), 'Indigenous standpoint theory', *International Journal of the Humanities*, 3 (8): 25–36.

Folman, A. (2008) *Waltz with Bashir* (film).

Fontaine, J.-L. (2006) *Croyances et Rituels Chez Les Innus, 1603–1650* (Québec).

Forsyth, D. R. (2010) *Group Dynamics* (5th edn, Belmont, CA).

Foucault, M. (1972) *The Archaeology of Knowledge and the Discourse on Language* (New York).

— (1973) 'La vérité et les formes juridiques', conference paper presented at the University of Rio de Janeiro, May 1973, reproduced in *DE*, 2, text no. 139.

— (1980) 'Entretien avec Michel Foucault' (with Duccio Trombadori, Paris, end of 1978), *Il Contributo*, 4 (1).

— (Oct–Nov 1983), 'Discourse and truth: the problematization of parrhesia' (six lectures), The University of California at Berkeley, http://www.lib.berkeley.edu/MRC/foucault/parrhesia.html (accessed 20 Jun. 2017).

— (1984) 'Le courage de la vérité. Le gouvernement de soi et des autres II'. Course at Collège de France (Paris).

— (1985) 'Entretien avec Michel Foucault', reproduced in *DE*, 3, text no. 192.

Francis, D. (1992) *The Imaginary Indian – the Image of the Indian in Canadian Culture* (Vancouver).

Frenette, P. (ed.) (1996) *Histoire de la Côte-Nord* (Québec).

— (1997) *La réserve d'Essipit: Revendication particulière de la bande des Montagnais d'Essipit contre la Couronne en Chef du Canada,* preliminary version.

— (2010) 'L'histoire d'Essipit', unpublished report.

Friedland, H. and V. Napoleon (2016a) 'Gathering the threads: developing a methodology for researching and rebuilding indigenous legal traditions', *Lakehead Law Journal* 1 (1).

— (2016b) 'Engaging with indigenous legal traditions through stories', *McGill Law Journal*, 61 (725): 4.

Friedland, H. (2018) *The Wetiko Legal Principles: Cree and Anishinabek Responses to Violence and Victimization* (Toronto).

Friedman, J. (1992) 'The past in the future: history and the politics of identity', *American Anthropologist*, 94 (4): 837–59.

— (2004) 'Culture et politique de la culture: une dynamique durkheimienne', *Anthropologie et Sociétés*, 28 (1): 28–9.

Gadamer, H. (1989) *Truth and Method* (2nd edn, London).

— (1999) *Truth and Method* (New York).

Garde-Hansen, J. and K. Worcman (2016) *Social Memory Technology: Theory, Practice, Action* (New York).

Garneau, J.-P. (2015) 'Contre-expertise du rapport de M. Paul Charest' (file SCT-2001-13).

Gaudreau, H. (2006) 'Un important employeur autochtone', Radio-Canada, 26 October.

Gaudry, A. and D. Leroux (2017) 'White settler revisionism and making metis everywhere: the contemporary evocation of metissage in Québec and Nova Scotia', *Jourrnal of Critical Ethnic Studies*, 3 (1).

Gendreau, P. and A. Lefèvre (2016) 'La souveraineté comme responsabilité: entretien avec Pierrot Ross-Tremblay', *Revue Liberté*, 310: 8–13.

Girard, N. (1981) 'La souveraineté des Amérindiens', *Journal de Québec*, 29 June 1981.

Goodwin, J., J.M. Jasper and F. Polletta (2008), 'Emotional dimensions of social movements', in D.S. Snow, S.A. Soule and H. Kriesi (eds.), *The Blackwell Companion to Social Movements* (London)

Greer, S. (1999) 'Making sense out of the self: a social constructionist perspective on the history and measurement of the self' (PhD thesis, York University).

Gross, M. and L. McGoey (2015), *Routledge International Handbook of Ignorance Studies* (London).

Hakemulder, J. (2000) *The Moral Laboratory: Experiments Examining the Effects of Reading Literature on Social Perception and Moral Self-Concept* (Amsterdam).

Halbwachs, M. (1997) *La Mémoire Collective* (Paris).

Hamidi, N. and N. Kanapé-Fontaine (2018) 'L'inexorable insurrection', *Liberté*, 321.

Hamidi, N. (forthcoming) 'Portraying Hogra: a multidimentional phenomenology of humiliation in Algeria' (PhD thesis, University of Essex).

Hamilton, P. (1991) *Max Weber: Critical Assessments I* (London).

Harper, D. (n.d.) 'Hypokrisis', in *Online Etymology Dictionary*, http://www.etymonline.com/index.php?term=hypocrisy (accessed Jun. 2011).

Harper, S. (2012) 'Statement by the prime minister at the Crown-First Nations Gathering', 24 Jan., http://news.gc.ca/web/article-en.do?nid=652889 (accessed 4 May 2016).

Hedges, C. (2015) *Wages of Rebellion: The Moral Imperative of Revolt* (New York).

Herzog, B. (2009) 'Collective forgetting – a reflection on a residual expression', in N. Packard (ed.), *Sociology of Memory: Papers from the Spectrum* (Cambridge), pp. 112–34.

Heuser, B. (2010) *The Evolution of Strategy: Thinking War from Antiquity to the Present* (Cambridge).

Higgleton, E. and A. Seaton (1995) *Harrap's Essential English Dictionary* (New York).

Hind, H. Y. (1863) *The Labrador Peninsula* (London).

Howard, R. E. (1995) *Human Rights and the Search for Community* (Boulder, CO).

Hunt, S. A. and R. D. Benford (2008) 'Collective identity, solidarity and commitment' in D. A. Snow, S. A. Soule and H. Kriesi (eds.), *The Blackwell Companion to Social Movements* (London).

Imai, S. (2007) 'The structure of the Indian Act: accountability in governance', research paper, National Centre for First Nations Governance, http://fngovernance.org/ncfng_research/shin_imai.pdf (accessed Apr. 2016).

Indigenous and Northern Affairs Canada (n.d.) https://www.aadnc-aandc.gc.ca/Mobile/Nations/profile_essipit-eng (accessed 28 Feb. 2017).

Iniguez, L., J. Valencia and F. Vazquez (1997) 'The construction of remembering and forgetfulness: memories and histories of the Spanish Civil War' in J. W. Pennebaker, N. Paez and B. Rimé (eds.), *Collective Memory of Political Events. Social Psychological Perspective* (Mahwah, NJ), pp. 237–52.

Jackson, M. (2004) 'Colonization as myth-making: a case study in Aotearoa', in S. Greymorning (ed.), *A Will to Survive: Indigenous Essays on the Politics of Culture, Language, and Identity* (New York).

Kanapé-Fontaine, N. (2017) *Tetepiska*, one of 13 productions in the project 'Legacies 150 stories', Canada's National Film Board.

Kanter, R. M. (1968) 'Commitment and Social Organisation: a Study of Commitment Mechanisms in Utopian Communities', *American Sociological Review*, 33 (4): 499–517.

— (1972) *Commitment and Community. Communes and Utopias in Sociological Perspective* (Boston, MA).

Kapesh, A. (1979) *Qu'as-Tu Fait de Mon Pays?* (Montréal).

Kappeler, S. (1986) *The Pornography of Representations* (London).

King, T. (2015) *Histoire(s) et vérité(s). Récits autochtones* (Montréal).

Klapp, O. E. (1969) *The Collective Search for Identity* (New York).

Klein, S. (2001) 'A self to remember: a cognitive neuropsychological perspective on how self creates memory and memory creates self', in C. Sedikides and M. Brewer (eds.), *Individual Self, Relational Self, Collective Self* (New York), pp. 25–46.

Kohn, M. (2006) 'Colonialism', *Stanford Encyclopaedia of Philosophy*, http://plato.stanford.edu/entries/colonialism/ (accessed May 2006).

Lacasse, J. (1996) *Les Innus et le territoire* (Sillery).

Laforest, R. (1983) *Occupation et utilisation du territoire par les Montagnais des Escoumins*, Report for the Conseil Attikamekw-Montagnais, Village-des-Hurons.

Langenberg, T. (2005) *Standardization and Expectations* (Berlin).

Leacock, E. (1997) 'The Montagnais-Naskapi of the Labrador Peninsula', in B. Morrison and R. Wilson (eds.), *Native Peoples: The Canadian Experience* (Toronto).

Legoff, J. (1986) *History and Memory* (New York).

Leroux, D. (2010) 'The spectacle of Champlain: commemorating Québec', *Borderlands*, 9 (1): 1–27.

Leroux, D. (2015a) 'Rejoinder', *Ethnic and Racial Studies*, 38 (9): 1665–6.

— (2015b) 'A genealogist's paradise: France, Québec, and the genealogics of race', *Ethnic and Racial Studies*, 38 (5): 718–33.

— (2016) 'Le grand livre de Champlain: cartography, colonialism, and commemoration in the French Atlantic', *Interventions: International Journal of Postcolonial Studies*, 18 (3): 404–21.

— (2017) Book review of *A Place in the Sun: Haiti, Haitians, and the Remaking of Québec*, *French Studies*, 71 (2).

— (2019) *Distorted Descent: White Claims to Indigenous Identity* (Manitoba).

Leroux, D. and L. Caldwell (2017) 'The settler-colonial imagination: comparing commemoration in Saskatchewan and Québec', *Memory Studies* 12 (4).

Leroux, D. and C. Vowel (2016) 'White settler antipathy and the Daniels decision', *TOPIA: Canadian Journal of Cultural Studies*, (36): 30–42.

Leslie, J. F. (1985) *Commissions of Inquiry into Indian Affairs in the Canadas, 1828–1858: Evolving a Corporate Memory for the Indian Department* (Ottawa).

Létourneau, J. (2011) 'Histoire – la relation complexe des Québécois avec leur histoire,' *Le Devoir*, 29 September.

Létourneau, R. and M. Létourneau (1985) *Les trente premières années de Les Escoumins 1845–1875* (Tadoussac).

Lévesque, F. (2015) 'Pensionnats indiens: il fallait qu'on oublie qui on était', *Le Nord-Côtier*, 3 June 2015.

Lippard, L. (1993) 'Jimmie Durham: Postmodernist Savage', *Art In America* 81 (2): 62–9.

Loranger-Saindon, A. (2008) 'Médias, Innus et Allochtones. L'image des Premières Nations dans les journaux de la Côte-Nord et ses effets sur les rapports interethniques' (MA thesis, Université Laval).

Lowenthal, D. (1985) *The Past is a Foreign Country* (Cambridge).

Luc, E. (2009) *Unleashing Your Leadership Potential: Seven Strategies for Success*, (Lanham, MD).

Mackenzie, A. (1993) 'The unilateral extinguishment of Innu people's rights by Canadian law: a case of violation of international standards for the protection of human rights', unpublished report submitted to the Royal Commission on Aboriginal Peoples.

Mailhot, J. (1996) 'La marginalisation des Montagnais', in P. Frenette (ed.), *Histoire de la Côte-Nord* (Québec).

Mailhot, J. and S. Vincent (1979) *La situation des Montagnais du Saguenay-Lac-St- Jean et de la Haute Côte-Nord au milieu du XIXe siècle*, report submitted to the Attikamekw-Montagnais Council.

— (1980) *Le discours montagnais sur le territoire*, Québec, report submitted to the Attikamekw-Montagnais Council, p. 213.

— (1982) 'Le droit foncier montagnais', *Interculture*, 15 (2–3): 280.

Manitowabi, D. (2017) 'Masking Anishinaabe Bimaadiziwin: uncovering cultural representations at Casino Rama', in B. Gercken and J. Pelletier (eds.), *Gambling on Authenticity: Gaming, the Noble Savage, and the Not-So-New Indian* (East Lansing, MI), pp. 135–58.

Mannheim, K. (1952) 'On the problem of generations', in *Collected Works of Karl Mannheim* (London).

Marger, M. N. (2009) *Race and Ethnic Relations: American and Global Perspectives* (Ware).

Markus, H. and Z. Kunda (1986) 'Stability and malleability of the self-concept', *Journal of Personality and Social Psychology*, 51 (4): 858–66.

Markus, H. and P. Nurius (1986) 'Possible selves', *American Psychologist*, 41 (9): 954–69.

Markus, H., J. Smith and L. R. Moreland (1985) 'Role of the self-concept in the perception of others', *Journal of Personality and Social Psychology*, 49 (6): 1494–512.

Marques, J., D. Páez and A. Serra (1997) 'Collective memory processes associated with traumatic war experiences: social sharing, emotional climate and the trangenerational transmission of information in the case of the Portuguese colonial war', in J. W. Pennebaker, D. Paez and B. Rimé (eds.), *Collective Memory of Political Events: Social Psychological Perspective* (Mahwah, NJ), pp. 253–76.

Marshall M., A. Marshall and C. Bartlett (2015), 'Two-eyed seeing in medicine', in M. Greenwood, S. de Leeuw, N. M. Lindsay and C. Reading (eds.), *Determinants of Indigenous Peoples' Health in Canada: Beyond the Social* (Toronto).

McAdam, S. (2015) *Nationhood Interrupted: Revitalizing nêhiyaw Legal Systems* (Vancouver).

McGoey, L. (2007) 'On the will to ignorance in bureaucracy', *Economy and Society*, 36 (2): 212–35.

— (2012a) 'The logic of strategic ignorance', *British Journal of Sociology*, 63 (3): 553–76.

— (2012b) 'Strategic unknowns: towards a sociology of ignorance', in L. McGoey (ed.), *An Introduction to the Sociology of Ignorance: Essays on the Limits of Knowing* (Abingdon).

McKenzie, G. and T. Vincent (2010) 'La "guerre du saumon" des années 1970–1980 entrevue avec Pierre Lepage', *Recherches Amérindiennes au Québec*, 40 (1–2): 103–11.

Memmi, A. (1957) *Portrait du Colonisé* (Paris).

Mestokosho, Rita (2010) *Comment je perçois la vie, grand-mère – Eshi Uapataman Nukum*, foreword by J. M. G. Le Clézio (Sweden).

Mol, H. (1977) *Identity and the Sacred* (Oxford).

— (1979) 'The identity model of religion: how it compares with nine other theories of religion and how it might apply to Japan', *Japanese Journal of Religious Studies*, Mar.–Jun.: 611–2.

Morin, M. (1997) *L'usurpation de la souveraineté autochtone. Le cas de la Nouvelle- France et des colonies Anglaises de l'Amérique du Nord* (Québec).

Morwood, J. and J. Taylor (2002) *Pocket Oxford Classical Greek Dictionary* (Oxford).

Munoz, J. E. (1999) *Disidentifications: Queers of Color and the Performance of Politics* (Minneapolis, MN).

Ministère des Affaires Autochtones et du Nord Canada (2016) 'Lettre aux Regroupement des familles traditionnelles chasseurs cueilleurs innuasht', 25 May.

Nabigon, H. (2006), *The Hollow Tree. Fighting Addiction with Traditional Native Healing* (Kingston, On).

Nakata, M. (2007) *Disciplining the Savages: Savaging the Disciplines* (Canberra, A.C.T.).

Nametau Innu: Memory and Knowledge of Nitassinan, 'Essipit – Community', http://www.nametauinnu.ca/en/culture/nation/detail/64/60.

— 'Essipit – Introduction', http://www.nametauinnu.ca/en/culture/nation/detail/64/72.

Napoleon, V. and H. Friedland (2016) 'An inside job: engaging with indigenous legal traditions through stories', *McGill Law Journal*, 61 (4): 725.

Neegan, W., C. Kauppi, E. Faries and H. Pallard (2012) *Will to Live: George Stephen On and Off the Street*, documentary video (Poverty, Homelessness and Migration: Centre for Research in Social Justice and Policy, Université Laurentienne).

Nepton-Philippe, K (2016) 'Marc Chalout: le grand manitou des communications', *Journal Haute Cote-Nord*, https://www.journalhcnouest.com/marc-chaloult-le-grand-manitou-des-communications/.

Nietzsche, F (1995) *Thus Spoke Zarathustra: A Book for All and For None*, trans. R. J. Hollingdale (New York).

— (2001) *Vie et vérité* (Paris).

Nora, P. (1989) 'Between memory and history: les lieux de la mémoire', *Representations*, 26 (special issue: Memory and Counter-Memory): 7–20.

Nouvel, H. (1664) 'Letters', in R. G. Thwaites (ed.) (1896–1901), *The Jesuit Relations and Allied Documents: travels and explorations of the Jesuit missionaries in New France, 1610–1791*, 73 vols. (Cleveland, OH).

Nungak, Z. (2017) *Wrestling with Colonialism on Steroids: Quebec Inuit Fight for Their Homeland* (Montréal).

Obomsawin, A. (1984) *Incident at Restigouche* (ONF).

— (1996) *150 Years Of Resistance* (ONF).

Office Québécois de la Langue Française (n.d.) 'Pourvoirie', Fiche Terminologique, http://www.granddictionnaire.com/ficheOqlf.aspx?Id_Fiche=1299222 (accessed 18 Jun. 2017).

Olick, J. K. (2007) 'Collective memory', in *International Encyclopaedia of the Social Sciences* (New York).

Olick, J. K. and J. Robbins (1998) 'Social memory studies: from "collective memory" to the historical sociology of mnemonic practices', *Annual Review of Sociology*, 24: 105–40.

Online Etymology Dictionary, http://www.etymonline.com/index.php (accessed 16 Mar. 2010).

Orwell, G. (1954) *Nineteen-Eighty Four* (Harmondsworth).

Palmater, P. D. (2011) *Beyond Blood: Rethinking Indigenous Identity* (Saskatoon).

— (2019) 'Canada continues to deny sex equality to First Nation woman and children', Rabble.ca (accessed 23 Jan. 2019).

Panasuk, A. (2018) 'Le silence des oblats, Radio-Canada', https://ici.radio-canada.ca/nouvelles/special/2018/10/pretres-pedophiles-oblats-innus-atikamekws/.

Panasuk, A. and J. Proulx (1979) 'Les rivières à saumon de la Côte-Nord ou Défense de pêcher – cette rivière est la propriété de...', *Recherches Amérindiennes au Québec*, 9 (3).

— (1981) 'La résistance des Montagnais à l'usurpation des rivières à saumon par les Euro-canadiens du 17e au 20e siècle' (MA thesis, University of Montréal).

Parent, R. (1985) 'Histoire des Amérindiens du Saint-Maurice jusqu'au Labrador, de la préhistoire à 1760' (MA thesis, Laval University).

Pasternak, S. (2016) 'A tale of two visions for Canada: the Trilateral Agreement versus the Land Claims Policy', in K. Burnett and G. Read (eds.), *Aboriginal History: A Reader* (2nd edn, Oxford).

— (2016) 'A tale of two visions for Canada: the Trilateral Agreement versus the Land Claims Policy', in K. Burnett and G. Read (eds.), *Aboriginal History: A Reader* (2nd edn, Oxford).

— (2017) *Grounded Authority – the Algonquins of Barriere Lake against the State* (Minnesota).

Peltier, C. (2018), 'An application of two-eyed seeing: indigenous research methods with participatory action research', *International Journal of Qualitative Methods*, 17 (1).

Pennebaker, J. W., D. Paez and B. Rimé (eds.) (1997) *Collective Memory of Political Events: Social Psychological Perspective* (Mahwah, NJ).

Petersen, M. (2001) 'Cultivating community: a story of cross-cultural learning and empowerment in the downtown eastside of Vancouver' (MA thesis, University of British Columbia).

Picard-Sioui, L.-K. (2017) *Chroniques de Kitchike. La grand débarque* (Wendake).

Plate, L. (2016) 'Amnesiology: towards the study of cultural oblivion', *Memory Studies*, 9 (2): 143–55.

Plourde, M. (1993) *D'Escanimes à Pletipishtuk, perspectives sur la préhistoire amérindienne de la HauteCôte-Nord du Saint-Laurent* (Québec), collection Patrimoines, Dossiers, pp. 80, 73.

Première Nation des Innus Essipit (2016) *Tipatshimun Essipit*, 13 (2), http://www.innu-essipit.com/fichiers/3457/Montage%20final.pdf (accessed 10 Nov. 2016).

Proctor, R. N. and L. Schiebinder (eds.) (2008) *Agnology. The Making and Unmaking of Ignorance* (Stanford, CA).

Releigh Yow, V. (2005) *Recording Oral History – a guide for the Humanities and Social Sciences* (Walnut Creek, CA).

Radio-Canada/CBC (1981) 'Les Escoumins' archives, 7:20 minutes.

— (2019) 'La légitimité des conseils de bande remise en question', Émission Médium Large (in French), https://ici.radio-canada.ca/premiere/emissions/medium-large/segments/entrevue/101853/conseil-bande-autochtone-premieres-nations-pipeline-gazoduc (accessed 19 Jan. 2019).

Ramos, A. (2010) 'The good memory of this land: reflections on the processes of memory and forgetting', *Memory Studies*, 3 (1): 55–72.

Redekop, V. (2002) *From Violence to Blessing: How an Understanding of a Deep-rooted Conflict Can Open Paths of Reconciliation* (Toronto).

Revel, J. (2009) *Le vocabulaire de Foucault* (Paris).

Richard, J. (2006) 'La gestion de la faune par les autochtones: l'exemple de l'autogestion du saumon atlantique chez les Innus de Ekuanitshit – Mingan', *Collection pêches autochtones no. 2,* Université Laval and CIERA.

Ricoeur, P. (2000) *Memory, History, Forgetting* (Chicago, IL).

Riis, O. (1998) 'Religion re-emerging: the role of religion in legitimating integration and power in modern societies', *International Sociology*, 13 (2): 249–72.

Rimé, B. and V. Christophe (1997) 'How individual emotional episodes feed collective memory', in J. W. Pennebaker, D. Paez and B. Rimé (eds.), *Collective Memory of Political Events: Social Psychological Perspective* (Mahwah, NJ), pp. 131–46.

Ross, S. (2014) 'Préface' in C. Girard and C. Brisson (eds.), *Nitassinan Notre Terre. Alliance et Souveraineté Partagée du Peuple Innu au Québec. Des Premiers Contacts à nos Jours* (Québec).

Ross-Tremblay, P. (2015) 'L'oubli n'est pas absolu: réminescences et prise de parole chez les Premiers Peuples de la francophonie des Amériques', *Linguistic Minorities and Society*, 5: 214–31.

Ross-Tremblay, P. and N. Hamidi (2019) "Pluralisme réel ou simulé? Perspectives critiques sur les interactions entre l'ordre juridique innu et celui de l'État au Canada", in G. Otis (ed.), *An Intersection of Indigenous Laws and and State Law. Confrontation or Cooperation?* (Laval), pp. 217 302.

Ross-Tremblay, P., G. Motard and S. Vincent (2015) 'Access to Land and Resource Management: Perspectives of Innu Law and Québec State Law, Integration Report I: How Legal Pluralism manifests, Partnership SSHRC-AUF 2012–2018 State and Indigenous Legal Cultures: A Right in Search of Legitimacy'.

Royal Commission of Aboriginal Peoples (n.d. a), 'Indian Act: Indian Women', *Report of the Royal Commission on Aboriginal Peoples* 1.

— (n.d. b) 'Women's Perspectives', in *Report of the Royal Commission on Aboriginal Peoples* 4, Perspectives and Realities, pp. 7–106.

— (1996) *Looking Forward, Looking Back, Vol. 1* (Ottawa).

Russell, A. L. (2005) 'Standardization in history: a review essay with an eye to the future', in S. Bolin (ed.), *The Standards Edge: Future Generations* (Ann Arbor, MI), pp. 247–60.

Ryan, L. (2011) 'Memory, power and resistance: the anatomy of a tripartite relationship', *Memory Studies*, 4 (2), pp. 154–69.

Samson, C. (ed.) (1999) *Health Studies: A Critical Multidisciplinary Reader* (Oxford).

— (2001) 'Sameness as a requirement for the recognition of the rights of the Innu of Canada: the colonial context', in J. Cowan, M. Dembour and R. Wilson (eds.), *Culture and Rights: Anthropological Perspectives* (Cambridge), pp. 226–48.

— (2003) *A Way of Life That Does Not Exist: Canada and the Extinguishment of the Innu* (London).

— (2008) 'A Colonial Double Bind: The social and historical contexts of Innu mental health', in L. J. Kirkmayer and G. Valaskakis (eds.), *The Mental Health of Canadian Aboriginal Peoples: Transformations of Identity and Community* (Vancouver), pp. 109–39.

— (2010a) 'The rule of *terra nullius* and the impotence of international human rights for indigenous peoples', *Essex Human Rights Review*, 5 (1).

— (2010b) 'Indigenous peoples rights: anthropology and the right to culture', in R. Morgan and B. Turner (eds.), *Interpreting Human Rights: Social Science Perspectives* (London).

— (2014) 'Dispossession and Canadian land claims: genocidal implications of the Innu nation land claim', in A. Hinton, A. Woolford and J. Benvenuto (eds.), *Colonial Genocide and Rights Cessions in Comprehensive Land Claims* (Durham, NC), pp. 246–72.

— (2016) 'Canada's strategy of dispossession: Aboriginal land and rights cessions in comprehensive land claims', *Canadian Journal of Law and Society*, 31 (1): 87–110.

Samson, C. and E. Cassell (2012) 'The long reach of frontier justice: Canadian land claims "negotiation" stragegies as human rights violations', *The International Journal of Human Rights*, 17 (1).

Samson, C. and J. Pretty (2006) 'Environmental and health benefits of hunting lifestyles and diets for the Innu of Labrador', *Food Policy*, 31 (6), pp. 528–53.

Samson, C. and D. Short (2006) 'Sociology and the human rights of indigenous peoples' in L. Morris (ed.), *Rights: Sociological Perspectives* (London), pp. 168–86.

Sartre, J. (1961) 'Introduction', in F. Fanon (ed.), *The Wretched of the Earth.*

Savard, R. (1971) *Carcajou et le sens du monde. Récits montagnais-naskapi* (Québec).

— (1973) 'Discours culturel montagnais, bilan d'une recherche en cours. Structure du récit L'enfant couvert de poux', *Signes et langages des Amériques, Recherches amérindiennes au Québec*, 3 (1–2).

— (1977a) 'Mythes et cosmologie des Indiens Montagnais: résultats préliminaires', in W. Cowan (ed.), *Actes du huitième congrès des algonquinistes* (Ottawa).

— (1977b) *Le Rire précolombien dans le Québec d'aujourd'hui* (Montréal).

— (1979) *Contes indiens de la Basse-Côte-Nord du Saint-Laurent,* Ottawa, Service Canadien d'ethnologie, Musée National de l'Homme, coll. ' Mercure', dossier 51.

— (1981) *Le sol américain: propriété privée ou terre-mère?... L'en-deçà et l'au-delà des conflits territoriaux entre autochtones et blancs au Canada* (Montréal).

— (1985) *La Voix des Autres. Positions Anthropologiques* (Montréal).

— (2002) 'Les peuples Américains et le système judiciaire Canadien: spéléologie d'un trou de mémoire', *Revue Canadienne Droit et Société* 17 (2), pp. 123–48.

— (2003) 'Obélix chez les Indiens: un scoop dépassé', *Le Devoir*, 25 November.

— (2004) *La forêt vive: Récits fondateurs du peuple Innu* (Montréal).

Schank, R. (1982) *Dynamic Memory: A Theory of Reminding and Learning in Computers And People* (New York).

Scheff, T. J. (1988) 'Shame and conformity: the deference/emotion system', *American Sociological Review*, 53 (6): 395–406.

Scheff, T. J. and S. Retzinger (1991) *Emotions and Violence: Shame and Rage in Destructive Conflicts* (Lexington, MA).

Schiffrin, D. (1996) 'Narrative as self-portrait: sociolinguistic constructions of identity', *Language in Society*, 25 (2): 167–203.

Schulte-Tenckhoff, I. (1998) 'Reassessing the paradigm of domestication: the problematic of indigenous treaties', *Review of Constitutional Studies*, 4: 239–89.

— (2000) 'A brief note on treaties, real and fictitious', *Indigenous Law Bulletin*, 12, 5 (1).

Scott, J. and G. Marshall (2005) *Oxford Dictionary of Sociology* (Oxford).

Sedikides, C. and M. B. Brewer (2001) *Individual Self, Relational Self, Collective Self* (Philadelphia, PA).

Sheflin, A. W. and D. Brown (1996) 'Repressed memory or dissociative amnesia: what the science says', *Journal of Psychiatry & Law*, 24 (2): 143–88.

Shewell, H. (1999) 'Jules Sioui and Indian political radicalism in Canada, 1943–1944', *Journal of Canadian Studies*, 34 (3): 211–42.

Shibutani, T. (1954) 'Reference groups as perspectives', *American Journal of Sociology*, 60 (5): 562–9.

Simonnet, E. (1982) 'Pour nos pères et nos enfants', *Science & Nature*.

Sioui J (n.d. but likely late 1944 or early 1945) *Who is Your Master?* (unpublished).

Smith, L. T. (1999) *Decolonizing Methodologies: Research and Indigenous Peoples* (New York).

Snow, D. A., S. A. Soule and H. Kriesi (2008) *The Blackwell Companion to Social Movements* (London).

Speck, F. G. (1918) 'Kinship terms and the family band among the northeastern Algonquian', *American Anthropologist*, n.s. 20 (2): 143–61.

— (1925) 'Montagnais and Naskapi tales from the Labrador Peninsula', *The Journal of American Folklore*, 38 (147): 1–32.

— (1927) 'Family hunting territories of the Lake St. John Montagnais and neighboring bands', *Anthropos*, 22: 387–403.

— (1931) 'Montagnais-Naskapi bands and early Eskimo distribution in the Labrador Peninsula', *American Anthropologist*, n.s. 33 (4): 557–600.

— (1933) 'Ethical attributes of the Labrador Indians', *American Anthropologist*, n.s. 35 (4): 559–94.

— (1935) *Naskapi: The Savage Hunters of the Labrador Peninsula* (Norman, OK).

— (1937) 'Montagnais art in birch-bark, a circumpolar trait', *Indian Notes and Monographs*, XI (2): 45–157.

— Personal notes of his meetings with the Escoumains band, recovered at the *American Philosophical Society*.

Speck, F. G. and G. G. Heye (1921) *Hunting Charms of the Montagnais and the Mistassini* (New York).

St-Georges, G. (2009) 'Préoccupations, valeurs et aspirations des Innus d'Essipit relativement à leur territoire ancestral, le Nitassinan' (MA thesis, Université Laval).

Staniforth, J. B. (2013) 'Québec in question: scholars attack province's colonial history', *The Nation*, 7 Oct. 2013, http://www.nationnewsarchives.ca/article/quebec-in-question-scholars-attack-provinces-colonial-history/ (accessed 22 Jun. 2017).

Stanley, T. J. (2014) 'The Aryan character of the future of British North America: Macdonald, Chinese exclusion, and the invention of Canadian white supremacy', in P. Dutil and R. Hall (eds.), *Macdonald at 200* (Toronto).

Statistics Canada (2007) *Essipit, Québec, 2006 Community Profiles*, 2006 Census, Statistics Canada Catalogue no. 92-591-XWE, Ottawa.

— (2017) 'Essipit, Indian reserve [Census subdivision], Québec and Québec [Province]', table appearing on 'Census Profile, 2016 Census', Statistics Canada Catalogue no. 98-316-X2016001, available at http://www12.statcan.gc.ca (search 'Essipit') (accessed 23 Mar. 2018).

Tangey, J. P., R. S. Miller, Flicker, L. and D. H. Barlow (1996) 'Are shame, guilt, and embarrassment distinct emotions?', *Journal of Personal Social Psychology*, 70 (6): 1256–69.

Thompson, P. (1994) 'Believe it or not: rethinking the interpretation of memory', in J. Jeffrey and G. Edwall (eds.), *Memory and History: Essays on Recalling and Interpreting Experience* (Lanham, MD).

— (2017) *The Voice of the Past – Oral History* (4th edn, Oxford).

Thompson, W. and J. Hickey (2005) *Society in Focus* (Boston, MA).

Tobias, J. L. (1976) 'Protection, civilization, assimilation: an outline history of Canada's Indian policy', *The Western Canadian Journal of Anthropology*, 6 (2).

Tremblay, J. (2006) 'La gestion de la faune par les autochtones: l'exemple de l'autogestion du saumon atlantique chez les Innus de Ekuanitshit – Mingan', *Collection pêches autochtones no. 2,* Université Laval and CIERA.

Trigger, B. G. (1981) 'Pour une histoire plus objective des relations entre colonisateurs et autochthones en Nouvelle-France', in *Recherches Amérindiennes au Québec*, 11 (3): 199–204.

Turgeon, L. (1986) 'Pour redécouvrir notre XVI siècle: les pêches à Terre-Neuve d'après les archives notariales de Bordeaux', *RHAF*, 39 (4): 1.

— (1990) 'Basque-Amerindian trade in the Saint-Lawrence during the sixteenth century: new documents, new perspectives', *Man in the Northeast*, 40: 81–7.

— (1994) 'Creuser les premiers contacts: pêcheurs basques et Amérindiens au Canada au XVI siècle', in J. Lintvelt, R. Ouellet and H. Hermans (eds.), *Culture et colonisation en Amérique du Nord* (Sillery), p. 66.

Turner, R. H. (1988) 'The self-conception in social interaction', in C. Gordon and K. J. Gergen (eds.), *The Self in Social Interaction* (New York).

Turner, R. H. and L. M. Killian (1987). Collective Behavior (3rd edn, Englewood Cliffs, NJ).

Turner, J. C., M. A. Hogg, P. J. Oakes, S. D. Reicher and M. S. Wetherell (1987) *Rediscovering the Social Group: A Self-categorization Theory* (Oxford and New York).

Van der Kolk, B. (1997) 'Post-traumatic stress disorder and memory', *Psychiatric Times*, 14 (3).

Vincent, S. (1976), 'L'implantation de l'ITT sur la Côte-Nord québécoise à la lumière de quatre siècles d'histoire montagnaise', *Actes du XLII Congrès international des Américanistes*, Congrès du Centenaire, 2–9 Sep., pp. 303–10.

Vincent, S. (1977a) 'Structures comparées du rite et des mythes de la tente tremblante', Proceedings of the Eighth Congress of Algonquinists.

— (1977b) 'L'histoire montagnaise jusqu'au 15 Novembre 1976: quatre siècles de dépossession', *Possibles*, I (3–4).

— (1978a) 'Tradition orale et action politique montagnaises: le cas de la rivière Natashquan', *Papers of the Ninth Algonquian Conference.*

— (1978b) *Atanutshe, nimushum* (Québec).

— (1982) 'La tradition orale montagnaise, comment l'interroger?', *Cahiers de Clio* (Brussels).

— (1991a) 'L'Indien n'est pas un fou : quelques réflexions montagnaises sur la gestion du territoire', *Recherches amérindiennes au Québec*, 12 (4): 245–9.

— (1991b) 'La présence des gens du large dans la version montagnaise de l'histoire', *Anthropologie et Sociétés*, 15 (1): 125–43.

— (1992) 'L'arrivée des Européens, récits et lectures d'aujourd'hui', *Recherches amérindiennes au Québec*, 22 (2–3): 3–6.

— (1994) *Tshishenniu-Maninuish umishta aiatshimun* (Montréal and Mingan).

Vincent, S. and J. Bacon (1992), 'L'arrivée des chercheurs de terres, récits et dires des Montagnais de la Moyenne et de la Basse-Côte-Nord', *Recherches amérindiennes au Québec*, 22 (2–3): 19–29.

White, R. (2008) 'Essipit: un effort collectif', in *Entreprenariat autochtone en plein essor.*

Widom, C. S. and R. L. Shepard (1996) 'Accuracy of adult recollections of childhood victimization: part 1. Childhood physical abuse', *Psychological Assessment* 8 (4): 412–21.

Widom, C. S. and S. Morris (1997) 'Accuracy of adult recollections of childhood victimization: part 2. Childhood sexual abuse', *Psychological Assessment*, 9 (1): 34–46.

Wurmser, L. (1987) 'Shame, the veiled companion of narcissism', in D. L. Nathanson (ed.) *The Many Faces of Shame* (New York).

Wilson, S. (2008), *Research is Ceremony. Indigenous Research Methods* (Winnipeg).

Yow, V. R. (2005) *Recording Oral History: A Guide for the Humanities and Social Sciences* (Walnut Creek, CA).

www.ingramcontent.com/pod-product-compliance
Lightning Source LLC
LaVergne TN
LVHW052015300826
846742LV00019B/67